The
BENSON and HEDGES
Top 10 of Everything 1994

Russell Ash

HEADLINE

First published in 1993
by HEADLINE BOOK PUBLISHING

10 9 8 7 6 5 4 3 2 1

British Library Cataloguing in Publication Data

Ash, Russell
  Benson & Hedges Top 10 of Everything. –
  1994
  I. Title
  032.02

ISBN 0–7472–0792–5

Cover photographs
Front (clockwise from top left): Science Photo Library; Tony Stone Worldwide; Patrick Eagar; Tony Stone Worldwide; Kobal Collection; Science Photo Library; Oxford Scientific Films; Life File

Back: Life File (top left); Christie's Colour Library (top right); Oxford Scientific Films

Designed by D&S Design Partnership, London

Colour reproduction by Koford, Singapore

Printed and bound in Great Britain by
Butler & Tanner Ltd,
Frome and London

HEADLINE BOOK PUBLISHING
A division of Hodder Headline PLC
Headline House
79 Great Titchfield Street
London W1P 7FN

ABOUT THE AUTHOR

Russell Ash was born in Surrey and went to school in Bedford. After obtaining a Joint Honours degree in Geography and Anthropology at the University of Durham, he worked briefly as an aviation insurance broker before his move into publishing in 1967. He has since written and contributed to more than 50 books on such subjects as art (particularly on the Impressionists and other late nineteenth-century painters, including Sir Lawrence Alma-Tadema, James Tissot, van Gogh, Toulouse-Lautrec and Burne-Jones), animals real and fictitious (he is the author of a book on post office cats, *The Pig Book* and *The Frog Book*, and is the official 'biographer' of Paddington Bear), popular reference books (including *The Londoner's Almanac*) and many humorous books (such as *The Cynic's Dictionary*, *Howlers*, and, as co-author, *Bizarre Books*). He is also a partner in a book production company specializing in illustrated books and gift and stationery items. He has contributed to numerous publications, among them the *Sunday Times*, the *Observer*, *Punch*, the *Connoisseur*, and the *Mail on Sunday*. Russell Ash lives in Lewes, East Sussex with his wife, Caroline, and two sons.

The Top 10 of Everything was first published in 1989, since when it has appeared annually. *The Top 10 of Sport* (co-authored with Ian Morrison) was published in 1992 and *The Top 10 of Music* (co-authored with Luke Crampton and Barry Lazell) in 1993.

CONTENTS

INTRODUCTION
— 6 —

INTRODUCTION

Welcome to this, the fifth annual edition of *The Top 10 of Everything.*

As ever, I want to extend my thanks to those readers who have taken the trouble to write with helpful suggestions – in many instances providing ideas for new lists or, even better, supplying lists that I could not otherwise have compiled.

I am often asked how much of the book changes from year to year, and the answer (judged, not least, by the amount of time I devote to updating established lists and compiling new ones!) is, a lot.

Some lists inevitably stay the same – although even here I have to watch carefully for alterations. I have often used the world's tallest mountains as an example of a list that does not change from year to year, but even this is not altogether true: as work was being finalized on this edition, word came through that a French-Italian scientific expedition to Mount Everest had calculated that it is 8,846.1 m/29,022.6 ft high, some 2 m/6.7 ft lower than the generally accepted height. Nevertheless, I await further corroboration before altering this supposedly 'fixed' figure. Some lists that might be assumed to change little still call for constant monitoring of even the smallest detail: as soon as I had completed a list of the 10 longest-running children's magazines, *Jackie*, the ninth entry, ceased publication.

Then there are the lists that appear every year, but which change annually, either completely or almost completely (such as the most watched films or bestselling books), and those where the same or similar entrants appear, but the figures change or the order is shuffled – such as the biggest motor manufacturers, the busiest members of the Royal Family or the most visited tourist attractions. This year the updates to some regular lists have surprisingly prompted the question, 'Recession, what recession?' Hardly a week has gone by without another auction record being broken (the world's most expensive photograph, for example, was sold in London on 7 May 1993), while in the past year all but one of the UK's Top 10 supermarkets managed to buck the trend and actually *increased* their turnover.

Finally, there are always a number of lists, both straightforward and quirky, that make a debut appearance. In this latter category this year are lists of the names most mentioned in the Bible, the tallest buildings that are no longer standing and the results of a recent poll of hoteliers that indicates what their customers most often leave behind, break or steal. Such lists may be revived for a future edition, or may never appear again...

Another, more fundamental question that comes up from time to time is 'Why make lists?' To some, such an enterprise is nothing short of obsessive and pointless – and I would agree that simply listing things for the sake of listing them is foolish and may even be a symptom of the incurable condition known as Asperger's Syndrome (or 'Train-spotter's Disease'). But there is no doubt that – taken in moderation – lists simplify or organize information in a form that we can digest and remember. Lists draw together disparate elements to make some meaningful connection while, as a form of shorthand, lists in their various forms reflect modern life in all its facets – serious, bizarre, trivial, important, fascinating, amusing, revealing or entertaining, and at best even amazing. Lists may be useful: we all make shopping lists, Christmas card lists, lists of New Year resolutions and lists of 'Things to Do' (sometimes doing the list is as far as we get, almost as if compiling it is the task itself). Lists as memory aids have a long history, from lists of who begat whom in the Bible (where the 10 Commandments is a classic list), to mnemonic lists to help us recall the sequence of British monarchs, and lists in literature (there's even an entire book on this subject!). Lists resulting from market surveys and polls and annually published lists – especially Top 10s – have become a staple press item: lists of the most watched TV shows of the week, the bestselling books, the record charts and the latest crime figures are all evidence of our national 'listomania'.

Fifteen years ago this widespread fascination with lists of all complexions gave rise to a celebrated series of *Books of Lists*, originally the brainchild of the American author David Wallechinsky and his family. Anyone who compiles books of this genre owes an inspirational debt to them and I would like publicly to acknowledge their influence. In a recent conversation with David Wallechinsky, we recognized that as children we had both been fans of the 'Believe It Or Not!' column and books by Robert Ripley, and no doubt Ripley was himself influenced by some other author, and so the enthusiasm for the odd facts of life goes on, from generation to generation.

The *Books of Lists* gave rise to others, some general or national, others on subjects as specific as films, food, cinema, royalty and business, and even places, including Texas and London – as in my own book, *The Londoner's Almanac*. Our approach contains one marked difference, however: 'The human animal differs from the lesser primates in his passion for lists of Ten Best', wrote H. Allen Smith (the author of some oddly titled humour books, including his memorable *My Life in a Putty-knife Factory)*. But the lists you will find in *The Top 10 of Everything* are hardly ever 'Ten Bests' because I take the view that for every compiler of such a list, however qualified she or he may be to do so, there will be someone else who will feel equally qualified to come forward and dispute it. Top 10 lists, by contrast, are lists of things that can be measured: the only '10 Bests' you will find here are bestsellers (because their sales can be quantified) and occasionally the results of polls – but only if they derive from a substantial survey. The lists therefore represent no one's opinions, least of all my own, in any area other than my personal choice of what I include and what I omit.

Partly in response to readers' letters, there is, this year, more concentration on famous people, especially film stars, more lists of 'firsts', some 50th anniversary lists and, as an innovation, a selection of 'celebrity lists' which are not quantifiable and are included for no better reason than that I like them.

It is always a pleasure to discover new sources of information and individuals with expert knowledge who can provide me (increasingly these days by having amassed a computer database) with material that used to be tortuous to acquire. The use of new methods of assembling and accessing information, especially CD-ROM, has been a significant change since I started compiling *The Top 10 of Everything*. Much is of a high standard, although glaring errors frequently appear in reference books. Though I am grateful when my mistakes are pointed out, the temptation to gloat over others' gaffes is hard to resist. Among my favourite recent examples is a respected book which declares that Manila has a population of 21 people per square foot! Are they standing on each other's heads 21 deep? Do they all live in skyscrapers? If you are planning a trip there and are worried about being squashed, you'll be relieved to know that the true figure is approximately 516 square feet *per person*.

It is frustrating *not* to be able to obtain certain information, and irritating how late some of it is in being made available, particularly data from 'official' bodies that is often a year out of date before it is published (what can they possibly have been doing with it that takes more than a year?). Figures for unified Germany are becoming available, but while the individual countries that were former members of the Soviet Union are now identified in *The Top 10 of Everything* in those lists relating to physical features (such as the list of the world's longest rivers), one is compelled to use the artificial designation 'Former USSR' in lists of, for example, figures relating to crop production. One day Russia, the Ukraine, Tajikstan and the rest might perhaps be considered as independent countries and not as components of a monolithic state that no longer exists.

I am asked if I'll ever run out of Top 10 lists. The answer, I think (and hope!) is no. Quite apart from new list ideas that appear all the time, whether suggested by others, inspired by something I read or spontaneously, almost every list is capable of generating other lists by a process resembling cell-division: a list of the 10 Types of Fruit Most Grown might include apples; this could give rise to a list of the 10 Countries that Produce Most Apples, or the 10 Varieties of Apples Most Grown, or perhaps the 10 Bestselling Products Made from Apples or the 10 Bestselling Brands of Cider. Four lists

have grown out of one – and that accounts only for apples; there are still nine more fruits to do!

We are said to be living in the 'Information Age', and in recent years there has certainly been a vast proliferation of specialist reference publications in the form of books, magazines and various electronic media. Question and answer columns of the 'Notes and Queries' ilk (led by the *Guardian*, but harking back to the journal *Notes and Queries*, which was first published in 1849) now appear in most daily newspapers and – inevitably – press articles have even appeared speculating on why we need so much information. Whatever the conclusion, the demand certainly seems insatiable, as evidenced by the continued popularity of Trivial Pursuit, of pub quiz leagues and TV quiz shows – and, indeed, it is gratifying to find, by the continuing popularity of *The Top 10 of Everything*.

RUSSELL ASH

If you have any comments or suggestions for new Top 10 lists, please write to:

Russell Ash
c/o Headline Book Publishing
Headline House
79 Great Titchfield Street
London W1P 7FN

THE 10 BRIGHTEST STARS

	Star	Constellation	Distance*	Mag†
1	Sun	Solar System	149,598,020 km	−26.8
2	Sirius	Canis Major	8.64	−1.46
3	Canopus	Carina	1,200	−0.72
4	Alpha Centauri	Centaurus	4.3	−0.27
5	Arcturus	Boötes	34	−0.04
6	Vega	Lyra	26	+0.03
7	Capella	Auriga	45	+0.08
8	Rigel	Orion	900	+0.12
9	Procyon	Canis Minor	11.4	+0.38
10	Achernar	Eridanus	85	+0.46

*From Earth in light years, unless otherwise stated. A light year is the distance travelled in one year by light at a speed of 299,792.458 km/186,282.397 miles per second.

†Apparent magnitude.

Based on apparent visual magnitude as viewed from Earth – the lower the number, the brighter the star. Sirius is actually 26 times brighter than the Sun, but its distance from the Earth relegates it into second place. If the Sun is excluded, the 10th brightest star is Beta Centauri in the constellation of Centaurus. At its brightest, the star Betelgeuse is brighter than some of these, but as it is variable its average brightness disqualifies it from the Top 10. The jury is out on a star known as VI Cygni No. 12 in the constellation of Cygnus, discovered in 1992 and arguably the brightest star in the galaxy, but still awaiting verification.

THE UNIVERSE

THE MOON QUIZ

1 What was the first manmade object to land on the Moon?

2 Who wrote the novel *The Moonstone*?

3 In what year were the first pictures taken of the far side of the Moon?

4 Who wrote the story, later filmed, *The Moon and Sixpence*?

5 The inhabitants of which English county are known as 'moonrakers'?

6 What US group had a 1961 No. 1 hit with *Blue Moon*?

7 Under what astrological sign is a 'moonchild' born?

8 Who popularized the dance step known as 'moonwalking'?

9 A poem by e.e. cummings contains the line 'the moon's a balloon'. Which British actor used this as the title of his autobiography?

10 In what year will the next total eclipse of the Moon be visible from the UK?

THE 10 LARGEST PLANETARY MOONS

Moon	Planet	Diameter km	miles
1 Ganymede	**Jupiter**	**5,262**	**3,270**

Discovered by Galileo in 1609–10 and believed to be the largest moon in the Solar System, Ganymede – one of Jupiter's 16 satellites – is thought to have a surface of ice about 97 km/60 miles thick. The 1979 *Voyager 1* and *2* space probes failed to detect evidence of an atmosphere. NASA's *Galileo* probe is scheduled to investigate the Jovian moons Ganymede, Callisto, Io and Europa in November 1995.

Moon	Planet	Diameter km	miles
2 Titan	**Saturn**	**5,150**	**3,200**

Titan, the largest of Saturn's 18 confirmed moons, is actually larger than two of the planets in the Solar System, Mercury and Pluto. It was discovered by the Dutch astronomer Christian Huygens in 1655. We have no idea what its surface looks like because it has a dense atmosphere containing nitrogen, ethane and other gases which shroud its surface – not unlike that of Earth 4 billion years ago – but data sent back by *Voyager 1* during 1980 and recent radio telescope observations suggest that it may have ethane 'oceans' and 'continents' of ice or other solid matter. Recent research has suggested that gases were deposited there by impacting comets. NASA and the European Space Agency have announced plans to send a space probe to Titan as part of the Cassini mission, to be launched in April 1996. It should touch down on Titan's surface in October 2002.

Moon	Planet	Diameter km	miles
3 Callisto	**Jupiter**	**4,820**	**2,995**

Possessing a similar composition to Ganymede, Callisto is heavily pitted with craters, perhaps more so than any other body in the Solar System.

Moon	Planet	Diameter km	miles
4 Io	**Jupiter**	**3,632**	**2,257**

Most of what we know about Io was reported back by the 1979 *Voyager* probe, which revealed a crust of solid sulphur with massive volcanic eruptions in progress, hurling sulphurous material 300 km/186 miles into space.

Moon	Planet	Diameter km	miles
5 Moon	**Earth**	**3,475**	**2,159**

Our own satellite is a quarter of the diameter and one-fiftieth the size of the Earth, the 5th largest in the Solar System and, to date, the only one to have been explored by Man.

Moon	Planet	Diameter km	miles
6 Europa	**Jupiter**	**3,126**	**1,942**

Although Europa's ice-covered surface is apparently smooth and crater-free, it is covered with mysterious black lines, some of them 64 km/40 miles wide and resembling canals.

Moon	Planet	Diameter km	miles
7 Triton	**Neptune**	**2,750**	**1,708**

Discovered on 10 October 1846 by brewer and amateur astronomer William Lassell, 17 days after he had discovered Neptune itself, Triton is the only known satellite in the Solar System that revolves around its planet in the opposite direction to the planet's rotation. It is getting progressively closer to Neptune, and it is believed that in several million years the force of the planet's gravity may pull it apart, scattering it into a form like the rings of Saturn. Information sent back to Earth by *Voyager 2* during August 1989 revealed the presence of three or four rings and 'ring arcs', or incomplete rings, at distances of between 17,110 km/10,625 miles and 38,100 km/23,674 miles from the planet's cloud tops, as well as six previously undiscovered moons, which were given the temporary names of 1989N1–1989N6. These range in size from the 400 km/249 miles of 1989N1 (making it larger than Neptune's other previously known moon, Nereid, which was discovered in 1948, at 340 km/211 miles) down to 1989N6's 54 km/34 miles. The probe also showed that Triton has an atmosphere composed largely of nitrogen and methane and a surface partly covered with nitrogen and methane ice glaciers. The average surface temperature of Triton was calculated to be –237°C, but the ice layer actually shifts from one pole to the other and back again once every 165 years, the length of time it takes for Neptune to orbit round the Sun. Photographs transmitted back to Earth also showed dark streaks shooting 8 km/5 miles into the atmosphere. These have been explained as resulting from seasonal temperature changes causing the methane to heat up and break through the nitrogen ice layers as geysers, or may perhaps be dust storms similar to those observed on Mars.

Moon	Planet	Diameter km	miles
8 Titania	**Uranus**	**1,580**	**982**

The largest of Uranus's 15 moons, Titania was discovered by William Herschel (who had discovered the planet six years earlier) in 1787 and has a snowball-like surface of ice. Its size estimate was revised by data from *Voyager 2*.

Moon	Planet	Diameter km	miles
9 Rhea	**Saturn**	**1,530**	**951**

Saturn's second largest moon was discovered by seventeenth-century Italian-born French astronomer Giovanni Cassini. *Voyager 1*, which flew past Rhea in November 1980, confirmed that its icy surface is pitted with craters, one of them 225 km/140 miles in diameter.

Moon	Planet	Diameter km	miles
10 Oberon	**Uranus**	**1,516**	**942**

Oberon was discovered by Herschel and given the name of the fairy king husband of Queen Titania, both characters in Shakespeare's *A Midsummer Night's Dream*. New information from *Voyager 2* has relegated Oberon from 9th to 10th place in this list.

The south pole of Triton, one of Neptune's moons, the seventh largest in the Solar System. The nitrogen ice cap 'migrates' between the poles during the 165 years it takes Neptune to complete its orbit round the Sun.

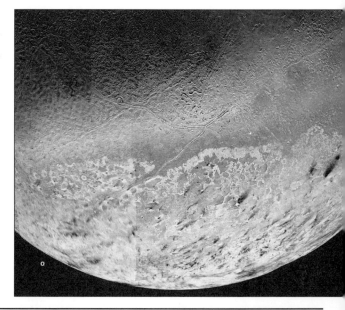

THE 10 STARS NEAREST TO EARTH*

	Star	Light years	Distance km	miles
1	Proxima Centauri	4.22	39,923,310,000,000	24,792,500,000,000
2	Alpha Centauri	4.35	41,153,175,000,000	25,556,250,000,000
3	Barnard's Star	5.98	56,573,790,000,000	35,132,500,000,000
4	Wolf 359	7.75	73,318,875,000,000	45,531,250,000,000
5	Lalande 21185	8.22	77,765,310,000,000	48,292,500,000,000
6	Luyten 726–8	8.43	79,752,015,000,000	49,526,250,000,000
7	Sirius	8.65	81,833,325,000,000	50,818,750,000,000
8	Ross 154	9.45	89,401,725,000,000	55,518,750,000,000
9	Ross 248	10.40	98,389,200,000,000	61,100,000,000,000
10	Epsilon Eridani	10.80	102,173,400,000,000	63,450,000,000,000

*Excluding the Sun.

A spaceship travelling at 40,237 kph/25,000 mph – which is faster than any human has yet reached in space – would take more than 113,200 years to reach Earth's closest star, Proxima Centauri (one light year = 9.4605 x 10^{12} km/5.875 x 10^{12} miles).

THE 10 LARGEST PLANETS IN THE SOLAR SYSTEM*

	Planet	Mass†	Distance from Earth km	miles	Maximum diameter km	miles
1	Jupiter	317.83	627,640,000	390,000,000	142,984	88,846
2	Saturn	95.19	1,276,210,000	793,000,000	120,536	74,898
3	Uranus	14.58	2,719,790,000	1,690,000,000	51,118	31,763
4	Neptune	17.20	4,345,230,000	2,700,000,000	49,600	30,820
5	Earth	1.00	–	–	12,756	7,926
6	Venus	0.82	41,840,000	26,000,000	12,103	7,520
7	Mars	0.11	78,053,000	48,500,000	6,794	4,222
8	Mercury	0.06	91,730,000	57,000,000	4,878	3,031
9	Pluto	0.01	5,750,190,000	3,573,000,000	2,284	1,419
10	'Planet X'	?	?	?	?	?

*Excluding 'minor planets' (asteroids).   †Compared with Earth = 1.00.

Most of the planets are visible with the naked eye and have been observed since ancient times. The exceptions are Uranus: discovered on 13 March 1781 by the British astronomer Sir William Herschel; Neptune: found by German astronomer Johann Galle on 23 September 1846 (Galle was led to his discovery by the independent calculations of the French astronomer Urbain Leverrier and the British mathematician John Adams); and Pluto: located using photographic techniques by American astronomer Clyde Tombaugh, its discovery was announced on 13 March 1930. The diameter and mass of Pluto are uncertain, but even more uncertain is the very existence of the so-called 'Planet X' that is believed to orbit beyond Pluto, and is hence the furthest planet from both the Sun and Earth. When Pluto was discovered, it was realized that such a small planet could not cause the irregularities discerned in the orbits of Uranus and Neptune. It was therefore concluded that there must be a 10th and as yet undiscovered planet, for which the name Persephone has been proposed. Since Chiron, which may be a comet or an asteroid orbiting between Saturn and Uranus, is about 200 km/124 miles in diameter, making it the smallest body yet observed in the outer reaches of the Solar System, it implies that if Planet X really does exist but is smaller and even more distant, it will not be detectable by terrestrial telescopes using current technology. However, the IRAS (Infra-Red Astronomical Satellite) also failed to detect it, while data sent back by Voyager 2 seemed to offer explanations for Neptune's orbit without the influence of a mysterious 10th planet. In 1992 optimistic reports suggesting that Planet X had at last been found were quickly refuted.

10 ASTRONOMICAL FEATURES NAMED AFTER PEOPLE

1 Baily's Beads

The name given to bright lights that appear round the edge of the Moon before and after a total eclipse, named after their discoverer, British astronomer and explorer Francis Baily, who observed the phenomenon in 1836 and 1842. Baily was also notable for his tireless work in calculating the weight of the Earth.

2 Dorsum Buckland

A 150-km/93-mile ridge on the Moon named after William Buckland, a British naturalist (celebrated for reputedly eating the mummified heart of Louis XIV, in the interests of scientific curiosity!). Other Moon features have been named after subjects as varied as printing pioneer Johann Gutenberg, aviator Charles Lindbergh, novelist H.G. Wells and Roman emperor Julius Caesar.

3 Gabi

An asteroid named in 1970 after East German women's ice-skating champion Gabriele Seyfert, who had been placed second in the 1968 Olympic figure-skating competition.

4 Herschel-Rigollet

A comet originally discovered in 1788 by Caroline, the sister of the British Astronomer Royal Sir William Herschel. It has a period of 156 years, and when it was next seen in 1939, by French astronomer Robert Rigollet, it was given a name that combines those of both its discoverers.

5 Hooveria

Asteroid 932, named after 35th US President Herbert Hoover; asteroid 1363 was named Herbertia, also after him.

6 Johanna

An asteroid discovered in 1872 and named by French astronomer Paul Henry in honour of Joan of Arc.

7 Nata

Asteroid 1086, discovered by Russian astronomer S.I. Belyavasky in 1927 and named after Russian female parachutist Natalya Babushkina; he named two other asteroids, Lyuba and Tamariva, after another two women parachutists. All three had in common the distressing fact that they had been killed in parachuting accidents.

8 Rotanev

The name of the star also known as Beta Delphini has a somewhat convoluted origin: the Latin version of the surname of Italian astronomer Niccolo Cacciatore is Venator – which spells Rotanev backwards!

9 George Smiley

A rock known as a planetesimal in the Kuiper Belt (itself named after Dutch astronomer Gerrit Pieter Kuiper), beyond Pluto's orbit, named by its discoverers David Jewitt and Jane Luu after the character in John Le Carré's novels; they also named a 1993 discovery Karla, after Smiley's opponent.

10 Victoria

An asteroid discovered in 1850 by the British astronomer John Russell Hind was controversially named after Queen Victoria, the first living monarch to be so-honoured.

THE 10 COLDEST PLACES IN THE SOLAR SYSTEM

	Planet	Lowest temperature (°C)
1	Triton*	−235
2	Pluto	−230
3	Uranus	−223
4 =	Mercury	−200
4 =	Neptune	−200
6	Saturn	−160
7	Jupiter	−145
8	Mars	−140
9	Earth	−89
10	Venus	+462

*A moon of Neptune. Various other moons of Neptune and other planets are nearly as cold.

Absolute zero, which has almost been attained on Earth under laboratory conditions, is −273.15°C, only 38.15°C below the surface temperature of Triton. At the other extreme, it has been calculated theoretically that the core of Jupiter attains 30,000°C, more than five times the boiling point of tungsten.

The bright zone seen at the edge of the Moon during a solar eclipse is called Baily's Beads after nineteenth-century astronomer Francis Baily.

THE 10 LONGEST RIVERS IN ASIA

	River	Countries	Length km	miles
1	Yangtze–Kiang	China	6,300	3,915
2	Yenisey–Angara–Selenga	Mongolia/Russia	5,540	3,442
3	Huang Ho (Yellow River)	China	5,464	3,395
4	Ob'–Irtysh	Mongolia/Kazakhstan/Russia	5,410	3,362
5	Lena–Kirenga	Russia	4,400	2,734
6	Mekong	Tibet/China/Myanmar/Laos/Cambodia/Vietnam	4,350	2,703
7	Amur–Argun	China/Russia	4,345	2,700
8	Volga	Russia	3,530	2,193
9	Strdayra–Naryn	Kyrgyzstan/Tajikstan/Uzbekistan/Kazakhstan	3,019	1,876
10	Nizhnaya Tunguska	Russia	2,989	1,857

An enhanced satellite photograph of the outflow of the Yangtze–Kiang shows that the delta is continuing to grow as silt is brought down by the river.

PLANET EARTH

THE BENSON AND HEDGES TOP 10 OF EVERYTHING 1994

THE 10 GREATEST* RIVERS IN THE WORLD

	River	Outflow/sea	Average flow (m³/sec)
1	Amazon	Brazil/South Atlantic	175,000
2	Zaïre	Angola–Zaïre/South Atlantic	39,000
3	Negro	Brazil/South Atlantic	35,000
4	Yangtze–Kiang	China/Yellow Sea	32,190
5	Orinoco	Venezuela/South Atlantic	25,200
6	Plata–Paraná–Grande	Uruguay/South Atlantic	22,900
7	Madeira–Mamoré–Grande	Brazil/South Atlantic	21,800
8	Yenisey–Angara–Selenga	Russia/Kara Sea	18,000
9	Brahmaputra	Bangladesh/Bay of Bengal	16,290
10	Lena–Kirenga	Russia/Arctic Ocean	16,100

*Based on rate of discharge at source.

THE 10 LONGEST RIVERS IN THE UK

	River	Length km	miles
1	Severn	354	220
2	Thames	346	215
3	Trent	298	185
4	Aire	259	161
5	Great Ouse	230	143
6	Wye	217	135
7	Tay	188	117
8	Nene	161	100
9	Clyde	159	98.5
10	Spey	158	98

During their courses, some rivers change their names, for example, Trent/Humber, Thames/Isis.

THE 10 LONGEST RIVERS IN THE WORLD

	River	Countries	Length km	miles
1	Nile	Tanzania/Uganda/ Sudan/Egypt	6,670	4,145
2	Amazon	Peru/Brazil	6,448	4,007
3	Yangtze–Kiang	China	6,300	3,915
4	Mississippi–Missouri–Red Rock	USA	5,971	3,710
5	Yenisey–Angara–Selenga	Mongolia/Russia	5,540	3,442
6	Huang Ho (Yellow River)	China	5,464	3,395
7	Ob'–Irtysh	Mongolia/Kazakhstan/ Russia	5,410	3,362
8	Zaïre (Congo)	Angola/Zaïre	4,700	2,920
9	Lena–Kirenga	Russia	4,400	2,734
10	Mekong	Tibet/China/ Myanmar/Laos/ Cambodia/Vietnam	4,350	2,703

THE 10 LONGEST RIVERS IN AUSTRALIA

	River	Length km	miles
1	Murray–Darling– Culgoa–Balonne– Condamine	3,750	2,330
2	Murray	1,754	1,090
3 =	Barwon–Macintyre– Dumaresq– Severn	1,577	980
3 =	Murrumbidgee	1,577	980
5	Lachlan	1,481	920
6	Fitzroy–Dawson	1,110	690
7	Macquarie	950	590
8	Namoi	853	530
9	Flinders	837	520
10	Bogan	724	450

THE 10 LONGEST RIVERS IN EUROPE*

	River	Countries	Length km	miles
1	Danube	Germany/Austria/ Czechoslovakia†/ Hungary/Yugoslavia†/ Romania/Bulgaria	2,842	1,766
2	Rhine	Switzerland/ Germany/Holland	1,368	850
3	Elbe	Czechoslovakia†/ Germany	1,167	725
4	Loire	France	1,014	630
5	Tagus	Portugal	1,009	627
6	Meuse	France/Belgium/ Holland	950	590
7	Ebro	Spain	933	580
8	Rhône	Switzerland/France	813	505
9	Guadiana	Spain/Portugal	805	500
10	Seine	France	776	482

*Excluding former USSR. †Former territory.

Without excluding those rivers in the territory of the former USSR in Europe, all 10 rivers would be Russian, with the 3,687-km/2,291-mile Volga heading the list.

THE 10 LONGEST RIVERS IN AFRICA

	River	Countries	Length km	miles
1	Nile	Tanzania/Uganda/ Sudan/Egypt	6,670	4,145
2	Zaïre (Congo)	Angola/Zaïre	4,700	2,920
3	Niger	Guinea/Nigeria	4,100	2,550
4	Zambezi	Zambia/ Mozambique	2,650	1,650
5	Shebeli	Somalia	2,490	1,550
6	Ubangi	Zaïre	2,460	1,530
7	Orange	Namibia/ South Africa	2,250	1,400
8	Kasai	Zaïre	1,930	1,200
9	Senegal–Bafing	Mauritania/ Senegal	1,700	1,050
10	Blue Nile	Sudan	1,610	1,000

THE 10 LONGEST RIVERS IN SOUTH AMERICA

	River	Countries	Length km	miles
1	Amazon	Peru/Brazil	6,448	4,007
2	Plata–Paraná	Brazil/Paraguay/ Argentina/Uruguay	4,000	2,485
3	Madeira– Mamoré– Grande	Bolivia/Brazil	3,380	2,100
4	Purus	Peru/Brazil	3,207	1,993
5	São Francisco	Brazil	3,198	1,987
6	Orinoco	Colombia/ Venezuela	2,736	1,700
7	Tocantins	Brazil	2,699	1,677
8	Paraguay	Paraguay/Brazil/ Argentina/Bolivia	2,549	1,584
9	Japurá– Caquetá	Colombia/Brazil	2,414	1,500
10	Negro	Colombia/ Venezuela/Brazil	2,253	1,400

THE 10 LONGEST RIVERS IN NORTH AMERICA

	River	Country	Length km	miles
1	Mackenzie–Peace	Canada	4,241	2,635
2	Missouri–Red Rock	USA	4,088	2,540
3	Mississippi	USA	3,779	2,348
4	Missouri	USA	3,726	2,315
5	Yukon	USA	3,185	1,979
6	St Lawrence	Canada	3,130	1,945
7	Rio Grande	USA	2,832	1,760
8	Nelson	Canada	2,575	1,600
9	Arkansas	USA	2,348	1,459
10	Colorado	USA	2,334	1,450

The Mississippi, Missouri and Red Rock rivers are often combined, thus becoming the 4th longest river in the world at 5,971 km/3,710 miles.

THE 10 DEEPEST OCEANS AND SEAS IN THE WORLD

	Ocean/sea	Greatest depth m	ft	Average depth m	ft
1	Pacific Ocean	10,918	35,820	4,028	13,215
2	Indian Ocean	7,455	24,460	3,963	13,002
3	Atlantic Ocean	9,219	30,246	3,926	12,880
4	Caribbean Sea	6,946	22,788	2,647	8,685
5	South China Sea	5,016	16,456	1,652	5,419
6	Bering Sea	4,773	15,659	1,547	5,075
7	Gulf of Mexico	3,787	12,425	1,486	4,874
8	Mediterranean Sea	4,632	15,197	1,429	4,688
9	Japan Sea	3,742	12,276	1,350	4,429
10	Arctic Ocean	5,625	18,456	1,205	3,953

For comparison, the North Sea is 660 m/2,165 ft at its deepest point, and has an average depth of 94 m/308 ft.

The Indian Ocean is the world's second deepest and third largest.

THE 10 LARGEST OCEANS AND SEAS IN THE WORLD

	Ocean/sea	Approx. area sq km	sq miles
1	Pacific Ocean	165,241,000	63,800,000
2	Atlantic Ocean	82,439,000	31,830,000
3	Indian Ocean	73,452,000	28,360,000
4	Arctic Ocean	13,986,000	5,400,000
5	Arabian Sea	3,864,000	1,492,000
6	South China Sea	3,447,000	1,331,000
7	Caribbean Sea	2,753,000	1,063,000
8	Mediterranean Sea	2,505,000	967,000
9	Bering Sea	2,269,000	876,000
10	Bay of Bengal	2,173,000	839,000

THE 10 HIGHEST MOUNTAINS IN THE WORLD

	Mountain	Country	Height* m	ft
1	Everest	Nepal/Tibet	8,848	29,029
2	K2	Kashmir/China	8,611	28,250
3	Kanchenjunga	Nepal/Sikkim	8,598	28,208
4	Lhotse	Nepal/Tibet	8,501	27,890
5	Makalu I	Nepal/Tibet	8,470	27,790
6	Dhaulagiri I	Nepal	8,172	26,810
7	Manaslu I	Nepal	8,156	26,760
8	Cho Oyu	Nepal	8,153	26,750
9	Nanga Parbat	Kashmir	8,126	26,660
10	Annapurna I	Nepal	8,078	26,504

*Height of principal peak; lower peaks of the same mountain are excluded.

Many of the Top 10 mountains have alternative names: in Tibetan Everest is known as Chomolungma ('Goddess Mother of the World'). K2 (so called because it was the second mountain in the Karakoram range counting from the Kashmir end) is also referred to by the local name Chogori and sometimes as Godwin-Austen, after Lieutenant Henry Haversham Godwin-Austen (1834–1923), who first surveyed it in 1865. Manaslu is also known as Kutang I and Nanga Parbat as Diamir.

THE 10 HIGHEST MOUNTAINS IN THE USA

	Mountain	Height m	ft
1	McKinley	6,194	20,320
2	St Elias	5,489	18,008
3	Foraker	5,304	17,400
4	Bona	5,044	16,550
5	Blackburn	4,996	16,390
6	Kennedy	4,964	16,286
7	Sanford	4,949	16,237
8	South Buttress	4,842	15,885
9	Vancouver	4,785	15,700
10	Churchill	4,766	15,638

All 10 tallest mountains in the United States are in Alaska or on the Alaska/Canada border. Mt Logan in Canada is the second tallest peak in the North American continent at 6,050 m/19,850 ft. Colorado and California also have a number of mountains of over 4,267 m/14,000 ft. Only one other state – Washington – has a mountain in the Top 80: Mt Rainier at 4,392 m/14,410 ft.

THE 10 HIGHEST MOUNTAINS IN AUSTRALIA

	Mountain	Height m	ft
1	Kosciusko	2,229	7,314
2	Townsend	2,209	7,249
3	Clarke	2,200	7,219
4	Twynham	2,195	7,203
5	Carruthers Peak	2,145	7,039
6	Sentinel	2,140	7,022
7	Northcote	2,131	6,992
8 =	Gungartan	2,068	6,786
8 =	Tate	2,068	6,786
10	Jagungal	2,062	6,766

All 10 of Australia's highest peaks are in New South Wales. None of the 10 tallest mountains in Oceania is in Australia, however, and there are at least six elsewhere in the continent that are more than twice the height of Kosciusko, led by Ngga Pulu in West Irian, Indonesia, which reaches 5,030 m/16,503 ft.

THE 10 HIGHEST MOUNTAINS IN ENGLAND

	Mountain	Height m	ft
1	Scafell Pike	977	3,206
2	Sca Fell	964	3,162
3	Helvellyn	949	3,113
4	Skiddaw	931	3,054
5	Bow Fell	902	2,960
6	Great Gable	899	2,949
7	Cross Fell	893	2,930
8	Pillar Fell	892	2,927
9	Esk Pike	885	2,903
10	Fairfield	873	2,863

All 10 of England's highest peaks are in Cumbria.

K2, relegated to second place in the league of the world's tallest mountains by just 237 m/779 ft – which is less than the height of the UK's tallest building.

PLANET EARTH

THE 10 HIGHEST MOUNTAINS IN WALES

	Mountain	Height m	ft
1	Snowdon	1,085	3,560
2	Carnedd Llewelyn	1,062	3,484
3	Carnedd Dafydd	1,044	3,426
4	Glyder Fawr	999	3,279
5	Glyder Fâch	994	3,262
6	Y Garn	946	3,104
7	Foel Fras	942	3,091
8	Elidir Fawr	923	3,029
9	Tryfan	917	3,010
10	Aran Fawddwy	905	2,970

All the tallest Welsh peaks are in the Snowdonia region of the county of Gwynedd. Several also have sub-peaks that are similarly tall, but are not included as separate mountains.

THE 10 HIGHEST MOUNTAINS IN IRELAND

	Mountain	Height m	ft
1	Carrauntual, Kerry	1,042	3,414
2	Beenkeraugh, Kerry	1,010	3,314
3 =	Caher, Kerry	975	3,200
3 =	Ridge of the Reeks, Kerry	975	3,200
5	Brandon, Kerry	953	3,127
6	Lugnaquilla, Wicklow	926	3,039
7	Galtymore, Tipperary	920	3,018
8 =	Baurtregaum, Kerry	852	2,796
8 =	Slieve Donard, Co Down	852	2,796
10	Mullaghcleevaun, Wicklow	850	2,788

Slieve Donard is the highest mountain in Northern Ireland. All the others are in the Irish Republic.

THE 10 HIGHEST MOUNTAINS IN SCOTLAND

	Mountain	Height m	ft
1	Ben Nevis, Highland	1,344	4,408
2	Ben Macdhui, Grampian	1,309	4,296
3	Braeriach, Grampian/Highland	1,296	4,252
4	Cairn Toul, Grampian	1,293	4,241
5	Cairn Gorm, Grampian/Highland	1,245	4,084
6	Aonach Beag, Highland	1,236	4,054
7	Carn Mór Dearg, Highland	1,223	4,012
8	Aonach Mór, Highland	1,219	3,999
9	Ben Lawers, Tayside	1,214	3,984
10	Beinn a' Bhùird, Grampian	1,196	3,924

Ben Nevis, Scotland and the UK's tallest mountain, derives its name from the Gaelic word for mountain and the name of the river nearby.

THE 10 HIGHEST MOUNTAINS IN EUROPE*

	Mountain	Country	Height† m	ft
1	Mont Blanc	France	4,807	15,771
2	Monte Rosa	Switzerland/Italy	4,634	15,203
3	Dom	Switzerland	4,545	14,911
4	Lyskamm	Switzerland/Italy	4,527	14,853
5	Weisshorn	Switzerland	4,505	14,780
6	Täschhorn	Switzerland	4,491	14,733
7	Matterhorn	Switzerland/Italy	4,475	14,683
8	Dent Blanche	Switzerland	4,357	14,293
9	Nadelhorn	Switzerland	4,327	14,196
10	Grand Combin	Switzerland	4,314	14,153

*Excluding Caucasus Mountains which include at least 15 peaks with elevations greater than that of Mont Blanc.

†Height of principal peak; lower peaks of the same mountain are excluded.

All 10 of Europe's 10 highest mountains are in the Alps. Some authorities regard Lyskamm as part of Mount Rosa; if excluded, 10th place goes to Lenzspitze (Switzerland; 4,294 m/14,087 ft).

THE 10 HIGHEST MOUNTAINS IN AFRICA

	Mountain	Country	Height m	ft
1	Kilimanjaro	Tanzania	5,895	19,340
2	Kenya	Kenya	5,199	17,058
3	Ngaliema	Uganda/Zaïre	5,109	16,763
4	Duwoni	Uganda	4,896	16,062
5	Baker	Uganda	4,843	15,889
6	Emin	Zaïre	4,798	15,741
7	Gessi	Uganda	4,715	15,470
8	Sella	Uganda	4,627	15,179
9	Ras Dashen	Ethiopia	4,620	15,158
10	Wasuwameso	Zaïre	4,581	15,030

THE 10 HIGHEST MOUNTAINS IN SOUTH AMERICA

	Mountain	Country	Height m	ft
1	Cerro Aconcagua	Argentina	6,960	22,834
2	Ojos del Salado	Argentina/Chile	6,885	22,588
3	Bonete	Argentina	6,873	22,550
4	Pissis	Argentina/Chile	6,780	22,244
5	Huascarán	Peru	6,768	22,205
6	Llullaillaco	Argentina/Chile	6,723	22,057
7	Libertador	Argentina	6,721	22,050
8	Mercadario	Argentina/Chile	6,670	21,884
9	Yerupajá	Peru	6,634	21,765
10	Tres Cruces	Argentina/Chile	6,620	21,720

THE 10 HIGHEST MOUNTAINS IN NORTH AMERICA

	Mountain	Country	Height* m	ft
1	McKinley	USA	6,194	20,320
2	Logan	Canada	6,050	19,850
3	Citlaltépetl (Orizaba)	Mexico	5,700	18,700
4	St Elias	USA/Canada	5,489	18,008
5	Popocatépetl	Mexico	5,452	17,887
6	Foraker	USA	5,304	17,400
7	Ixtaccihuatl	Mexico	5,286	17,343
8	Lucania	Canada	5,226	17,147
9	King	Canada	5,173	16,971
10	Steele	Canada	5,073	16,644

*Height of principal peak; lower peaks of the same mountain are excluded.

THE 10 DEEPEST DEPRESSIONS IN THE WORLD

	Depression	Country	Maximum depth below sea level m	ft
1	Dead Sea	Israel/Jordan	394	1,293
2	Turfan Depression	China	154	505
3	Qattâra Depression	Egypt	133	436
4	Poluostrov Mangyshlak	Kazakhstan	132	433
5	Danakil Depression	Ethiopia	117	383
6	Death Valley	USA	86	282
7	Salton Sink	USA	72	235
8	Zapadny Chink Ustyurta	Kazakhstan	70	230
9	Prikaspiyskaya Nizmennost	Russia/Kazakhstan	67	220
10	Ozera Sarykamysh	Uzbekistan/Turkmenistan	45	148

The shore of the Dead Sea is the lowest exposed ground below sea level, but the bed of the Sea actually reaches 728 m/2,388 ft below sea level, and that of Lake Baikal, Russia, attains 1,485 m/4,872 ft below sea level. Much of Antarctica is below sea level (some as low as 2,538 m/8,326 ft) – but is covered by an ice cap. The lowest land in the UK is the Holme Fen, Cambridgeshire (2.7 m/9 ft below sea level), although the bed of Loch Morar, Inverness, is 301 m/987 ft below sea level.

The Dead Sea is the lowest place on Earth.

THE 10 LARGEST METEORITES FOUND IN THE UK

	Location	Date found	Approx. weight kg	lb
1	Barwell, Leicestershire	24 Dec 1965	46.0	101
2 =	Appley Bridge, Lancashire	13 Oct 1914	33.0	73
2 =	Hatford, Berkshire (3 rocks)	9 Apr 1628	33.0	73
4	Wold Cottage, Yorkshire	13 Dec 1795	25.4	56
5	Strathmore, Tayside (4 rocks)	3 Dec 1917	13.0	29
6	Strechleigh, Devon	10 Jan 1623	12.0	26
7	Perth	17 May 1830	11.0	24
8	High Possil, Strathclyde	5 Apr 1804	4.5	10
9	Crumlin, Antrim	13 Sep 1902	4.1	9
10	Rowton, Shropshire	20 Apr 1876	3.2	7

Treasure from outer space: an American collector and dealer's array of meteorites, with a necklace made from meteoric fragments.

The Barwell meteorite broke up on impact and not all the pieces were recovered, some entering private collections (the miserly Geological Museum offer of 10 shillings [50p] an ounce clearly dissuaded many finders from parting with their treasures, or persuaded them to sell privately for larger sums). Since the Strechleigh meteorite of 1623, there have been 23 recorded instances of meteorite falls in the British Isles, including one at Adare, Co. Limerick, on 10 September 1813, the total weight of which exceeded 48 kg/106 lb, with the largest stone weighing 29.5 kg/65 lb.

THE 10 LARGEST METEORITE CRATERS IN THE WORLD

	Crater	Location	Diameter km	miles
1 =	Sudbury	Ontario, Canada	140	87
1 =	Vredefort	South Africa	140	87
3 =	Manicouagan	Quebec, Canada	100	62
3 =	Popigai	Russia	100	62
5	Puchezh-Katunki	Russia	80	50
6	Kara	Russia	60	37
7	Siljan	Sweden	52	32
8	Charlevoix	Quebec, Canada	46	29
9	Araguainha Dome	Brazil	40	25
10	Carswell	Saskatchewan, Canada	37	23

Dispute rages about Earth's notable meteor craters: unlike on the Solar System's other planets and moons, many astroblemes (collision sites) on Earth have been weathered over time and obscured, and one of the ongoing debates in geology is thus whether or not certain crater-like structures are of meteoric origin or the remnants of long-extinct volcanoes. The Vredefort Ring, for example, long thought to be meteoric, was declared in 1963 to be volcanic, but has since been claimed as a definite meteor crater, as are all the giant meteorite craters in the Top 10 which are listed as such (along with 106 others) by the International Union of Geological Sciences Commission on Comparative Planetology. The relatively small Barringer Crater in Arizona (1.265 km/0.79 miles) is, however, the largest that all scientists agree is indisputably an astrobleme. Recently, by using photographs taken from space, many new possible astroblemes have been discovered, including a massive 320-km/199-mile diameter site centred on Prague, Czech Republic, which has been named the Praha Basin. It has been postulated that what may turn out to be Europe's biggest crater was caused 15,000,000 years ago by a meteorite of some 80 km/50 miles diameter which impacted with a force a million times more powerful than the atomic bomb that destroyed Hiroshima.

THE 10 LARGEST METEORITES EVER FOUND

	Location	Estimated weight (tonnes)
1	Hoba West, Grootfontein, South Africa	54.4
2	Ahnighito ('The Tent'), Cape York, West Greenland	30.9
3	Bacuberito, Mexico	27.0
4	Mbosi, Tanganyika	26.0
5	Agpalik, Cape York, West Greenland	20.1
6	Armanti, Western Mongolia	20.0
7 =	Chupaderos, Mexico	14.0
7 =	Willamette, Oregon	14.0
9	Campo del Cielo, Argentina	13.0
10	Mundrabila, Western Australia	12.0

Meteorites have been known since early times: fragments of meteorite have been found mounted in a necklace in an Egyptian pyramid and in ancient American Indian burial sites and there is a well-documented fall on 16 November 1492 of a 118-kg/260-lb meteorite that was later preserved in the museum at Ensisheim in Switzerland. It was not until about 200 years ago, however, that the notion of meteorites falling from the sky was taken seriously (the word meteorite itself was not used until 1834); thus prior to 1790 only 20 incidents were recorded in the world. From that year until 1940, however, there were 1,400 recorded instances of meteorites falling to Earth – a reflection of the spread of awareness of their existence and nature (especially in highly populated areas) rather than any increase in the number of meteorites falling, which has been calculated to amount to some 500 a year across the whole globe, although many fall in the sea and in unpopulated areas where their descent goes unnoticed. The actual risk of being struck by a falling meteorite has also been estimated, and for citizens of the USA placed at one occurrence every 9,300 years. Apart from occasional unfounded legends, there is in fact no certain case of anyone being killed by a meteorite, although animals are occasional victims and humans have been slightly injured by meteorite fragments. The Hoba meteorite, the largest in the world, was found on a farm in 1920. A 2.73 m/9 ft x 2.43 m/8 ft slab, it consists of 82 per cent iron and 16 per cent nickel. 'The Tent', known by its original Eskimo name, Ahnighito, was discovered in 1897 by the American Arctic explorer Admiral Robert Peary and is now in the Hayden Planetarium at the New York Museum of Natural History. It is the largest meteorite in the world on exhibition.

THE 10 LONGEST CAVES IN THE WORLD

	Cave	Location	Length* m	ft
1	Mammoth cave system	Kentucky, USA	560,000	1,837,270
2	Optimisticeskaja	Ukraine	178,000	583,989
3	Holloch	Switzerland	137,000	449,475
4	Jewel Cave	South Dakota, USA	127,000	416,667
5	Siebenhengsteholensystem	Switzerland	110,000	360,892
6	Ozernaya	Ukraine	107,300	352,034
7	Réseau de la Coume d'Hyouernede	France	90,500	296,916
8	Sistema de Ojo Guarena	Spain	89,100	292,323
9	Wind Cave	South Dakota, USA	88,500	290,354
10	Fisher Ridge cave system	Kentucky, USA	83,000	273,950
16	*Ease Gill cave system*	*West Yorkshire, UK*	*66,000*	*216,535*

*Total length of known system.

CAVES QUIZ

1 What is the cave on the Isle of Staffa that inspired Mendelssohn's *Hebridean Overture*?

2 What is the name given to a person who studies caves?

3 Where are the Spanish caves in which fine Stone Age paintings were found in 1879?

4 Who wrote the novel *Clan of the Cave Bear*?

5 Having once performed in Liverpool's Cavern Club, who appeared in a 1981 film called *Caveman*?

6 Which Kent caves were used in the Second World War as an air raid shelter, complete with church, cinema and shops?

7 What is a cave-dweller called?

8 In the Bible, who fled from King Saul and took refuge in the Cave of Adullam?

9 Do stalagmites grow down from a cave roof or up from the floor?

10 In what cave system would you find the Star Chamber, Frozen Niagara and Charlotte's Grotto?

THE 10 OLDEST BOTANIC GARDENS IN THE UK

	Garden	Founded
1	University Botanic Garden, Oxford	1621
2	Royal Botanic Garden, Edinburgh	1670
3	Chelsea Physic Garden, London	1673
4	Royal Botanic Gardens, Kew	1759
5	Cambridge University Botanic Garden, Cambridge	1762*
6	Bath Botanical Gardens, Bath	1779
7	Glasgow Botanic Gardens, Glasgow	1817
8	Museum Gardens, York	1827
9	Belfast Botanic Garden, Belfast	1828
10	Birmingham Botanical Gardens, Birmingham	1839

Moved to present site 1846.

The first botanic gardens for the study of plants date from the medieval era. Plants were then widely used in the preparation of remedies, so gardens were often attached to medical schools, such as that at the first European medical school at Salerno, Italy, dating from 1309, which became the model for gardens set up in Venice, Pisa and Padua. Other European universities such as Leiden, Leipzig and Heidelberg followed suit, with the University of Oxford creating the first in the British Isles. In the eighteenth century botanic gardens were set up in various parts of the world, including Pamplemousses, Mauritius (1735), Sibpur, India (1787) and the Dublin National Botanic Gardens, Glasnevin (1795). As well as those in the Top 10, Westonbirt Arboretum was established in 1839, but is not technically a botanic garden. Others founded during the nineteenth century include Bristol University Botanic Garden which dates from 1882.

The magnificent recently restored Palm House at Kew, one of England's oldest established botanic gardens, dates from 1848.

PLANTS & CROPS

PLANTS & CROPS

THE 10 COUNTRIES WITH THE LARGEST AREAS OF FOREST

	Country	Area hectares	acres
1	Former USSR	947,000,000	2,340,084,350
2	Brazil	493,030,000	1,218,301,780
3	Canada	359,000,000	887,106,950
4	USA	293,600,000	725,500,280
5	Zaïre	174,310,000	430,728,720
6	China	126,515,000	312,624,890
7	Indonesia	113,433,000	280,298,610
8	Australia	106,000,000	261,931,300
9	Peru	68,400,000	169,019,820
10	India	66,700,000	164,819,030
	UK	2,135,000	5,275,692
	World total	4,205,288,000	10,391,476,000

THE 10 MOST FORESTED COUNTRIES IN THE WORLD

	Country	% forest cover
1	Surinam	91
2	Solomon Islands	89
3	Papua New Guinea	83
4	French Guiana	81
5	Guyana	76
6	Gabon	75
7 =	Cambodia	74
7 =	North Korea	74
9	Finland	69
10	Japan	66

These are the 10 countries with the greatest area of forest and woodland as a percentage of their total land area. With increasing deforestation, the world average has fallen below 25 per cent. That of the UK stands at less than 10 per cent, with Ireland under five per cent. The least forested large countries in the world are the desert lands of the Middle East and North Africa, such as Libya with under 0.4 per cent.

THE 10 LARGEST FORESTS IN THE UK

	Forest	Area hectares	acres
1	Kielder	39,380	97,310
2	Newton Stewart	35,275	87,166
3	Dornoch	35,180	86,932
4	Ayrshire and Arran	29,189	72,127
5	Castle Douglas	27,415	67,774
6	Kintyre	26,287	64,956
7	Loch Awe	25,202	62,275
8	Aberfoyle	24,431	60,370
9	Easter Ross	23,795	58,799
10	Cowal	23,521	58,122

The Kielder Forest is in Northumberland, but the other nine largest forests under the aegis of the Forestry Commission are all located in Scotland.

THE TOP 10 FRUIT-PRODUCING COUNTRIES

	Country	Annual production (tonnes)
1	Brazil	31,348,000
2	India	28,388,000
3	USA	24,668,000
4	China	22,992,000
5	Italy	17,632,000
6	Former USSR	14,700,000
7	Spain	12,542,000
8	France	10,313,000
9	Mexico	9,605,000
10	Turkey	9,391,000
	UK	502,000
	World total	348,140,000

THE TOP 10 BANANA-PRODUCING COUNTRIES

	Country	Annual production (tonnes)
1	India	6,400,000
2	Brazil	5,630,000
3	Philippines	3,545,000
4	Ecuador	2,954,000
5	Indonesia	2,400,000
6	China	2,105,000
7	Mexico	1,868,000
8	Colombia	1,630,000
9	Thailand	1,620,000
10	Burundi	1,580,000
	World total	*47,660,000*

The banana was eaten by Alexander the Great's army in India, which remains the world's foremost producer.

THE TOP 10 ORANGE-PRODUCING COUNTRIES

	Country	Annual production (tonnes)
1	Brazil	18,942,000
2	USA	7,258,000
3	China	5,385,000
4	Spain	2,504,000
5	Mexico	2,175,000
6	Italy	1,942,000
7	India	1,890,000
8	Egypt	1,600,000
9	Iran	1,270,000
10	Pakistan	1,100,000
	World total	*55,308,000*

During the 1980s, orange production progressively increased from a world total of less than 40,000,000 tonnes. China's, in particular, rocketed up almost sevenfold during the decade, from under 800,000 tonnes to its present 3rd position in the world league table. Iran has also experienced a boost in production, entering the Top 10 for the first time in 1991 and thereby ousting Morocco (920,000 tonnes).

Orange production experienced an international surge in recent years.

THE TOP 10 APPLE-PRODUCING COUNTRIES

	Country	Annual production (tonnes)
1	Former USSR	6,000,000
2	China	4,816,000
3	USA	4,477,000
4 =	France	2,000,000
4 =	Turkey	2,000,000
6	Italy	1,793,000
7	Iran	1,515,000
8	Poland	1,146,000
9	Argentina	1,100,000
10	Germany	1,081,000
	World total	39,404,000

Japan (1,046,000 tonnes) and India (1,020,000 tonnes) are the only other countries in the world with annual apple production of more than 1,000,000 tonnes. Having steadily declined during the 1980s in the face of cheap imports, the UK's commercial production of apples has recently increased again and in 1991 totalled 334,000 tonnes.

THE TOP 10 LEMON/LIME-PRODUCING COUNTRIES

	Country	Annual production (tonnes)
1	Italy	832,000
2	Mexico	707,000
3	USA	670,000
4	India	570,000
5	Spain	516,000
6	Argentina	430,000
7	Egypt	415,000
8	Turkey	357,000
9	Iran	210,000
10	China	173,000
	World total	6,786,000

THE TOP 10 PINEAPPLE-PRODUCING COUNTRIES

	Country	Annual production (tonnes)
1	Thailand	1,876,000
2	Philippines	1,160,000
3	China	927,000
4	Brazil	787,000
5	Vietnam	507,000
6	USA	504,000
7	Mexico	345,000
8	Indonesia	285,000
9	Kenya	245,000
10	Colombia	240,000
	World total	10,076,000

THE TOP 10 COCONUT-PRODUCING COUNTRIES

	Country	Annual production (tonnes)
1	Indonesia	14,000,000
2	Philippines	8,923,000
3	India	6,550,000
4	Thailand	1,328,000
5	Malaysia	1,155,000
6	Mexico	1,101,000
7	Vietnam	1,000,000
8	Papua New Guinea	900,000
9	Argentina	792,000
10	Côte d'Ivoire	515,000
	World total	42,385,000

FRUIT QUIZ

1. What fruit did Eve eat in the Garden of Eden?
2. In what year did the Beatles release their single *Strawberry Fields Forever*?
3. What fruit did the botanist Linnaeus call *Musa sapientum*, 'the fruit of the wise men'?
4. What fruit did Nell Gwynn sell?
5. What fruit is known in Polish as *gruszki* and German as *birne*?
6. A shipload of a fruit previously cultivated only in hot-houses arrived in England in 1847. What was it?
7. Name Eddie Calvert's 1955 No. 1 instrumental hit record which contains the names of two fruits.
8. From what fruit is *kamraddin* made?
9. What is the common name for the alligator pear?
10. What are Laxtons, Early Rivers and Mirabelles?

THE TOP 10 PEAR-PRODUCING COUNTRIES

	Country	Annual production (tonnes)
1	China	2,728,000
2	Italy	864,000
3	USA	824,000
4	Former USSR	500,000
5 =	Japan	420,000
5 =	Turkey	420,000
7	Spain	412,000
8	France	280,000
9	Argentina	220,000
10	South Africa	204,000
	UK	*39,000*
	World total	*9,359,000*

The sunflowers that inspired Van Gogh's paintings remain a significant crop in France.

THE TOP 10 STRAWBERRY-PRODUCING COUNTRIES

	Country	Annual production (tonnes)
1	USA	635,300
2	Poland	262,625
3	Japan	218,100
4	Italy	191,200
5	Spain	181,300
6	Former USSR	125,000
7	Republic of Korea	101,000
8	Mexico	96,794
9	France	88,000
10	UK	55,000
	World total	*2,469,117*

THE TOP 10 SUNFLOWER SEED-PRODUCING COUNTRIES

	Country	Annual production (tonnes)
1	Former USSR	5,800,000
2	Argentina	3,970,000
3	France	2,563,000
4	USA	1,637,000
5	China	1,250,000
6	Spain	994,000
7	Hungary	855,000
8	India	850,000
9	Turkey	800,000
10	Romania	612,000
	World total	*22,803,000*

THE TOP 10 AVOCADO-PRODUCING COUNTRIES

	Country	Annual production (tonnes)
1	Mexico	866,000
2	USA	151,000
3	Dominican Republic	130,000
4	Brazil	115,000
5	Colombia	81,000
6	Indonesia	72,000
7	Haiti	57,000
8	Venezuela	51,000
9	Zaïre	46,000
10 =	Chile	45,000
10 =	Israel	45,000
10 =	Spain	45,000
	World total	*2,036,000*

Rice is one of the world's most important food crops.

THE TOP 10 FOOD CROPS IN THE WORLD

	Crop	Annual production (tonnes)
1	Sugar cane	1,090,802,000
2	Wheat	550,993,000
3	Rice	519,869,000
4	Maize	478,775,000
5	Sugar beet	296,519,000
6	Potatoes	261,162,000
7	Barley	169,385,000
8	Cassava	153,689,000
9	Sweet potatoes	126,187,000
10	Soybeans	103,065,000

THE TOP 10 TOMATO-PRODUCING COUNTRIES

	Country	Annual production (tonnes)
1	USA	11,379,000
2	Former USSR	6,600,000
3	Turkey	6,200,000
4	Italy	6,069,000
5	China	5,690,000
6	India	3,100,000
7	Spain	2,764,000
8	Brazil	2,309,000
9	Greece	1,990,000
10	Mexico	1,772,000
	UK	139,000
	World total	69,145,000

THE TOP 10 BARLEY-PRODUCING COUNTRIES IN THE WORLD

	Country	Annual production (tonnes)
1	Former USSR	42,000,000
2	Germany	14,449,000
3	Canada	12,463,000
4	France	10,651,000
5	USA	10,113,000
6	Spain	9,141,000
7	Turkey	7,800,000
8	UK	7,700,000
9	Denmark	4,978,000
10	Poland	4,257,000
	World total	169,385,000

THE TOP 10 SWEET POTATO-PRODUCING COUNTRIES IN THE WORLD

	Country	Annual production (tonnes)
1	China	107,190,000
2	Vietnam	2,105,000
3	Indonesia	1,976,000
4	Uganda	1,800,000
5	Japan	1,460,000
6	India	1,195,000
7	Rwanda	850,000
8	Brazil	700,000
9	Burundi	680,000
10	Philippines	662,000
	World total	126,187,000

Top popcorn: the USA is by far the world's leading producer of maize.

THE TOP 10 MAIZE-PRODUCING COUNTRIES IN THE WORLD

	Country	Annual production (tonnes)
1	USA	188,867,000
2	China	93,350,000
3	Brazil	22,604,000
4	Mexico	13,527,000
5	France	12,787,000
6	Romania	10,493,000
7	Former Yugoslavia	8,800,000
8	Former USSR	8,500,000
9	South Africa	8,200,000
10	Argentina	7,768,000
	World total	*478,775,000*

THE TOP 10 CASSAVA-PRODUCING COUNTRIES IN THE WORLD

	Country	Annual production (tonnes)
1	Brazil	24,632,000
2	Thailand	20,300,000
3	Nigeria	20,000,000
4	Zaïre	18,227,000
5	Indonesia	16,330,000
6	Tanzania	6,266,000
7	India	5,600,000
8	Paraguay	3,900,000
9	Mozambique	3,690,000
10	Ghana	3,600,000
	World total	*153,689,000*

THE TOP 10 RICE-PRODUCING COUNTRIES IN THE WORLD

	Country	Annual production (tonnes)
1	China	187,450,000
2	India	110,945,000
3	Indonesia	44,321,000
4	Bangladesh	28,575,000
5	Thailand	20,040,000
6	Vietnam	19,428,000
7	Myanmar (Burma)	13,201,000
8	Japan	12,005,000
9	Philippines	9,670,000
10	Brazil	9,503,000
	World total	*519,869,000*

THE TOP 10 WHEAT-PRODUCING COUNTRIES IN THE WORLD

	Country	Annual production (tonnes)
1	China	95,003,000
2	Former USSR	80,000,000
3	India	54,522,000
4	USA	53,915,000
5	France	34,483,000
6	Canada	32,822,000
7	Turkey	20,400,000
8	Germany	16,669,000
9	Pakistan	14,505,000
10	UK	14,300,000
	World total	*550,993,000*

THE TOP 10 SUGAR CANE-PRODUCING COUNTRIES IN THE WORLD

	Country	Annual production (tonnes)
1	Brazil	261,907,000
2	India	240,290,000
3	Cuba	74,000,000
4	China	73,103,000
5	Thailand	40,661,000
6	Mexico	36,683,000
7	Pakistan	35,989,000
8	Indonesia	32,563,000
9	USA	28,332,000
10	Philippines	25,551,400
	World total	1,090,802,000

THE TOP 10 SUGAR BEET-PRODUCING COUNTRIES IN THE WORLD

	Country	Annual production (tonnes)
1	Former USSR	79,000,000
2	France	29,280,000
3	Germany	25,926,000
4	USA	25,263,000
5	China	16,237,000
6	Turkey	14,900,000
7	Italy	13,085,000
8	Poland	11,412,000
9	Netherlands	7,500,000
10	UK	7,340,000
	World total	296,519,000

THE TOP 10 SOYBEAN-PRODUCING COUNTRIES IN THE WORLD

	Country	Annual production (tonnes)
1	USA	54,039,000
2	Brazil	14,771,000
3	Argentina	11,250,000
4	China	9,807,000
5	India	2,100,000
6	Indonesia	1,549,000
7	Italy	1,325,000
8	Paraguay	1,304,000
9	Former USSR	760,000
10	Mexico	718,000
	World total	103,065,000

THE TOP 10 POTATO-PRODUCING COUNTRIES IN THE WORLD

	Country	Annual production (tonnes)
1	Former USSR	64,500,000
2	China	35,533,000
3	Poland	29,038,000
4	USA	18,970,000
5	India	15,254,000
6	Germany	10,225,000
7	Netherlands	6,735,000
8	UK	6,700,000
9	France	6,300,000
10	Spain	5,300,000
	World total	261,162,000

THE 10 MOST POPULAR PEDIGREE CAT BREEDS IN THE UK

	Breed	No. registered by Cat Fancy	
		1991	1992
1	Persian Long Hair	12,515	11,107
2	Siamese	6,642	5,618
3	Burmese	4,433	3,808
4	British Short Hair	3,555	3,588
5	Birman	2,228	2,046
6	Oriental Short Hair	1,270	1,275
7	Maine Coon	889	975
8	Abyssinian	716	662
9	Exotic Short Hair	504	607
10	Russian Blue	507	458

Based on a total of 32,767 cats registered with the Governing Council of the Cat Fancy in 1992 (1991: 35,756).

A Birman kitten: such breeds are among the most popular pedigree cats in the UK.

ANIMALS & BIRDS

10 FAMOUS CAT-LOVERS AND THEIR CATS

Owner	Cat
1 **Winston Churchill**	*Margate*

The cat turned up at 10 Downing Street and was adopted by Churchill on 10 October 1953, the day of an important speech at Margate, hence its name. Subsequent feline occupants of No. 10 have included Harold Wilson's Siamese cat Nemo and Mrs Thatcher's Wilberforce.

2 **Bill Clinton**	*Socks*

The White House cat of President Bill Clinton, Socks is already the subject of a bestselling book. As the President and First Lady are allergic to cats, their daughter Chelsea is Socks's official custodian.

3 **Charles Dickens**	*Williamina*

Williamina was called William until she gave birth to a litter of kittens, one of which, known as 'The Master's Cat', gained Dickens' attention by putting out his candle with its paw.

4 **Ernest Hemingway**	*Crazy Christian*

Crazy Christian, Ecstasy and about 40 other cats overran Hemingway's Cuba home until a special tower was built for them.

5 **Edward Lear**	*Foss*

Foss was the subject of a number of Lear's nonsense poems and comic drawings. When the cat died in 1887, Lear imaginatively claimed he was 31 years old.

6 **Abraham Lincoln**	*Tabby*

Cared for by Lincoln's son Tad, Tabby was an early example of what became a White House cat tradition that continued with Theodore Roosevelt, Kennedy, Carter and now Clinton.

7 **Cardinal Richelieu**	*Racan*

Named, with Perruque, after the Marquis de Racan's wig in which they were born. When Richelieu died in 1642, Racan, Perruque and a dozen others were left a trust fund for their welfare.

8 **Sir Walter Scott**	*Hinse of Hinsfield*

Hinse was a tomcat that terrorized Scott's dogs until 1826, when he lost a fight with a bloodhound called Nimrod.

9 **Mark Twain**	*Tammany*

Tammany was one of many; the others included Apollinaris, Beelzebub, Blatherskite, Buffalo Bill, Sour Mash and Zoroaster. Twain described how one of Tammany's kittens liked to sit in the pocket of his billiard table watching games in progress.

10 **Queen Victoria**	*White Heather*

A Buckingham Palace resident, White Heather outlived her mistress and thus became official court cat to King Edward VII (proving that a cat *may* look at a king...).

THE 10 SMALL ANIMALS MOST OFTEN SEEN BY VETS IN THE UK

1	Dog	**6**	Budgerigar
2	Cat	**7**	Gerbil
3	Rabbit	**8**	Tortoise
4	Guinea pig	**9**	Goldfish
5	Hamster	**10**	Parrot

THE 10 FARM ANIMALS MOST OFTEN TREATED BY VETS IN THE UK

1	Cattle	**7**	Deer
2	Sheep	**8**	Poultry
3	Goats	**9**	Farmed fish
4	Pigs	**10 =**	Llamas
5	Horses	**10 =**	Ostriches
6	Donkeys		

The commonest livestock naturally receives the greatest proportion of British vets' time (there are almost 116,000,000 chickens, 30,000,000 sheep and more than 13,000,000 cows alone in the UK to occupy their attention). It is therefore surprising to find two rare species that are farmed in comparatively minute numbers jostling for position at the bottom of the British Veterinary Association's Top 10.

Sheep are among the farm animals most often treated by vets.

THE 10 MOST POPULAR CATS' NAMES IN THE UK*

1	Sooty	**6**	Tom
2	Tigger	**7**	Fluffy
3	Tiger	**8**	Lucy
4	Smokey	**9**	Sam
5	Ginger	**10**	Lucky

*Based on an RSPCA survey conducted during National Pet Week, 1991.

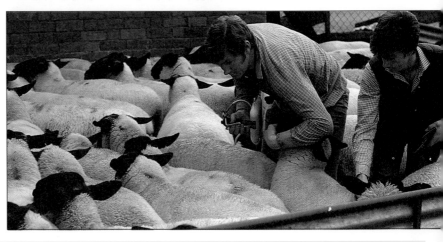

THE 10 MOST POPULAR DOG BREEDS IN THE UK

	Breed	No. registered by Kennel Club
1	Labrador	25,488
2	German Shepherd (Alsatian)	17,715
3	Yorkshire Terrier	16,646
4	West Highland White Terrier	16,113
5	Golden Retriever	14,678
6	Cavalier King Charles Spaniel	13,918
7	Cocker Spaniel	12,815
8	English Springer Spaniel	11,137
9	Boxer	7,597
10	Staffordshire Bull Terrier	5,501

As in the previous year, the 10 principal breeds of dogs registered by the Kennel Club in 1992 remained identical, but with some slight adjustments to the order, with German Shepherds making the biggest climb, from 4th to 2nd place, and with increasing numbers of Boxers registered. Independent surveys of dog ownership present a similar picture, though with certain other popular breeds (among them the Jack Russell, Border Collie and Poodle) making a stronger showing than in the Kennel Club's list.

THE TOP 10 DOGS' NAMES IN THE UK

Female		Male
Gemma	1	Ben
Rosy	2	Sam
Sam(antha)	3	Pip
Lucky	4	Prince
Candy	5	Captain
Gypsy	6	Buster
Mitzy	7	Scamp
Honey	8	Oscar
Bess	9	Rusty
Sandy	10	Max

As we have observed in previous editions of *The Top 10 of Everything*, a move away from traditional dogs' names occurred during the 1980s, with the demise of perennial (and specifically canine) names such as Shep, Brandy, Whisky, Butch, Rex, Lassie and, of course, Rover, and an increasing tendency toward human first names. The latest research by the National Canine Defence League shows that this fashion has continued, with Ben and Sam holding their respective positions while certain names (including Tessa, a former No. 1, Bella, Toby and Charlie) have fallen out of the Top 10 to be replaced by trendy newcomers such as Rosy, Candy, Mitzy, Pip, Captain and Oscar.

THE 10 SMALLEST MAMMALS IN THE WORLD

	Mammal	Weight g	oz	Length cm	in
1	Kitti's hognosed bat	2.0	0.07	2.9	1.1
2	Pygmy shrew	1.5	0.05	3.6	1.4
3	Pipistrelle bat	3.0	0.11	4.0	1.6
4	Little brown bat	8.0	0.28	4.0	1.6
5	Masked shrew	2.4	0.08	4.5	1.8
6	Southern blossom bat	12.0	0.42	5.0	2.0
7	Harvest mouse	5.0	0.18	5.8	2.3
8	Pygmy glider	12.0	0.42	6.0	2.4
9	House mouse	12.0	0.42	6.4	2.5
10	Common shrew	5.0	0.18	6.5	2.5

The pygmy glider and another that does not quite make the Top 10, the pygmy possum (15.0 g/0.53 oz; 8.5 cm/3.4 in) are marsupials, more closely related to kangaroos than to anything else in this list. Some classifications exclude marsupials from the mammal class. Among other contenders for the small world are the water shrew (12.0 g/0.42 oz; 7.0 cm/2.8 in) and bank vole (15.0 g/0.53 oz; 8.0 cm/3.2 in). The Kitti's hognosed bat and several other rare bats not included here are represented only by a few specimens in museum collections, so may well turn out to have been short-changed. And when such tiny dimensions and minute differences are involved, it's a job to tell where anything stands in the batting order.

The Latin name of the pygmy shrew, *Sorex minutus*, emphasizes its miniature status as the world's second smallest mammal.

THE 10 HEAVIEST PRIMATES IN THE WORLD

	Primate	Length* cm	in	Weight kg	lb
1	Gorilla	200	79	220	485
2	Man	177	70	77	170
3	Orangutan	137	54	75	165
4	Chimpanzee	92	36	50	110
5 =	Baboon	100	39	45	99
5 =	Mandrill	95	37	45	99
7	Gelada baboon	75	30	25	55
8	Proboscis monkey	76	30	24	53
9	Hanuman langur	107	42	20	44
10	Siamung gibbon	90	35	13	29

*Excluding tail.

The largest primates (including Man) and all the apes are rooted in the Old World (Africa, Asia and Europe): only one member of a New World species of monkeys (the Guatemalan howler at 91 cm/36 in; 9 kg/20 lb) is a close contender for the Top 10. The difference between the prosimians (primitive primates), great apes, lesser apes and monkeys is more to do with shape than size, though the great apes mostly top the table anyway. Lower down the list, the longer, skinnier and lighter forms of the lemurs, langurs, gibbons and monkeys, designed for serious monkeying round in trees, send the length column haywire.

Though outclassed by the gorilla and Man, the orangutan is nonetheless one of the largest primates.

THE 10 HEAVIEST MARINE MAMMALS

	Mammal	Length m	ft	Weight (tonnes)
1	Blue whale	30.5	100.0	130.0
2	Fin whale	25.0	82.0	45.0
3	Right whale	17.5	57.4	40.0
4	Sperm whale	18.0	59.0	36.0
5	Gray whale	14.0	46.0	32.7
6	Humpback whale	15.0	49.2	26.5
7	Baird's whale	5.5	18.0	11.0
8	Southern elephant seal	6.5	21.3	3.6
9	Northern elephant seal	5.8	19.0	3.4
10	Pilot whale	6.4	21.0	2.9

Probably the largest animal that ever lived, the blue whale dwarfs even the other whales listed here, all but one of which far outweigh the biggest land animal, the elephant. Among the mammals that frequent inland waters, the dugong is heaviest at 907 kg/2,000 lb (4.1 m/13.5 ft).

THE 10 HEAVIEST TERRESTRIAL MAMMALS

	Mammal	Length m	ft	Weight kg	lb
1	African elephant	7.3	24.0	5,000	11,023
2	Great Indian rhinoceros	4.2	13.8	4,000	8,818
3	Hippopotamus	4.9	16.1	2,000	4,409
4	Giraffe	5.8	19.0	1,200	2,646
5	American bison	3.9	12.8	1,000	2,205
6	Grizzly bear	3.0	9.8	780	1,720
7	Dromedary	3.0	9.8	600	1,323
8	Moose	3.0	9.8	595	1,312
9	Tiger	2.8	9.2	300	661
10	Gorilla	2.0	6.6	220	485

The list excludes domesticated cattle and horses. It also avoids comparing close kin such as the African and Indian elephants, highlighting instead the sumo stars within distinctive large mammal groups such as the bears, deer, big cats, primates and bovines (ox-like mammals). Sizes are not necessarily the top of the known range: records exist, for instance, of African elephant specimens weighing more than 6,000 kg/13,228 lb.

THE 10 FASTEST MAMMALS IN THE WORLD

	Mammal	Maximum recorded speed kph	mph
1	Cheetah	105	65
2	Pronghorn antelope	89	55
3 =	Mongolian gazelle	80	50
3 =	Springbok	80	50
5 =	Grant's gazelle	76	47
5 =	Thomson's gazelle	76	47
7	Brown hare	72	45
8	Horse	69	43
9 =	Greyhound	68	42
9 =	Red deer	68	42

Although some authorities have alleged higher speeds, this list is based on data from reliable sources using accurate methods of measurement. In addition to these speeds, estimated over distances of up to 0.4 km/¼ mile, charging lions can achieve 80 kph/50 mph over very short distances, while various members of the antelope family, wildebeests, elks, dogs, coyotes, foxes, hyenas, zebras and Mongolian wild asses, have all been credited with unsustained spurts of 64 kph/40 mph or more. Just failing to make the list is the Sei whale, the fastest of the large sea mammals at 64 kph/40.2 mph.

THE 10 FASTEST FISH IN THE WORLD

	Fish	Maximum recorded speed kph	mph
1	Sailfish	110	68
2	Marlin	80	50
3	Bluefin Tuna	74	46
4	Yellowfin Tuna	70	44
5	Blue shark	69	43
6	Wahoo	66	41
7 =	Bonefish	64	40
7 =	Swordfish	64	40
9	Tarpon	56	35
10	Tiger shark	53	33

Flying fish have a top speed in the water of only 37 kph/23 mph, but airborne they can reach 56 kph/35 mph. Many sharks qualify for the list: only two are listed here to prevent the list becoming overly shark-infested. But just in case you thought it was safe to go back in the water, the great white shark (of Jaws fame) can manage 48 kph/30 mph with ease. For any smaller fish (up to the size of a pike or salmon) a handy formula for estimating an individual's top swimming speed is just over 10 times its own length in centimetres per second: thus a trout 15 cm long swims at 160 cm per second, or 5.8 kph/3.6 mph.

THE 10 LARGEST FLIGHTLESS BIRDS

	Bird	Weight kg	lb	oz	Height cm	in
1	Ostrich	156.5	345	0	274.3	108.0
2	Emu	40.0	88	3	152.4	60.0
3	Cassowary	33.5	73	14	152.4	60.0
4	Rhea	25.0	55	2	137.1	54.0
5	Kiwi	29.0	63	15	114.3	45.0
6	Emperor penguin	29.4	64	13	114.0	44.9
7	King penguin	15.8	34	13	94.0	37.0
8	Southern gentoo	5.4	11	14	71.0	28.0
9 =	Adelie penguin	4.9	10	13	71.0	28.0
9 =	Magellanic penguin	4.9	10	13	71.0	28.0

There are 46 living and 16 recently extinct flightless birds on record. The smallest known bird, the bee hummingbird, weighs 1.7 g/0.06 oz and measures 6.4 cm/2.5 in from beak to tail. Almost 100,000 bee hummingbirds would be needed to balance one ostrich on a pair of scales. The largest bird in recorded history was the flightless elephant bird (Aepyornis) of Madagascar. It weighed around 438 kg/966 lb and stood 3 m/10 ft tall. Its eggs were nearly 38 cm/15 in long and weighed over 18 kg/40 lb. It became extinct in the late 1640s.

THE 10 LARGEST FLIGHTED BIRDS

	Bird	Weight kg	lb	oz
1	Great bustard	20.9	46	1
2	Trumpeter swan	16.8	37	1
3	Mute swan	16.3	35	15
4 =	Albatross	15.8	34	13
4 =	Whooper swan	15.8	34	13
6	Manchurian crane	14.9	32	14
7	Kori bustard	13.6	30	0
8	Grey pelican	13.0	28	11
9	Black vulture	12.5	27	8
10	Griffon vulture	12.0	26	7

Wing size does not necessarily correspond to weight in flighted birds. The 4 m/13 ft wingspan of the marabou stork beats all the birds listed here, even the mighty 3.6 m/12 ft span of the albatross, yet its body weight is normally no heavier than any of these. When laden with a meal of carrion, however, the marabou can double its weight and needs all the lift it can get to take off. It often fails altogether and has to put up with flightlessness until digestion takes its course.

ANIMALS & BIRDS

THE 10 LARGEST BIRDS IN THE UK

	Bird	Length* cm	Length* in
1	Mute swan	145–160	57–63
2	Bewick's swan	116–128	46–50
3	Canada goose	up to 110	up to 43
4	Grey heron	90–100	35–39
5	Cormorant	84–98	33–39
6	Gannet	86–96	34–38
7	Golden eagle	76–91	30–36
8	Capercaillie (male)	82–90	32–35
9	Greylag goose	71–89	28–35
10	Great black-backed gull	69–76	27–30

*Beak to tail.

The whooper swan once qualified for equal first position on this list, but as it no longer breeds in the British Isles it has been excluded, as has another former resident, the white-tailed sea eagle (69–91 cm/27–36 in). Pheasants sometimes measure 91 cm/36 in, but more than half the total is tail.

THE 10 FASTEST BIRDS IN THE WORLD

	Bird	Maximum recorded speed kph	Maximum recorded speed mph
1	Spine-tailed swift	171	106
2	Frigate bird	153	95
3	Spur-winged goose	142	88
4	Red-breasted merganser	129	80
5	White-rumped swift	124	77
6	Canvasback duck	116	72
7	Eider duck	113	70
8	Teal	109	68
9 =	Mallard	105	65
9 =	Pintail	105	65

Until aeroplane pilots cracked 306 kph/190 mph in 1919, birds were the fastest animals on Earth: stooping (diving) peregrine falcons clock up speeds approaching 298 kph/185 mph. However, most comparisons of air speed in birds rule out diving or wind-assisted flight: most small birds on migration can manage a ground speed of 97 kph/60 mph to 113 kph/70 mph if there is even a moderate following wind. So this listing picks out star performers among the medium- to large-sized birds (mainly waterfowl) that do not need help from wind or gravity to hit their top speed.

The mute swan is the largest bird in the UK and the third largest in the world.

THE TOP 10 TYPES OF LIVESTOCK IN THE WORLD

	Animal	World total
1	Chickens	11,061,000,000
2	Cattle	1,294,604,000
3	Sheep	1,202,920,000
4	Pigs	857,099,000
5	Goats	594,286,000
6	Ducks	560,000,000
7	Turkeys	267,000,000
8	Buffaloes	142,189,000
9	Horses	61,620,000
10	Asses	44,143,000

The world chicken population is more than double the human population, and both cattle and sheep outnumber the population of China. There are more pigs in the world than the entire population of India, enough turkeys for every citizen of the USA to have one each for Thanksgiving, and sufficient horses for every inhabitant of the UK to go riding.

GROUP NAMES QUIZ

A group of lions is a pride, but what collective name belongs with which animal here?

	Animal		Group		Animal		Group
1	Larks	A	Leap	6	Kittens	F	Unkindness
2	Apes	B	Crash	7	Storks	G	Colony
3	Ferrets	C	Array	8	Hedgehogs	H	Business
4	Ravens	D	Kindle	9	Rhinoceros	I	Exaltation
5	Leopards	E	Shrewdness	10	Beavers	J	Mustering

THE TOP 10 GOAT COUNTRIES

	Country	Goats
1	India	112,000,000
2	China	97,378,000
3	Pakistan	36,673,000
4	Nigeria	36,000,000
5	Iran	23,500,000
6	Bangladesh	22,000,000
7	Somalia	20,500,000
8	Ethiopia	18,000,000
9	Sudan	15,277,000
10	Brazil	12,500,000
	World total	594,286,000

The goat is one of the most widely distributed of all domesticated animals, its resilience to diseases such as the tuberculosis that affects cattle and its adaptability to harsh conditions making it ideally suited to the environments encountered in some of the less developed parts of the world: even some of the smaller African countries have 1,000,000 or more goats.

THE TOP 10 DUCK COUNTRIES

	Country	Ducks
1	China	369,000,000
2	India	30,000,000
3	Vietnam	29,000,000
4 =	France	17,000,000
4 =	Thailand	17,000,000
6	Bangladesh	12,000,000
7 =	Egypt	8,000,000
7 =	Philippines	8,000,000
9 =	Mexico	7,000,000
9 =	Poland	7,000,000
	World total	560,000,000

While it is extraordinary to consider that 66 per cent of the world's domesticated ducks live in China, an examination of the menu of any Chinese restaurant would remind us of the prominent role played by the duck in oriental cuisine. In contrast, the traditional Aylesbury duck and its British relatives account for a UK population of barely 2,000,000.

THE TOP 10 BUFFALO COUNTRIES

	Country	Buffaloes
1	India	77,000,000
2	China	21,635,000
3	Pakistan	15,031,000
4	Thailand	4,743,000
5	Indonesia	3,500,000
6	Nepal	3,101,000
7	Vietnam	2,929,000
8	Philippines	2,710,000
9	Egypt	2,550,000
10	Myanmar	2,080,000
	World total	142,189,000

Approximately 95 per cent of the world's total buffalo population resides in the Top 10 countries. Only two European countries have significant herds: Romania with 180,000 and Italy with 112,000 – milk from the latter country's buffaloes was traditionally used in the manufacture of mozzarella cheese. Considering there were once as many as 50,000,000 bison – the North American buffalo – surprisingly there are reckoned to be fewer than 35,000 surviving today in the USA and Canada, with up to 9,000 European and other types.

THE TOP 10 ASS COUNTRIES

	Country	Asses
1	China	11,198,000
2	Ethiopia	5,100,000
3	Pakistan	3,279,000
4	Mexico	3,188,000
5	Egypt	2,000,000
6	Iran	1,937,000
7	India	1,500,000
8	Brazil	1,340,000
9	Afghanistan	1,300,000
10	Turkey	985,000
	World total	44,143,000

The ass or donkey is used extensively throughout the world as a beast of burden, although its role in such countries as the UK (with an estimated population of around 10,000) has been largely reduced to providing

THE TOP 10 HORSE COUNTRIES

	Country	Horses
1	China	10,174,000
2	Brazil	6,200,000
3	Mexico	6,175,000
4	Former USSR	5,900,000
5	USA	5,650,000
6	Argentina	3,400,000
7	Ethiopia	2,700,000
8	Mongolia	2,255,000
9	Colombia	1,980,000
10	India	965,000
	World total	61,620,000

Mongolia makes an appearance in few Top 10 lists – but here it scores doubly as it is also the only country in the world where the human population is outnumbered by horses. Throughout the world, and especially in the USA where there were once more than 10,000,000 horses, the population has declined as they have been replaced by motor vehicles. Horses are still used extensively in agriculture in many developing countries, while in the West they tend to be kept for sport and other recreational purposes. The UK horse population is estimated to be around 170,000.

Sorting the sheep from the goats: there is one sheep for every four people on earth, and one goat for every nine.

rides for children. It should not be confused with the mule (the offspring of a horse and donkey), of which there is a world population of almost 15,000,000, one-third of which are in China.

THE TOP 10 PIG COUNTRIES

	Country	Pigs
1	China	363,975,000
2	Former USSR	75,600,000
3	USA	54,427,000
4	Brazil	35,000,000
5	Germany	30,819,000
6	Poland	21,868,000
7	Mexico	16,902,000
8	Spain	16,100,000
9	Netherlands	13,788,000
10	France	12,239,000
	World total	*857,099,000*

The distribution of the world's pig population is determined by cultural, religious and dietary factors – few pigs are found in African and Islamic countries, for example – with the result that there is a disproportionate concentration of pigs in those countries that do not have such prohibitions – 75 per cent of the world total is found in the Top 10 countries. Denmark, with 9,489,000 pigs, is the only country where the pig population outnumbers the human population (by almost two to one). The UK has 7,379,000 pigs, or one pig for every eight people.

THE TOP 10 TURKEY COUNTRIES

	Country	Turkeys
1	USA	97,000,000
2	Former USSR	46,000,000
3	France	28,000,000
4	Italy	24,000,000
5	UK	10,000,000
6	Israel	7,000,000
7 =	Brazil	6,000,000
7 =	Mexico	6,000,000
7 =	Portugal	6,000,000
10	Canada	5,000,000
	World total	*267,000,000*

Some 88 per cent of the world's turkeys are found in the Top 10 countries – with the largest number, appropriately, in North America, their country of origin. The name turkey was applied originally to guinea fowl because they were brought to the West from Turkish territory, and then confusingly applied to the birds from the New World. The name is equally misleading in French where they are known as *dinde* in the erroneous belief that they came from India.

THE TOP 10 SHEEP COUNTRIES

	Country	Sheep
1	Australia	162,774,000
2	Former USSR	134,000,000
3	China	112,820,000
4	New Zealand	57,000,000
5	India	55,700,000
6	Iran	45,000,000
7	Turkey	40,553,000
8	South Africa	32,580,000
9	Pakistan	30,160,000
10	UK	29,954,000
	World total	*1,202,920,000*

This is one of the few world lists in which the UK ranks considerably higher than the USA, which has only 11,200,000 head of sheep. As has been pointed out in past editions of *The Top 10 of Everything*, there are a number of countries in which sheep outnumber people – most notably the Falkland Islands which has 365,000 sheep to a human population of 2,121 (172 sheep per person), followed by New Zealand (17 sheep per person).

THE TOP 10 CHICKEN COUNTRIES

	Country	Chickens
1	China	2,077,000,000
2	USA	1,520,000,000
3	Former USSR	1,160,000,000
4	Indonesia	590,000,000
5	Brazil	570,000,000
6	India	380,000,000
7	Japan	335,000,000
8	Mexico	246,000,000
9	France	213,000,000
10	Pakistan	192,000,000
	World total	*11,061,000,000*

The Top 10 countries have 67 per cent of the world's chicken population. In the UK chickens – 122,000,000 of them – outnumber people more than twice over.

THE TOP 10 CATTLE COUNTRIES

	Country	Cattle
1	India	198,400,000
2	Brazil	152,000,000
3	Former USSR	115,600,000
4	USA	98,896,000
5	China	81,407,000
6	Argentina	50,080,000
7	Ethiopia	30,000,000
8	Mexico	29,847,000
9	Colombia	24,875,000
10	Bangladesh	23,500,000
	World total	*1,294,604,000*

The Top 10 countries own 62 per cent of the world's cattle. The UK's cattle population is 11,846,000, equivalent to more than one animal for every five people.

Christmas is coming: turkeys await their seasonal fate.

THE 10 MOST ABUNDANT CLASSES OF ANIMAL

Microbes exist in staggering numbers: some nine trillion (9,000,000,000,000) of medium size could be packed into a box with sides 2.5 cm/1 inch long. But whether they are plants, animals, both or neither is a matter of endless debate and we shall therefore disregard them.

The four trillion trillion trillion world population claimed by some for nematodes (microscopic worm-like parasites) is a dubious sum based on birthrate without proper adjustments for survival rate or gaps in distribution.

Of animals that can be seen without a microscope, insects unquestionably top the numbers league: there are at least 1,000,000 insects for each of the Earth's 5,292,000,000 humans. Put together, they would weigh at least 12 times as much as the human race and at least three times more than the combined weight of all other living animals.

Estimates of the populations of other classes are at best 'guesstimates', and this Top 10 should be viewed as a general picture of the relative numbers of each type of animal. Primitive sea animals like the sponges and corals have not been factored into the list. Their occurrence in massed colonies makes them hard to differentiate by number and their global distribution is not well known.

1 Insects and spiders

At least 5,000,000,000,000,000 individuals. Among the commonest insects are ants, fleas, flies and the little-known springtails, which inhabit moist topsoil the world over. The latter alone probably outnumber the human race.

2 Crustaceans

Besides crabs, woodlice and so on, this class also includes the krill and other tiny shrimp-like creatures that form a major animal ingredient in plankton, mainstay of life in the oceans.

3 Worms

Earthworms and other tube-like animals, including parasitic worms, can occur in great numbers in some habitats: more than 1,000,000 earthworms were counted in 0.4 hectare/1 acre of British farmland, for example. But their distribution is variable compared with the teeming arthropods higher up the list.

4 Fish

Total fish population of the world's oceans has been estimated at around 760,000,000 tonnes – at least 100,000,000,000,000 individuals.

5 Molluscs

Includes snails, slugs, most shellfish, squids and octopus and many tiny animals in the plankton horde.

6 Amphibians

Frogs, toads, newts etc: an estimated trillion (1,000,000,000,000) creatures.

7 Birds

Many birds share human habitats yet avoid conflict with us, so have the edge in numbers over most other larger wildlife outside the oceans. There are probably about 100,000,000,000 birds in the world and the commonest must include poultry species and specialist townies such as the sparrows.

8 Mammals (excluding humans)

Despite exploding human numbers and heavy pressures on many rare mammal species in the wild, other mammals probably still outnumber humans by at least four to one, boosted by the huge numbers of herd animals, pets and 'commensal' or scavenging animals such as rats and mice that share our habitat.

9 Humans

The baby that pushed the world's human population meter past the 5,000,000,000 mark was born in the late 1980s.

10 Reptiles

Reptiles never recovered from the unknown cataclysm that finished off the dinosaurs, well before *Homo sapiens* arrived on the scene. Now largely through conflict and competition with humans, the world's snakes, lizards, turtles, crocodiles and other scaly-skinned beasts are once more in decline and may number fewer than 2,000,000,000 individuals at present.

Red weaver ants, representatives of one of the commonest insects, the most abundant class of creatures to inhabit the planet.

THE 10 DEADLIEST SNAKES IN THE WORLD

Species	Native region
1 = Taipan Mortality is nearly 100% unless antivenin is administered promptly.	Australia and New Guinea
1 = Black mamba Mortality nearly 100% without antivenin.	Southern and Central Africa
3 Tiger snake Very high mortality without antivenin.	Australia
4 Common krait Up to 50% mortality even with antivenin.	South Asia
5 Death adder Over 50% mortality without antivenin.	Australia
6 Yellow or Cape cobra The most dangerous type of cobra, with high mortality.	Southern Africa
7 King cobra At 4.9 m/16 ft long, the king cobra is the largest poisonous snake in the world. It also injects the most venom into its victims.	India and southeast Asia
8 = Bushmaster	Central and South America
8 = Green mamba	Africa
10 Coral snake	North, Central and South America

Most people fear snakes, but only a few dozen of the 3,000-odd snake species that exist can cause serious harm and many more are beneficial because they prey on vermin and on other snake species of worse repute. Measuring the strength of the venom of snakes is scientifically possible, but this does not indicate how dangerous they may be: the Australian smooth-scaled snake, for example, is believed to be the most venomous land snake, but no human victims have ever been recorded. The Top 10 takes account of the degree of threat posed by those snakes that have a record of causing fatalities – although it can only be approximate, since circumstances such as the amount of venom injected, speed of administering antivenin (an antitoxin that counteracts the venom), age and health of victim and so on, can vary enormously. Among venomous snakes, the saw-scaled or carpet viper (Africa and Asia) is probably the world's most dangerous solely in terms of numbers of victims. Its aggressive behaviour is combined with highly toxic venom and a nasty habit of lying concealed in the sand and grass verges of pathways in areas densely populated by people who mostly go barefoot. Small wonder it causes one in six of the 10,000–12,000 cases of serious snakebite injury recorded in India each year.

Venom yield increases with body size, but the venom of the cobras and other slender snakes is often less toxic than that of the stockier vipers and rattlers lower down this list. Longer snakes also tend to avoid contact with people, or use venom only for defence – although the black mamba is a fearsome exception. Among other notable dangerous snakes are the boomslang (Africa), the Eastern diamond rattlesnake (North America), the Gaboon viper (Africa) and the sand viper (Europe). The yellow-bellied sea snake, found in the tropical Pacific, is a fish-eating relative of the cobras and lives almost entirely in the sea, coming ashore only to lay eggs. Its venom is 100 times more powerful than the deadliest viper venom, but though there have been two recorded attacks on scuba divers (causing their instant death), sea snakes so rarely encounter humans they can scarcely be called dangerous. Reassuringly, Britain has only one poisonous snake, the adder. Reported UK cases of snakebite have rarely reached double figures in any postwar year and no deaths from this cause have been recorded since 1967.

The black mamba is feared as one of the world's most venomous snakes.

Diversity is one of the most impressive features of the animal kingdom, and even within a single species huge variations in size can be encountered. There are practical problems that make measurement difficult – it is virtually impossible to weigh an elephant in the wild, or to estimate the flight speed of a speeding bird, for example. The lists therefore represent 'likely averages' based on the informed observations of specialist researchers, rather than one-off assessments or rare and extreme record-breaking cases.

Many fossils of the long-necked Diplodocus, a dinosaur from the late Jurassic period, were excavated in the American West around the turn of the century.

THE FIRST 10 DINOSAURS TO BE NAMED

	Name	Meaning	Named by	Year
1	Megalosaurus	Great lizard	William Buckland	1824
2	Iguanodon	Iguana tooth	Gideon Mantell	1825
3	Hylaeosaurus	Woodland lizard	Gideon Mantell	1832
4	Macrodontophion	Large tooth snake	A. Zborzewski	1834
5 =	Thecodontosaurus	Socket-toothed lizard	Samuel Stutchbury and H. Riley	1836
5 =	Palaeosaurus	Ancient lizard	Samuel Stutchbury and H. Riley	1836
7	Plateosaurus	Flat lizard	Hermann von Meyer	1837
8 =	Cladeiodon	Branch tooth	Richard Owen	1841
8 =	Cetiosaurus	Whale lizard	Richard Owen	1841
10	Pelorosaurus	Monstrous lizard	Gideon Mantell	1850

The first 10 dinosaurs were all identified and named within a quarter of a century – although subsequent research has since cast doubt on the authenticity of certain specimens. The name Megalosaurus, the first to be given to a dinosaur, was proposed by William Buckland (1784–1856), an English geologist who was also Dean of Westminster and a noted eccentric (out of scientific curiosity he ate the mummified heart of the French King, Louis XIV). Acknowledging that the name had been suggested to him by another clergyman-geologist, the Rev William Daniel Conybeare (who later named Plesiosaurus), Buckland first used it in an article, 'Notice on the Megalosaurus or Great Fossil Lizard of Stonesfield', which was published in 1824 in the *Transactions of the Geological Society of London*.

The Iguanodon, the second dinosaur to be named, was identified by Gideon Algernon Mantell (1790–1852). A shoemaker's son, he became a doctor in his home town of Lewes in Sussex, but devoted much of his life to the study of geology. Mantell (or, according to some authorities, his wife Mary) found the first Iguanodon teeth in 1822 in a pile of stones being used for road repairs in the Tilgate Forest area of Sussex. After detailed study, he concluded that they resembled an enormous version of the teeth of the Central American iguana lizard, and hence, in an article in *Philosophical Transactions*, suggested the name Iguanodon; seven years later he was to assign the name Hylaeosaurus to another of his finds. Following the first two, a Polish nobleman, Count Zborzewski, named Macrodontophion, British geologists Samuel Stutchbury and H. Riley christened Thecodontosaurus and Palaeosaurus and German paleontologist Hermann von Meyer gave Plateosaurus its name.

Curiously, all the first seven dinosaurs had been named before the world 'dinosaur' itself had been coined: 'Dinosauria' ('terrible lizards') was proposed as a name for the group by Richard Owen in July 1841 at the Plymouth meeting of the British Association for the Advancement of Science. Owen himself named a number of dinosaurs and was the driving force behind the creation in 1854 of the life-sized dinosaur models at Crystal Palace (which can be seen to this day). After the 1850s, the hunting, identifying and naming of dinosaurs became highly competitive, with dinosaurologists vying with each other to discover and assign names to every new find.

THE 10 LARGEST DINOSAURS

1 'Seismosaurus'

Length: 30–36 m/98–119 ft
Estimated weight: 50–80 tonnes

A single skeleton of this colossal plant-eater was excavated in 1985 near Albuquerque, New Mexico, by US paleontologist David Gillette and given an unofficial name (i.e. one that is not yet an established scientific name) that means 'earth-shaking lizard'. It is currently being studied by the New Mexico Museum of Natural History, which may confirm its position as the largest dinosaur yet discovered.

2 Supersaurus

Length: 24–30 m/80–100 ft
Height: 16 m/54 ft
Estimated weight: 50 tonnes

The remains of Supersaurus were found in Colorado in 1972 (like those of Ultrasaurus, by James A. Jensen). Some scientists have suggested a length of up to 42 m/138 ft and a weight of 75–100 tonnes.

3 Antarctosaurus

Length: 18–30 m/60–98 ft
Estimated weight: 40–50 tonnes

Named Antarctosaurus ('southern lizard') by German paleontologist Friedrich von Huene in 1929, this creature's thigh bone alone measures 2.3 m/7 ft 6 in.

4 Barosaurus

Length: 23–27.5 m/75–90 ft
Height and weight uncertain

Barosaurus (meaning 'heavy lizard', so named by US paleontologist Othniel C. Marsh in 1890) has been found in both North America and Africa, thus proving the existence of a land link in Jurassic times (205–140 million years ago).

5 Mamenchisaurus

Length: 27 m/89 ft
Height and weight uncertain

An almost complete skeleton discovered in 1972 showed it had the longest neck of any known animal, comprising more than half its total body length – perhaps up to 15 m/49 ft. It was named by Chinese paleontologist Young Chung Chien after the place in China where it was found.

6 Diplodocus

Length: 23–27 m/75–89 ft
Estimated weight: 12 tonnes

As it was long and thin, Diplodocus was a relative lightweight in the dinosaur world. It was also probably one of the most stupid dinosaurs, having the smallest brain in relation to its body size. Diplodocus was given its name (which means 'double beam') in 1878 by Marsh. One skeleton was named *Diplodocus carnegii*, in honour of Scottish-American millionaire Andrew Carnegie, who financed the excavations that discovered it.

7 'Ultrasaurus'

Length: Over 25 m/82 ft
Height: 16 m/52 ft
Estimated weight: 50 tonnes

Ultrasaurus was discovered by US paleontologist James A. Jensen in Colorado in 1979 but has not yet been fully studied. Some authorities have claimed its weight as an unlikely 100–140 tonnes. Confusingly, although its informal name (which means 'ultra lizard') was widely recognized, another, smaller dinosaur has been given the same official name.

8 Brachiosaurus

Length: 25 m/82 ft
Height: 16 m/52 ft
Estimated weight: 50 tonnes

Its name (given to it in 1903 by US paleontologist Elmer S. Riggs) means 'arm lizard'. Some paleontologists have put the weight of Brachiosaurus as high as 190 tonnes, but this seems improbable (if not impossible, in the light of theories of the maximum possible weight of terrestrial animals).

9 Pelorosaurus

Length: 24 m/80 ft
Height and weight uncertain

The first fragments of Pelorosaurus ('monstrous lizard') were found in Sussex and named by British doctor and geologist Gideon Algernon Mantell as early as 1850.

10 Apatosaurus

Length: 20–21 m/66–70 ft
Estimated weight: 20–30 tonnes

Apatosaurus (its name, coined by Marsh, means 'deceptive lizard') is better known by its former name of Brontosaurus ('thunder reptile'). The bones of the first one ever found, in Colorado in 1879, caused great confusion for many years because its discoverer attached a head from a different species to the rest of the skeleton.

The first dinosaur bones were found in Sussex in 1822. The name 'dinosaur' was given to them by the naturalist Sir Richard Owen, and first appeared in print in 1841. It comes from two Greek words, *deinos*, fearful, and *sauros*, lizard.

The Top 10 is based on the most reliable recent evidence of their lengths and indicates the probable ranges; as more and more information is assembled, these are undergoing constant revision. Lengths have often been estimated from only a few surviving fossilized bones, and there is much dispute even among experts about these and even more about the weights of most dinosaurs. Some, such as Diplodocus, had squat bodies but extended necks, which made them extremely long but not necessarily immensely heavy.

Everyone's favourite dinosaur, *Tyrannosaurus rex* ('tyrant lizard'), does not appear in the Top 10 list because although it was one of the fiercest flesh-eating dinosaurs, it was not as large as many of the herbivorous ones. However, measuring a probable 12 m/39 ft and weighing more than six tonnes, it certainly ranks as one of the largest flesh-eating animals yet discovered. Bones of an earlier dinosaur called Epanterias were found in Colorado in 1877 and 1934, but incorrectly identified until recently, when studies suggested that this creature was possibly larger than Tyrannosaurus.

To compare these sizes with living animals, note that the largest recorded crocodile measured 6.2 m/20 ft 4 in and the largest elephant 10.7 m/35 ft from trunk to tail and weighed about 12 tonnes. The largest living creature ever measured is the blue whale at 33.6 m/110 ft – slightly smaller than the size claimed for Seismosaurus.

THE 10 COMMONEST PHOBIAS

	Object of phobia	Medical term
1	Spiders	Arachnephobia or arachnophobia
2	People and social situations	Anthropophobia or sociophobia
3	Flying	Aerophobia or aviatophobia
4	Open spaces	Agoraphobia, cenophobia or kenophobia
5	Confined spaces	Claustrophobia, cleisiophobia, cleithrophobia or clithrophobia
6	Heights	Acrophobia, altophobia, hypsophobia or hypsiphobia
7	Cancer	Carcinomaphobia, carcinophobia, carcinomatophobia, cancerphobia or cancerophobia
8	Thunderstorms	Brontophobia or keraunophobia; related phobias are those associated with lightning (astraphobia), cyclones (anemophobia) and hurricanes and tornadoes (lilapsophobia)
9	Death	Necrophobia or thanatophobia
10	Heart disease	Cardiophobia

A phobia is a morbid fear that is out of all proportion to the object of the fear. Many people would admit to being uncomfortable about these principal phobias, as well as others, such as snakes (ophiophobia), injections (trypanophobia) or ghosts (phasmophobia), but most do not become obsessive about them and allow such fears to rule their lives. True phobias often arise from some incident in childhood when a person has been afraid of some object and has developed an irrational fear that persists into adulthood. Nowadays, as well as the valuable work done by the Phobics Society and other organizations, phobias can be cured by taking special desensitization courses, for example, to conquer one's fear of flying.

Arachnophobia is the commonest of all phobias – but how would *you* like to find this tarantula in *your* bath?

HUMAN BODY & HEALTH

There are many phobias that are much less common than those appearing in the Top 10. Even if only one person has ever been observed with a specific phobia, psychologists have often given it a name – some more bizarre than others:

Beards
Pogonophobia

Chickens
Alektorophobia

Chins
Geniophobia

Eggshells
No medical term

Everything
Pantophobia, panophobia, panphobia or pamphobia

Gravity
Barophobia

Hair
Chaetophobia

Mirrors
Eisoptrophobia

Money
Chrometophobia

Opening one's eyes
Optophobia

Satellites plunging to Earth
Keraunothnetophobia

Slime
Blennophobia or myxophobia

String
Linonophobia

Teeth
Odontophobia

The number thirteen
Terdekaphobia, tridecaphobia, triakaidekaphobia or triskaidekaphobia

THE 10 BESTSELLING PRESCRIPTION DRUGS IN THE WORLD

	Brand name	Manufacturer	Prescribed for	Annual revenue (US$)
1	Zantac	Glaxo	Ulcers	3,023,000,000
2	Vasotec	Merck & Co	High blood pressure, etc	1,745,000,000
3	Capoten	Bristol-Myers-Squibb	High blood pressure, etc	1,580,000,000
4	Voltaren	Ciba-Geigy	Arthritis	1,185,000,000
5	Tenormin	ICI	High blood pressure	1,180,000,000
6	Adalat	Bayer	Angina; high blood pressure	1,120,000,000
7	Tagamet	Smith Kline Beecham	Ulcers	1,097,000,000
8	Mevacor	Merck	High fat level in blood	1,090,000,000
9	Naproxen	Syntex	Arthritis	954,000,000
10	Ceclor	Eli Lilly	Infections	935,000,000

The revenues of the international drug industry attain staggering levels: in 1991, the total revenue of the top 25 drug companies was $94,598,000,000. To put this in perspective, fewer than 25 countries in the world have a gross domestic product (the total production of goods and services of the entire country) of more than this figure – which is approximately equivalent to the GDP of Norway. Of this total, the Top 10 drugs alone accounted for earnings of $13,909,000,000.

THE 10 MOST POPULAR NON-PRESCRIPTION MEDICINES IN THE UK

	Medicine	Sales (£)
1	Analgesics (painkillers such as aspirin)	179,500,000
2	Food supplements	130,000,000
3	Skin treatments	126,300,000
4	Cold remedies	85,700,000
5	Vitamins and minerals	81,000,000
6	Cough remedies	67,300,000
7	Sore throat remedies	57,700,000
8	Indigestion remedies	55,900,000
9	Oral hygiene products	38,700,000
10	Laxatives	33,200,000

In 1992 we spent an estimated £1,036,100,000 on non-prescription or 'over-the-counter' home remedies, with the Top 10 product categories accounting for almost 83 per cent of the total. Such items appear to be largely 'recession proof': while the markets for many products were static or declined in 1992, sales of many of these increased – those of food supplements, oral hygiene products and others outside the Top 10, such as hayfever remedies, growing by more than 20 per cent, although it should be borne in mind that some of these increases reflect price rises and the growing availability of remedies that were previously obtainable only by doctor's prescription.

THE 10 MOST ABUSED DRUGS

1	Cocaine/crack
2	Prescribed drugs
3	Cannabis
4	Ecstasy
5	A mixture of drugs
6	Heroin/opium-derived drugs
7	Solvents
8	Amphetamines
9	Hallucinogenics (LSD, etc)
10	Others

These are the 10 types of drug for which people most sought help in the period 1991–92 from Release, founded in 1967 and today Britain's largest drug-help agency. Since the late 1980s the so-called 'designer drug' ecstasy has moved steadily up the list while cocaine and crack have ascended from the middle to the top.

Opium poppies: though linked with the opium dens of Dickens' era, opium and its derivatives remain among the 10 most abused drugs.

THE TOP 10 COUNTRIES FOR HEALTH SPENDING

	Country	Average annual health spending per person (US$)
1	USA	2,051
2	Canada	1,483
3	Iceland	1,241
4	Sweden	1,233
5	Switzerland	1,225
6	Norway	1,149
7	France	1,105
8	(West) Germany	1,093
9	Luxembourg	1,050
10	Netherlands	1,041
	UK	758

The USA not only spends the most per head on health care, but also the most as a percentage of gross domestic product (11.2 per cent, compared with the UK's 6.1 per cent). Among European countries, Turkey spends the least – just $148 per capita.

THE 10 COUNTRIES WITH THE HIGHEST MALE LIFE EXPECTANCY

	Country	Life expectancy at birth (years)
1	Japan	75.9
2	Iceland	75.7
3	Macau	75.1
4	Hong Kong	74.6
5	Sweden	74.2
6 =	Andorra	74.0
6 =	Switzerland	74.0
8	Israel	73.9
9	Malta	73.8
10	Netherlands	73.7
	UK	72.7

The relatively high, and generally increasing life expectancy for males in the Top 10 countries contrasts sharply with that in many underdeveloped countries, particularly the majority of African countries, where it rarely exceeds 45 years, with Sierra Leone at the bottom of the league with 39.4 years.

THE 10 COUNTRIES WITH THE HIGHEST FEMALE LIFE EXPECTANCY

	Country	Life expectancy at birth (years)
1	Japan	81.8
2	Andorra	81.0
3	Switzerland	80.9
4	France	80.5
5 =	Hong Kong	80.3
5 =	Iceland	80.3
5 =	Macau	80.3
8	Netherlands	80.2
9	Sweden	80.1
10 =	Canada	80.0
10 =	Monaco	80.0
	UK	77.9

For the first time, female life expectancy in all the Top 10 countries exceeds 80 years. Since this represents the average, as many women are now living beyond this age as die before attaining it.

THE 10 COMMONEST CAUSES OF DEATH IN THE UK

	Cause	England & Wales	Scotland	Northern Ireland	Total
1	Diseases of the circulatory system	261,834	29,166	6,983	297,983
2	Cancer	145,355	15,031	3,551	163,937
3	Diseases of the respiratory system	63,273	7,068	2,494	72,835
4	Diseases of the digestive system	18,508	2,059	395	20,962
5	Accidents and violence	17,286	2,532	719	20,537
6	Mental disorders	13,500	1,110	68	14,678
7	Diseases of the nervous system	11,889	947	168	13,004
8	Endocrine, nutritional and metabolic diseases and immunity disorders	10,538	776	68	11,382
9	Diseases of the genito-urinary system	6,964	805	272	8,041
10	Diseases of the musculo-skeletal system	5,417	270	54	5,741
	Total deaths from all causes*	*570,044*	*61,041*	*15,096*	*646,181*

*Including some that do not appear in the Top 10.

The 10 principal causes of death remain the same and in approximately the same order from year to year, with only slight fluctuations in total numbers (total UK deaths in 1991 were 4,382 or 0.68 per cent higher than in the previous year). Deaths resulting from accidents and violence overtook diseases of the digestive system in 1990 after several years in 5th place, but reverted to its former position in 1991. In the former category, motor vehicle accidents accounted for most deaths, 5,178 in total, but representing a drop of 523, or nine per cent, on the 1990 figure.

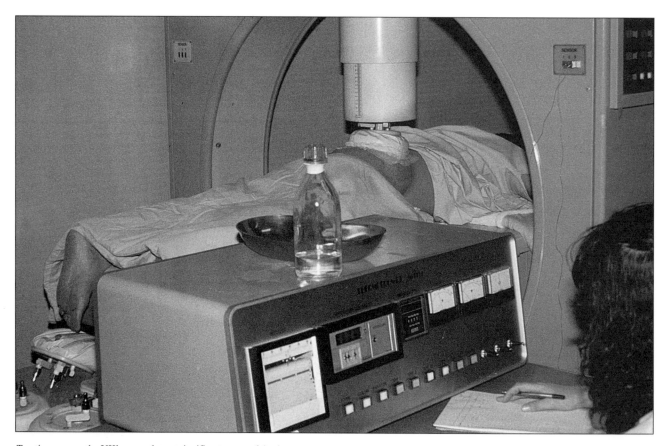

Treating cancer, the UK's second most significant cause of death.

10 CELEBRITY SUICIDES

1 Barney Barnarto

South African diamond magnate and rival of Cecil Rhodes, inexplicably jumped off an ocean liner en route for England, 2 June 1897. His body was recovered and buried in the Jewish Cemetery, Willesden, London.

2 Jerome Cardan

Italian physician, mathematician and astrologer, died in Rome on 2 September 1576 after deliberately starving himself to death to ensure that his own prediction of his death would come true.

3 Hart Crane

American poet, killed himself by jumping off the liner *Orizaba* in the Caribbean, 27 April 1927; his body was never recovered. Crane (whose father, ironically, had invented the lifebelt-shaped sweet Life Savers) and Hemingway (*see* number 6) were born on the same day, 21 July 1899, and both committed suicide.

4 Emily Davison

British suffragette, threw herself under the King's horse Anmer at Tattenham Corner during the Epsom Derby, 4 June 1913. She is buried at Morpeth, Northumberland.

5 George Eastman

American camera pioneer, founder of the Kodak photographic company and multi-millionaire philanthropist, killed himself on 14 March 1932 in Rochester, New York.

6 Ernest Hemingway

American author, committed suicide (as had his father and brother), with a shotgun, 2 July 1961. He was buried at Ketchum, Idaho.

7 Donny Hathaway

33-year-old American R & B singer, plunged 15 floors to his death at the Essex House Hotel, New York, 13 January 1979. Despite suggestions to the contrary, his demise was officially registered as suicide.

8 Adolf Hitler

Shot himself at his bunker in Berlin as the Soviet army occupied the city, 30 April 1945. Eva Braun, who he had married the day before, took poison and both bodies were burned. New evidence, including film of 'Hitler's body', has recently emerged from KGB archives.

9 Vincent Van Gogh

Turbulent Dutch painter (and record-holder for the world's most expensive painting), died 29 July 1890, two days after shooting himself with a revolver. He was buried at Auvers, his brother Theo later buried alongside him.

10 Virginia Woolf

British novelist, drowned herself in the River Ouse near her Sussex home, 28 March 1941. Her ashes were buried beneath an elm in her garden.

THE 10 MOST SUICIDAL COUNTRIES IN THE WORLD

	Country	Suicides per 100,000 population
1	Hungary	43.1
2	Austria	24.8
3	Switzerland	24.1
4	Denmark	23.3
5	Germany	22.2
6 =	Bermuda	19.0
6 =	Sweden	19.0
8	Luxembourg	18.5
9	Japan	17.6
10	Canada	14.2

Egypt has one of the lowest rates – 0.1 per 100,000.

THE 10 EUROPEAN COUNTRIES WITH THE MOST DEATHS FROM HEART ATTACK

	Country	Death rate per 100,000 population
1	Irish Republic	89.25
2	Finland	82.73
3	UK	74.99
4	Denmark	58.81
5	Norway	58.61
6	Sweden	50.83
7	Netherlands	48.13
8	Luxembourg	45.04
9	Germany	44.70
10	Belgium	39.49

France has one of the lowest rates – 21.35 per 100,000.

THE TOP 10 IN LINE TO THE BRITISH THRONE

1   HRH The Prince of Wales (Prince Charles Philip Arthur George)
b. 14 November 1948   *then his elder son:*

2   HRH Prince William of Wales (Prince William Arthur Philip Louis)
b. 21 June 1982   *then his younger brother:*

3   HRH Prince Henry of Wales (Prince Henry Charles Albert David)
b. 15 September 1984   *then his uncle:*

4   HRH The Duke of York (Prince Andrew Albert Christian Edward)
b. 19 February 1960   *then his elder daughter:*

5   HRH Princess Beatrice of York (Princess Beatrice Elizabeth Mary)
b. 8 August 1988   *then her younger sister:*

6   HRH Princess Eugenie of York (Princess Eugenie Victoria Helena)
b. 23 March 1990   *then her uncle:*

7   HRH Prince Edward (Prince Edward Antony Richard Louis)
b. 10 March 1964   *then his sister:*

8   HRH The Princess Royal (Princess Anne Elizabeth Alice Louise)
b. 15 August 1950   *then her son:*

9   Master Peter Mark Andrew Phillips
b. 15 November 1977   *then his sister:*

10   Miss Zara Anne Elizabeth Phillips
b. 15 May 1981

The birth in 1988 of Princess Beatrice altered the order of succession, ousting David Albert Charles Armstrong-Jones, Viscount Linley (b. 3 November 1961), from the No. 10 position, while the birth in 1990 of her sister, Princess Eugenie, evicted HRH Princess Margaret, Countess of Snowdon (Princess Margaret Rose, b. 21 August 1930) from the Top 10.

Monarch in waiting: Prince Charles has been first in line to the throne since the age of three.

THE 10 YOUNGEST BRITISH MONARCHS

	Monarch	Reign	Age at accession years	months
1	Henry VI	1422–61	0	8
2	Henry III	1216–72	9	1
3	Edward VI	1547–53	9	3
4	Richard II	1377–99	10	5
5	Edward V	1483	12	5
6	Edward III	1327–77	14	2
7	Jane	1553	15	8
8	Henry VIII	1509–47	17	10
9	Victoria	1837–1901	18	1
10	Charles II	1649–85	18	8

Henry VI was born on 6 December 1421 and became King of England on 1 September 1422, the day after the death of his father, Henry V. At the age of 10 months (following the death of his grandfather, Charles VI, on 21 October 1422), he also became King of France. Before the Norman Conquest, Edward the Martyr became king in 975 when aged about 12 and Ethelred II ('the Unready') in 978 at the age of about 10.

THE 10 OLDEST MONARCHS TO ASCEND THE BRITISH THRONE

	Monarch	Reign	Age at accession
1	William IV	1830–37	64
2	Edward VII	1901–10	59
3	George IV	1820–30	57
4	George I	1714–27	54
5	James II	1685–88	51
6	George V	1910–36	44
7	George II	1727–60	43
8	Edward VIII	1936	41
9	George VI	1936–52	40
10	William I	1066–87	39

If Prince Charles were to ascend the throne between October 1993 and July 2000, he would become the 6th oldest ever to become reigning monarch.

THE 10 LONGEST-LIVED BRITISH MONARCHS

	Monarch	Born	Reign	Age at death
1	Victoria	1819	1837–1901	81
2	George III	1738	1760–1820	81
3	Edward VIII	1894	1936 (abdicated; d.1972)	77
4	George II	1683	1727–60	76
5	William IV	1765	1830–37	71
6	George V	1865	1910–36	70
7	Elizabeth I	1533	1558–1603	69
8	Edward VII	1841	1901–10	68
9	Edward I	1239	1272–1307	68
10	James II	1633	1685–88	67

Queen Victoria and George III are close rivals for the title of longest-lived British monarch, and George's dates might suggest that he lived slightly longer than Victoria. However, during his lifetime, in 1752, the Gregorian Calendar was adopted in Great Britain, as a result of which 11 days were lost. Taking this into account, Queen Victoria lived for 81 years 243 days and George III for 81 years 239 days. The difference between the lifetimes of Edward VII and Edward I is also very slight, with Edward VII the winner by just six months; in fact, there is just a two-month difference between the life spans of Edward I and James II, who ranks 10th.

Longest-lived and longest-reigning, Queen Victoria gave her name to an entire age.

THE 10 LONGEST-REIGNING BRITISH MONARCHS

	Monarch	Reign	Age at accession	Age at death	Reign years
1	Victoria	1837–1901	18	81	63
2	George III	1760–1820	22	81	59
3	Henry III	1216–72	9	64	56
4	Edward III	1327–77	14	64	50
5	Elizabeth I	1558–1603	25	69	44
6	Elizabeth II	1952–	25	–	41
7	Henry VI	1422–61 (deposed; d.1471)	8 months	49	38
8	Henry VIII	1509–47	17	55	37
9	Charles II	1649–85	19	54	36
10	Henry I	1100–35	31/32 *	66/67 *	35

Henry I's birthdate is unknown, so his age at accession and death are uncertain.

This list excludes the reigns of monarchs before 1066, so omits such rulers as Ethelred II who reigned for 37 years. Queen Elizabeth II overtook Henry VI's 38 years and 185 days reign in August 1990. If she is still on the throne on 11 September 2015, she will have beaten Queen Victoria's record by one day. She will then be 89 years old.

THE 10 OLDEST BRITISH TITLES

	Title	Created
1	Earl of Mar	c1115
2	Baron de Ros	12 December 1264
3	Baron Mowbray & Stourton	28 June 1283
4	Baron Hastings	before 1290
5	Baron Clinton	6 February 1298
6 =	Baron de Clifford	29 December 1299
6 =	Baron Strange of Knokin	29 December 1299
8	Baron Zouche	16 August 1308
9	Baron Beaumont	4 March 1309
10	Baron Audley	8 January 1313

THE WORLD'S 10 LONGEST-REIGNING MONARCHS

	Monarch	Country	Reign	Age at accession	Reign years
1	Louis XIV	France	1643–1715	5	72
2	John II	Liechtenstein	1858–1929	18	71
3	Franz-Josef	Austria–Hungary	1848–1916	18	67
4	Victoria	Great Britain	1837–1901	18	63
5	Hirohito	Japan	1926–89	25	62
6	George III	Great Britain	1760–1820	22	59
7	Louis XV	France	1715–74	5	59
8	Pedro II	Brazil	1831–89	6	58
9	Wilhelmina	Netherlands	1890–1948	10	58
10	Henry III	England	1216–72	9	56

Some authorities have claimed a 73-year reign for Alfonso I of Portugal, but his father, Henry of Burgundy, who conquered Portugal, ruled as Count, and it was this title that Alfonso inherited on 30 April 1112, at the age of two. His mother, Theresa of Castile, ruled until he took power in 1128, but he did not assume the title of king until 25 July 1139, during the Battle of Ourique at which he vanquished the Moors. He thus ruled as king for 46 years until his death on 6 December 1185. Even more extravagant claims are sometimes made for long-reigning monarchs in the ancient world, such as the alleged 94 years of Phiops II, a Sixth Dynasty Egyptian pharaoh, but since it is uncertain when he was either born or died, he has not been included.

THE 10 SHORTEST-REIGNING BRITISH MONARCHS

	Monarch	Reign	Duration
1	Jane	1553	14 days
2	Edward V	1483	75 days
3	Edward VIII	1936	325 days
4	Richard III	1483–85	2 years
5	James II	1685–88	3 years
6	Mary I	1553–58	5 years
7	Mary II	1689–94	5 years
8	Edward VI	1547–53	6 years
9	William IV	1830–37	7 years
10	Edward VII	1901–10	9 years

THE 10 LONGEST-REIGNING LIVING MONARCHS IN THE WORLD*

	Monarch	Country	Date of birth	Accession
1	Bhumibol Adulyadej	Thailand	5 Dec 1927	9 Jun 1946
2	Prince Rainier III	Monaco	31 May 1923	9 May 1949
3	Baudouin	Belgium	7 Sep 1930	17 Jul 1951
4	Elizabeth II	United Kingdom	21 Apr 1926	6 Feb 1952
5	Hussein	Jordan	14 Nov 1935	11 Aug 1952
6	Hassan II	Morocco	9 Jul 1929	26 Feb 1961
7	Isa bin Sulman al-Khalifa	Bahrain	3 Jul 1933	2 Nov 1961
8	Malietoa Tanumafili II	Western Samoa	4 Jan 1913	1 Jan 1962
9	Grand Duke Jean	Luxembourg	5 Jan 1921	12 Nov 1964
10	Taufa'ahau Tupou IV	Tonga	4 Jul 1918	16 Dec 1965

*Including hereditary rulers of principalities, dukedoms, etc.

There are 25 countries that have emperors, kings, queens, princes, dukes, sultans or other hereditary rulers as their heads of state. Malaysia, uniquely, has an elected monarchy.

THE 10 BUSIEST MEMBERS OF THE ROYAL FAMILY

		A	B	C	D
1	Princess Royal	299	94	78	471
2	The Queen	127	51	269	447
3	Prince of Wales	151	65	99	315
4	Duke of Edinburgh	125	96	29	250
5	Princess of Wales	188	28	19	235
6	Prince Edward	104	65	30	199
7	Duke of Kent	116	42	34	192
8	Duke of Gloucester	131	25	17	173
9	Duchess of Gloucester	113	26	15	154
10	Duchess of Kent	122	21	7	150

In 1992 the members of the Royal Family appearing in this list attended a total of 2,586 events in the United Kingdom, while five others members (Princess Alexandra, Princess Margaret, the Duke of York, the Queen Mother and Princess Alice, Duchess of Gloucester) attended 500 events between them. In addition, those in the Top 10 spent a total of 338 days abroad on official tours. On these the Duke of Edinburgh carried out 384 further engagements, Prince Edward 218, the Princess Royal 215, the Prince of Wales 145 and The Queen 141.

A: Official visits, opening ceremonies and other appearances.

B: Receptions, lunches, dinners and banquets.

C: Other engagements including investitures, meetings attended and audiences given.

D: Home total.

The Princess of Wales's 235 engagements in 1992 placed her fifth among the busy royals.

10 UNUSUAL DEATHS OF KINGS

1   Alexander of Greece

King Alexander died in October 1920 of blood poisoning after being bitten by his pet monkey.

2   Charles II of Navarre

Called 'Charles the Bad', he was imprisoned by King John of England in 1356, but escaped. He later contracted leprosy and as part of a bizarre 'cure' his physicians swathed him in cloth soaked in brandy and sulphur. On 1 January 1387 his page accidentally set his highly inflammable wrappings on fire, as a result of which the king was burned to death.

3   Charles VIII of France

Known as 'Charles the Affable', 27-year-old Charles was escorting his queen, Anne of Brittany, to a tennis court when he accidentally hit his head on a low beam and fractured his skull, as a result of which he died on 7 April 1498.

4   Henry I of England

Henry died on 1 December 1135 at St Denis-le-Ferment six days after contracting a fever, apparently after eating 'a surfeit of lampreys' (a kind of eel). Ptomaine poisoning contracted from the fish has been suggested as the cause of death, and is reinforced by reports that the man who removed the king's brain also caught a fever and died in agony.

5   Henry II of France

On 30 June 1559, having survived several years of hazardous warfare virtually unscathed, Henry was wounded during a tournament to celebrate the marriages of Margaret of Valois and Elisabeth of France. The lance of Scottish nobleman Gabriel de Montmorency pierced his eye, and he died on 10 July 1559.

6   Henry IV of England

Suffering from leprosy, devoutly religious King Henry proposed launching a crusade in the belief that he might be cured, although a soothsayer had prophesied that he would die in Jerusalem. On 20 March 1413 the king visited Westminster Abbey to say prayers before embarking on his journey. As he kneeled, he was seized with a stroke and carried to a room in the Abbey where he soon died. The room is known as the Jerusalem Chamber.

7   John of England

Already suffering from dysentery, King John arrived at Newark where he unwisely consumed a huge meal that included unripe peaches and new cider. As a result, his gastric condition worsened and on 19 October 1216 he died. A rumour later arose that John had been poisoned by a monk using venom extracted from a toad.

8   Ludwig II of Bavaria

Best known as the patron of Wagner, often watching performances of his works as the sole member of the audience, Ludwig became increasingly deranged and in 1886, at the age of 40, was declared incapable of ruling and committed to an asylum. On 13 June 1886 he drowned himself in the Starnbergersee, Germany, and in struggling to save him his 'minder' Bernhard von Gudden also lost his life.

9   Umberto I of Italy

On 28 July 1900 Umberto was dining in a restaurant in Monza when he was amazed to discover that the proprietor looked exactly like him, was also called Umberto, that they had both been born in Turin on the same day in 1844, and both had married women called Margherita, also on the same day. Astonished by the coincidences, the king invited his 'double' to a sports event the following day. The king duly arrived but was horrified to learn that the other Umberto had been killed in a mysterious shooting accident. As he expressed his sorrow, an anarchist called Bresci leaped forward and shot him dead.

10   William II of England

Known as 'William Rufus', the king was hunting deer in the New Forest on 2 August 1100 when he was shot in the heart by an arrow fired by Sir Walter Tyrrell which glanced off a tree. Theories have abounded ever since, ranging from accidental death to murder, as well as human sacrifice as part of a witch cult. William was not the only English king killed by an arrow: according to tradition, Harold lost his life through being shot in the eye at the Battle of Hastings, and Richard I ('Richard the Lionheart') was shot at Chaluz, France.

THE 10 OLDEST DUKEDOMS IN BRITAIN

	Dukedom	Order of succession	Title created
1	Norfolk	17th	28 June 1483
2	Somerset	19th	16 February 1547
3	Richmond (Lennox & Gordon)	10th	9 August 1675
4	Grafton	11th	11 September 1675
5	Beaufort	11th	2 December 1682
6	St Albans	14th	10 January 1684
7	Bedford	13th	11 May 1694
8	Devonshire	11th	12 May 1694
9	Marlborough	11th	14 December 1702
10	Rutland	10th	29 March 1703

THE 10 BRITISH PEERS WITH THE HIGHEST SUCCESSION NUMBERS

	Title	Current holder	Created	Number
1	Baron Kingsale	John de Courcy	1223	35th
2	Countess of Mar	Margaret	c1115	31st
3	Earl of Crawford	Robert	1398	29th
4 =	Baron de Ros	Peter	1264	28th
4 =	Baron Dunboyne	Patrick	1324	28th
6 =	Baroness Dacre	Rachel	1321	27th
6 =	Baron de Clifford	John	1299	27th
6 =	Baroness Willoughby de Eresby	Nancy	1313	27th
9	Baron Mowbray	Charles	1283	26th
10	Baron Audley	Richard	1313	25th

THE TOP 10 GIRLS' AND BOYS' NAMES ANNOUNCED IN THE BIRTHS COLUMN OF *THE INDEPENDENT* (1992)

	Girls		Boys
1	Emily	1	Thomas
2	*Isobel*	2	James
3	*Katherine*	3	Oliver
4	Alice	4	Edward
5 =	*Elizabeth*	5 =	*Benjamin*
5 =	*Emma*	5 =	William
5 =	*Rachel*	7	George
8	*Anna*	8	Alexander
9	Charlotte	9	*Richard*
10	Sophie	10 =	*Robert*
		10 =	*Samuel*

Names in italics do not also appear in The Times First Names Top 10.

THE TOP 10 GIRLS' AND BOYS' NAMES IN THE UK*

Girls

1	Hannah	↑
2	Emily	↑
3	Rebecca	↑
4	Charlotte	↑
5	Sophie	↑
6	Jessica	↑
7	Emma	↑
8	Sarah	↓
9	Laura	↓
10	Katie	↓

Boys

1	Thomas	↑
2	James	↓
3	Matthew	↓
4	Daniel	↑
5	Christopher	↓
6	Jack	↑
7	Joshua	↑
8	Michael	→
9	Robert	↑
10	Alexander	↑

According to a 1992 survey of the 300,000 members of the children's book club, The Red House.

↑ Higher position than in previous year.

↓ Lower position.

→ No change.

THE TOP 10 GIRLS' AND BOYS' NAMES ANNOUNCED IN THE BIRTHS COLUMN OF *THE TIMES* (1992)

FIRST NAME ONLY

		Girls	No.				Boys	No.
1	(4)	Sophie	74		1	(3)	Thomas	135
2	(2)	Charlotte	73		2	(1)	James	124
3	(1)	Emily	68		3	(2)	Alexander	118
4	(3)	Olivia	60		4	(4)	William	100
5	(5)	Lucy	57		5	(7)	Oliver	76
6	(–)	Alexandra	52		6	(8)	George	74
7	(–)	Harriet	48		7	(6)	Charles	73
8 =	(10)	Hannah	44		8	(5)	Edward	68
8 =	(8=)	Alice	44		9	(9)	Henry	61
8 =	(8=)	Georgina	44		10	(–)	Nicholas	57

ALL NAMES (INCLUDING MIDDLE NAMES)

		Girls	No.				Boys	No.
1	(1)	Eliz(s)abeth	194		1	(1)	James	318
2	(3)	Charlotte	130		2	(2)	William	239
3	(4)	Rose	126		3	(3)	Alexander	221
4	(2)	Louise	114		4	(4)	Thomas	191
5	(6)	Alice	103		5	(6)	Charles	160
6	(7=)	Sophie	98		6	(8)	George	155
7	(5)	Emily	97		7	(5)	Edward	152
8	(–)	Lucy	86		8	(7)	John	134
9	(–)	Victoria	83		9	(10)	Henry	111
10	(7=)	Alexandra	82		10	(–)	Robert	94

1991 position in brackets.

In 1947, when the names announced in *The Times* were first monitored, the most popular were Ann(e) and John – neither of which now makes an appearance in the first names Top 10s. In 1992 a total of 4,919 births were recorded — 2,434 girls and 2,485 boys (down on 1991, when it was 5,508: 2,577 girls and 2,931 boys). James had been the most popular boy's name consistently since 1964, but in 1992 was overtaken by Thomas. George and Olivia both entered the first name list in 1989, with Georgina joining them in 1990 (along with Samuel and Jessica, whose popularity was less sustained) and Hannah in 1991 (with Sarah, another short-term resident). Among first names only, Alexandra dropped out of the Top 10 in 1991, but returned to 6th place in 1992, while the top nine boys' names – which tend to be less subject to changes of fashion – remained the same, but with slight changes of order, Nicholas being the only new entry. The list of all names indicates that two 1991 newcomers, Louise and Rose, have maintained their Top 10 status, to which Lucy, Victoria and Robert have also aspired, while Michael (2nd in 1947, but thereafter in decline), experienced a brief resurgence in 1991 but is now once again out of the Top 10.

THE TOP 10 GIRLS' AND BOYS' NAMES IN THE USA

Girls

	White	Ethnic
1	Ashley	Ashley
2	Jessica	Brittany
3	Amanda	Jessica
4	Sarah	Sierra
5	Megan	Danielle
6	Jennifer	Tiffany
7	Katherine	Erica
8	Rachel	Crystal
9	Stephanie	Jasmine
10	Heather	Tanisha

Boys

	White	Ethnic
1	Michael	Michael
2	Matthew	Christopher
3	Christopher	Brandon
4	Joshua	Anthony
5	Andrew	James
6	Justin	Joshua
7	Daniel	Steven
8	Ryan	Charles
9	James	Darryl
10	David	Brian/Kevin/Robert/William

American name fashions are even more volatile than those in the UK, and vary considerably according to the child's ethnic background. Back in 1984, Ashley, which now tops the girls' lists, was already being noted as *the* girl's name of the year, just as Angela had been 10 years earlier. Heather has surprisingly maintained its momentum and has actually grown in popularity since the 1970s, despite the decline of other names derived from flowers, such as Daisy, Violet and Lily. It has been claimed that Jennifer (recently overtaken by Jessica) rose to prominence after the heroine of the book and film *Love Story*, and that Tiffany entered the Top 10 in 1980, influenced by the character Tiffany Welles in the TV series, *Charlie's Angels*. Among boys' names, Joshua appeared in the Top 10 for the first time in 1983, while Richard plummeted out of the Top 10 after Richard Nixon's disgrace during the Watergate scandal. Michael has topped every US list since 1964.

THE TOP 10 LIVERY COMPANIES OF THE CITY OF LONDON

1	Mercers
2	Grocers
3	Drapers
4	Fishmongers
5	Goldsmiths
6/7	Skinners
7/6	Merchant Taylors
8	Haberdashers
9	Salters
10	Ironmongers

The livery companies, so called from the distinctive costume, or livery, worn by their members, grew out of the city craft guilds of the fourteenth century, but today they function more as charitable, educational and social institutions than as trade associations. At one time all had halls with collections of art treasures and often extensive grounds, but as companies such as the Bonnet Makers, Virginals Makers and Heumers (helmet makers) were disbanded or absorbed and buildings were destroyed (many of them during the Blitz) or sold to raise funds, the number of halls has dwindled to fewer than 40. Today the liverymen elect the sheriffs of London and the Lord Mayor. In the time of Henry VIII, long and bitter disputes over the rank of the various livery companies were resolved when their governing body, the Court of Aldermen, established a list in order of precedence, headed by the so-called 'Great Twelve' (the other two are: 11 – Vintners and 12 – Clothworkers). An argument over precedence between the Skinners and Merchant Taylors was resolved by their order switching in alternate years. Over the centuries, the order of this list has remained the same, although many companies have left and new ones joined: in modern times these have included the Guild of Air Pilots' and Navigators (81 in precedence), Chartered Accountants (86) and Environmental Cleaners (97).

THE TOP 10 MEMBERSHIP ORGANIZATIONS IN THE UK

	Organization		Membership
1	Trades Union Congress		7,700,000
2	Automobile Association		7,600,000
3	National Alliance of Women's Organizations		5,500,000
4	Royal Automobile Club		5,400,000
5	National Trust		2,186,384
6	Amalgamated Engineering and Electrical Union		
	Engineering section	620,000	
	Electrical section	750,000	
		Total:	1,370,000
7	Transport & General Workers' Union		1,100,000
8	Royal Society for the Protection of Birds		870,000
9	GMB (formerly General, Municipal, Boilermakers and Allied Trades Union)		860,000
10	National and Local Government Officers' Union*		759,000

The 1 July 1993 merger of NALGO with NUPE (National Union of Public Employees) and COHSE (the Confederation of Health Service Employees) created a new union, UNISON, with approximately 1,500,000 members.

AA Box 161 at Tretower, Powys, the oldest in use in the UK: the AA is one of the top membership organizations in the country.

THE 10 OLDEST-ESTABLISHED CLUBS* IN THE UK

	Club	Location	Year est.
1	White's Club	London	1693
2	Boodle's	London	1762
3	Brooks's	London	1764
4	Norfolk Club	Norwich	1770
5	Royal Thames Yacht Club	London	1775
6	New Club	Edinburgh	1787
7	Marylebone Cricket Club	London	1787
8	The Athenaeum	Liverpool	1797
9	Royal Anglesey Yacht Club	Beaumaris	1802
10	City Club	Chester	1807

*Other than golf clubs.

Although the New Club, Edinburgh, and the Marylebone Cricket Club (MCC) were both founded in 1787, the New Club has the slight edge, having been established on 1 February, whereas Marylebone is traditionally dated from its first cricket match, played on 1 June.

Boodle's Club, founded in 1762, had such illustrious members as Beau Brummell and the Duke of Wellington.

THE TOP 10 NOBEL PRIZE WINNING COUNTRIES

	Country	Phy	Che	Ph/ Med	Lit	Pce	Eco	Total
1	USA	55	37	68	9	17	19	205
2	UK	20	23	22	8	10	6	89
3	Germany	19	27	14	6	4	–	70
4	France	10	7	7	12	9	1	46
5	Sweden	4	4	7	7	5	2	29
6	Switzerland	2	5	5	2	3	–	17
7	USSR	7	1	2	3	2	1	16
8	Stateless institutions	–	–	–	–	14	–	14
9	Italy	3	1	3	5	1	–	13
10 =	Denmark	3	–	5	3	1	–	12
10 =	Netherlands	6	2	2	–	1	1	12

Phy – Physics; Che – Chemistry; Ph/Med – Physiology or Medicine; Lit – Literature; Pce – Peace; Eco – Economic Sciences. Germany includes the united country before 1948, West Germany to 1990 and the united country since 1990.

At his death in 1896, the Swedish scientist Alfred Nobel left his fortune of some £1,750,000, amassed through his invention of dynamite, to establish a trust fund, which is now estimated to be worth over £150,000,000. Interest earned from this has enabled annual prizes to be awarded since 1901 to those who have achieved the greatest common good in the fields of Physics, Chemistry, Physiology or Medicine, Literature, Peace and, since 1969, Economic Sciences. All the award ceremonies take place in Stockholm, Sweden, with the exception of the Peace Prize, which is awarded in Oslo, Norway. The list includes all winners up to 1992, when the prizes were each worth over £400,000. Austria has produced 10 and Belgium nine Nobel Prize laureates, and some 30 other countries between one and eight winners. However, it should be noted that the prizes are won by individuals, and not the countries from which they come. The stateless institutions in 8th place include the Red Cross, and two national institutions, the British Friends' Service Council and the American Friends' Service Committee – both bodies affiliated to the Society of Friends (Quakers) – who were also winners in 1947.

THE FIRST BRITISH WINNERS OF THE NOBEL PRIZE FOR LITERATURE

	Winner	Dates	Prize year
1	Rudyard Kipling	1865–1936	1907
2	George Bernard Shaw	1856–1950	1925
3	John Galsworthy	1867–1933	1932
4	Thomas Stearns Eliot*	1888–1965	1948
5	Bertrand Russell	1872–1970	1950
6	Winston Churchill	1874–1965	1953
7	Elias Canetti†	b.1906	1981
8	William Golding	1911–93	1983

*US-born.

†Bulgarian-born.

France, with 12 winners, is the only nation to have won the Nobel Prize for Literature more than nine times. The United States has had nine winners, the UK eight and Germany seven.

Since it was inaugurated in 1969, there have also been six British winners of the Nobel Prize for Economic Sciences – placing the UK in 2nd position after the United States (12 winners).

Rudyard Kipling was the first of only eight British winners of the Nobel Prize for Literature.

THE FIRST 10 BRITISH WINNERS OF THE NOBEL PEACE PRIZE

	Winner	Dates	Prize year
1	Sir William Cremer	1838–1908	1903
2	Sir Joseph Austen Chamberlain	1863–1937	1925
3	Sir Norman Angell	1872–1967	1933
4	Arthur Henderson	1863–1935	1934
5	Lord Robert Cecil	1864–1958	1937
6	The Friends' Service Council*	–	1947
7	Lord John Boyd Orr	1880–1971	1949
8	Lord Philip Noel-Baker	1889–1982	1959
9 =	Mairead Corrigan	b.1944	1976
9 =	Betty Williams	b.1943	1976

*Shared with the American Friends' Service Committee.

To date, the first 10 are also the only 10 British winners of the Nobel Peace Prize.

THE FIRST 10 BRITISH WINNERS OF THE NOBEL PRIZE FOR PHYSICS

	Winner	Dates	Prize year
1	John Strutt (Lord Rayleigh)	1842–1919	1904
2	Sir Joseph Thomson	1856–1940	1906
3 =	Sir William Henry Bragg	1862–1942	1915
3 =	Sir William L. Bragg	1890–1971	1915
5	Charles Barkla	1877–1944	1917
6	Charles Wilson*	1869–1959	1927
7	Sir Owen Richardson	1879–1959	1928
8	Paul Dirac*	1902–84	1933
9	Sir James Chadwick	1891–1974	1935
10	Sir George Thomson	1892–1975	1937

*Prize shared with other nationalities.

Britons have won the Nobel Prize for Physics a total of 20 times since it was first awarded in 1901.

THE FIRST 10 BRITISH WINNERS OF THE NOBEL PRIZE FOR CHEMISTRY

	Winner	Dates	Prize year
1	Sir William Ramsay	1852–1916	1904
2	Lord Ernest Rutherford	1871–1937	1908
3	Frederick Soddy	1877–1956	1921
4	Francis Aston	1877–1945	1922
5	Sir Arthur Harden*	1865–1940	1929
6	Sir Walter Haworth*	1883–1950	1937
7	Sir Robert Robinson	1886–1975	1947
8 =	Archer Martin	b.1910	1952
8 =	Richard Synge	b.1914	1952
10	Sir Cyril Hinshelwood*	1897–1967	1956

*Prize shared with other nationalities.

Britons have won the Nobel Prize for Chemistry a total of 23 times since it was first awarded in 1901.

THE FIRST 10 BRITISH WINNERS OF THE NOBEL PRIZE FOR MEDICINE

	Winner	Dates	Prize year
1	Sir Ronald Ross	1857–1932	1902
2	Sir Archibald Hill*	1886–1977	1922
3	Sir Frederick Hopkins	1861–1947	1929
4 =	Lord Edgar Adrian	1889–1977	1932
4 =	Sir Charles Sherrington	1857–1952	1932
6	Sir Henry Dale*	1875–1968	1936
7 =	Sir Ernest Boris Chain	1906–79	1945
7 =	Sir Alexander Fleming	1881–1955	1945
7 =	Lord Howard Florey	1898–1968	1945
10	Sir Hans Krebs*†	1900–81	1953

*Prize shared with other nationalities.

†German-born.

Britons have won the Nobel Prize for Medicine a total of 22 times since it was first awarded in 1901.

THE TOP 10 ADVICE SERVICES IN THE UK

	Organization	Branches	Clients
1	Citizens Advice Bureaux	2,111	7,648,900
2	Samaritans	185	470,000
3	Law Centres Federation	60	452,400
4	Young People's Counselling and Advisory Service	125	113,000
5	Disablement Information and Advice Lines	100	75,000
6	Relate	133	70,000
7	Alcoholics Anonymous	2,800	45,000
8	Cruse Bereavement Care	185	22,500
9	Catholic Marriage Advisory Council	82*	17,100
10	Al-Alon Family Groups	1,090	13,100

THE FIRST 10 WEDDING ANNIVERSARY GIFTS

1	Cotton
2	Paper
3	Leather
4	Fruit and flowers
5	Wood
6	Sugar (or iron)
7	Wool or copper
8	Bronze (or electrical appliances)
9	Pottery (or willow)
10	Tin (or aluminium)

The custom of celebrating different wedding anniversaries by presenting specific types of gift has a long tradition, but has been much modified over the years, the association of 'electrical appliances' with the 8th anniversary testifying to the intrusion of modern commercialism into the practice. It varies considerably from country to country, and in the UK most of the earlier themes are generally disregarded in favour of the 'milestone' anniversaries: the 25th (silver), 40th (ruby), 50th (gold) and 60th (diamond). Correctly, the 75th anniversary is the 'diamond', but few married couples live long enough to celebrate it, and since Queen Victoria's so-called 'Diamond Jubilee' was celebrated on the 60th anniversary of her succession to the throne, it has usually been commemorated as the 60th.

10 NORTH POLE FIRSTS

1 The First to Reach the Pole?

Dispute continues to rage as to which – if either – of two men was the first to reach the North Pole: American adventurer Frederick Albert Cook (1865–1940) announced that he had attained his goal, accompanied by two Eskimos, on 21 April 1908, but his claim appears to have little foundation – and he is known to have committed various other fraudulent actions. It is more likely that another American, Robert Edwin Peary (1856–1920), his companion Matthew Alexander Henson (1866–1955) and four Eskimos were first at the Pole on 6 April 1909. If Peary's claim is valid, Henson also becomes the first black man to reach the Pole.

2 The First to Fly over the Pole in an Aeroplane

Two Americans, Lt-Cdr (later Admiral) Richard Evelyn Byrd (1888–1957; team-leader and navigator) and Floyd Bennett (1890–1928; pilot) traversed the Pole on 9 May 1926 in a three-engined Fokker F.VIII-3m named *Josephine Ford* after motor magnate Henry Ford's granddaughter (Ford and John D. Rockefeller sponsored the exploit). On 29 November 1929, Byrd also became the first to fly over the South Pole.

3 The First to Fly over the Pole in an Airship

A team of 16 led by Roald Amundsen (1872–1928), the Norwegian explorer who first reached the South Pole in 1911, flew across the North Pole on 12 May 1926 in the Italian-built airship *Norge*. One of his companions, Oscar Wisting, was with him at the South Pole and hence both men became the first to see both Poles.

4 The First to Land at the Pole in an Aircraft

A Soviet team comprising Pavel Afanaseyevich Geordiyenko, Mikhail Yemel'yenovich Ostrekin, Pavel Kononovich Sen'ko and Mikhail Mikhaylovich Somov arrived at and departed from the Pole by air on 23 April 1948. The first US landing at the Pole was that of Lt-Col William Pershing Benedict with 10 Air Force officials and scientists on 3 May 1952. In the same year, SAS became the first airline to fly scheduled flights over the Pole.

5 The First Solo Flight over the Pole in a Single-engined Aircraft

Capt Charles Francis Blair Jr of the USA became the first to fly over the Pole in a single-engined aircraft, a Mustang fighter *Excalibur III*, on 29 May 1951, crossing from Bardufoss, Norway, to Fairbanks, Alaska.

6 The First Confirmed Overland Journey to the Pole

American explorer Ralph S. Plaisted, with companions Walter Pederson, Gerald Pitzel and Jean Luc Bombardier, reached the Pole on 18 April 1968.

7 The First Woman at the Pole

Fran Phipps, a Canadian, arrived at the Pole by aeroplane on 5 April 1971.

8 The First Solo Overland Journey to the Pole

Japanese explorer Naomi Uemura (1941–84) reached the Pole on 1 May 1978, travelling by dog sled, but was then picked up by an aircraft. (Jean-Louis Etienne, who achieved the first solo journey without dogs on 11 May 1986, also flew out.)

9 The First Crossing on a Pole to Pole Expedition

British explorer Sir Ranulph Fiennes and his partner Charles Burton achieved this feat by walking over the North Pole on 10 April 1982, having crossed the South Pole on 15 December 1980.

10 The First to Reach the Pole on a Motorcycle

Fukashi Kazami of Japan arrived at the Pole on 20 April 1987 on a specially adapted 250cc motorcycle, after which he was picked up by aeroplane.

THE FIRST 10 PEOPLE TO REACH THE SOUTH POLE

Name	Nationality	Date
1 = Roald Amundsen*	Norwegian	14 December 1911
1 = Olav Olavsen Bjaaland	Norwegian	14 December 1911
1 = Helmer Julius Hanssen	Norwegian	14 December 1911
1 = Helge Sverre Hassel	Norwegian	14 December 1911
1 = Oscar Wisting	Norwegian	14 December 1911
6 = Robert Falcon Scott*	British	17 January 1912
6 = Henry Robertson Bowers	British	17 January 1912
6 = Edgar Evans	British	17 January 1912
6 = Lawrence Edward Grace Oates	British	17 January 1912
6 = Edward Adrian Wilson	British	17 January 1912

*Expedition leader.

Just 33 days separate the first two expeditions to reach the South Pole. Although several voyages had sailed close to Antarctica, no one had set foot on the mainland until the nineteenth century, when the first explorations were mounted. Scott, a naval lieutenant, first landed in the Antarctic in 1902 and examined the feasibility of reaching the South Pole. In 1909 Ernest Shackleton marched to within 113 miles of the Pole, and a multi-nation race for its conquest began. With Scott as its leader, a British Antarctic Expedition was organized in 1910 with its avowed goal 'to reach the South Pole and to secure for the British Empire the honour of this achievement'. En route, on his arrival in Australia, Scott learned for the first time that the Norwegian explorer Roald Amundsen had also embarked on an expedition to the Pole. After reaching the Antarctic, Scott undertook scientific research and acclimatized his team to local conditions. His party, leaving later than Amundsen's, experienced severe weather conditions and, after difficulties with motor sleds, ponies and dogs, relied entirely on fatiguing man-hauled sleds. Amundsen, in contrast, depended exclusively on dog-power, and even used them as part of his team's food supply, regarding the animals as a 'mobile larder' – behaviour that the British expedition regarded as barbaric. When Scott eventually reached the Pole, his party discovered that the Norwegians had beaten them. Plagued by illness, hunger, bad weather and exhaustion, they began the arduous journey back to their base during which Evans died after injuring himself. Recognizing that they had insufficient rations, Oates stepped out into a blizzard in a famous act of self-sacrifice. At precisely the time that Amundsen's achievement was being reported to the world, the remaining three died in their tent.

Captain Scott (standing, centre) with the other members of his ill-fated South Pole expedition.

10 CIRCUMNAVIGATION FIRSTS

1   The First Circumnavigation

Juan Sebastian de Elcano and his crew of 17 on board *Vittoria* sailed from Spain, returning to Italy 6 September 1522 (the expedition was led by Ferdinand Magellan, but he did not survive the voyage; he was murdered in the Philippines, 27 April 1521).

2   The First British Circumnavigation

Sir Francis Drake and his crew of 50 on the *Golden Hind*, returning to Plymouth 26 September 1580.

3   The First Circumnavigation in Less Than 80 Days

Nellie Bly, 1889 (*see* Around the World in 72 Days).

4   The First Solo Circumnavigation

Captain Joshua Slocum (1844–1910) in *Spray*, an oyster boat he built himself, returned to Massachusetts on 3 July 1898 after a voyage of more than three years.

5   The First Circumnavigation by Air

Two Douglas DCW amphibian aircraft, *Chicago* piloted by Lt Lowell Smith and Lt Leslie P. Arnold and *New Orleans* piloted by Lt Erik H. Nelson and Lt John Harding, in a series of 'hops', 6 April–28 September 1924.

6   The First Non-stop Air Circumnavigation

USAF B-50A bomber *Lucky Lady II* piloted by Capt James Gallagher, flying from and returning to Fort Worth, Texas on 2 March 1949 after 94 hours 1 minute in the air, refuelling four times.

7   The First Underwater Circumnavigation

US Navy nuclear submarine *Triton* completed its journey on 25 April 1960.

8   The First Non-stop Solo Circumnavigation

British yachtsman Robin Knox-Johnston in *Suhali*, returning to Falmouth 22 April 1969.

9   The First Helicopter Circumnavigation

H. Ross Perot Jr (son of the 1992 US presidential candidate), and Jay Coburn, in Bell 206L *Spirit of Texas*, from and to Dallas, Texas, 1–30 September 1982.

10   The First Air Circumnavigation Without Refuelling

Richard Ruttan and Jeana Yeager in *Voyager*, from and to Edwards Air Force Base, California, 14–23 December 1986.

AROUND THE WORLD IN 72 DAYS

In 1870, an eccentric American businessman, George Train, circumnavigated the world in 80 days (or, more accurately, 80 days if one discounts the time he spent in jail in France). The French novelist Jules Verne claimed he had never heard of Train or his achievement; nor that of William Perry Fogg, another American, who travelled round the world and in 1872 published an account of his journey entitled *Round the World*. Verne explained that in 1871 he had spotted a Thomas Cook brochure that declared travel facilities to be so advanced that it was now possible to journey round the world with ease; indeed, Cook's were planning such a tour for 1872 – a trip that in the event took 222 days. In this same year, Verne wrote his best-known novel, calling it *Around the World in Eighty Days* – and, coincidentally, naming his principal character Phileas Fogg.

The book became an immediate bestseller in France and the following year was translated into English and published in Britain and America. The idea of a race around the world, the central theme of Verne's novel, captivated many readers, some of whom attempted to emulate Fogg's journey. The first of them was Nellie Bly. Her real name was Elizabeth Cochrane. At the age of 18 she was writing for the *Pittsburgh Dispatch* whose managing editor suggested the pseudonym, Nellie Bly, which he took from a popular song by Stephen Foster. She soon gained fame through her fearless investigative journalism: working for the New York *World*, she had pretended to be insane in order to have herself committed to a mental asylum so as to expose the conditions there.

Inspired by Verne's novel, she set out to beat Phileas Fogg's record, travelling light with her belongings in just two satchels – and, much to the consternation of many female readers, *without a parasol,* a breach of Victorian etiquette that marked her as irresponsible. She sailed to England by steamer, and made her way to Amiens to visit Jules Verne. Although it was well off her proposed route, she was never one to pass up the chance of extra publicity, and reported Verne's response in detail. 'Is it possible that this child is travelling around the world alone?' he asked, astonished by her youth. Showing her a map of Fogg's imaginary voyage, he told her, 'If you do it in 79 days, I shall applaud you with both hands. But 75 days – *mon dieu* – that would be a miracle!'

On she travelled, via Brindisi, Port Said, Ishmailia, Suez, Aden, Colombo, Penang, Singapore, Hong Kong, Yokohama, San Francisco and then back to a heroine's welcome in New York on 25 January 1890 – a record circumnavigation of 72 days, 6 hours, 11 minutes and 14 seconds.

Bly's record became the new target to beat: the following year another female journalist, Elizabeth Bisland, attempted to do so, but failed by one day; George Train tried to regain his record, achieving 67 days in 1890 and 60 in 1892. Eventually even Verne himself got fed up with round the world record-breakers and in 1892 wrote a satire, *Claudius Bombarnac*, in which the hero attempts to do the journey in 39 days, but by missing every boat and train succeeds in taking 187.

THE 10 LONGEST ENTRIES IN THE *DICTIONARY OF NATIONAL BIOGRAPHY**

	Name	Dates	Length (pages)†
1	William Shakespeare	1564–1616	49
2	First Duke of Wellington	1769–1852	34
3	Francis Bacon	1561–1626	32
4	Oliver Cromwell	1599–1658	31
5	Sir Robert Walpole	1676–1745	28
6	Queen Elizabeth I	1533–1603	28
7	First Duke of Marlborough	1650–1722	26
8	Sir Walter Scott	1771–1832	25
9	Edward I	1239–1307	24
10	Charles II	1630–85	24

**Up to 1900.*

†*Fractions of pages have been taken into account in establishing the ranking order.*

In 1882 the publisher George M. Smith inaugurated the monumental *Dictionary of National Biography*, a huge collection of biographical accounts of notable British men and women, both heroes and villains, from the earliest times to the present, a qualification for entry being that subjects should no longer be alive. Volumes were issued alphabetically (starting with Abbadie to Anne) over the ensuing years, but it was not until 1900 that the series was completed, with the publication of the 63rd volume (containing entries from Wordsworth to Zuylestein). This was followed in 1901 by a supplement adding a further 1,000 biographies that had been omitted, since when a new volume has been added every ten years or so up to the present day, with the 1993 publication of the so-called *Missing Persons* featuring biographies of individuals who for one reason or another were previously overlooked. The first editor of the series was Leslie Stephen, the father of the novelist Virginia Woolf, who commissioned specialist writers in various fields, each of whom was allocated a number of entries to compile. Up to 1900 there were 29,120 entries, with each decennial volume adding approximately 750 new entries. After the initial A–Z volumes had been completed, a 'statistical account' was published which provided such information as the list of longest entries (the Top 10 being closely followed by Lord Byron, Sir Isaac Newton, Jonathan Swift, Edward III, Laurence Sterne and John Wycliffe). However, in the supplement appearing the following year, even Shakespeare's superlative entry was eclipsed by that of Queen Victoria, which ran to a massive 112 pages.

THE 10 COMMONEST FIRST LETTERS OF NAMES IN THE *DICTIONARY OF NATIONAL BIOGRAPHY**

	Letter	Entries
1	B	3,078
2	C	2,542
3 =	H	2,420
3 =	S	2,420
5	M	2,310
6	P	1,807
7	W	1,797
8	G	1,490
9	R	1,462
10	D	1,316

**Up to 1900.*

No one appears with a surname beginning with X, but there are 21 Zs, 31 Qs and 75 Us.

THE 10 COMMONEST SURNAMES IN THE *DICTIONARY OF NATIONAL BIOGRAPHY**

	Name†	Entries
1	Smith	195
2	Jones	132
3	Stewart	112
4	Hamilton	106
5	Brown	102
6	Clark	99
7	Moore	88
8	Taylor	86
9	Douglas	85
10	Scott	83

**Up to 1900.*

†*Including variant spellings: Smith/Smyth; Clark/Clarke, etc.*

THE 10 YOUNGEST ENTRANTS IN *WHO'S WHO*

	Name	Date of birth
1	Master of Lindasy	5 Aug 1991
2	Lord Cochrane	14 Mar 1991
3	Viscount Garnock	30 Dec 1990
4	Viscount Chichester	19 Nov 1990
5	Viscount Alexander	15 Oct 1990
6	Lord Worsley	9 Aug 1990
7	Lord Mountstuart	21 Dec 1989
8	Lord Kenlis	18 Jun 1989
9	The Earl of Craven	13 Jun 1989
10	Viscount Knebworth	7 Mar 1989

The qualification for entry to *Who's Who* is either through notable achievement or through aristocratic birth: those on the list have all gained their *Who's Who* entries via the latter route, as at the time this book is published, even the oldest of them would only just qualify for entry to primary school. The youngest person ever to receive his entry on merit was the violinist Yehudi Menuhin, aged 15 when he appeared in the 1932 edition.

THE 10 LONGEST ENTRIES IN *WHO'S WHO*

	Name	Profession	Date of birth	Length (lines)
1	Dame Barbara Cartland	Author/playwright	9 Jul 1901	199
2	Peter Maxwell Davies	Composer/conductor	8 Sep 1934	118
3	Rt Rev John Vockler	Writer/theologian	22 Jul 1924	81
4	Sir Karl Popper	Scientist	28 Jul 1902	76
5	Sir John Gielgud	Actor	14 Apr 1904	74
6	Joseph Needham	Scientist	1900	73
7	Nicholas Polunin	Environmentalist	?	71
8 =	Sir Peter Hall	Theatre director	22 Nov 1930	65
8 =	Wendy Toye	Theatre director, etc	1 May 1917	65
10	Very Rev Professor Thomas Torrance	Academic	30 Aug 1913	64

Dame Barbara Cartland achieved her current record for the longest *Who's Who* entry by the simple expedient of listing virtually every book and play she has ever written. As she is one of the most prolific authors of all time, the result is a very long list – as is that of Peter Maxwell Davies, who includes all his musical compositions. The longest entry of all time was the 211 lines of Sir Winston Churchill. While revealing everything else about their professional lives, two entrants are curiously reticent about their birth dates: Joseph Needham provides only the year, while Nicholas Polunin does not even supply that.

Barbara Cartland's 199-line entry, effectively a complete bibliography of her novels, is the longest in *Who's Who*.

THE 10 MOST HIGHLY POPULATED CITIES IN THE WORLD

	City	Country	Population (1991)
1	Tokyo/Yokohama	Japan	27,245,000
2	Mexico City	Mexico	20,899,000
3	São Paulo	Brazil	18,701,000
4	Seoul	South Korea	16,792,000
5	New York	USA	14,625,000
6	Osaka/Kobe/Kyoto	Japan	13,872,000
7	Bombay	India	12,101,000
8	Calcutta	India	11,898,000
9	Rio de Janeiro	Brazil	11,688,000
10	Buenos Aires	Argentina	11,657,000
17	*London*	*UK*	*9,115,000*

Calculating the populations of the world's cities is fraught with difficulties, not least that of determining whether the city is defined by its administrative boundaries or by its continuously built-up areas or conurbations. Since different countries adopt different schemes, and some have populations concentrated in city centres while others are spread out in suburbs sprawling over hundreds of square miles, it has been impossible to compare them meaningfully. In order to resolve this problem, the US Bureau of the Census has adopted the method of defining cities as population clusters or 'urban agglomerations' with densities of more than 5,000 inhabitants per square mile (equivalent to 1,931 per sq km). It should be stressed that totals based on this system will differ considerably from those based on other methods: by it, for example, the hugely spread-out city of Shanghai is reckoned to have a population of 6,936,000, compared with the total of 12,670,000 estimated for its metropolitan area. On this basis, the city in the Top 10 with the greatest area is New York (3,300 sq km/1,274 sq miles) and the smallest Bombay (246 sq km/95 sq miles) – which also means that Bombay has the greatest population density, 49,191 inhabitants per sq km/127,379 per sq mile – more than 12 times that of London. One recent change to note in the Top 10 is the inexorable rise in the population of Brazil's second-largest city, Rio de Janeiro, the total of which has now overtaken that of Buenos Aires. They remain the most populous cities in the southern hemisphere, with Jakarta, Indonesia, the runner-up (9,882,000 in 1991, using this method of calculation).

With a population of more than 20 million and climbing, Mexico City is the world's second largest.

THE 10 LARGEST CITIES IN ENGLAND, SCOTLAND AND WALES

	ENGLAND		SCOTLAND		WALES	
	City	Population	City	Population	City	Population
1	London	6,735,400	Glasgow	725,100	Cardiff	281,500
2	Birmingham	1,004,100	Edinburgh	438,232	Swansea	187,000
3	Leeds	710,900	Aberdeen	215,300	Ogwr	135,000
4	Sheffield	534,300	Renfrew	204,000	Newport	129,500
5	Liverpool	483,000	Dundee	176,200	Glamorgan	118,500
6	Bradford	463,100	Kirkaldy	148,900	Wrexham	115,800
7	Manchester	451,400	Motherwell	147,500	Rhymney	104,700
8	Bristol	391,500	Falkirk	144,400	Taff-Ely	93,600
9	Leicester	279,700	West Lothian	142,600	Torfaen	91,200
10	Nottingham	276,800	Cunninghame	137,100	Monmouth	79,400

THE 10 MOST DENSELY POPULATED CITIES IN THE WORLD

	City	Country	Population per sq mile (1991)
1	Hong Kong	Hong Kong	247,501
2	Lagos	Nigeria	142,821
3	Jakarta	Indonesia	130,026
4	Bombay	India	127,379
5	Ho Chi Minh City	Vietnam	120,168
6	Ahamadabad	India	115,893
7	Shenyang	China	109,974
8	Tianjin	China	98,990
9	Cairo	Egypt	97,106
10	Bangalore	India	96,041
	London	*UK*	*10,429*

According to the US Bureau of the Census method of calculating population and population density, the main island of Hong Kong, the capital of which is Victoria, is the most densely populated area in the world, a cramped 113 sq ft per person (London appears positively spacious with 2,673 sq ft per person). For any purist who may wish to exclude Hong Kong as having the status of a colony rather than a city, the new No. 10 becomes Chengdu, China (94,870 per sq mile).

THE 10 MOST HIGHLY POPULATED CITIES IN THE WORLD 100 YEARS AGO

	City	Population
1	London	4,231,431
2	Paris	2,423,946
3	Peking	1,648,814
4	Canton (Kwangchow)	1,600,000
5	Berlin	1,579,244
6	Tokyo	1,552,457
7	New York	1,515,301
8	Vienna	1,364,548
9	Chicago	1,099,850
10	Philadelphia	1,046,964

In 1890, Nanking in China was the only other city in the world with a population of more than 1,000,000, with another Chinese city, Tientsing, close behind. Several other cities, including Constantinople (called Istanbul since 1930), St Petersburg (known as Petrograd 1914–24 and Leningrad 1924–91) and Moscow, all had populations in excess of 750,000. However, it is remarkable to consider that, as a result of the rapid growth of American cities in the second half of the nineteenth century, Brooklyn, with a population in 1890 of 806,343, was marginally larger than Bombay (804,470 in 1891), whereas Bombay's present population of 12,571,720 makes it more than five times the size of the whole of Brooklyn county.

THE 10 MOST HIGHLY POPULATED CITIES IN THE WORLD 1893–1993

	1893	1943	1993
1	London	London	Mexico City
2	Paris	New York	Cairo
3	Peking	Tokyo	Shanghai
4	Canton	Berlin	Bombay
5	Berlin	Moscow	Tokyo
6	Tokyo	Shanghai	Calcutta
7	New York	Chicago	Peking
8	Vienna	Leningrad	São Paulo
9	Chicago	Osaka	Seoul
10	Philadelphia	Paris	Paris

THE 10 MOST HIGHLY POPULATED CITIES IN EUROPE

	City	Country	Population (1991)
1	Moscow*	Russia	10,446,000
2	London*	UK	9,115,000
3	Paris*	France	8,720,000
4	Essen	Germany	7,452,000
5	Istanbul†	Turkey	6,678,000
6	Milan	Italy	4,749,000
7	St Petersburg	Russia	4,672,000
8	Madrid*	Spain	4,513,000
9	Barcelona	Spain	4,227,000
10	Manchester	UK	4,030,000

*Capital city.

†Located in Turkey in Europe.

The problem of defining a city's boundaries means that population figures generally relate to 'urban agglomerations', which often include suburbs sprawling over very large areas. The US Bureau of the Census method of identifying city populations (see The 10 Most Highly Populated Cities in the World) produces this list – although one based on cities minus their suburbs would present a very different picture. Using this method with other cities shows that Athens, Berlin and Rome have populations in excess of 3,000,000, Naples, Ankara, Kiev, Lisbon, Vienna, Birmingham, Valencia and Budapest over 2,000,000 and more than a dozen European cities have populations in excess of 1,000,000.

THE 10 MOST HIGHLY POPULATED CITIES IN NORTH AMERICA

	City	Country	Population (1991)
1	Mexico City	Mexico	20,899,000
2	New York	USA	14,625,000
3	Los Angeles	USA	10,130,000
4	Chicago	USA	6,529,000
5	Philadelphia	USA	4,003,000
6	San Francisco	USA	3,987,000
7	Miami	USA	3,471,000
8	Guadalajara	Mexico	3,370,000
9	Toronto	Canada	3,145,000
10	Detroit/Windsor	USA/Canada	2,969,000

The US Bureau of the Census method of calculating city populations (see The 10 Most Highly Populated Cities in the World) takes account of often widely spread 'urban agglomerations' – in the instance of Detroit and Windsor giving rise to the anomaly of a 'city' that straddles two countries.

THE 10 MOST HIGHLY POPULATED CITIES IN SOUTH AMERICA

	City	Country	Population (1991)
1	São Paulo	Brazil	18,701,000
2	Rio de Janeiro	Brazil	11,688,000
3	Buenos Aires	Argentina	11,657,000
4	Lima	Peru	6,815,000
5	Bogota	Colombia	5,913,000
6	Santiago	Chile	5,378,000
7	Belo Horizonte	Brazil	3,812,000
8	Caracas	Venezuela	3,217,000
9	Porto Alegre	Brazil	3,114,000
10	Salvador	Brazil	2,298,000

THE 10 MOST HIGHLY POPULATED CITIES IN AFRICA

	City	Country	Population
1	Cairo	Egypt	6,513,000
2	Kinshasa	Zaïre	3,562,122
3	Casablanca	Morocco	3,500,000
4	Alexandria	Egypt	3,183,000
5	Cape Town	South Africa	1,911,521
6	Giza	Egypt	1,670,000
7	Johannesburg	South Africa	1,609,000
8	Luanda	Angola	1,544,000
9	Algiers	Algeria	1,507,241
10	Addis Ababa	Ethiopia	1,495,266

A busy market in Lagos, Nigeria, Africa's most populous country.

THE 10 MOST HIGHLY POPULATED CITIES IN ASIA

	City	Country	Population (1991)
1	Tokyo/Yokohama	Japan	27,245,000
2	Seoul	South Korea	16,792,000
3	Osaka/Kobe/Kyoto	Japan	13,872,000
4	Bombay	India	12,101,000
5	Calcutta	India	11,898,000
6	Manila	Philippines	10,156,000
7	Jakarta	Indonesia	9,882,000
8	Tehran	Iran	9,779,000
9	Delhi	India	8,778,000
10	Karachi	Pakistan	8,014,000

THE 10 MOST HIGHLY POPULATED COUNTRIES IN AFRICA

	Country	Population
1	Nigeria	108,542,000
2	Egypt	53,513,000
3	Ethiopia	49,240,000
4	Zaïre	35,562,000
5	South Africa	35,282,000
6	Morocco	27,575,000
7	Tanzania	25,635,000
8	Sudan	25,203,000
9	Algeria	24,960,000
10	Kenya	24,032,000

TOWN & COUNTRY

THE 10 MOST HIGHLY POPULATED COUNTRIES IN THE WORLD

	Country	Population* 1983	1993
1	China	1,008,175,288	1,143,330,000
2	India	683,880,051	843,930,861
3	USA	226,545,805	248,709,873
4	Indonesia	153,000,000	179,300,000
5	Brazil	119,098,922	150,368,000
6	USSR/Russia	271,203,000	147,022,000
7	Japan	118,390,000	123,537,000
8	Pakistan	83,780,000	112,049,000
9	Nigeria	85,000,000	108,542,000
10	Bangladesh	94,700,000	108,000,000
	UK	*55,776,422*	*57,701,000*

*Based on closest census or most recent estimate.

In the 1980s world population increased from 4,450,000,000 at the beginning of the decade to 5,292,000,000 at the end – a growth of almost 19 per cent. The figures for the past 10 years show that the population of China is now almost 20 times that of the UK and represents almost 22 per cent of the total population of the world, proving the commonly stated statistic that 'one person in five is Chinese'. Although differential rates of population increase result in changes in the order, the members of the Top 10 remain largely the same from year to year. Despite the anomaly that the USSR no longer exists, Russia, its largest former component state, maintains an independent place in the ranking.

Colombia's population, as with that of all other countries in South America, appears well below that of Brazil.

THE 10 MOST DENSELY POPULATED COUNTRIES IN EUROPE

	Country	Population per sq km
1	Monaco	14,359
2	Vatican City	2,288
3	Malta and Gozo	1,148
4	Netherlands	439
5	San Marino	393
6	Belgium	327
7	UK	235
8	Germany	223
9	Italy	192
10	Liechtenstein	180

THE 10 MOST HIGHLY POPULATED COUNTRIES IN SOUTH AMERICA

	Country	Population
1	Brazil	150,368,000
2	Argentina	33,370,298
3	Colombia	32,987,000
4	Peru	22,332,000
5	Venezuela	19,735,000
6	Chile	13,173,000
7	Ecuador	10,782,000
8	Bolivia	7,400,000
9	Paraguay	4,277,000
10	Uruguay	3,094,000

The least populated country in South America is the Falkland Islands, with a resident population of 2,121 – 1,643 of whom live in the capital Port Stanley.

THE 10 MOST HIGHLY POPULATED COUNTRIES IN ASIA

	Country	Population
1	China	1,143,330,000
2	India	843,930,861
3	Indonesia	179,300,000
4	Japan	123,537,000
5	Pakistan	112,049,000
6	Bangladesh	108,000,000
7	Vietnam	66,200,000
8	Philippines	61,480,000
9	Thailand	57,196,000
10	Turkey*	56,473,000

*Including Turkey in Europe.

That part of the territory of the former USSR in Asia previously placed the country in 7th place, but following the break-up of the Soviet Union no one of its individual states qualifies for the Top 10 (Uzbekistan is the largest with a population of 19,810,000). Part of Turkey falls in Europe; if only Turkey in Asia is taken into account, it would be replaced in the list by Iran with a population of 54,607,000.

THE 10 MOST HIGHLY POPULATED COUNTRIES IN OCEANIA

	Country	Population
1	Australia	17,335,900
2	Papua New Guinea	3,699,000
3	New Zealand	3,435,000
4	Fiji	764,000
5	Solomon Islands	320,000
6	Samoa (US & Western)	236,773
7	French Polynesia	206,000
8	New Caledonia	167,000
9	Vanuatu	142,900
10	Guam	133,152

THE 10 COUNTRIES OUTSIDE THE USA WITH THE MOST RESIDENT US CITIZENS

	Country	US citizens
1	Mexico	425,400
2	Canada	259,700
3	UK	170,100
4	Germany	152,300
5	Philippines	120,600
6	Italy	83,400
7	Israel	77,200
8	Australia	67,000
9	Spain	61,400
10	Greece	54,000

THE 10 LONGEST PLACE NAMES IN THE UK

	Name	Letters
1	Gorsafawddachaidraigddanheddogleddollônpenrhynareurdraeth-ceredigion (see The 10 Longest Place Names in the World)	67
2	Llanfairpwllgwyngyllgogerychwyrndrobwllllantysiliogogogoch (see The 10 Longest Place Names in the World)	58
3	Sutton-under-Whitestonecliffe, North Yorkshire	27
4	Llanfihangel-yng-Ngwynfa, Powys	22
5 =	Llanfihangel-y-Creuddyn, Dyfed	21
5 =	Llanfihangel-y-traethau, Gwynedd	21
7	Cottonshopeburnfoot, Northumberland	19
8 =	Blakehopeburnhaugh, Northumberland	18
8 =	Coignafeuinternich, Inverness-shire	18
10 =	Claddochbaleshare, North Uist, Outer Hebrides	17
10 =	Claddochknockline, North Uist, Outer Hebrides	17

These are all single and hyphenated names. The longest multiple name in England is North Leverton with Habblesthorpe, Nottinghamshire (30 letters), followed by Skidbrooke cum Saltfeet Haven, Lincolnshire (26) and Preston upon the Weald Moors, Shropshire (24). In Wales it is Lower Llanfihangel-y-Creuddyn, Dyfed (26) followed by Llansantffraid Cwmdeuddwr, Powys (24), and in Scotland Huntingtower and Ruthvenfield (27) – although there is also a loch on the island of Lewis called Loch Airidh Mhic Fhionnlaidh Dhuibh (31) (see The 10 Longest Place Names in the World).

If the parameters are extended to encompass Ireland, the single word Muckanaghederdauhaulia (22) is scooped into the net. Runners-up include Doddiscombsleigh, Moretonhampstead, Woolfardisworthy (pronounced 'Woolsery'), Combe-in-Teignhead and Stoke-in-Teignhead, all of which are in Devon and have 16 letters.

The longest parish name in the UK was for many years Saint Andrew, Holborn above the Bars, with Saint George the Martyr (54) in London, until the formation on 5 April 1971 of Saint Mary le More and All Hallows with Saint Leonard and Saint Peter, Wallingford (68).

A sign-painter's dream comes true in Wales.

THE 10 LONGEST PLACE NAMES IN THE WORLD

Name	Letters
1 Krung Thep Mahanakhon Bovorn Ratanakosin Mahintharayutthaya Mahadilok pop Noparatratchathani Burirom Udomratchanivetmahasathan Amornpiman Avatarnsathit Sakkathattiyavisnukarmprasit	**167**

When the poetic name of Bangkok, capital of Thailand, is used, it is usually abbreviated to 'Krung Thep' (city of angels).

2 Taumatawhakatangihangakoauauotamateaturipukakapiki-maungahoronukupokaiwhenuakitanatahu	**85**

This is the longer version (the other has a mere 83 letters) of the Maori name of a hill in New Zealand. It translates as 'The place where Tamatea, the man with the big knees, who slid, climbed and swallowed mountains, known as land-eater, played on the flute to his loved one'.

3 Gorsafawddachaidraigddanheddogleddollônpenrhynareurdraethceredigion	**67**

A name contrived by the Fairbourne Steam Railway, Gwynedd, North Wales, for publicity purposes and in order to outdo No. 4.

4 Llanfairpwllgwyngyllgogerychwyrndrobwllllantysiliogogogoch	**58**

This is the place in Gwynedd famed especially for the length of its railway tickets. It means 'St Mary's Church in the hollow of the white hazel near to the rapid whirlpool of Llantysilio of the Red Cave'. Its official name comprises only the first 20 letters.

5 El Pueblo de Nuestra Señora la Reina de los Angeles de la Porciuncula	**57**

The site of a Franciscan mission and the full Spanish name of Los Angeles; it means 'the town of Our Lady the Queen of the Angels of the Little Portion'. Nowadays it is customarily known by its initial letters, 'LA', making it also one of the shortest-named cities in the world.

6 Chargoggagoggmanchauggagoggchaubunagungamaugg	**45**

America's longest place name, a lake near Webster, Massachusetts. Its Indian name, loosely translated, means 'You fish on your side, I'll fish on mine, and no one fishes in the middle'. It is pronounced 'Char-gogg-a-gogg (pause) man-chaugg-a-gogg (pause) chau-bun-a-gung-a-maugg'.

7 = Lower North Branch Little Southwest Miramichi	**40**

Canada's longest place name – a short river in New Brunswick.

7 = Villa Real de la Santa Fe de San Francisco de Asis	**40**

The full Spanish name of Santa Fe, New Mexico, translates as, 'Royal city of the holy faith of St Francis of Assisi'.

9 Te Whakatakanga-o-te-ngarehu-o-te-ahi-a-Tamatea	**38**

The Maori name of Hammer Springs, New Zealand; like the second name in this list, it refers to a legend of Tamatea, explaining how the springs were warmed by 'the falling of the cinders of the fire of Tamatea'.

10 Loch Airidh Mhic Fhionnlaidh Dhuibh	**31**

The name of a loch on the island of Lewis, Scotland.

Monaco is the world's most densely populated and second smallest country.

The list of the world's largest countries, the Top 10 of which comprise 53.8 per cent of the total Earth's surface, have undergone substantial revision of late: the break-up of the former Soviet Union has effectively introduced two new countries, with Russia taking pre-eminent position (since it occupies a vast 76 per cent of the area of the old USSR which it replaces and, for comparison, is 70 times the size of the UK), while Kazakhstan, which enters in 9th position, ousts Algeria from the bottom of the list.

THE 10 LARGEST COUNTRIES IN THE WORLD

	Country	Area sq km	sq miles
1	Russia	17,070,289	6,590,876
2	Canada	9,970,537	3,849,646
3	China	9,596,961	3,705,408
4	USA	9,372,614	3,618,787
5	Brazil	8,511,965	3,286,488
6	Australia	7,686,848	2,967,909
7	India	3,287,590	1,269,346
8	Argentina	2,766,889	1,068,302
9	Kazakhstan	2,716,626	1,048,895
10	Sudan	2,505,813	967,500
	UK	*244,046*	*94,227*
	World total	*136,597,770*	*52,740,700*

THE 10 SMALLEST COUNTRIES IN THE WORLD

	Country	Area sq km	sq miles
1	Vatican City	0.44	0.17
2	Monaco	1.81	0.7
3	Gibraltar	6.47	2.5
4	Macau	16.06	6.2
5	Nauru	21.23	8.2
6	Tuvalu	25.90	10.0
7	Bermuda	53.35	20.6
8	San Marino	59.57	23.0
9	Liechtenstein	157.99	61.0
10	Antigua	279.72	108.0

THE 10 COUNTRIES WITH THE LONGEST OFFICIAL NAMES

	Official name*	Common English name	Letters
1	al-Jamāhīrīyah al-'Arabīya al-Lībīyah ash-Sha'biyah al-Ishtirākīyah	Libya	56
2	al-Jumhūrīyah al-Jazā'irīyah ad-Dīmuqrāṭīyah ash-Sha'biyah	Algeria	49
3	United Kingdom of Great Britain and Northern Ireland	United Kingdom	45
4	Sri Lankā Prajathanthrika Samajavadi Janarajaya	Sri Lanka	43
5	Jumhūrīyat al-Yaman ad-Dimuqrātīyah ash-Sha'bīyah	People's Democratic Republic of Yemen	42
6 =	Republika Popullore Socialiste e Shqipërisë	Albania	39
6 =	YeĒtiyop'iya Hezbawi Dimokrasīyawī Republēk	Ethiopia	39
8	République Fédérale Islamique des Comores	The Comores	37
9 =	al-Jumhūrīyah al-Islāmīyah al-Mūrītānīyah	Mauritania	36
9 =	The Federation of St Christopher and Nevis	St Christopher and Nevis	36

Some official names have been transliterated from languages that do not use the Roman alphabet; their length may vary according to the method used.

There is clearly no connection between the length of names and the longevity of the nation states that bear them, for since we last published this list in 1991, three countries have ceased to exist: Socijalistička Federativna Republika Jugoslavija (Yugoslavia, 45 letters), Soyuz Sovetskikh Sotsialisticheskikh Respublik (USSR, 43) and Československá Socialistická Republika (Czechoslovakia, 36).

TOWN & COUNTRY

THE 10 LARGEST COUNTRIES IN AFRICA

	Country	Area sq km	sq miles
1	Sudan	2,505,813	967,500
2	Algeria	2,381,741	919,595
3	Zaïre	2,345,409	905,567
4	Libya	1,759,540	679,362
5	Chad	1,284,000	495,755
6	Niger	1,267,080	489,191
7	Angola	1,246,700	481,354
8	Mali	1,240,000	478,791
9	Ethiopia	1,221,900	471,778
10	South Africa	1,221,031	471,445

Sudan, the largest country in Africa, has an area 10 times that of the UK.

THE 10 LARGEST COUNTRIES IN OCEANIA

	Country	Area sq km	sq miles
1	Australia	7,686,848	2,967,909
2	Papua New Guinea	461,691	178,260
3	New Zealand	268,676	103,736
4	Solomon Islands	28,446	10,983
5	New Caledonia	19,058	7,358
6	Fiji	18,274	7,055
7	Vanuatu	12,190	4,706
8	French Polynesia	4,000	1,544
9	Western Samoa	2,842	1,097
10	Kiribati	728	281

Australia is over nine times as large as the rest of the Top 10 Oceanian countries put together. The virtually uninhabited Ross Dependency which comes under New Zealand's control is actually larger than New Zealand itself (750,310 sq km/286,696 sq miles, including permanent ice shelf).

THE 10 LARGEST COUNTRIES IN EUROPE

	Country	Area sq km	sq miles
1	Russia (in Europe)	4,710,227	1,818,629
2	Ukraine	603,700	233,090
3	France	547,026	211,208
4	Spain	504,781	194,897
5	Sweden	449,964	173,732
6	Germany	356,999	137,838
7	Finland	337,007	130,119
8	Norway	324,220	125,182
9	Poland	312,676	120,725
10	Italy	301,226	116,304
11	UK	244,046	94,227

THE 10 LARGEST COUNTRIES IN ASIA

	Country	Area sq km	sq miles
1	China	9,596,961	3,705,408
2	India	3,287,590	1,269,346
3	Kazakhstan	2,716,626	1,049,155
4	Saudi Arabia	2,149,640	830,000
5	Indonesia	1,904,569	735,358
6	Iran	1,648,000	636,296
7	Mongolia	1,565,000	604,250
8	Pakistan	803,950	310,407
9	Turkey (in Asia)	790,200	305,098
10	Myanmar (Burma)	676,552	261,218

THE 10 COUNTRIES WITH MOST NEIGHBOURS

Country/neighbours	Number of neighbours
1　China Afghanistan, Bhutan, Hong Kong, India, Kazakhstan, Kyrgyzstan, Laos, Macau, Mongolia, Myanmar, Nepal, North Korea, Pakistan, Russia, Tajikstan, Vietnam	16
2　Russia Azerbaijan, Belarus, China, Estonia, Finland, Georgia, Kazakhstan, Latvia, Lithuania, Mongolia, North Korea, Norway, Poland, Ukraine	14
3　Brazil Argentina, Bolivia, Colombia, French Guiana, Guyana, Paraguay, Peru, Suriname, Uruguay, Venezuela	10
4 = Germany Austria, Belgium, Czech Republic, Denmark, France, Luxembourg, Netherlands, Poland, Switzerland	9
4 = Zaïre Angola, Burundi, Central African Republic, Congo, Rwanda, Sudan, Tanzania, Uganda, Zambia	9
6 = Austria Czech Republic, Germany, Hungary, Italy, Liechtenstein, Slovac Republic, Slovenia, Switzerland	8
6 = Saudi Arabia Iraq, Jordan, Kuwait, Oman, People's Democratic Republic of Yemen, Qatar, United Arab Emirates, Yemen Arab Republic	8
6 = Sudan Central African Republic, Chad, Egypt, Ethiopia, Kenya, Libya, Uganda, Zaïre	8
6 = Tanzania Central African Republic, Chad, Ethiopia, Kenya, Libya, Uganda, Zaïre	8
10 = Mali Algeria, Burkina Faso, Cote d'Ivoire, Guinea, Mauritania, Niger, Senegal	7
10 = Niger Algeria, Benin, Burkina Faso, Chad, Libya, Mali, Nigeria	7
10 = Ukraine Belarus, Hungary, Moldova, Poland, Romania, Russia, Slovac Republic	7
10 = Zambia Angola, Malawi, Mozambique, Namibia, Tanzania, Zaïre, Zimbabwe	7

Keeping out the neighbours: China's Great Wall traverses 3,460 km/2,150 miles of a country with no fewer than 16 others adjoining it.

10 CITIES AND COUNTRIES NAMED AFTER BRITISH PEOPLE

1 Baltimore, Maryland, USA
Named after Lord Baltimore, founder of the city in 1729.

2 Cook Islands
Partly discovered by British explorer Captain James Cook (1728–79) in 1773.

3 Darwin, Australia
Originally called Palmerston, but renamed in 1911 to honour British scientist Charles Darwin (1809–82), who had stopped off there briefly in 1836.

4 Falkland Islands
First called Davis Land (after their discoverer John Davis), then Hawkins Maidenland (after Sir Richard Hawkins and Elizabeth I, the 'Maiden queen'), in 1690 the islands were finally named after Viscount Falkland, who financed an expedition there.

5 Kingston, Jamaica
Port Royal was destroyed by an earthquake in 1692, and the next city founded on the site was named in honour of King William III (1650–1702).

6 New York, USA
Captured by the British from the Dutch in 1664, it was named in honour of the Duke of York, brother of Charles II.

7 Raleigh, North Carolina, USA
Named in 1792 after Sir Walter Raleigh (1552–1618), the would-be colonist of the area.

8 Rhodesia, Africa
Named in 1884 after the British founder of the South Africa Company, Cecil Rhodes (1853–1902).

9 Vancouver, British Columbia, Canada
The island took its name from British explorer George Vancouver (1758–98), who was the first to survey it.

10 Wellington, New Zealand
Founded in 1840, it was named after the famous British general Arthur Wellesley, the Duke of Wellington (1769–1852).

PLACE NAME CHANGES QUIZ
What were the previous names of these cities and countries?

	Previous		Current
1	Leningrad	A	Albany
2	Burma	B	Cincinnati
3	Southern Rhodesia	C	Burkina Faso
4	New Amsterdam	D	Ottawa
5	New Holland	E	Zimbabwe
6	Constantinople	F	St Petersburg
7	Upper Volta	G	Myanmar
8	Fort Orange	H	Istanbul
9	Losantiville	I	Australia
10	Bytown	J	New York

THE 10 SMALLEST STATES IN THE USA

	State	Area*	
		sq km	sq miles
1	Rhode Island	4,002	1,545
2	Delaware	6,447	2,489
3	Connecticut	14,358	5,544
4	New Jersey	22,590	8,722
5	New Hampshire	24,219	9,351
6	Vermont	24,903	9,615
7	Massachusetts	27,337	10,555
8	Hawaii	28,313	10,932
9	Maryland	32,135	12,407
10	West Virginia	62,759	24,231

*Total, including water.

The District of Columbia has a total area of 179 sq km/69 sq miles.

THE 10 LARGEST STATES IN THE USA

	State	Area*	
		sq km	sq miles
1	Alaska	1,700,139	656,427
2	Texas	695,676	268,602
3	California	424,002	163,708
4	Montana	380,850	147,047
5	New Mexico	314,939	121,599
6	Arizona	295,276	114,007
7	Nevada	286,368	110,567
8	Colorado	269,620	104,101
9	Oregon	254,819	98,386
10	Wyoming	253,349	97,819

*Total, including water.

Alaska, the largest state, has the second smallest population (550,043; Wyoming is the smallest with 453,588). Alaska also has the greatest area of inland water of any state: 86,051 sq km/222,871 sq miles. By comparison, the UK (244,046 sq km/94,227 sq miles) is smaller than the 10th largest state, and the area of England (130,440 sq km/50,363 sq miles) slightly smaller than that of Alabama (the 30th largest state at 135,775 sq km/52,423 sq miles).

THE 10 LARGEST LANDLOCKED COUNTRIES IN ASIA

	Country	Area sq km	sq miles
1	Kazakhstan	2,716,626	1,049,155
2	Mongolia	1,565,000	604,250
3	Afghanistan	647,497	250,000
4	Turkmenistan	488,100	188,417
5	Uzbekistan	447,400	172,742
6	Laos	231,800	91,429
7	Kyrgyzstan	198,500	76,642
8	Nepal	140,747	54,342
9	Tajikstan	143,100	54,019
10	Bhutan	47,000	18,147

South America has just two landlocked countries: Bolivia (1,098,581 sq km/424,165 sq miles) and Paraguay (406,752 sq km/157,048 sq miles).

THE 10 LARGEST LANDLOCKED COUNTRIES IN AFRICA

	Country	Area sq km	sq miles
1	Chad	1,284,000	495,755
2	Niger	1,267,080	489,191
3	Mali	1,240,000	478,791
4	Zambia	752,614	290,586
5	Central African Republic	622,984	240,535
6	Botswana	581,730	224,607
7	Zimbabwe	390,580	150,804
8	Burkina Faso	274,200	105,869
9	Uganda	236,036	91,259
10	Malawi	118,484	45,747

THE 10 LARGEST LANDLOCKED COUNTRIES IN EUROPE

	Country	Area sq km	sq miles
1	Belarus (Byelorussia)	207,897	80,300
2	Hungary	93,030	35,919
3	Azerbaijan	86,565	33,436
4	Austria	83,849	32,374
5	Czech Republic	78,864	30,441
6	Slovak Republic	49,035	18,298
7	Switzerland	41,293	15,943
8	Moldova	36,018	13,912
9	Armenia	29,271	11,306
10	Luxembourg	2,586	998

THE 10 LARGEST NATURE RESERVES IN WALES

	Nature Reserve	Area hectares	acres
1	Dyfi, Dyfed	2,095	5,177
2	Y Wyddfa, Gwynedd	1,677	4,144
3	Newborough Warren, Gwynedd	1,301	3,215
4	Morfa Harlech, Gwynedd	884	2,184
5	Cors Caron, Dyfed	792	1,957
6	Whiteford, West Glamorgan	782	1,932
7	Rhinog, Gwynedd	598	1,478
8	Kenfig Pool and Dunes, Mid Glamorgan	518	1,280
9	Cader Idris, Gwynedd	430	1,063
10	Ogof Ffynnon Ddu, Powys	413	1,021

THE 10 LARGEST NATURE RESERVES IN SCOTLAND

	Nature Reserve	Area hectares	acres
1	Cairngorms, Grampian and Highland Regions	25,949	64,121
2	Inverpolly, Highland Region	10,857	26,828
3	Rum, Highland Region	10,684	26,401
4	Ben Wyvis, Highland Region	5,673	14,026
5	Caerlaverock, Dumfries and Galloway Region	5,501	13,593
6	Beinn Eighe, Highland Region	4,758	11,757
7	Glen Tanar, Grampian Region	4,185	10,341
8	Ben Lawers, Tayside and Central Regions	3,974	9,820
9	Craeg Meagaidh, Highland Region	3,948	9,756
10	Caenlochan, Tayside Region	3,639	8,992

National Nature Reserves are sites designated under the National Parks and Access to the Countryside Act of 1949 for the study and preservation of flora and fauna or geological or physiological features. They are either owned or controlled by English Nature or approved bodies such as Wildlife Trusts. In 1992 there were 140 such sites in England, a total of 47,327 hectares/116,947 acres. A further 290 sites (1992 total: 13,000 hectares/32,124 acres) are maintained by local authorities as Local Nature Reserves.

THE 10 LARGEST NATURE RESERVES IN ENGLAND

	Nature Reserve	Area hectares	acres
1	The Wash, Lincolnshire	9,899	24,461
2	Ribble Marshes, Lancashire/Mersey	4,116	10,171
3	Moor House, Cumbria	4,047	10,000
4	Holkham, Norfolk	3,926	9,701
5	Upper Teesdale, North Yorkshire	3,493	8,631
6	Lindisfarne, Northumberland	3,278	8,100
7	Bridgewater Bay, Somerset	2,559	6,323
8	Dengie, Essex	2,293	5,666
9	Lizard, Cornwall	1,376	3,400
10	Blackwater Estuary, Essex	1,032	2,550

The Wash is England's largest National Nature Reserve.

THE 10 LARGEST REFLECTING TELESCOPES IN THE WORLD

	Telescope name	Location	Opened*	Aperture (m)
1	Keck Telescope	Mauna Kea Observatory, Hawaii	1992	10.0
2	Bolshoi Teleskop Azimutal'ny	Special Astrophysical Observatory of the Russian Academy of Sciences, Mount Pastukhov, Russia	1976	6.0
3	Hale Telescope	Palomar Observatory, California	1948	5.0
4	William Herschel Telescope	Observatorio del Roque de los Muchachos, La Palma, Canary Islands	1987	4.2
5 =	Mayall Telescope†	Kitt Peak National Observatory, Arizona, USA	1973	4.0
5 =	4-metre Telescope†	Cerro Tololo Inter-American Observatory, Chile	1976	4.0
7	Anglo-Australian Telescope	Siding Spring Observatory, New South Wales, Australia	1974	3.9
8 =	ESO 3.6-metre Telescope	European Southern Observatory, La Silla, Chile	1975	3.6
8 =	Canada-France-Hawaii Telescope	Mauna Kea Observatory, Hawaii	1970	3.6
8 =	United Kingdom Infrared Telescope	Mauna Kea Observatory, Hawaii	1979	3.6

*Dedicated or regular use commenced.

†Northern/southern hemisphere 'twin' telescopes.

If the Keck Telescope at No. 1 is discounted because its 'mirror' is not in one piece, but comprises 36 hexagonal segments slotted together, then the 10th entry in the list becomes the 3.5 m New Technology Telescope at the European Observatory, La Silla, Chile, which started operations in 1990. The Multiple Mirror Telescope at the Fred Lawrence Whipple Observatory, Arizona, opened in 1979, has six linked 1.8-metre mirrors, together equivalent to a 4.5-metre telescope. These are to be replaced by a single 6.5-metre mirror which is currently under construction.

The 4-metre Cerro Tololo Observatory in Chile is the largest in the southern hemisphere.

BUILDINGS & STRUCTURES

THE 10 TALLEST CHURCHES IN THE WORLD

	Church	Location	Year completed	Height m	ft
1	Chicago Methodist Temple	Chicago, USA	1924	173	568
2	Ulm Cathedral	Ulm, Germany	1890	161	528
3	Cologne Cathedral	Cologne, Germany	1880	156	513
4	Rouen Cathedral	Rouen, France	1876	148	485
5	St Nicholas	Hamburg, Germany	1847	145	475
6	Notre Dame	Strasbourg, France	1439	142	465
7	St Peter's	Rome, Italy	1612	140	458
8	St Stephen's Cathedral	Vienna, Austria	1433	136	446
9 =	Amiens Cathedral	Amiens, France	1260	134	440
9 =	St Michael	Hamburg, Germany	1906	134	440

With the exception of the world-beating Chicago Methodist Temple and St Joseph's Oratory, Montreal, Canada (completed 1922; 126 m/412 ft), which does not quite make the Top 10, most of the world's tallest churches are in Europe. To make the world Top 10 a European-only list, the first entry should be deleted and St Peter, Hamburg, Germany (completed 1842; 133 m/436 ft) added. Several other European churches, including Antwerp Cathedral, Belgium (1525; 124 m/406 ft), are taller than the UK's record-holder, Salisbury Cathedral (1375; 123 m/404 ft).

UK CATHEDRALS QUIZ

1 Which British group had a No. 4 hit in 1966 with *Winchester Cathedral*?

2 In which cathedral is St Cuthbert buried?

3 Who wrote the play *Murder in the Cathedral*?

4 Who is buried in St Paul's Cathedral in a tomb originally designed for Cardinal Wolsey?

5 Which cathedral contains a stained-glass window by Marc Chagall?

6 In which cathedral is the *Mappa Mundi* kept?

7 In which cathedral is the tomb of King Edward II?

8 Which cathedral houses a copy of the *Magna Carta*?

9 Which cathedral once had the tomb of Mary Queen of Scots and still has that of Catharine of Aragon?

10 In which cathedral is William Shakespeare's brother Edmund buried?

THE 10 TALLEST HABITABLE* BUILDINGS IN THE UK

	Building		Year completed	Height m	ft
1	Canary Wharf Tower, London E14		1991	244	800
2	National Westminster Tower, London EC2		1979	183	600
3	Post Office Tower, London W1		1966	177	580
4	Blackpool Tower		1894	158	519
5	Barbican, London EC2:	Shakespeare Tower	1971	128	419
		Cromwell Tower	1973	128	419
		Lauderdale Tower	1974	128	419
6	Euston Centre, Euston Road, London NW1		1969	124	408
7	Cooperative Insurance Society Building, Miller Street, Manchester		1962	122	399
8	Centrepoint, New Oxford Street, London WC1		1966	121	398
9	Britannic House, Moor Lane, London EC2		1967	120	395
10 =	Millbank Tower, Millbank, London SW1		1963	118	387
10 =	Commercial Union, Undershaft, London EC3		1969	118	387

*Excludes radio masts, chimneys and church spires.

The 244 m/800 ft Canary Wharf Tower is now not only the tallest habitable building in the UK, but also the second tallest in Europe, after the Frankfurt Messeturm (256 m/840 ft). On a global scale, however, it would appear in 48th position, and is only 2.4 m/8 ft taller than one of the world's first skyscrapers, the Woolworth Building, New York, built in 1913. The Barbican towers are the tallest blocks of flats in the UK.

THE 10 TALLEST HABITABLE BUILDINGS IN THE WORLD

	Building	Location	Year completed	Storeys	Height m	Height ft
1	Sears Tower	Chicago, USA	1974	110	443	1,454
2	World Trade Center*	New York City, USA	1973	110	417	1,368
3	Empire State Building	New York City, USA	1931	102	381	1,250
4	Amoco Building	Chicago, USA	1973	80	346	1,136
5	John Hancock Center	Chicago, USA	1968	100	343	1,127
6	C & S Plaza	Atlanta, USA	1993	57	324	1,063
7	Yu Kyong Hotel	Pyong Yang, North Korea	1992	105	320	1,050
8	Central Plaza	Hong Kong	1992	78	313	1,028
9	First Interstate World Center	Los Angeles, USA	1990	73	310	1,017
10	Texas Commerce Tower	Houston, USA	1981	75	305	1,002

*Twin towers; the second tower, completed in 1973, has the same number of storeys but is slightly smaller at 415 m/1,362 ft – although its spire takes it up to 521 m/1,710 ft.

Heights are of buildings less their TV and radio antennae and uninhabited extensions – the aerials on both the Sears Tower and one of the World Trade Center buildings take them up to 475 m/1,558 ft, while the Empire State Building's TV tower raises it to 431 m/1,414 ft. The recent completion of the C & S Plaza, the Yu Kyong Hotel and Central Plaza buildings marks the end of an era which has been dominated by American skyscrapers: two out of the Top 10 are now in Asia, and after more than 60 years – most of them with the status of the world's second tallest, after the Empire State Building – the Chrysler Building, New York (282 m/925 ft; 319 m/1,046 ft with its spire) has finally been relegated from the Top 10. The 445 m/1,460ft Central Place skyscraper in Brisbane, Australia was planned to become the world's tallest inhabited building, but local objections halted its construction. If it is ever finished, Trump City Tower, under construction in New York and scheduled for completion in 1999, is intended to top them all at 559 m/1,835 ft. The devastation caused by the terrorist bombing of the World Trade Center on 26 February 1993 has raised the spectre of potential collapse or of a massive fire engulfing one of these gigantic buildings, a threat formerly confined to the fiction of disaster movies such as *Towering Inferno* and *Die Hard*.

THE WORLD'S 10 TALLEST BUILDINGS BEFORE THE AGE OF SKYSCRAPERS

	Building	Location	Year completed	Height m	Height ft
1	Eiffel Tower	Paris, France	1889	300	984
2	Washington Memorial	Washington DC, USA	1885	169	555
3	Ulm Cathedral	Ulm, Germany	1890	161	528
4	Lincoln Cathedral	Lincoln, England	c1307 (destroyed 1548)	160	525
5	Cologne Cathedral	Cologne, Germany	1880	156.4	513
6	Notre-Dame	Rouen, France	1530	156	512
7	St Pierre Church	Beauvais, France	1568 (collapsed 1573)	153	502
8	St Paul's Cathedral	London, England	1315 (destroyed 1561)	149	489
9	Rouen Cathedral	Rouen, France	1876	148	485
10	Great Pyramid	Giza, Egypt	c2580BC	146.5	480.9

The first tall office buildings of 10 storeys or more were constructed in Chicago and New York in the 1880s, with the Eiffel Tower following at the end of the decade. It was not until 1913 that the first true 'skyscraper' – a secular building exceeding the height of the great medieval cathedrals – was built: the Woolworth Building, New York. At 241 m/792 ft it remained the tallest habitable building in the world until 1930, when the Chrysler Building (*see* The 10 Tallest Habitable Buildings in the World) overtook both it *and* the Eiffel Tower. A year later the Empire State Building topped them all, and remained the world's tallest for 40 years.

The height of the Washington Memorial is less than it was when it was erected, as it has steadily sunk into the ground. Lincoln Cathedral was the tallest building in the world for over 200 years, but fell in a storm. St Pierre at Beauvais collapsed in 1573. 'Old St Paul's' was destroyed by lightning on 4 June 1561; the present St Paul's Cathedral is only 112 m/366 ft high. The Great Pyramid stood as the world's tallest building for nearly 4,000 years, and was numbered among the Seven Wonders of the World. The loss of its topstone reduced its height to 137 m/449 ft.

BUILDINGS & STRUCTURES

THE 10 TALLEST HABITABLE BUILDINGS IN EUROPE

	Building	Location	Year completed	Height m	ft
1	Messeturm	Frankfurt, Germany	1991	256	840
2	Canary Wharf	London, UK	1991	244	800
3	Moscow State University	Moscow, Russia	1953	240	787 *
4	Palace of Science & Culture	Warsaw, Poland	1955	234 **	768
5	Tour Maine-Montparnasse	Paris, France	1973	210	689
6	National Westminster Tower	London, UK	1979	183	600
7	Tour Elf (La Défense)	Paris, France	1985	179	587
8	Tour Fiat (La Défense)	Paris, France	1985	178	584
9 =	Kotelnitchenkaïa	Moscow, Russia	1952	170	558
9 =	Ukraine Hotel	Moscow, Russia	1953	170	558

*303 m/994 ft with tower. **Including TV mast.*

The Frankfurt Messeturm is Europe's tallest building.

THE 10 TALLEST TOWERS* IN EUROPE

	Tower	Location	Year completed	Height m	ft
1	Gerbrandytoren TV Tower	Lopik, Netherlands	1960	383	1,257
2	TV Tower	Berlin, Germany	1969	365	1,198
3	Telecommunications Tower	Frankfurt, Germany	1977	331	1,086
4	Eiffel Tower	Paris, France	1889	300	984
5	Olympic Tower	Munich, Germany	1968	290	951
6	TV Tower	Hamburg, Germany	1968	271	889
7	Donauturm	Vienna, Austria	1964	252	827
8	TV Tower	Frejlev, Denmark	1956	231	758
9	TV Tower	Stuttgart, Germany	1956	217	712
10	TV Tower	Beromünster, Switzerland	1931	215	705

TV and other communications towers.

THE WORLD'S 10 TALLEST STRUCTURES THAT ARE NO LONGER STANDING

	Structure	Location	Completed	Destroyed	Height m	ft
1	Warszawa Radio Mast	Konstantynow, Poland	1974	1991	646	2,120
2	KSWS TV Mast	Roswell, New Mexico, USA	1956	1960	491	1,610
3	IBA Mast	Emley Moor, UK	1965	1969	385	1,265
4	Chimney, Matla Power Station	Kriel, South Africa	1980 *	1981	275	902
5	New Brighton Tower	Merseyside, UK	1900	1919	171	562
6	Lincoln Cathedral	Lincoln, England	c1307	1548	160	525
7	St Pierre Church	Beauvais, France	1568	1573	153	502
8	St Peter's	Louvain, Flanders	1425	1606	150	500
9	St Paul's Cathedral	London, England	1315	1561	149	489
10	Pharos†	Alexandria, Egypt	c270BC	1375	122	400

Never fully operational; demolished after accident. †The first lighthouse, one of the Seven Wonders of the World, destroyed by an earthquake.

THE 10 TALLEST HABITABLE BUILDINGS IN ASIA

	Building	Location	Year completed	Storeys	Height m	ft
1	Yu Kyong Hotel	Pyong Yang, North Korea	1992	105	320	1,050
2	Central Plaza	Hong Kong	1992	78	313	1,028
3	Bank of China Tower	Hong Kong	1989	72	305	1,001
4	Landmark Tower	Yokohama, Japan	1993	70	296	971
5 =	Overseas Union Bank	Singapore	1984	63	280	919
5 =	UOB Plaza	Singapore	1992	66	280	919
7	City Hall Tower	Tokyo, Japan	1992	60	243	798
8	Metropolitan Tower	Tokyo, Japan	1992	50	242	796
9	Treasury Building	Singapore	1986	52	235	770
10	Korea Insurance Centre	Seoul, Korea	1988	63	233	764

Of the 100 tallest buildings in the world, 72 (if the World Trade Center is counted as two buildings) are in the USA, the original home of the skyscraper. However, the rest of the world is steadily catching up, and of the remaining 28 buildings, 14 are in Asia, five in Australia, six in Canada (all of them in Toronto) and three in Europe.

Hong Kong boasts two of Asia's 10 tallest buildings.

THE 10 LARGEST RESERVOIRS IN THE WORLD

	Reservoir	Location	Completed	Capacity litres	gallons
1	Owen Falls	Lake Victoria/Nile, Uganda	1954	2,699,981,000,000,000	593,916,300,000,000
2	Kariba	Zambezi, Zimbabwe/Zambia	1959	180,599,860,000,000	39,726,401,000,000
3	Bratsk	Angara, Russia	1964	169,269,870,000,000	37,234,152,000,000
4	Aswan High	Nile, Egypt	1970	168,899,860,000,000	37,152,764,000,000
5	Akosombo	Volta, Ghana	1965	147,999,840,000,000	32,555,412,000,000
6	Daniel Johnson	Manicouagan, Canada	1968	141,185,352,000,000	31,203,420,000,000
7	Guri (Raul Leoni)	Caroni, Venezuela	1986	137,999,890,000,000	30,355,722,000,000
8	Krasnoyarsk	Yenisey, Russia	1967	73,299,823,000,000	16,123,727,000,000
9	Bennett W.A.C.	Peace, Canada	1967	70,308,949,000,000	15,465,800,000,000
10	Zeya	Zeya, Russia	1978	68,399,909,000,000	15,045,879,000,000

THE 10 LARGEST VOLUME* DAMS IN THE WORLD

	Dam	Location	Completed	Volume cu m	cu ft
1	Syncrude Tailings	Alberta, Canada	1992	540,000,000,000	19,069,921,000,000,000
2	Pati	Paraná, Argentina	1990	230,180,000,000	8,128,730,700,000,000
3	New Cornelia Tailings	Ten Mile Wash, Arizona, USA	1973	209,500,000,000	7,398,423,300,000,000
4	Tarbela	Indus, Pakistan	1976	105,922,000,000	3,740,600,400,000,000
5	Fort Peck	Missouri, Montana, USA	1937	96,050,000,000	3,391,974,000,000,000
6	Lower Usuma	Usuma, Nigeria	1990	93,000,000,000	3,284,264,300,000,000
7	Atatürk	Euphrates, Turkey	1990	84,500,000,000	2,984,089,600,000,000
8	Yacyreta-Apipe	Paraná, Paraguay/Argentina	1991	81,000,000,000	2,860,488,200,000,000
9	Guri (Raul Leoni)	Caroni, Venezuela	1986	77,971,000,000	2,753,520,100,000,000
10	Rogun	Vakhsh, Tajikstan	1987	75,500,000,000	2,666,257,500,000,000

*Material used in construction (earth, rocks, concrete, etc).

The Chapeton dam under construction on the Paraná, Argentina, scheduled for completion in 1998, will have a volume of 296,200,000,000 cu m/10,460,205,000,000,000 cu ft and will thus become the second largest dam in the world. The Cipasang dam under construction on the Cimanuk, Indonesia, will have a volume of 90,000,000,000 cu m/3,178,320,300,000,000 cu ft.

THE 10 LARGEST RESERVOIRS IN THE UK

	Reservoir	County	Capacity litres	gallons
1	Kielder	Northumberland	200,027,870,000	44,000,000,000
2	Loch Awe	Strathclyde	159,722,201,000	35,133,948,000
3	Rutland	Leicestershire	122,744,370,000	27,000,000,000
4	Elan Valley	Dyfed	100,013,930,000	22,000,000,000
5	Loch Lomond	Central/Strathclyde Regions	86,249,436,000	18,972,232,000
6	Loch Doon	Strathclyde	81,957,360,000	18,028,107,000
7	Haweswater	Cumbria	81,829,584,000	18,000,000,000
8	Loch Katrine	Central Region	64,553,649,000	14,199,824,000
9	Megget	Borders Region	63,722,515,000	14,017,000,000
10	Vyrnwy	Powys	63,645,232,000	14,000,000,000

THE 10 OLDEST CLOCKS IN THE UK

	Clock/location	Manufactured
1	**Salisbury Cathedral, Wiltshire**	**c1386**

A faceless clock, and probably the oldest working timepiece in the world, it was restored in 1956.

2	**Wells Cathedral, Somerset**	**c1392**

Now displayed in the Science Museum, London.

3	**Ottery St Mary, Devon**	**late 14th century**

Much altered from its original construction.

4	**Hexagonal Burgundian clock, British Museum**	**c1450**

On permanent loan from the Victoria & Albert Museum collection.

5	**St Mary's church, Launceston, Cornwall**	**c1480**

A clock with a 24-hour stone face.

6	**Cothele House, Cornwall**	**c1495**

Mostly original construction.

7	**Exeter Cathedral, Exeter, Devon**	**late 15th century**

With an astronomical dial; the striking train probably dates from the sixteenth century.

8	**Durham Cathedral, Durham**	**c1500**

In an elaborately carved case with dials.

9	**Domestic clock, British Museum**	**early 16th century**

A clock with a castellated dial.

10	**St Augustine of Canterbury church, East Hendred, Berkshire**	**1535**

A clock with three trains made by John Seymour of Wantage; the earliest British clock that can be precisely dated.

THE 10 MOST EXPENSIVE PAINTINGS BY J.M.W. TURNER

	Painting/sale	Price (£)
1	**Seascape, Folkestone** Sotheby's, London, 5 July 1984	6,700,000
2	**Juliet and her Nurse** Sotheby's, New York, 29 May 1980 ($6,400,000)	2,844,440
3	**Landscape – Woman with Tambourine** Christie's, London, 14 April 1989	1,000,000
4 =	**Bonneville – Savoy with Mont Blanc** Christie's, London, 13 July 1984	600,000
4 =	**The Temple of Jupiter Pallenius Restored** Christie's, London, 16 July 1982	600,000
6	**Seascape with Squall Coming Up** Sotheby's, London, 15 November 1989	580,000
7	**Hampton Court Palace** Sotheby's, London, 15 March 1990	430,000
8	**Venice – The Grand Canal with S. Maria della Salute** Phillips, London, 18 April 1988	400,000
9	**Venice – Storm Approaching San Giorgio and the Dogana** Sotheby's, New York, 17 November 1986 ($525,000)	367,133
10	**Bridgewater Sea Piece** Christie's, London, 18 June 1976	340,000

In addition to these paintings, Turner's *Channel Sketchbook,* a collection of pencil drawings, fetched £480,000 at Sotheby's, London, on 10 July 1986.

★ ★ ★ ★ ★ ★ ★ **ARTIST FACTS** ★ ★ ★ ★ ★ ★ ★
Joseph Mallord William Turner (born London, 23 April 1775; died London, 19 December 1851) is Britain's foremost painter of landscapes. His works are ranked second only to Constable's among British painters' record auction prices. ★ ★ ★ ★ ★ ★ ★

Turner's *Landscape – Woman with Tambourine* was the third of the artist's works to achieve £1 million or more at auction.

THE 10 MOST EXPENSIVE PAINTINGS BY HENRI MATISSE

	Painting/sale	Price (£)
1	**Harmonie Jaune** Christie's, New York, 11 November 1992 ($13,200,000)	8,741,723
2	**Femme à l'Ombrelle Rouge, Assise de Profil** Sotheby's, New York, 18 October 1989 ($11,250,000)	7,075,472
3	**L'Asie** Sotheby's, New York, 10 November 1992 ($10,000,000)	6,622,517
4	**Femme au Bijou Bleu, Hélène Galitzine au Cabochon** Christie's, New York, 15 May 1990 ($5,000,000)	2,958,580
5	**Odalisque** Ader, Picard & Tajan, Paris, 18 November 1989 (FF127,350,000)	2,808,008
6	**Nature Morte aux Citrons sur Fond Fleurdelise** Sotheby's, New York, 10 May 1988 ($5,200,000)	2,765,958
7	**Bouquet de Fleurs** Guy Loudmer, Paris, 25 March 1990 (FF23,500,000)	2,524,168
8	**La Robe Persane** Sotheby's, New York, 7 May 1991 ($4,100,000)	2,369,942
9	**Figure Décorative** Sotheby's, New York, 17 May 1990 ($3,800,000)	2,248,521
10	**Sylphide** Christie's, New York, 10 May 1989 ($3,100,000)	1,901,841

THE 10 MOST EXPENSIVE PAINTINGS BY DAVID HOCKNEY

	Painting/sale	Price (£)
1	**Grand Procession of Dignitaries in the semi-Egyptian Style** Sotheby's, New York, 2 May 1989 ($2,000,000)	1,204,819
2	**Deep and Wet Water** Sotheby's, New York, 8 November 1989 ($1,300,000)	822,785
3	**Henry Geldzahler and Christopher Scott** Sotheby's, New York, 17 November 1992 ($1,000,000)	662,252
4	**The Room, Manchester Street** Christie's, New York, 3 May 1989 ($800,000)	481,928
5	**A Neat Lawn** Sotheby's, London, 1 December 1988	320,000
6	**Different Kinds of Water Pouring into Swimming Pool, Santa Monica** Sotheby's, New York, 2 May 1989 ($460,000)	277,108
7	**The Room, Tarzana** Christie's, London, 3 December 1987	260,000
8	**The Actor** Sotheby's, London, 27 June 1991	240,000
9	**Fall Pool with Two Flat Blues** Christie's, New York, 12 November 1991 ($380,000)	212,291
10	**California Landscape** Sotheby's, New York, 31 October 1984 ($250,000)	206,612

ARTIST FACTS

Henri Matisse (born Le Câteau, 31 December 1869; died Nice, 3 November 1954), leader of the Fauves (literally, 'wild beasts') and a pioneer of modern art, was a painter of boldly coloured nudes and still-lifes in a variety of media. An enormously popular exhibition of his work was held in New York and Paris in 1992–93.

ARTIST FACTS

David Hockney (born Bradford, 9 July 1937) studied at the Royal College of Art and achieved early acclaim in England as a representative of 'Pop Art' before settling in California, where the colourful urban landscape ideally suited his evolving style. As well as his paintings, which are avidly collected by the fashionable wealthy, he has produced stage sets and worked in a variety of novel media such as Polaroid photocollages and even faxes, while many of his popular subjects have become widely known at a more affordable level through reproduction as decorative posters.

THE 10 MOST EXPENSIVE PAINTINGS BY SIR EDWARD BURNE-JONES

	Painting	Sale	Price (£)
1	*Nativity*	Sotheby's, London, 21 November 1989	700,000
2	*The King and the Shepherd*	Sotheby's, London, 21 November 1989	620,000
3	*The Sleeping Princess*	Christie's, London, 25 November 1988	400,000
4	*Philip Comyns Carr*	Sotheby's, London, 20 June 1989	370,000
5	*Flamma Vestalis*	Sotheby's, London, 20 June 1989	310,000
6	*King Cophetua and the Beggar Maid**	Sotheby's, London, 20 June 1989	290,000
7	*King Cophetua and the Beggar Maid**	Sotheby's, London, 20 June 1989	220,000
8 =	*The Heart of the Rose*	Sotheby's, London, 9 April 1980	130,000
8 =	*The Mirror of Venus*	Sotheby's, London, 21 June 1983	130,000
10 =	*The Fall of Lucifer*	Sotheby's, London, 23 June 1981	110,000
10 =	*Garden of Idleness – Largesse and Richesse*	Sotheby's, London, 19 June 1990	110,000
10 =	*Portrait of Amy Gaskell*	Sotheby's, London, 23 March 1981	110,000

*Two different versions of the same painting, the principal version of which is in the Tate Gallery, London.

★ ★ ★ ★ ★ ★ ★ ★ ★ ★ ★ ★ ★ ★ ★ ARTIST FACTS ★ ★ ★ ★ ★ ★ ★ ★ ★ ★ ★ ★ ★ ★ ★

Edward Burne-Jones (born Birmingham, 28 August 1833; died London, 17 June 1898) was a close friend and associate of William Morris and the Pre-Raphaelites. He produced many often very large paintings of Arthurian legends and mythological subjects as well as book illustrations and decorative art, including numerous stained-glass commissions. He was knighted in 1894. ★ ★ ★ ★ ★ ★ ★ ★ ★ ★ ★ ★ ★ ★ ★ ★

The Sleeping Princess from Burne-Jones' 'Briar Rose' series made £400,000 at auction in 1988.

THE 10 MOST EXPENSIVE PAINTINGS BY CLAUDE MONET

	Painting	Sale	Price (£)
1	*Dans la Prairie (Camille in the Meadow)*	Sotheby's, London, 28 June 1988	13,000,000
2	*Le Parlement, Coucher de Soleil*	Christie's, New York, 10 May 1989 ($13,000,000)	7,975,460
3	*Le Bassin aux Nymphéas*	Christie's, New York, 11 November 1992 ($13,000,000)	7,284,770
4 =	*Nymphéas*	Christie's, New York, 14 November 1989 ($10,500,000)	6,774,194
4 =	*Le Grand Canal*	Sotheby's, New York, 15 November 1989 ($10,500,000)	6,774,194
6	*Le Pont du Chemin de Fer à Argenteuil*	Christie's, London, 28 November 1988	6,200,000
7	*Garden House on the Banks of the Zaan*	Sotheby's, New York, 9 May 1989 ($10,000,000)	6,134,970
8	*S. Maria della Salute et le Grand Canal, Venise*	Sotheby's, London, 4 April 1989	6,100,000
9	*Le Parlement, Soleil Couchant*	Christie's, New York, 14 November 1989 ($9,000,000)	5,806,452
10	*Le Pont Japonais, Bassin aux Nymphéas, Les Iris d'Eau*	Christie's, London, 28 November 1988	5,500,000

By a remarkable coincidence, the current 8th most expensive painting by Monet is of an identical Venetian subject to that of the 8th most expensive painting by Turner.

★ ★ ★ ★ ★ ★ ★ ★ ★ ★ ★ ★ ★ ★ **ARTIST FACTS** ★ ★ ★ ★ ★ ★ ★ ★ ★ ★ ★ ★ ★ ★

Claude Monet (born Paris, 14 November 1840; died Giverny, 5 December 1926) was a leading French Impressionist (the title of one of his works gave the group its name). His many paintings of water-lilies (nymphéas) in his garden at Giverny are among his most popular works and are represented by three out of the Top 10. ★

THE TOP 10 TREASURE HOUSES IN THE UK*

	House	Owner	Value (£)
1	Chatsworth, Derbyshire	Duke of Devonshire	800,000,000
2	Castle Howard, North Yorkshire	Howard family	750,000,000
3	Eaton Hall, Cheshire	Duke of Westminster	700,000,000
4	Syon House, London	Duke of Northumberland	550,000,000
5	Arundel Castle	Duke of Norfolk	500,000,000
6	Burghley House, Lincolnshire	Trustees of the Salisbury family	450,000,000
7	Dorney Court, Buckinghamshire	Palmer family	400,000,000
8	Holkham Hall, Norfolk	Earl of Leicester	350,000,000
9	Woburn Abbey, Bedfordshire	Marquess of Tavistock	300,000,000
10	Longleat House, Wiltshire	Marquess of Bath	250,000,000

*Excluding royal palaces.

The valuation is of the contents of the properties, not of the houses and estates themselves. In reality, if the entire contents of some of these repositories of huge collections of art treasures came on the market, there would probably not be sufficient wealthy buyers, individual or institutional, to absorb them.

THE 10 MOST EXPENSIVE PAINTINGS EVER SOLD AT AUCTION

Painting	Price (£)

1 Vincent Van Gogh, *Portrait of Dr Gachet*   49,107,142

Christie's, New York, 15 May 1990   ($82,500,000)

Bought by Ryoei Saito, chairman of the Japanese firm Daishowa Paper Manufacturing.

2 Pierre-Auguste Renoir, *Au Moulin de la Galette*   46,488,095

Sotheby's, New York, 17 May 1990   ($78,100,000)

Also purchased by Ryoei Saito.

3 Vincent Van Gogh, *Irises*   30,187,623

Sotheby's, New York, 11 November 1987   ($53,900,000)

After much speculation, its mystery purchaser was eventually confirmed as Australian businessman Alan Bond. However, as he was unable to pay for it in full, its former status as the world's most expensive work of art has been disputed and regarded by some as 'artificial'. In 1990 it was sold to the J. Paul Getty Museum, Malibu, for an undisclosed sum, with speculation ranging from $60,000,000 to as little as $35,000,000.

4 Pablo Picasso, *Les Noces de Pierrette*   33,083,023

Binoche et Godeau, Paris, 30 November 1989   (FF315,000,000/$51,895,000)

Is this the third or fourth most expensive painting ever sold at auction? The answer depends on whether the 315,000,000 French francs paid for it is converted into pounds or US dollars. As a result of exchange rate fluctuations, if converted into sterling it breaks the record set by *Irises*. However, if the price is converted into dollars, it falls short by over $2,000,000. Another consideration is that the price includes a five per cent buyer's premium, whereas the prices of paintings sold in New York and London are inflated by a 10 per cent premium. If this is deducted, *Les Noces de Pierrette* becomes the more expensive by $424,000. Whatever its place in the league table, it is the most expensive twentieth-century work of art. It was sold by Swedish financier Fredrik Roos and bought by Tomonori Tsurumaki, a Japanese property developer, bidding from Tokyo by telephone. He exhibits it with other art treasures in a gallery at 'Autopolis', a motor racing circuit he has built (at a cost of some £290,000,000) in a remote part of Kyushu, Japan's southern island.

5 Pablo Picasso, *Self Portrait: Yo Picasso*   28,825,301

Sotheby's, New York, 9 May 1989   ($47,850,000)

The purchaser has remained anonymous but unconfirmed reports have identified him as Stavros Niarchos, the Greek shipping magnate.

6 Pablo Picasso, *Au Lapin Agile*   25,710,675

Sotheby's, New York, 15 November 1989   ($40,700,000)

The painting depicts Picasso as a harlequin at the bar of the café Lapin Agile. The owner of the café acquired the picture in exchange for food and drink at a time when Picasso was hard up. In 1989 it was bought by the Walter Annenberg Foundation.

7 Vincent Van Gogh, *Sunflowers*   24,750,000

Christie's, London, 30 March 1987

At the time, the most expensive picture ever sold, it was bought by the Yasuda Fire and Marine Insurance Company of Tokyo.

8 Jacopo da Carucci (Pontormo), *Portrait of Duke Cosimo I de Medici*   22,370,511

Christie's, New York, 31 May 1989   ($35,200,000)

The world record price for an Old Master – and the only one in the Top 10 – it was bought by the J. Paul Getty Museum, Malibu. The previous record for an Old Master was held by Andrea Mantegna's *Adoration of the Magi*, sold at Christie's, London, on 18 April 1985 for £8,100,000.

9 Pablo Picasso, *Acrobate et Jeune Arlequin*   20,900,000

Christie's, London, 28 November 1988

Until the sale of *Yo Picasso*, this held the world record for a twentieth-century painting. It was bought by Mitsukoshi, a Japanese department store (in Japan, many major stores have important art galleries).

10 Edouard Manet, *La rue Mosnier aux drapeaux*   16,708,860

Christie's, New York, 14 November 1989   ($26,400,000)

Until the sale of Renoir's *Au Moulin de la Galette*, this held the world record price for a French Impressionist painting. Few top quality Impressionist works were auctioned during the art boom period of the late 1980s, with the result that Van Gogh (a Post-Impressionist) and Picasso have dominated the scene. When the same painting was previously sold in 1958, it held the then record price for a Manet of £113,000.

All prices include buyer's premium; $/£ conversion at rate then prevailing.

It is perhaps a telling reflection of the elevated – some commentators say ludicrous – heights to which paintings soared in the late 1980s, that this list has not altered at all during three years of global recession and seems unlikely to change dramatically during the coming years.

PHOTOGRAPHERS QUIZ

1 Which British pioneer photographer lived at Lacock Abbey in Wiltshire?

2 Which notable photographer won Oscars for his costume and set designs for the film *My Fair Lady*?

3 Who is the wife of a former member of the Beatles who has had books of her photographs published?

4 Which former deputy leader of the Labour party has had books of his photographs published?

5 What war did the photographer Roger Fenton cover as photographer in 1855?

6 Which British photographer was married to French actress Catherine Deneuve and Hawaiian model Marie Helvin?

7 Which photographer designed an aviary at London Zoo?

8 Who stars as a fashion photographer in the 1966 film *Blow Up*?

9 The real name of which photographer, who features in the Most Expensive Photographs Top 10, was Emmanuel Rudnitzky?

10 Portrait photographer Yousuf Karsh signed himself as 'Karsh of' which city?

THE 10 MOST EXPENSIVE PHOTOGRAPHS EVER SOLD AT AUCTION

	Photographer/photograph/sale	Price (£)
1	**Man Ray (American, 1890–1976),** ***Glass Tears, c1930*** Sotheby's, London, 7 May 1993	122,500
2	**Alexander Rodchenko (Russian, 1891–1956),** ***Girl with Leica*** Christie's, London, 29 October 1992	115,500
3	**Tina Modotti (Mexican, 1896–1942),** ***Roses, Mexico,* 1925** Sotheby's, New York, 17 April 1991 ($165,000)	97,923
4	**Edward Weston (American, 1886–1958),** ***Palm Trunk, Cuernavaca,* 1925** Sotheby's, New York, 17 April 1991 ($154,000)	91,395
5	**El(iezer) Lissitzky (Russian, 1890–1941),** ***Photomontage*** Christie's, New York, 16 April 1991 ($132,000)	78,338
6	**Man Ray,** ***The Primacy of Matter over Thought*** Sotheby's, New York, 1 November 1989 ($121,000)	77,864
7	**Alexander Rodchenko,** ***Morning Wash*** Christie's, London, 29 October 1992	77,000
8	**Edward Weston,** ***Nautilus Shell,* 1927** Sotheby's, New York, 26–27 April 1989 ($115,500)	74,324
9	**Alvin Langdon Coburn (American, 1882–1966),** ***Vortograph*** Christie's, London, 29 October 1992	68,000
10	**Man Ray, Untitled (rayograph)** Christie's, New York, 17 October 1990 ($126,500)	67,539

*Two examples achieved identical prices.

The Top 10 represents only individual photographic prints, but two collections of photographs have achieved even higher prices: 'Set 21 Equivalents', a set of prints by Alfred Stieglitz (American, 1864–1946) was sold at Christie's, New York, on 30 October 1989, and 20 volumes and 20 portfolios of images of North American Indians (1907–30) by Edward S. Curtis (American, 1868–1952) by Christie's, New York, on 13 October 1992, each achieving $396,000.

Even higher prices than those in the Top 10 have been paid privately for single photographs, the highest known being $250,000 for *Chez Mondrian*, a photograph by André Kertész (Hungarian-American, 1894–1985), sold by the G. Ray Hawkins Gallery in Santa Monica, California, in 1991, followed by another Kertész, *Pipes and Glasses*, which fetched $225,000 in a private sale in 1992; several further works by Kertész have achieved prices in excess of $100,000. The previous record was held by a Californian collector who in 1990 paid $190,000/£101,442 for a print of Edward Weston's *Nautilus Shell*, one of only 16 in existence (*see also* number 8 in the Top 10). In 1985 *Wall Street* (1915), a photograph by Paul Strand (American, 1890–1976), was sold to the Canadian Center for Architecture for $170,000, a price that was exceeded in 1989 when Strand's *Twin Lakes (Portrait)* was sold for $180,000. Another Strand, *Grand Canyon* (1915), made $150,000 in 1988. Graham Nash, the British member of the rock groups the Hollies and Crosby, Stills and Nash, an avid collector of rare photographs, was reported in 1990 to have equalled the current number three auction record by paying $165,000/£88,094 for *Self Portrait with Clara on their Honeymoon* (1903) by Edward Steichen (American, 1879–1973). A print of *Triumph of the Egg* by Paul Outerbridge (American, 1896–1958) was reported to have changed hands in 1990 for $160,000/£85,424, while several further works by Man Ray and other photographers represented in the Top 10 have been sold for more than $100,000. *Wheels* by Charles Sheeler (American, 1883–1965), a photograph of a railway locomotive's wheels, was purchased in 1988 by the Getty Museum for about $130,000. A photograph by Anthony Berger of Abraham Lincoln and his son Tad (1864) was sold at Sotheby's, New York, on 27 March 1985 for $104,500, but its high value derived less from the photograph itself than from the fact that it was autographed by Lincoln. It is now in the Forbes Magazine Collection, New York.

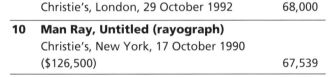

Alexander Rodchenko's *Girl with Leica* is the second most expensive photograph ever sold at auction.

THE 10 MOST EXPENSIVE FOUNTAIN PENS SOLD AT AUCTION BY BONHAMS, LONDON

	Pen/sale	Price (£)
1	Waterman Model 418, American, c1907 Red hard rubber with silver filigree overlay, 26 June 1992	6,100
2	De La Rue *Pelikan*, English, c1897 9ct pink and yellow gold with floral chasing, 13 July 1990	5,500
3	Waterman Model 504, American or French, c1901–10 18ct yellow gold with floral and scroll decoration, 27 March 1992	4,000
4 =	Dunhill Namiki *Cloisonne*, Japanese, c1930 Silver with Maki-E lacquer floral inlay, 2 October 1992	3,300
4 =	Waterman Model 504, American, c1901 14ct pink gold with snail decoration, 5 October 1990	3,300
4 =	Namiki Maki-E pen and pencil set, Japanese, c1927 Decorated with pheasants, 13 July 1990	3,300
4 =	Namiki customized Maki-E pen with watch, Japanese, c1926. With gold dust decoration of six cranes, 13 July 1990	3,300
8	Waterman Model 0558, American, c1920–25 Gold plated basket-weave filigree overlay, 12 April 1992	3,100
9	Montblanc Model 2, German, c1924 14ct gold safety pen, 30 March 1990	2,900
10	Montblanc Model 4, German, c1927 Silver octagonal safety pen, 26 July 1992	2,600

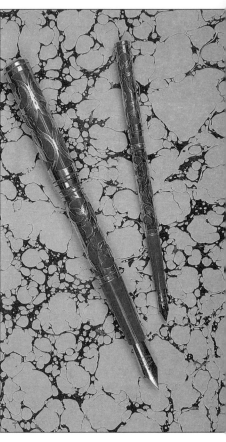

The rare Waterman Model 418 fountain pen (left) was sold at auction for a record £6,100 in June 1992.

Fountain pens and other writing instruments are much prized among collectors, and Bonhams, the London auctioneers who hold the world's largest auctions of vintage fountain pens, have achieved some of the highest prices ever paid.

THE 10 MOST VALUABLE *VANITY FAIR* CARICATURES

	Subject	Profession	Caption	Date	Value (£)
1 =	Lord Hawke	Cricketer	'Yorkshire Cricket'	24 Sep 1892	500
1 =	Jack Hobbs	Cricketer	'A Tested Centurion'	7 Aug 1912	500
1 =	Frederick Spofforth	Cricketer	'The Demon Bowler'	13 Jul 1878	500
4	Lord Harris	Cricketer	'Kent'	16 Jul 1881	485
5	Winston Churchill	Politician	'Winnie'	8 Mar 1911	450
6	Winston Churchill	Politician	'Winston'	27 Sep 1900	400
7 =	W.S. Gilbert	Dramatist	'Patience'	21 May 1881	300
7 =	Tod Sloane	Jockey	'An American Jockey'	25 May 1899	300
9 =	William Gillette	Actor	'Sherlock Holmes'	27 Feb 1907	275
9 =	Oscar Wilde	Writer	'Oscar'	24 May 1884	275

When *Vanity Fair* magazine was first published 1865, it contained popular coloured caricatures of men of the day, from sportsmen and soldiers to artists and royalty. They were produced initially by an Italian-born aristocrat Carlo Pellegrini, working under the pseudonym 'Ape'. He was briefly succeeded by James Tissot (pseudonym Coïdé) who produced caricatures from 1869 to 1877, and then by Sir Leslie Ward, working under the name 'Spy', whose caricatures appeared over a long period (1877–1909). Other contributors included Jean de Paleologu ('Pal'), Adriano Cecioni, Walter Sickert ('Sic') and Max Beerbohm ('Max'). The individual elongated style of the Vanity Fair caricatures made them instantly recognizable and they have become highly collectable: there is scarcely a solicitor's office in the country that does not display one of an eminent judge or barrister. Cricketers are especially popular – outside the Top 10, W.G. Grace is much sought-after, but as his caricature appeared twice, it is less rare than many consider. One subject ought correctly to head the list, but it is so rare and valuable that collectors have made us swear not to reveal its identity!

THE 10 TALLEST FREE-STANDING STATUES IN THE WORLD

	Statue	Height m	ft
1	**Chief Crazy Horse** Thunderhead Mountain, South Dakota, USA	172	563

Started in 1948 by Polish-American sculptor Korczak Ziolkowski and continued after his death in 1982 by his widow and eight of his children, this gigantic equestrian statue is even longer than it is high (195 m/641 ft). It is being carved out of the granite mountain by dynamiting and drilling more than 5,000,000 tonnes of rock in total, and is not expected to be completed until the next century.

	Statue	Height m	ft
2	**The Indian Rope Trick** Riddersberg Säteri, Jönköping, Sweden	103	337

Sculptor Calle Örnemark's 144-tonne wooden sculpture depicts a long strand of 'rope' held by a fakir, while another figure ascends.

	Statue	Height m	ft
3	**Motherland, 1967** Volgograd, Russia	82	270

Unveiled in 1967, this concrete statue of a woman with raised sword, designed by Yevgeniy Vuchetich, commemorates the Soviet victory at the Battle of Stalingrad (1942–43).

	Statue	Height m	ft
4	**Buddha** Bamian, Afghanistan	53	173

Near this third–fourth century AD statue lie the remains of the even taller Sakya Buddha, said to have measured 305 m/1,000 ft.

	Statue	Height m	ft
5	**Kannon** Otsubo-yama, near Tokyo, Japan	52	170

The immense statue of the goddess of mercy was unveiled in 1961 in honour of the dead of the Second World War.

	Statue	Height m	ft
6	**Statue of Liberty** New York, USA	46	151

Designed by Auguste Bartholdi and presented to the USA by the people of France, the statue was shipped in sections to Liberty (formerly Bedloes) Island where it was assembled. It was unveiled on 28 October 1886, and restored and reinaugurated on 4 July 1986. It consists of sheets of copper on an iron frame, which weighs 229 tonnes in total. The height of the statue itself is 46 m/151 ft from the base to the top of the torch, and 34 m/111 ft from the heel to the tip of the crown. It stands on a massive pedestal which more than doubles the overall height to 93 m/305 ft from the base to the torch.

	Statue	Height m	ft
7	**Christ** Rio de Janeiro, Brazil	38	125

The work of sculptor Paul Landowski and engineer Heitor da Silva Costa, the figure of Christ weighs 1,163 tonnes. It was unveiled in 1931 and has recently been restored. The Uspallata Pass in the Andes, on the border of Chile and Argentina, also boasts a huge figure of Christ. This is the work of Argentine artist Mateo Alonso, unveiled in 1904 and consisting of an 8 m/26 ft bronze statue on a 6 m/20 ft pedestal.

	Statue	Height m	ft
8	**Colossi of Memnon** Karnak, Egypt	21	70

Two seated sandstone figures of Pharaoh Amenhotep III.

The 21 m/70 ft Colossi of Memnon are the largest surviving statues dating from before the birth of Christ.

	Statue	Height m	ft
9	**Sphinx** Giza, Egypt	20	66

The huge body of a lion, with the face of fourth-dynasty Pharaoh Chepren, was carved from limestone and measures 73 m/240 ft in length.

	Statue	Height m	ft
10	**Hermanns-Denkmal** Teutoburger Forest, Lower Saxony, Germany	19	62

Unveiled in 1875, this copper statue of a figure holding a 7 m/23 ft sword has an additional 29 m/95 ft base. There are many other heroic figures of heights approaching this elsewhere in Germany and Eastern Europe, among them a massive stone figure of Bismarck in Hamburg. However, since the fall of Communism, most of the Eastern Bloc's colossal statues of Lenin have been consigned to scrapyards.

Two of the Seven Wonders of the World were giant free-standing statues: the Colossus of Rhodes, a 36 m/117 ft bronze of the sun-god Helios or Apollo by the sculptor Chares of Lindus, which fell in an earthquake in 224BC and the 12 m/40 ft statue of Zeus in the temple at Olympia, created by Phidias in 457BC. The Ancient World also boasted other large statues, including one of Nero in Rome, said to have stood 37 m/120 ft high.

The tallest statue in the United Kingdom is the 4 m/18 ft (9 m/30 ft with base), 34-tonne bronze Achilles (1822) in Hyde Park, London. The stone statue of Nelson on Nelson's Column (1843) measures 5 m/17 ft, but stands at an elevation of 44 m/145 ft. What is less well known is that there is an even higher statue in London – a 3.7 m/12 ft figure of George I incongruously surmounting the steeple of St George's Church, Bloomsbury Way, London, at a height of 44.8 m/147 ft.

Auguste Bartholdi, the designer of the Statue of Liberty, was also responsible for the 22 m/72 ft long, 11 m/36 ft high 'Lion of Belfort' (1880), built with granite blocks and set into a hillside in Alsace.

Yes Ya Oui
Hai Si Da

2+2=4

CULTURE & LEARNING

THE 10 MOST WIDELY SPOKEN LANGUAGES IN THE WORLD

	Country	Approximate no. of speakers
1	Chinese (Mandarin)	901,000,000
2	English	451,000,000
3	Hindustani	377,000,000
4	Spanish	360,000,000
5	Russian	291,000,000
6	Arabic	207,000,000
7	Bengali	190,000,000
8	Portuguese	178,000,000
9	Malay-Indonesian	148,000,000
10	Japanese	126,000,000

According to 1992 estimates by Sidney S. Culbert of the University of Washington, in addition to those languages appearing in the Top 10, there are only two other languages that are spoken by more than 100,000,000 individuals: French (122,000,000) and German (118,000,000). A further 10 languages are spoken by between 50,000,000 and 100,000,000 people: Urdu (98,000,000), Punjabi (89,000,000), Korean (73,000,000), Telugu (70,000,000), Tamil (68,000,000), Marathi (67,000,000), Italian (63,000,000), Javanese (61,000,000), Vietnamese (60,000,000) and Turkish (57,000,000).

Chinese-speakers outnumber English-speakers two-to-one, but learn other languages in order to be understood by the rest of the world.

THE 10 COUNTRIES WITH THE MOST ENGLISH LANGUAGE SPEAKERS

	Country	Approximate no. of English speakers
1	USA	215,000,000
2	UK	56,000,000
3	Canada	17,000,000
4	Australia	14,000,000
5	Irish Republic	3,300,000
6	New Zealand	3,000,000
7	Jamaica	2,300,000
8	South Africa	2,000,000
9	Trinidad and Tobago	1,200,000
10	Guyana	900,000

The Top 10 represents the countries with the greatest numbers of inhabitants who speak English as their mother-tongue. After the 10th entry, the figures dive to around 250,000 in the case of both Barbados and the Bahamas, while Zimbabwe occupies 13th place with some 200,000 English speakers. In addition to these and others that make up a world total that is probably in excess of 451,000,000, there are perhaps as many as 1,000,000,000 who speak English as a second language: a large proportion of the population of the Philippines, for example, speaks English, and there are many countries, such as India, Nigeria and other former British colonies in Africa, where English is either an official language or is widely understood and used in conducting legal affairs, in government and business.

THE 10 MOST WIDELY SPOKEN LANGUAGES IN THE EC*

	Language	Approximate no. of speakers*
1	German	75,667,000
2	English	59,595,000
3	French	56,943,000
4	Italian	55,370,000
5	Spanish	28,672,000
6	Dutch	20,463,000
7	Portuguese	10,431,000
8	Greek	10,120,000
9	Catalan	6,370,000
10	Danish	5,005,000

*As 'first language', including speakers resident in EC countries other than those where it is the main language, such as German-speakers living in France.

THE TOP 10 GCSE SUBJECTS IN 1992

	Subject	Total taking exam
1	English	641,937
2	Science	572,327
3	Mathematics	556,199
4	English Literature	450,282
5	French	300,876
6	Geography	268,235
7	Art and Design	214,425
8	History	207,395
9	CTD*	149,448
10	Home Economics	116,446

*Craft, Technology and Design.

GCSE French is taken by almost half as many students as take English.

THE 10 GCSE SUBJECTS WITH THE HIGHEST PERCENTAGE OF GRADE A PASSES IN 1992

	Subject	Total taking exam	Grade A %
1	Greek	1,285	71.1
2	Latin	13,286	61.0
3	Spanish	29,245	29.7
4	Classical Civilization	4,775	23.6
5	German	98,930	22.8
6	Physics	78,275	21.5
7	Music	32,712	20.9
8	French	300,876	19.1
9	Chemistry	72,214	18.9
10	Biology	103,247	15.5

THE 10 GCSE SUBJECTS WITH THE LOWEST PERCENTAGE OF GRADE A PASSES IN 1992

	Subject	Total taking exam	Grade A %
1	Home Economics	116,446	7.3
2	Social Science	5,420	7.5
3	Mathematics	556,199	9.0
4	CTD*	149,448	9.1
5	Science	572,327	9.4
6	Computer Studies	45,057	9.5
7	English	641,937	9.6
8	Economics	19,787	11.8
9	English Literature	450,282	12.0
10	Business Studies	97,282	12.5

*Craft, Technology and Design.

THE TOP 10 'A' LEVEL SUBJECTS IN 1992

	Subject	Total taking exam
1	English	86,685
2	Mathematics	72,357
3	General Studies	53,651
4	Biology	48,707
5	History	46,680
6	Geography	45,603
7	Chemistry	42,695
8	Physics	41,273
9	Economics	40,194
10	French	31,254

THE 10 LARGEST UNIVERSITIES IN THE UK*

	University	Full-time students†
1	London	51,392
2	Manchester	20,098
3	Leeds	14,453
4	Oxford	14,288
5	Cambridge	13,920
6	Glasgow	13,638
7	Edinburgh	12,607
8	Birmingham	12,304
9	Ulster	10,972
10	Liverpool	9,565

*Excluding Open University.

†Undergraduates and post-graduates.

The universities featured in the Top 10 for 1992–93 remain the same as the previous year, although with some changes of order. All those listed have increased their total numbers of students.

THE 10 COUNTRIES WITH THE LOWEST LITERACY LEVELS

	Country	Literacy %
1	Burkina Faso	8
2 =	Mali	10
2 =	Senegal	10
4 =	Afghanistan	12
4 =	Gambia	12
6	Niger	13
7	Mozambique	14
8 =	Bhutan	15
8 =	Comoros	15
8 =	Sierra Leone	15

At the other end of the scale, Liechtenstein, Luxembourg and Norway are the only three nations credited with 100 per cent literacy levels.

THE 10 LARGEST LIBRARIES IN THE WORLD

	Library	Location	Founded	Books
1	Library of Congress	Washington, DC, USA	1800	27,000,000
2	British Library	London, UK	1753*	18,000,000
3	Harvard University Library	Cambridge, MA, USA	1638	12,169,049
4	State V.I. Lenin Library†	Moscow, Russia	1862	11,750,000
5	New York Public Library	New York, NY, USA	1848	10,000,000#
6	Yale University Library	New Haven, CT, USA	1701	9,937,751
7	Biblioteca Academiei Romăne	Bucharest, Romania	1867	9,397,260
8	Bibliothèque Nationale	Paris, France	1480	9,000,000
9	State M.E. Saltykov-Shchedrin State Public Library	Leningrad, Russia	1795	8,000,000
10	University of Illinois	Urbana, IL, USA	1867	7,918,951

*Founded as part of the British Museum, 1753; became an independent body, 1973.   †Founded as Rumyantsev Library.

#Reference holdings only, excluding books in lending library branches.

Old-established rivalries between Eastern European libraries and the West seem to have been responsible for the hugely inflated figures claimed for the State M.E. Saltykov-Shchedrin (28,500,000) and State V.I. Lenin Libraries (over 30,000,000). As these appear to include individual copies of newspapers and periodicals, they cannot be compared with the holdings of bound books in Western libraries. It is also known that a very large number of books were destroyed in a disastrous fire at the Saltykov-Shchedrin. The figures for books in such vast collections as those of the British Library represent only the tip of a cultural iceberg which encompasses millions of additional items, including manuscripts, microfilms, maps, prints and records. The Library of Congress has perhaps 73,000,000 and the New York Public Library 36,000,000 manuscripts, maps, audio-visual and other catalogued items in addition to books.

The Reading Room of the British Library, the largest library in the UK and second largest in the world.

THE 10 LARGEST LIBRARIES IN THE UK

	Library	Location	Founded	Books
1	British Library	London	1753	18,000,000
2 =	Bodleian Library	Oxford	1602	6,000,000
2 =	National Library of Scotland	Edinburgh	1682	6,000,000
4	National Library of Wales	Aberystwyth	1907	5,000,000
5	University of Cambridge	Cambridge	c1400	4,850,000
6	Lancashire County Library	Preston	1924	3,697,640
7 =	Hampshire County Library	Winchester	1925	3,500,000
7 =	John Rylands University Library of Manchester*	Manchester	1851	3,500,000
9	Kent County Library	Maidstone	1921	3,300,000
10	Birmingham Public Library	Birmingham	1861	2,600,000

*In 1972 the John Rylands Library (founded 1900) was amalgamated with Manchester University Library (1851).

In addition to the books held by these libraries, many have substantial holdings of manuscripts, periodicals and other printed material: the Bodleian Library, for example, has almost 1,000,000 maps.

THE 10 MOST-QUOTED AUTHORS IN THE OXFORD ENGLISH DICTIONARY

	Author	Dates	Approximate number of references*
1	William Shakespeare	1564–1616	29,142
2	Sir Walter Scott	1771–1832	15,732
3	John Milton	1608–74	12,000
4	Geoffrey Chaucer	c1343–1400	11,013
5	John Wyclif	c1330–84	10,776
6	William Caxton	c1422–91	9,553
7	John Dryden	1631–1700	8,777
8	Charles Dickens	1812–70	8,189
9	Philemon Holland	1552–1637	7,947
10	Alfred, Lord Tennyson	1809–92	6,680

*These figures may not be absolutely precise because of variations in the way in which sources are quoted, where there is more than one example from the same author, etc.

THE 10 LONGEST WORDS IN THE OXFORD ENGLISH DICTIONARY

	Word	Letters
1	Pneumonoultramicroscopicsilicovolcanoconiosis	45
2	Supercalifragilisticexpialidocious	34
3	Pseudopseudohypoparathyroidism	30
4 =	Floccinaucinihilipilification	29
4 =	Triethylsulphonemethylmethane	29
6 =	Antidisestablishmentarianism	28
6 =	Octamethylcyclotetrasiloxane	28
6 =	Tetrachlorodibenzoparadioxin	28
9	Hepaticocholangiogastronomy	27
10 =	Radioimmunoelectrophoresis	26
10 =	Radioimmunoelectrophoretic	26

Words that are hyphenated, including such compound words as 'transformational-generative' and 'tristhio-dimethyl-benzaldehyde', have not been included. Only one unhyphenated word did not quite make it into the Top 10, the 25-letter psychophysicotherapeutics. After this, there is a surprisingly large number of words containing 20–24 letters (pneumonoencephalographic, pneumonoventriculography, psychoneuroendocrinology, radioimmunoprecipitation, spectro-photofluorometric, thyroparathyroidectomize, hypergammaglo-bulinaemia, hypergammaglobulinaemic, roentgenkymographically, tribothermoluminescence, photomorphogenetically, honorific-abilitudinity and immunosympathectomized, for example) – few of which are ever used by anyone except scientists and crossword compilers.

THE 10 MOST-QUOTED SOURCES IN THE OXFORD ENGLISH DICTIONARY

	Source	Approximate number of references*
1	The Times	19,098
2	Cursor Mundi**	11,035
3	Encyclopaedia Britannica	10,102
4	Daily News	9,650
5	Nature	9,150
6	Transactions of the Philological Society	8,972
7	Chronicle	8,550
8	Westminster Gazette	7,478
9	History of England	7,180
10	Listener	7,139

*These figures may not be absolutely precise because of variations in the way in which source books and journals are quoted, where there is more than one example from the same source, etc.

**Cursor Mundi is a long fourteenth-century Northumbrian poem which is extensively cited for early uses of English words.

References to Daily News, Chronicle and History of England may include several different works with similar titles.

THE 10 LONGEST WORDS IN THE ENGLISH LANGUAGE

1 Acetylseryltyrosylserylisoleucylthreonylserylprolylserylglutaminylphenylalanylvalylphenylalanylleucylserylserylvalyltryptophylalanylaspartylprolylisoleucylglutamylleucylleucyllasparaginylvalylcysteinylthreonylserylserylleucylglycllasparaginylglutaminylphenylalanylglutaminylthreonylglutaminylglutaminylalanylarginylthreonylthreonylglutaminylvalylglutaminylglutaminylphenylalanylserylglutaminylvalyltryptophyllysylprolylphenylalanylprolylglutaminylserylthreonylvalylarginylphenylalanylprolylglycylaspartylvalyltyrosyllsyslvalyltyrosylarginyltyrosylasparaginylalanylvalylleucylaspartylprolylleucylisoleucylthreonylalanylleucylleucylglycylthreonylphenylalanylaspartylthreonylarginylasparaginylarginylisoleucylisoleucylglutamylvalylglutamylasparaginylglutaminylglutaminylserylprolylthreonylthreonylalanylglutamylthreonylleucylaspartylalanylthreonylarginylarginylvalylaspartylaspartylalanylthreonylvalylalanylisoleucylarginylserylalanylasparaginylisoleucylasparaginylleucylvallasparaginylglutamylleucylvalylarginylglycylthreonylglycylleucyltyrosylasparaginylglutaminylasparaginylthreonylphenylalanylglutamylserylmethionylserylglycylleucylvalyltryptophylthreonylserylalanylprolylalanylserine **(1,185 letters)**

The word for the Tobacco Mosaic Virus, Dahlemense Strain, qualifies as the longest word in English because it has actually been used in print (in the American Chemical Society's *Chemical Abstracts* – and in the first edition of *The Top 10 of Everything*, where a typesetting error robbed it of a single 'l', which surprisingly went unnoticed by its readers) whereas certain even longer words for chemical compounds, which have been cited in such sources as *The Guinness Book of Records*, are bogus in the sense that they have never been used by scientists or appeared in print. Long words for chemical compounds may be regarded by purists as cheating, since such words as trinitrophenylmethylnitramine (29 letters) – a type of explosive – can be created by linking together the scientific names of their components. Other words that are also discounted are those that have been invented with the sole intention of being long words, such as James Joyce's 100-letter examples in *Finnegans Wake*.

2 Aopadotenachoselachogaleokranioleipsanodrimhipotrimmatosilphioparaomelitokatakechymenokichlepikossyphophattoperisteralektryonoptekephalliokigklopeleiolagoiosiraiobaphetraganopterygon **(182 letters)**

The English transliteration of a 170-letter Greek word that appears in *The Ecclesiazusae* (a comedy on government by women) by the Greek playwright, Aristophanes (c448–380BC). It is used as a description of a 17-ingredient dish.

3 Aequeosalinocalcinosetaceoaluminosocupreovitriolic **(52 letters)**

Invented by a medical writer, Dr Edward Strother (1675–1737), to describe the spa waters at Bath.

4 Asseocarnisanguineoviscericartilaginonervomedullary **(51 letters)**

Coined by writer and East India Company official Thomas Love Peacock (1785–1866), and used in his satire *Headlong Hall* (1816) as a description of the structure of the human body.

5 Pneumonoultramicroscopicsilicovolcanoconiosis **(45 letters)**

It first appeared in print (though ending in '-koniosis') in F. Scully's *Bedside Manna* [sic] (1936), then found its way into *Webster's Dictionary* and is now in the *Oxford English Dictionary* – but with the note that it occurs 'chiefly as an instance of a very long word'. It is said to mean a lung disease caused by breathing fine dust.

6 Hepaticocholangiocholecystenterostomies **(39 letters)**

A surgical operation to create channels of communication between gall bladders and hepatic ducts or intestines.

7 = Pseudoantidisestablishmentarianism **(34 letters)**

A word meaning 'false opposition to the withdrawal of state support from a Church', derived from that perennial favourite long word, antidisestablishmentarianism (a mere 28 letters). Another composite made from it (though usually hyphenated) is ultra-anti-disestablishmentarianism, which means 'extreme opposition to the withdrawal of state support from a Church' (33 letters).

7 = Supercalifragilisticexpialidocious **(34 letters)**

An invented word, but perhaps now eligible since it has appeared in the *Oxford English Dictionary*. It was popularized by the song of this title in the film *Mary Poppins* (1964) where it is used to mean 'wonderful', but it was originally written in 1949 in an unpublished song by Parker and Young who spelt it 'supercalafajalistickespialadojus' (32 letters). In 1965–66, Parker and Young unsuccessfully sued the makers of *Mary Poppins*, claiming infringement of copyright. In summarizing the case, the US Court decided against repeating this mouthful, stating that 'All variants of this tongue-twister will hereinafter be referred to collectively as "the word".'

9 = Encephalomyeloradiculoneuritis **(30 letters)**

A syndrome caused by a virus associated with encephalitis.

9 = Hippopotomonstrosesquipedalian **(30 letters)**

Appropriately, the word that means 'pertaining to an extremely long word'.

9 = Pseudopseudohypoparathyroidism **(30 letters)**

First used (hyphenated) in the USA in 1952 and (unhyphenated) in Great Britain in *The Lancet* in 1962 to describe a medical case in which a patient appeared to have symptoms of pseudohypoparathyroidism, but with 'no manifestations suggesting hypoparathyroidism'.

If the rules are changed and No. 1 is disqualified as a compound chemical name, and No. 2 because it is a transliteration from Greek, the next longest word is Floccinaucinihilipilification (29 letters). Alternatively spelt 'Flocci-nauci-nihili-pilification' or, by Sir Walter Scott, in his *Journal* (18 March 1829), 'Floccipaucinihilipilification', it means the action of estimating as worthless. Until supercalifragilisticexpialidocious, floccinaucinihilipilification was the longest word in the *Oxford English Dictionary*. Honorificabilitudinitatibus, a 27-letter monster word, is used by Shakespeare in *Love's Labour's Lost* (Act V, Scene i) to mean 'with honourableness'.

THE 10 MOST EXPENSIVE BOOKS AND MANUSCRIPTS EVER SOLD AT AUCTION

Book/manuscript	Price (£)*
1 The Gospels of Henry the Lion, c1173–75 Sotheby's, London, 6 December 1983	**7,400,000**
The most expensive manuscript, book or work of art other than a painting ever sold.	
2 The Gutenberg Bible, 1455 Christie's, New York, 22 October 1987 ($5,390,000)	**2,934,131**
One of the first books ever printed, by Johann Gutenberg and Johann Fust in 1455, it holds the record for the most expensive printed book.	
3 The Northumberland Bestiary, c1250–60 Sotheby's, London, 29 November 1990	**2,700,000**
The highest price ever paid for an English manuscript.	
4 Autograph manuscript of nine symphonies by Wolfgang Amadeus Mozart, c1773–74 Sotheby's, London, 22 May 1987	**2,350,000**
The record for a music manuscript and for any post-medieval manuscript.	
5 John James Audubon's *The Birds of America*, 1827–38 Sotheby's, New York, 6 June 1989 ($3,600,000)	**2,292,993**
The record for any natural history book. Another copy of the same book, a collection of large, hand-coloured engravings, was sold at Sotheby's, London, on 21 June 1990 for £1,600,000 and a further copy, auctioned by Christie's, New York, on 24 April 1992, fetched $2,120,000/£1,187,000. A facsimile reprint of Audubon's *The Birds of America* published in 1985 by Abbeville Press, New York, and now listed at $30,000 or £15,000, is the most expensive book ever published.	
6 The Bible in Hebrew, a manuscript written in Iraq, Syria or Babylon in the ninth or tenth century Sotheby's, London, 5 December 1989	**1,850,000**
The record for any Hebrew manuscript.	

7 The Monypenny Breviary, illuminated
manuscript, c1490–95
Sotheby's, London, 19 June 1989   **1,700,000**

The record for any French manuscript.

**8 The Hours and Psalter of Elizabeth de Bohun,
Countess of Northampton,** c1340–45
Sotheby's, London, 21 June 1988   **1,400,000**

9 *Biblia Pauperum*
Christie's, New York, 22 October 1987
($2,200,000)   **1,320,000**

A block-book bible printed in the Netherlands in c1460 (the pages of block-books, with text and illustrations, were printed from single carved woodblocks rather than moveable type).

10 The Gospels of St Hubert, c860–80
Sotheby's, London, 26 November 1985   **1,300,000**

Excluding premiums.

Franz Kafka's manuscript of *The Trial*, sold at Sotheby's, London, on 17 November 1988 for £1,000,000, holds the record for any modern literary manuscript.

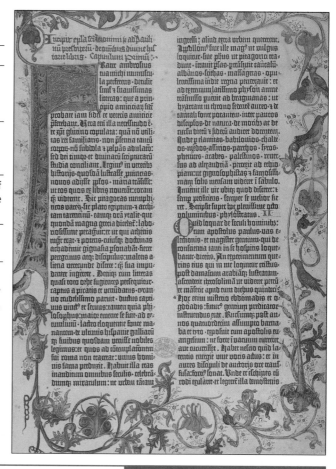

The 1455 Gutenberg Bible, with printed text and hand-drawn illuminations, is the most expensive printed book ever sold at auction.

THE 10 BESTSELLING BOOKS OF ALL TIME

Title	No. sold
1 The Bible	**3,000,000,000**

No one really knows how many copies of the Bible have been printed, sold or distributed. The Bible Society's attempt to calculate the number printed between 1816 and 1975 produced the figure of 2,458,000,000. It is now thought to be closer to 3,000,000,000 in over 300 languages. Whatever the precise figure, it is by far the bestselling book of all time.

2 Quotations from the Works of **Mao Tse-tung**	**800,000,000**

Chairman Mao's 'Little Red Book' could scarcely fail to become a bestseller: between the years 1966 and 1971 it was compulsory for every Chinese adult to own a copy. It was both sold and distributed to the people of China – though what proportion voluntarily bought it must remain open to question. Some 100,000,000 copies of his *Poems* were also disseminated.

3 American Spelling Book **by Noah Webster**	**100,000,000**

First published in 1783, this reference book by American man of letters Noah Webster (1758–1843) – of *Webster's Dictionary* fame – remained a bestseller throughout the nineteenth century.

4 The Guinness Book of Records	**73,000,000 +**

First published in 1955, *The Guinness Book of Records* stands out as the greatest contemporary publishing achievement. In the UK there have now been 36 editions (it was not published annually until 1964), as well as numerous foreign language editions.

5 The McGuffey Readers **by William Holmes McGuffey**	**60,000,000**

Published in numerous editions from 1853, some authorities have put the total sales of these educational textbooks, originally compiled by American anthologist William Holmes McGuffey (1800–73), as high as 122,000,000. It has also been claimed that 60,000,000 copies of the 1879 edition were printed, but as this is some 10,000,000 more than the entire population of the USA at the time, the publishers must have been extremely optimistic about its success.

6 A Message to Garcia **by Elbert Hubbard**	**40–50,000,000**

Now forgotten, Hubbard's polemic on the subject of labour relations was published in 1899 and within a few years had achieved these phenomenal sales largely because many American employers purchased bulk supplies to distribute to their employees. The literary career of Elbert Hubbard (1856–1915) was cut short in 1915 when he went down with the *Lusitania*, but even in death he was a record-breaker: his posthumous *My Philosophy* (1916) was published in the largest-ever 'limited edition' of 9,983 copies!

7 The Common Sense Book of Baby and Child **Care by Benjamin Spock**	**39,200,000 +**

Dr Spock's 1946 manual became the bible of infant care for subsequent generations of parents. Most of the sales have been of the paperback edition of the book.

8 World Almanac	**36,000,000 +**

Having been published annually since 1868 (with a break from 1876 to 1886), this wide-ranging reference book has remained a bestseller ever since.

9 Valley of the Dolls **by Jacqueline Susann**	**28,712,000 +**

This racy tale of sex, violence and drugs by Jacqueline Susann (1921–74), first published in 1966, is perhaps surprisingly the world's bestselling novel.

10 In His Steps: 'What Would Jesus Do?' **by Rev. Charles Monroe Sheldon**	**28,500,000**

Though virtually unknown today, Charles Sheldon (1857–1946) achieved fame and fortune with this 1896 religious treatise.

It is extremely difficult to establish precise sales even of contemporary books, and virtually impossible to do so with books published long ago. How many copies of the *Complete Works of Shakespeare* or Conan Doyle's Sherlock Holmes books have been sold in countless editions? The publication of variant editions, translations and pirated copies all affect the global picture, and few publishers or authors are willing to expose their royalty statements to public scrutiny. As a result, this Top 10 list offers no more than the 'best guess' at the great bestsellers of the past, and it may well be that there are other books with a valid claim to a place in it.

There are problems of definition: what, for example, is the status of a book that is revised and reissued annually, and what precisely is a 'book'? A UNESCO conference in 1950 decided it was 'a non-periodical literary publication containing 49 or more pages, not counting the covers' (which is baffling in itself, since all publications have to contain an even number of pages, while, according to this criterion, a 32-page children's book would not be regarded as a book at all!). If *Old Moore's Almanac* is classed as a book rather than a periodical or a pamphlet, it would appear high on the list. Having been published annually since 1697, its total sales to date are believed to be over 112,000,000. More than 107,000,000 copies of the Jehovah's Witness tract, *The Truth That Leads to Eternal Life*, first published in 1968, are believed to have been distributed in 117 languages, usually in return for a donation to the sect, but as they were not sold through bookshops it does not technically rank as a 'bestseller'.

Almost the double: Andrew Morton's royal exposé *Diana: Her True Story* was the bestselling non-fiction hardback but second bestselling paperback of 1992.

THE TOP 10 CHILDREN'S BOOKS BORROWED FROM LIBRARIES IN THE UK

	Title	Author
1	Matilda	Roald Dahl
2	George's Marvellous Medicine	Roald Dahl
3	The Very Hungry Caterpillar	Eric Carle
4	The BFG	Roald Dahl
5	The Witches	Roald Dahl
6	The Twits	Roald Dahl
7	Whatever Next	Jill Murphy
8	Peace at Last	Jill Murphy
9	Dogger	Shirley Hughes
10	Alfie's Feet	Shirley Hughes

A survey of 60,000 libraries conducted by the Libraries Association revealed a list of children's favourites that, interestingly, bore no resemblance to the 'approved' list drawn up by the National Curriculum Council – which excludes Britain's undeniably most popular children's author, Roald Dahl, altogether.

THE 10 BESTSELLING CHILDREN'S BOOKS OF 1992 IN THE UK

	Title	Author
1	Matilda	Roald Dahl
2	Fudga-a-mania	Judy Blume
3	The Very Hungry Caterpillar	Eric Carle
4	Esio Trot	Roald Dahl
5	Animals of Farthing Wood	Colin Dann
6	Incredible Cross Sections	Stephen Biesty
7	The Minpins	Roald Dahl
8	Where's Spot?	Eric Hill
9	The Baby's Catalogue	Janet and Allan Ahlberg
10	The Carpet People	Terry Pratchett

THE 10 MOST BORROWED AUTHORS IN THE UK IN 1992

1	Catherine Cookson
2	Agatha Christie
3	Danielle Steel
4	Dick Francis
5	Ruth Rendell
6	Roald Dahl
7	Enid Blyton
8	Jack Higgins
9	Stephen King
10	Allan and Janet Ahlberg

According to figures produced by the Public Lending Right office (the organization that pays registered authors fees according to the number of times their books are borrowed from public libraries), books by a total of 19 authors – including all those in the Top 10 – were borrowed more than 1,000,000 times.

THE 10 MOST BORROWED CLASSIC AUTHORS IN THE UK IN 1992

1	Thomas Hardy
2	J.R.R. Tolkien
3	Charles Dickens
4	A.A. Milne
5	Jane Austen
6	D.H. Lawrence
7	Anthony Trollope
8	Rudyard Kipling
9	George Orwell
10	Sir Arthur Conan Doyle

Public Lending Right figures indicate that each of the top seven authors featured in this list was borrowed more than 200,000 times.

THE 10 BESTSELLING HARDBACK NON-FICTION BOOKS OF 1992 IN THE UK

	Title	Author	Estimated sales*
1	Diana: Her True Story	Andrew Morton	240,000
2	Sex	Madonna	165,000
3	Pole to Pole	Michael Palin	160,000
4	The Guinness Book of Records	Peter Matthews (ed.)	120,000
5	Mr Bean's Diary	Rowan Atkinson & Robin Driscoll	90,000
6	A Brief History of Time	Stephen Hawking	70,000
7	One Hundred Days	Sandy Woodward	68,000
8	Michelin Red Guide: France 1992	Michelin	55,000
9	Storm Command	Peter de la Billière	45,000
10	Wild Swans	Jung Chang	40,000

*UK book trade only, excluding book club sales and exports.

The list excludes perennial bestsellers such as the Bible and various dictionaries.

THE TOP 10 US AUTHORS IN THE UK*

1. Danielle Steel
2. Stephen King
3. Tom Clancy
4. Sidney Sheldon
5. Robert Ludlum
6. Thomas Harris
7. Virginia Andrews
8. Judith Krantz
9. Dean Koontz
10. David Eddings

*Ranking based on publishers' annual declared sales since 1980.

THE 10 BESTSELLING HARDBACK FICTION BOOKS OF 1992 IN THE UK

	Title	Author	Estimated sales*
1	The Queen and I	Sue Townsend	50,000
2	Mostly Harmless	Douglas Adams	42,000
3	Driving Force	Dick Francis	37,000
4	Fatherland	Robert Harris	30,000
5	The Silence of the Lambs and Red Dragon	Thomas Harris	28,000
6	Gerald's Game	Stephen King	20,000
7	A Dubious Legacy	Mary Wesley	19,000
8	Small Gods	Terry Pratchett	15,000
9	The Way Through the Woods	Colin Dexter	14,000
10	The House of Women	Catherine Cookson	13,000

*UK book trade only, excluding book club sales and exports.

THE 10 BESTSELLING PAPERBACK FICTION BOOKS OF 1992 IN THE UK

	Title	Author	Estimated sales*
1	Polo	Jilly Cooper	500,000
2	As the Crow Flies	Jeffrey Archer	490,000
3	The Liar	Stephen Fry	400,000
4	My Beloved Son	Catherine Cookson	390,000
5	The Rag Nymph	Catherine Cookson	380,000
6	Remember	Barbara Taylor Bradford	365,000
7	The Rector's Wife	Joanna Trollope	350,000
8	Elephant Song	Wilbur Smith	345,000
9	Needful Things	Stephen King	330,000
10	Heartbeat	Danielle Steel	320,000

*UK book trade only, excluding book club sales and exports.

Leading paperback novelist of 1992, and with two entries in the Top 10 books by female authors, Jilly Cooper is one of Britain's bestselling writers.

THE 10 BESTSELLING PAPERBACK NON-FICTION BOOKS OF 1992 IN THE UK

	Title	Author	Estimated sales*
1	A Year in Provence	Peter Mayle	280,000
2	Diana: Her True Story	Andrew Morton	260,000
3	Toujours Provence	Peter Mayle	250,000
4	Seasons of My Life	Hannah Hauxwell	150,000
5	The Tree and Shrub Expert	Dr David Hessayon	140,000
6	Proms 1992	–	125,000
7	The Flower Expert	Dr David Hessayon	115,000
8	Gardens of England and Wales Open to the Public 1992	–	110,000
9	Complete Hip and Thigh Diet	Rosemary Conley	100,000
10	Complete Cookery Course	Delia Smith	95,000

*UK book trade only, excluding book club sales and exports.

The list excludes annual bestsellers such as The Highway Code.

THE 10 BESTSELLING PENGUIN CLASSICS IN 1992

	Author	Title	First published*
1	Emily Brontë	Wuthering Heights	1847
2	Charlotte Brontë	Jane Eyre	1847
3	George Eliot	Silas Marner	1861
4	Thomas Hardy	Tess of the D'Urbervilles	1891
5	Jane Austen	Pride and Prejudice	1813
6	Thomas Hardy	Far from the Madding Crowd	1874
7	Charles Dickens	Great Expectations	1862
8	Jane Austen	Emma	1816
9	Charles Dickens	Hard Times	1854
10	Thomas Hardy	Jude The Obscure	1886

*In book form (some nineteenth-century novels were originally issued in weekly parts before appearing as books).

The Penguin Classics series was started in 1944 by E.V. Rieu, whose own translation of Homer's Odyssey, the first title published, has sold over 1,000,000 copies and remains in the Top 25 to this day (at No. 23). The Top 10 of the more than 700 books now in print is dominated by nineteenth-century novels, to some extent reflecting their use as 'set books' in English literature courses, but the same authors, with others such as Oscar Wilde and Mark Twain, also predominate in the Top 100, with only a handful of earlier writers making an appearance, among them classical writers such as Plato and Ovid and English mainstays Geoffrey Chaucer, Jonathan Swift and Daniel Defoe. Little affected by the dictates of literary fashion, the bestsellers in the series remain much the same from year to year, with only slight adjustments in the overall order.

THE 10 HIGHEST RECORDED SALES IN THE FIRST WEEK OF PUBLICATION*

	Title	Author	Year	Copies sold
1	The Growing Pains of Adrian Mole	Sue Townsend	1985	110,000
2	Stark	Ben Elton	1989	70,000
3	First Among Equals	Jeffrey Archer	1985	68,000
4	The Thorn Birds	Colleen McCulloch	1984	56,000
5	Hold the Dream	Barbara Taylor Bradford	1986	55,000
6	To Be the Best	Barbara Taylor Bradford	1989	52,000
7	A Matter of Honour	Jeffrey Archer	1987	45,000
8	Hot Money	Dick Francis	1988	42,000
9	A Woman of Substance	Barbara Taylor Bradford	1984	40,000
10	Polo	Jilly Cooper	1992	39,000

*Paperbacks only; UK book trade, excluding book club sales and exports.

This Top 10 list is based on sales in the first week in which the books in question were officially released (although, traditionally, many novels are published on a Thursday, so the first week's sale may actually comprise only a Thursday to Sunday). It should be noted that the practice of 'early selling' by booksellers – putting the titles on display before the official publication date – is commonplace, and often a title may be selling widely before its launch date.

THE 10 BESTSELLING PENGUIN FICTION PAPERBACKS IN 1992

	Title	Author
1	Paradise News	David Lodge
2	Having it All	Mave Haran
3	The Feather Men	Ranulph Fiennes
4	King Solomon's Carpet	Barbara Vine
5	Basic Instinct	Richard Osborne
6	Time's Arrow	Martin Amis
7	Wuthering Heights	Emily Brontë
8	Jericho	Dirk Bogarde
9	On the Trail of the Assassins	Jim Garison
10	A Moment of War	Laurie Lee

THE 10 BESTSELLING FICTION TITLES BY MALE AUTHORS IN THE UK*

	Title	Author	Year
1	A Matter of Honour	Jeffrey Archer	1987
2	The Prodigal Daughter	Jeffrey Archer	1983
3	A Twist in the Tale	Jeffrey Archer	1989
4	The Negotiator	Frederick Forsyth	1990
5	The Eagle Has Landed	Jack Higgins	1977
6	Watership Down	Richard Adams	1974
7	The Hitchhiker's Guide to the Galaxy	Douglas Adams	1979
8	As the Crow Flies	Jeffrey Archer	1992
9	A Perfect Spy	John Le Carré	1987
10	The Silence of the Lambs	Thomas Harris	1990

*UK book trade only, excluding book club sales and exports, since bestseller lists began (1974), based on sales in first year of publication.

THE 10 LONGEST-RUNNING BESTSELLERS IN THE UK

	Title	Author	Published*	Appear-ances†
1	A Brief History of Time	Stephen Hawking	H 1988	210
2	The Country Diary of an Edwardian Lady	Edith Holden	H 1977	183
3	The Complete Hip and Thigh Diet	Rosemary Conley	P 1989	155
4	A Year in Provence	Peter Mayle	P 1990	152
5	Life on Earth	David Attenborough	H 1979	139
6	The Secret Diary of Adrian Mole, Aged 13³/₄	Sue Townsend	P 1983	119
7	The Ascent of Man	Jacob Bronowski	H 1974	114
8	Delia Smith's Complete Cookery Course	Delia Smith	H 1989	105
9	RHS Gardeners Encyclopedia of Plants and Flowers	Chris Brickell (ed.)	H 1989	104
10	America	Alistair Cooke	H 1974	99

*H = hardback, P = paperback.

†As at 23 May 1993, based on number of appearances in Sunday Times bestseller lists.

Jeffrey Archer dominates the Top 10 of male authors with no fewer than four titles.

10 ROYAL AUTHORS AND THEIR BOOKS

1 Henry VIII

Henry was the author of *A Necessary Doctrine and Erudition for any Christian Man* (1543), written with the help of Archbishop Cranmer. He also wrote other, mainly theological, works.

2 King James I

James was the author of a dozen books including *Demonology* (1597), a treatise on witchcraft, and *Counterblaste on the Use of Tobacco* (1604).

3 Queen Victoria

Leaves from a Journal of Our Life in the Highlands, 1848–61 (1868) and its sequel, *More Leaves* (1883), were the only books Queen Victoria published in her lifetime, but numerous books containing extracts from her letters and her more than 100 volumes of diaries and journals, her other writings and watercolours have been published since her death.

4 Duchess of Windsor

The wife of Edward VIII, the Duchess published her autobiography *The Heart Has its Reasons*, in 1956.

5 Prince Philip

The Duke of Edinburgh has published a number of books, among them *Wildlife Crisis*, *A Question of Balance*, *Windsor Correspondence* and *Survival or Extinction*.

6 Lord Snowdon

Lord Snowdon's photographic and travel books include his *Private View* (1965).

7 Prince Charles

HRH The Prince of Wales wrote his children's book *The Old Man of Lochnagar* in 1986, since when he has produced such books as *Vision of Britain*, *Watercolours* and, most recently, *Highgrove: Portrait of an Estate*.

8 Duchess of York

Among the Duchess's publications are her *Budgie the Helicopter* books and *Victoria & Albert: Life at Osborne House*.

9 Princess Alice, Duchess of Gloucester

Princess Alice published her *Memories of Ninety Years* in 1991.

10 Lord Lindley

Professional furniture-maker and designer Lord Lindley's *Classical Furniture* appeared in 1993.

THE 10 BESTSELLING FICTION TITLES BY FEMALE AUTHORS IN THE UK*

	Title	Author	Year
1	*The Secret Diary of Adrian Mole, Aged 13³/₄*	Sue Townsend	1984
2	*Hold the Dream*	Barbara Taylor Bradford	1986
3	*The Growing Pains of Adrian Mole*	Sue Townsend	1985
4	*The Moth*	Catherine Cookson	1987
5	*The Parson's Daughter*	Catherine Cookson	1988
6	*Rivals*	Jilly Cooper	1989
7	*Hollywood Wives*	Jackie Collins	1984
8	*Hollywood Husbands*	Jackie Collins	1987
9	*Polo*	Jilly Cooper	1992
10	*Act of Will*	Barbara Taylor Bradford	1987

UK book trade only, excluding book club sales and exports, since bestseller lists began (1974), based on sales in first year of publication.

PEN NAMES QUIZ

What are the real names of these well-known writers?

	Pseudonym		Real name
1	John Le Carré	A	Eric Blair
2	Jean Plaidy and Victoria Holt	B	Amandine-Aurore-Lucille Dudevant
3	Mark Twain	C	David Cornwell
4	Lewis Carroll	D	René Raymond
5	George Sand	E	Leslie Yin
6	George Orwell	F	Mary Ann Evans
7	James Hadley Chase	G	Charles Dodgson
8	Leslie Charteris	H	Eleanor Hibbert
9	Ellery Queen	I	Samuel Clemens
10	George Eliot	J	Frederic Dannay and Manfred Lee

THE 10 BESTSELLING FICTION TITLES BY FOREIGN AUTHORS IN THE UK*

Title	Author	Nationality	Year	Position
1 = *The Thorn Birds*	Colleen McCulloch	Australian	1979	1
1 = *The Silence of the Lambs*	Thomas Harris	American	1991	1
3 = *Alien*	Allen Dean Foster	American	1979	2
3 = *Red Dragon*	Thomas Harris	American	1991	2
3 = *Gorky Park*	Martin Cruz Smith	American	1982	2
6 = *The Great Gatsby*	F. Scott Fitzgerald	American	1974	3
6 = *A Sparrow Falls*	Wilbur Smith	South African	1978	3
6 = *Circle of Friends*	Maeve Binchy	Irish	1991	3
9 = *Star Wars*	George Lucas	American	1977/78	5/5
9 = *Jaws*	Peter Benchley	American	1975/76	5/10

UK book trade only, excluding book club sales and exports, since bestseller lists began (1974).

Ranking is based on positions achieved in the annual bestseller lists for paperback fiction. Both *Jaws* and *Star Wars* may be deserving of a higher placing since they appeared in two successive lists. Having gained their place in the 1991 list, *The Silence of the Lambs* and *Red Dragon* were reissued as a low-priced hardback edition and spent most of the following year repeating their success in the hardback bestseller lists – a reverse of the customary practice of paperbacks following some time after hardbacks. Sales of five of the 10 books listed were helped more than a little by the simultaneous appearance of blockbuster movies (the film of *Gorky Park*, however, appeared a year later than the book's success), while *The Great Gatsby* was unusual in that the book was a reissue published to coincide with the film starring Robert Redford, F. Scott Fitzgerald's novel having been first published almost 50 years earlier.

THE TOP 10 LITERARY PRIZES AND AWARDS IN THE UK

	Prize/award	Category	Total value (£)
1	David Cohen British Literature Prize	'Lifetime's achievement' award of £30,000 + £10,000 to enable the writer to produce new work	40,000
2	Whitbread Book of the Year	Books by residents of the UK or Ireland; first prize £20,500 + five other prizes of £2,000	30,500
3	NCR Book Award for Non-fiction	Best non-fiction book; first prize £25,000 + three prizes of £1,500	29,500
4	The Ian St James Awards	Unpublished fiction; 12 prizes	28,000
5 =	Eric Gregory Award	For poets under 30; total varies, but at least:	25,000
5 =	Betty Trask Awards	First novel of a traditional or romantic nature by authors under 35; total value more than:	25,000
5 =	Wolfson History Prizes	Historical works	25,000
8	Kraszna-Kranz Award	Books on still and movie photography; three prizes	22,500
9 =	Booker Prize	Best novel in English	20,000
9 =	Science Book Prizes	Sponsored by Rhône-Poulenc Ltd, for science books; adult and junior categories	20,000
9 =	Sunday Express Book of the Year	Fiction	20,000

While the Booker Prize attracts the most publicity, there are numerous other valuable literary prizes awarded in the UK. Those that are not exclusively British, and writing bursaries awarded to enable writers to survive while working on their books, are not included. The newly established David Cohen British Literature Prize was first awarded in 1993 (to V.S. Naipaul). In addition, there are many other awards of £10,000 or less – some for as little as £100 or just a certificate or gift, such as the bronze eggs given to winners of the Mother Goose Award or the diamond dagger received by Crime Writers' Association Award winners. The qualifications for entry for some prizes are very specialized, such as the Calvin and Rose G. Hoffman Prize, worth at least £7,500, which is awarded for the best work on Christopher Marlowe, and the Pro Dogs Open Creative Writing Competition, with £200 prizes for the best short stories or poems about a dog. Citizens of Ireland (or residents of more than three years) are in a more privileged position than British writers, as they alone are eligible for the biggest literary award in the British Isles – the triennial IR£50,000 Guinness Peat Aviation Prize for Irish Writing.

10 CHILD AUTHORS

1 Hans Christian Andersen (1805–1875)

Danish author of fairy tales, he published his appropriately titled *Youthful Attempts* when he was 17. Of 300 copies printed, just 17 were sold, the rest being acquired by a grocer who used the paper to wrap goods. However, a novel and his *Fairy Tales Told for Children*, both dating from 1835, made Andersen's international reputation.

2 Daisy Ashford (1881–1972)

Living in Lewes, Daisy Ashford wrote *The Young Visiters* [sic] when she was nine. It was published in 1919 with a foreword by Peter Pan author, J.M. Barrie – who was consequently believed by many to have written it. The book became a bestseller and has been in print ever since, along with other childhood writings issued after its success.

3 Jane Austen (1775–1817)

Regarded as one of England's greatest novelists, Jane Austen wrote an ambitious *History of England* at the age of 15, which her sister Cassandra illustrated with watercolours that are as naïve in their style as Jane's early spelling.

4 Mina Drouet (born 1947)

French poet Mina Drouet issued *Arbre Mon Ami* ('My Friend The Tree'), which was published in English as *First Poems*, in 1956, when she was eight. Mina was put to various tests by literary experts who could not believe she had written the poems unaided, but she passed them with flying colours.

5 John Evelyn (1620–1706)

British writer Evelyn began to keep notes for his *Diary*, one of the best-known records of daily life in England during the seventeenth century, when he was an 11-year-old schoolboy – coincidentally in Lewes, where Daisy Ashford later embarked on her precocious writing career.

6 Mary Godwin (1797–1851)

Later famous under her married name, Mary Shelley, as the author of *Frankenstein*, she wrote *Mounseer Nongtonpaw; or, the Discoveries of John Bull in a Trip to Paris* when aged 11. It was published by her father, William Godwin, in 1808.

7 Francis Hawkins (1628–81)

British writer Hawkins was aged eight when he translated *Youths Behaviour* [sic] from the French, although it was not published until about 1641.

8 Felicia Hemans (1793–1835)

British poet Hemans, who wrote 'The Boy Stood on the Burning Deck', had her first verses published in 1808, when she was aged 14. In 1836 they were reissued with the descriptive title *Early Blossoms: A collection of poems written between eight and fifteen years of age*.

9 S.E. (Susan Eloise) Hinton (born 1950?)

At the age of 17 (or possibly 19 – different authorities give her year of birth as 1948 or 1950) American children's novelist Hinton published *The Outsiders*, which was made into a 1983 Hollywood film (in which she herself appeared in a cameo role as a nurse). Her 1975 novel *Rumble Fish* also became a film.

10 Jerome Siegel (born 1914)

American writer Siegel (and artist Joseph Shuster, also born 1914) was aged 19 when he created *Superman* in 1933, originally designing it as a newspaper comic strip. Siegel and Shuster sold the rights to their creation to Detective Comics, which first published it in comic book form in June 1938.

THE TOP 10 BRITISH NATIONAL DAILY NEWSPAPERS

	Newspaper	Average daily sale (1992)
1	*Daily Mirror/Daily Record* (Scotland)	3,558,753
2	*The Sun*	3,554,833
3	*Daily Mail*	1,735,737
4	*Daily Express*	1,529,273
5	*Daily Telegraph*	1,038,792
6	*Daily Star*	805,571
7	*Today*	539,284
8	*The Guardian*	411,509
9	*The Times*	381,854
10	*The Independent*	372,243

The 11th bestselling daily newspaper in Great Britain is the *Financial Times*, with total average worldwide daily sales during this period of 288,495 copies (including editions published in Frankfurt and New York). The combined sales of all the 'quality' daily newspapers (*Daily Telegraph*, *Guardian*, *The Times*, *Independent* and *Financial Times*) are more than 1,000,000 fewer than those of the *Sun* and the *Daily Mirror*.

THE TOP 10 BRITISH NATIONAL SUNDAY NEWSPAPERS

	Newspaper	Average sales per issue (1992)
1	News of the World	4,700,208
2	Sunday Mirror	2,692,654
3	The People	2,079,902
4	Mail on Sunday	1,984,123
5	Sunday Express	1,765,278
6	Sunday Times	1,195,227
7	Sunday Telegraph	573,897
8	Observer	533,325
9	Independent on Sunday	404,534
10	Sunday Sport	299,477

A total of more than 16 million copies of the Top 10 Sunday newspapers are sold every week.

THE TOP 10 DAILY NEWSPAPERS IN THE WORLD*

	Newspaper	Country	Average daily circulation
1	Yomiuri Shimbun	Japan	8,700,000
2	Asahi Shimbun	Japan	7,400,000
3	People's Daily	China	6,000,000
4	Bild Zeitung	Germany	5,900,000
5	Wall Street Journal	USA	1,857,131 **
6	USA Today	USA	1,429,024
7	Los Angeles Times	USA	1,242,864 †
8	New York Times	USA	1,209,225 ‡
9	New York Daily News	USA	1,180,139
10	Washington Post	USA	838,902 §

*Excluding the UK – see The Top 10 British National Daily Newspapers.

**National edition; Eastern edition average 798,515.

†Daily; Sunday 1,576,425.

‡Daily; Sunday 1,762,015.

§Daily; Sunday 1,165,567.

The Russian joke used to be that there was no news in *Pravda* (which means 'truth') and no *pravda* in the news; now, as a result of the upheavals in the former Soviet Union, there is no *Pravda*, the newspaper which formerly topped this list with (probably untruthful) sales of 10,700,000 copies a day. Sales of another Russian daily, *Isvestia*, were once reported as exceeding 8,600,000, but in the absence of recent accurate data for any Russian newspaper, it is misleading to include them.

THE TOP 10 UK REGIONAL NEWSPAPERS

	Newspaper	Average sales per issue
1	Evening Standard (London)	483,626
2	Manchester Evening News	237,722 *
3	West Midlands Express & Star	228,066
4	Birmingham Evening Mail	213,889 **
5	Liverpool Echo	183,662 #
6	Glasgow Evening Times	156,969 †
7	Birmingham Sunday Mercury	153,684
8	Belfast Telegraph (Evening)	138,001
9	Newcastle Evening Chronicle	133,277 ‡
10	Yorkshire Evening Post (Leeds)	129,629 §

*Monday to Friday (Saturday 216,358).

**Monday to Friday (Saturday 201,565).

#Monday to Friday (Saturday 150,454).

†Monday to Friday (Saturday 104,171).

‡Monday to Friday (Saturday 114,567).

§Monday to Friday (Saturday 110,809).

THE 10 LONGEST-RUNNING CHILDREN'S COMICS AND MAGAZINES IN THE UK

	Publication	First issue
1	Scouting (name changed from The Scouter, 1971)	1 Jan 1923
2	Dandy	4 Dec 1937
3	Beano	30 Jul 1938
4	Beezer and Topper	21 Jan 1956/7 Feb 1953 *
5	Bunty	14 Jan 1958
6	Mandy and Judy	21 Jan 1967/16 Jan 1960 †
7	Buster (incorporating Whizzer & Chips#)	28 May 1960
8	Victor	25 Feb 1961
9	The Brownie (monthly)	Jan 1962
10	Plus (monthly)	Jan 1966

*Amalgamated 22 September 1990.

†Amalgamated 18 May 1991.

#First published 18 October 1969; amalgamated 3 November 1990.

THE 10 OLDEST PERIODICALS IN PRINT IN THE UK

	Periodical*	Founded
1	Philosophical Transactions of the Royal Society	1665
2	Archaeologia (Journal of the Society of Antiquaries)	1770
3	Curtis's Botanical Magazine	1787
4	The Lancet	1823
5	The Spectator	1828
6	Royal Society of Edinburgh Proceedings	1832
7	Gospel Standard	1835
8	British Medical Journal	1840
9	Jewish Chronicle	1841
10	The Friend	1843

*Includes only those continuously published under their original titles.

The Philosophical Transactions of the Royal Society was first published on 6 March 1665. The magazine Tatler, which appeared on 12 April 1709, ceased publication in 1711; the present-day magazine of this name was founded at a later date, and is hence ineligible for this list. Punch, first published on 17 July 1841, was a member of this august body until its closure in 1992, its last issue appearing on 8 April. Once Britain's foremost humour magazine, it had reached its peak circulation in the 1940s, selling about 170,000 copies a week , but had declined to little more than 30,000 by the time it ceased publication.

THE TOP 10 MAGAZINES IN THE UK

	Magazine	Average sale per issue
1	Radio Times	1,562,770
2	Reader's Digest	1,542,885
3	What's on TV	1,401,031
4	Take a Break	1,368,792
5	Bella	1,161,442
6	National Trust Magazine	1,125,625
7	TV Times	1,109,358
8	Viz	922,338
9	Woman's Weekly	864,305
10	Prima	740,787

Billed as 'The Official Organ of the BBC', the Radio Times, the UK's bestselling magazine, was first published on 28 September 1923 priced twopence. Its sales have been overtaken on occasions by its close rival, Reader's Digest, which had its origins during the First World War. In 1916, American bank clerk DeWitt Wallace published a booklet called Getting the Most Out of Farming, which consisted of extracts from various US Government agricultural publications. While recovering after being wounded in France during the war, he contemplated applying the same principle to a general interest magazine and in 1920 produced a sample copy of Reader's Digest. He and his new wife, Lila Acheson, solicited sales by subscription and published 5,000 copies of the first issue in February 1922. It was an enormous success, rapidly becoming America's bestselling monthly magazine. The British office opened in 1938 followed by further branches throughout the world: today 41 editions are published in 17 languages. The Wallaces became notable philanthropists, supporting in particular the Arts. Lila Wallace, for example, sponsored the restoration of Monet's garden at Giverny. DeWitt died in 1981 and Lila Wallace in 1984.

Madonna's tally of Top 10 hits puts her well ahead of the rest of the field.

THE 10 FEMALE SINGERS WITH THE MOST TOP 10 HITS IN THE USA AND UK*

	Artist	Hits
1	Madonna	30
2	Diana Ross (including one duet each with Marvin Gaye and Lionel Richie)	22
3 =	Aretha Franklin (including one duet each with George Michael and the Eurythmics)	18
3 =	Olivia Newton-John (including two duets with John Travolta and one with ELO)	18
3 =	Donna Summer (including one duet with Barbra Streisand)	18
6	Connie Francis	17
7 =	Brenda Lee	16
7 =	Kylie Minogue (including one duet with Jason Donovan, and one with Keith Washington)	16
9 =	Petula Clark	14
9 =	Whitney Houston	14

*To 31 December 1992.

The hitmaking careers of some of these artists have either slowed down or ceased altogether in recent years. Only Madonna, Kylie Minogue, Diana Ross and Whitney Houston, of those listed, have had Top 10 hits so far in the 1990s, and Ms Ciccone seems likely to further widen the gap between herself and the rest of the field as the decade progresses, while the likes of Tina Turner, Janet Jackson and Paula Abdul are waiting in the wings to join the list.

THE 10 ACTS WITH MOST GOLD ALBUMS IN THE USA

	Artist	Gold albums
1	Elvis Presley	60
2	Rolling Stones	34
3	Barbra Streisand	30
4	Elton John	26
5	Beatles	25
6	Neil Diamond	23
7	Bob Dylan	21
8	Kenny Rogers	20
9 =	Frank Sinatra	19
9 =	Chicago	19

This award, made by the Recording Industry Association of America, the trade association of record companies in the United States, confirms a minimum sale of 500,000 copies of an album. The RIAA began certification for gold records in 1958, when the *Oklahoma Original Soundtrack* was awarded the first such honour.

50 YEARS ON

Pop music is so avowedly an offshoot of the youth cult that emerged in the 1960s that it seems incongruous to note that increasing numbers of rockers from that era are approaching (or, in some instances have passed) their half-centuries. Some, of course, didn't make it: Elvis Presley would have been 50 in 1985, Buddy Holly in 1986, John Lennon in 1990 and Jimi Hendrix in 1992. But surviving and ever-youthful stars such as Little Richard turned 50 in 1985, Bill Wyman in 1986 and Tina Turner in 1989. Gary Glitter, who has made a profession of being a geriatric songster, as exemplified in his advertisements for young persons' railcards, hit 50 in 1990 – as did Cliff Richard, followed in 1991 by Charlie Watts of the Stones, Bob Dylan and both Paul Simon and Art Garfunkel. Paul McCartney reached 50 in 1992 and Mick Jagger in 1993. Two members of the Who will be 50 in 1995: Pete Townshend and Roger Daltrey, who may find some irony in singing the *My Generation* lyrics 'I hope I die before I get old'. Is advancing age a drawback in the chart singles business? Only three singers have topped the UK charts after their 50th year, Frank Sinatra and Telly Savalas at 51, with Louis Armstrong holding the record with *What A Wonderful World* which attained the No. 1 spot when he was aged 67 years 10 months, while Honor Blackman is the only artist apart from Sinatra and Armstrong to have a Top 10 hit after the age of 60 (she was 64 when her novelty record *Kinky Boots* entered the Top 10).

THE TOP 10 BEACH BOYS SINGLES IN THE UK

	Title	Year
1	*Good Vibrations*	1966
2	*Sloop John B*	1966
3	*God Only Knows*	1966
4	*Do It Again*	1968
5	*Cottonfields*	1970
6	*I Get Around*	1964
7	*Then I Kissed Her*	1967
8	*Barbara Ann*	1966
9	*Break Away*	1969
10	*Lady Lynda*	1979

Good Vibrations was also a Top 20 hit when reissued a decade after its initial success, cementing its status as the Beach Boys' biggest UK seller by far. By contrast, the group's belated all-time United States top-seller, 1988's *Kokomo*, was only a middling British success, and registers nowhere near the Top 10 listing. The group were also co-vocalists on the Fat Boys' revival of *Wipe Out* in 1987; this single would appear at number 8 if included here.

Dennis Wilson, drummer/vocalist with the Beach Boys, and brother of group co-founder Brian Wilson, was born in Inglewood, California, on 4 December 1944. He would have celebrated his 50th birthday in 1994, but was tragically drowned in a swimming accident on 28 December 1983.

THE TOP 10 SONGS OF 1944 IN THE UK

	Title	Artist
1	*All Or Nothing At All*	Frank Sinatra
2	*Cocktails For Two*	Spike Jones
3	*Don't Fence Me In*	Bing Crosby
4	*Into Each Life Some Rain Must Fall*	Ella Fitzgerald and the Ink Spots
5	*Is You Is Or Is You Ain't My Baby?*	Louis Jordan
6	*Moonlight In Vermont*	Margaret Whiting
7	*Rum And Coca Cola*	Andrews Sisters
8	*Swinging On A Star*	Bing Crosby
9	*Too-Ra-Loo-Ra-Loo-Ral*	Bing Crosby
10	*You Always Hurt The One You Love*	Mills Brothers

Since there were no actual charts, either of record or sheet music sales, 50 years ago in the UK, determining popularity in strict rank order is not possible, so the 10 songs above are listed alphabetically by title. All are claimed or estimated to have sold 1,000,000 copies in 1944 (though gold discs were unknown at the time too), on a global basis. Clearly, Bing Crosby was the biggest-selling artist of the year.

Frank Sinatra's *All Or Nothing At All* was the No. 1 single of 1944.

THE TOP 10 WHO SINGLES IN THE UK

	Title	Year
1	Substitute	1966/1976
2	My Generation	1965
3	I'm A Boy	1966
4	Happy Jack	1966
5	Pinball Wizard	1969
6	Pictures Of Lily	1966
7	I Can't Explain	1965
8	I Can See For Miles	1967
9	Won't Get Fooled Again	1971
10	Anyway, Anyhow Anywhere,	1965

Substitute was the Who's largest UK seller by virtue of having been issued and charted twice – the 1966 original reaching the Top 5 (a legal battle at the time meant that three different pressings, with forced withdrawals in between, all appeared with different B-sides), and the 1976 reissue, which was the UK's first commercially released 12" single, climbing to No. 7.

John Alex Entwistle, guitarist with the Who, was born in Chiswick, London on 9 October 1944.

THE TOP 10 QUEEN SINGLES IN THE UK

	Title	Year
1	Bohemian Rhapsody	1975/1991
2	Under Pressure (with David Bowie)	1981
3	We Are The Champions	1977
4	Radio Ga-Ga	1984
5	Killer Queen	1974
6	I Want To Break Free	1984
7	Crazy Little Thing Called Love	1979
8	Somebody To Love	1976
9	A Kind Of Magic	1986
10	Innuendo	1991

Ironically, it was Freddie Mercury's death in 1991 that resulted in Queen's achieving the UK's all-time second-bestselling single with Bohemian Rhapsody, which topped 2,000,000 UK sales after it returned to No. 1 16 years after its original triumph. Oddly, Queen's best-ever US seller, Another One Bites the Dust (1980), does not appear in the list here, having climbed to only No. 7 on the UK chart.

THE TOP 10 DIANA ROSS SINGLES IN THE UK

	Title	Year
1	Chain Reaction	1986
2	I'm Still Waiting	1971
3	Upside Down	1980
4	When You Tell Me That You Love Me	1991
5	Theme From 'Mahogany' (Do You Know Where You're Going To?)	1976
6	Why Do Fools Fall In Love	1981
7	Ain't No Mountain High Enough	1970
8	Endless Love (duet with Lionel Richie)	1981
9	You Are Everything (duet with Marvin Gaye)	1974
10	Touch Me In The Morning	1973

The ageless Diana Ross has been making hit records since 1964.

This Top 10 does not include records on which Diana Ross sang as lead vocalist of the Supremes in the 1960s, but if it did, numbers 5 to 10 in the list would all be ousted by Supremes' hits. Worth noting is the fact that three of Diana's four top UK sellers were not even Top 40 hits in the United States (Upside Down being the exception).

Diana Ross was born in Detroit, Michigan, on 26 March 1944.

A wish unfulfilled: The Who were born in 1964 and, contrary to their My Generation lyrics – and with the exception of drummer Keith Moon – they did not die before they got old.

THE 10 MOST EXPENSIVE ITEMS OF ROCK STARS' CLOTHING SOLD AT AUCTION IN THE UK

	Item/sale	Price (£)*
1	Elvis Presley's one-piece 'Shooting Star' stage outfit, c1972	
	Phillips, London, 24 August 1988	28,600
2	John Lennon's black leather jacket, c1960–62	
	Christie's, London, 7 May 1992	24,200
3	Four 'super hero'-style costumes worn by glam rock group Kiss in the film *Kiss Meets the Phantom* (1978)	
	Christie's, London, 14 May 1993	20,900
4	Michael Jackson's white rhinestone glove	
	Christie's, London, 19 December 1991	16,500
5	Elvis Presley's blue stage costume, c1972	
	Phillips, London, 24 August 1988	15,400
6	Jimi Hendrix's black felt hat	
	Sotheby's, London, 22 August 1991	14,300
7	Elvis Presley's one-piece stage costume, as worn on the cover of his *Burning Love* album	
	Phillips, London, 25 August 1992	13,200
8	Elton John's giant Dr Marten boots from the film *Tommy*	
	Sotheby's, London, 6 September 1988	12,100
9 =	Michael Jackson's black sequinned jacket	
	Sotheby's, London, 22 August 1991	11,000
9 =	Prince's *Purple Rain* stage costume, 1984	
	Christie's, London, 19 December 1991	11,000

*Including 10 per cent buyer's premium.

Close runners-up in the second-hand rock star clothing market include two of Madonna's gold basques, designed by Jean Paul Gaultier, one of which made £9,900 at Sotheby's, London, on 27 August 1992, and another, which was auctioned twice – at Sotheby's, London, on 22 August 1991, when it fetched £8,800 and again on 27 August 1992, when it realized £9,000. Another of Prince's *Purple Rain* stage costumes was sold at Christie's, London, on 8 May 1992 for £9,020, and Michael Jackson's studded black leather jacket at Sotheby's, London, on 22 August 1991 for £7,480.

THE 10 MOST EXPENSIVE ITEMS OF POP MEMORABILIA EVER SOLD AT AUCTION*

	Item/sale	Price (£)**
1	John Lennon's 1965 Rolls-Royce Phantom V touring limousine, finished in psychedelic paintwork	
	Sotheby's, New York, 29 June 1985 ($2,299,000)	1,768,462
2	Jimi Hendrix's Fender *Stratocaster* guitar	
	Sotheby's, London, 25 April 1990	198,000
3	Buddy Holly's Gibson acoustic guitar, c1945, in a tooled leather case made by Holly	
	Sotheby's, New York, 23 June 1990 ($242,000)	139,658
4	John Lennon's 1970 Mercedes-Benz 600 Pullman four-door limousine	
	Christie's, London, 27 April 1989	137,500
5	Elvis Presley's 1963 Rolls-Royce Phantom V touring limousine	
	Sotheby's, London, 28 August 1986	110,000
6	Elvis Presley's Martin D-18 guitar (formerly with a $5,000,000 asking price)	
	Red Baron Antiques, Atlanta, Georgia, 3 October 1991 ($180,000)	106,825
7	Elvis Presley's 1942 Martin D18 acoustic guitar (used to record his first singles, 1954–56)	
	Christie's, London, 14 May 1993	99,000
8	Buddy Holly's Fender *Stratocaster* guitar, 1958	
	Sotheby's, New York, 23 June 1990 ($110,000)	63,481
9	John Lennon's handwritten lyrics for *A Day In The Life*	
	Sotheby's, London, 27 August 1992	48,400
10	Elton John's 1977 Panther de Ville Coupé	
	Sotheby's, London, 22 August 1991	46,200

*Excluding rock stars' clothing – see separate list.

**Including 10 per cent buyer's premium, where appropriate.

Pioneered particularly by Sotheby's in London, pop memorabilia has become big business – especially if it involves personal association with mega-stars such as the Beatles and, latterly, Buddy Holly. In addition to the Top 10, high prices have also been paid for other musical instruments once owned by notable rock stars, such as a guitar belonging to John Entwistle of the Who and pianos that were once owned by Paul McCartney and John Lennon.

MUSIC

U2's *The Joshua Tree* was voted one of Radio 1 listeners' favourite albums of all time.

BBC RADIO 1 LISTENERS' 10 FAVOURITE ALBUMS OF ALL TIME

	Title	Artist	Year
1	*Stars*	Simply Red	1991
2	*Sgt Pepper's Lonely Hearts Club Band*	Beatles	1967
3	*The Joshua Tree*	U2	1987
4	*Bat Out Of Hell*	Meat Loaf	1978
5	*Dark Side Of The Moon*	Pink Floyd	1973
6	*Out Of Time*	R.E.M.	1991
7	*Thriller*	Michael Jackson	1982
8	*Brothers In Arms*	Dire Straits	1985
9	*Automatic For The People*	R.E.M.	1992
10	*Nevermind*	Nirvana	1991

This Top 10 comes from an 'All-time Top 100' chart compiled in 1993 by Radio 1 and the *Daily Mail* from some 35,000 votes cast. As with the Radio 1 Listeners' 10 Favourite Singles list, there is a mixture of 'classics' and relative newcomers, with some perhaps surprising omissions from the Top 100, among them Whitney Houston, the Rolling Stones, Tina Turner and Stevie Wonder, while the presence (at number 35) of an album by the Levellers is a reflection of the loyalty of the band's following – and hence high-volume voting – rather than a measure of its national popularity.

BBC RADIO 1 LISTENERS' 10 FAVOURITE SINGLES OF ALL TIME

	Title	Artist
1	*Bohemian Rhapsody*	Queen
2	*Stairway To Heaven*	Led Zeppelin
3	*(Everything I Do) I Do It For You*	Bryan Adams
4	*Imagine*	John Lennon
5	*Baker Street*	Gerry Rafferty
6	*Layla*	Derek & The Dominos
7	*Careless Whisper*	George Michael
8	*I'm Not In Love*	10cc
9	*Hey Jude*	Beatles
10	*Bat Out Of Hell*	Meat Loaf

Based on a survey conducted by BBC Radio 1FM in association with Pepsi, 31 August 1992.

THE TOP 10 FEMALE GROUPS OF ALL TIME IN THE UK*

	Group	No. 1	Top 10	Top 20
1	Supremes	1	13	17
2	Bananarama	–	9	14
3	Three Degrees	1	5	7
4	Sister Sledge	1	4	7
5	Nolans	–	3	7
6	Bangles	1	3	5
7	Mel and Kim	–	4	4
8	Salt'n'Pepa	–	3	4
9	Pointer Sisters	–	2	5
10	Beverley Sisters	–	2	4

*To 31 March 1992. Ranked according to total number of hits.

The Supremes also had three other Top 20 hits which have not been included because they were recorded in partnership with Motown male groups Four Tops and Temptations. However, Bananarama's charity revival of *Help!*, shared with comediennes Dawn French and Jennifer Saunders, has been included since all the participants are female.

THE FIRST TOP 10 SINGLES CHART IN THE USA

	Title	Artist
1	I'll Never Smile Again	Tommy Dorsey
2	The Breeze And I	Jimmy Dorsey
3	Imagination	Glenn Miller
4	Playmates	Kay Kyser
5	Fools Rush In	Glenn Miller
6	Where Was I	Charlie Barnet
7	Pennsylvania 6-5000	Glenn Miller
8	Imagination	Tommy Dorsey
9	Sierra Sue	Bing Crosby
10	Make-Believe Island	Mitchell Ayres

This was the first singles Top 10 compiled by *Billboard* magazine, for its issue dated 20 July 1940. Since the 7" 45-rpm single was still the best part of a decade in the future, all these would have been 10" 78-rpm discs. Note the almost total domination of big-name big bands more than a half century ago – and spare a thought for Mitchell Ayres, who crept in at the bottom of this very first chart, and then never had a hit again.

Tommy Dorsey's *I'll Never Smile Again* topped the first singles chart in the USA.

THE TOP 10 SINGLES OF ALL TIME WORLDWIDE

	Title	Artist	Sales exceed
1	White Christmas	Bing Crosby	30,000,000
2	Rock Around The Clock	Bill Haley & His Comets	17,000,000
3	I Want To Hold Your Hand	Beatles	12,000,000
4	It's Now Or Never	Elvis Presley	10,000,000
5 =	Hound Dog/Don't Be Cruel	Elvis Presley	9,000,000
5 =	Diana	Paul Anka	9,000,000
7 =	Hey Jude	Beatles	8,000,000
7 =	I'm A Believer	Monkees	8,000,000
9 =	Can't Buy Me Love	Beatles	7,000,000
9 =	Do They Know It's Christmas?	Band Aid	7,000,000
9 =	We Are The World	USA For Africa	7,000,000

Global sales are notoriously difficult to calculate, particularly in countries outside the UK and USA and especially in the Far East. 'Worldwide' is thus usually taken to mean the known minimum 'western world' sales. Bing Crosby's 1942 record, *White Christmas*, is indisputably the all-time bestselling single, and the *song*, recorded by others and sold as sheet music, has also achieved such enormous sales that it would additionally appear in first position in any list of bestselling songs.

THE TOP 10 ONE-HIT WONDERS IN THE UK

	Artist	Title	Year
1	Simon Park Orchestra	Eye Level	1973
2	Archies	Sugar Sugar	1969
3	Clive Dunn	Grandad	1971
4	Joe Dolce Music Theatre	Shaddup You Face	1981
5	St Winifred's School Choir	There's No One Quite Like Grandma	1980
6	Phyllis Nelson	Move Closer	1985
7	Fern Kinney	Together We Are Beautiful	1980
8	Lee Marvin	Wand'rin' Star	1970
9	Kalin Twins	When	1958
10	Ricky Valance	Tell Laura I Love Her	1960

These represent the 10 biggest-selling UK No. 1 hits by acts who never had another chart success in this country apart from that solitary chart-topper. One-off acts like Band Aid are excluded from the list because they were made up of individuals who were hitmakers in their own right.

THE BENSON AND HEDGES TOP 10 OF EVERYTHING 1994

THE TOP 10 SINGLES OF ALL TIME IN THE UK

	Title	Artist	Year	Approximate UK sales
1	Do They Know It's Christmas?	Band Aid	1984	3,510,000
2	Bohemian Rhapsody	Queen	1975/1991	2,130,000
3	Mull Of Kintyre	Wings	1977	2,050,000
4	Rivers Of Babylon/Brown Girl In The Ring	Boney M	1978	1,995,000
5	She Loves You	Beatles	1963	1,890,000
6	You're The One That I Want	John Travolta and Olivia Newton-John	1978	1,870,000
7	Relax	Frankie Goes To Hollywood	1984	1,800,000
8	Mary's Boy Child/Oh My Lord	Boney M	1978	1,790,000
9	I Just Called To Say I Love You	Stevie Wonder	1984	1,775,000
10	I Want To Hold Your Hand	Beatles	1963	1,640,000

A total of 46 singles have sold over 1,000,000 copies apiece in the UK during the last 40 years, and these are the cream of that crop. The Band Aid single had a host of special circumstances surrounding it, and it is difficult to imagine, even if a similarly special case arose in the future, such sales ever being approached again by a single in this country. Two years, 1978 and 1984, were the all-time strongest for million-selling singles, and this chart fittingly has three representatives from each. Prior to the huge sales of Queen's *Bohemian Rhapsody* in the wake of Freddie Mercury's death in 1991, it stood at number 23 in this list, its elevation to the Top 10 ousting Ken Dodd's *Tears* (1965).

THE 10 SINGLES THAT STAYED LONGEST IN THE UK CHARTS

	Title	Artist	First chart entry	Weeks in charts
1	My Way	Frank Sinatra	1969	122
2	Amazing Grace	Judy Collins	1970	67
3	Rock Around The Clock	Bill Haley & His Comets	1955	57
4	Release Me	Engelbert Humperdinck	1967	56
5	Stranger On The Shore	Mr Acker Bilk	1961	55
6	Relax	Frankie Goes To Hollywood	1983	52
7	Blue Monday	New Order	1983	49
8	I Love You Because	Jim Reeves	1964	47
9	Let's Twist Again	Chubby Checker	1961	44
10	White Lines (Don't Don't Do It)	Grandmaster Flash and Melle Mel	1983	43

THE TOP 10 CHRISTMAS SINGLES OF ALL TIME IN THE UK

	Title	Artist	Year
1	Do They Know It's Christmas?	Band Aid	1984
2	Mary's Boy Child/Oh My Lord	Boney M	1978
3	Last Christmas	Wham!	1984
4	Merry Christmas Everybody	Slade	1973
5	Mary's Boy Child	Harry Belafonte	1957
6	White Christmas	Bing Crosby	1977 *
7	Mistletoe And Wine	Cliff Richard	1988
8	When A Child Is Born	Johnny Mathis	1976
9	Happy Xmas (War Is Over)	John Lennon	1980 *
10	Lonely This Christmas	Mud	1974

Year of highest chart position.

Band Aid's *Do They Know It's Christmas?* has now sold over 3,500,000 copies in the UK alone. Slade's *Merry Christmas Everybody* has charted on eight seasonal occasions. Bing Crosby's *White Christmas*, despite having sold over 30,000,000 copies worldwide since 1942, charted for the first time in the UK as late as 1977, a few weeks after the singer's death.

THE 10 UK CHART SINGLES WITH THE LONGEST TITLES

	Title	Artist	Highest chart position	Year	No. of letters
1	I'm In Love With The Girl On A Certain Manchester Megastore Checkout Desk	Freshies	54	1981	60
2	If I Said You Had A Beautiful Body Would You Hold It Against Me?	Bellamy Brothers	3	1979	50
3	Gilly Gilly Ossenfeffer Katzenallen Bogen By The Sea	Max Bygraves	7	1954	45
4 =	There's A Guy Works Down The Chipshop Swears He's Elvis	Kirsty MacColl	14	1981	44
4 =	Have You Seen Your Mother, Baby, Standing In The Shadow?	Rolling Stones	5	1966	44
6	When The Girl In Your Arms Is The Girl In Your Heart	Cliff Richard	3	1961	41
7 =	I'm Gonna Sit Right Down And Write Myself A Letter	Billy Williams	22	1957	40
7 =	I'm Gonna Sit Right Down And Write Myself A Letter	Barry Manilow	36	1982	40
8 =	Loving You's A Dirty Job But Someone's Got To Do It	Bonnie Tyler	73	1985	39
8 =	Itsy Bitsy Teeny Weeny Yellow Polka Dot Bikini	Bryan Hyland	8	1960	39
8 =	You Don't Have To Be In The Army To Fight In The War	Mungo Jerry	13	1971	39
8 =	Two Pints Of Lager And A Packet Of Crisps Please	Splodgenessabounds	7	1980	39

This list includes only titles that do not contain words or phrases in brackets. It also includes only chart hits, and thus does not contain such memorable gems as Fairport Convention's 172-letter album track, *Sir B. MacKenzie's Daughter's Lament For The 77th Mounted Lancers' Retreat From The Straits Of Loch Knombe In The Year Of Our Lord 1717, On The Occasion Of The Announcement Of Her Marriage To The Laird Of Kinleakie.*

THE TOP 10 INSTRUMENTAL SINGLES OF ALL TIME IN THE UK

	Title	Artist
1	Stranger On The Shore	Mr Acker Bilk
2	Eye Level	Simon Park Orchestra
3	Telstar	Tornados
4	The Harry Lime Theme (The Third Man)	Anton Karas
5	Amazing Grace	Royal Scots Dragoon Guards Band
6	Chi Mai	Ennio Morricone
7	Wonderful Land	Shadows
8	Apache	Shadows
9	Albatross	Fleetwood Mac
10	Mouldy Old Dough	Lieutenant Pigeon

If this Top 10 reveals anything, it is that non-vocal hits are more likely to be found in the 'middle-of-the-road' sector than in Rock 'n' Roll. Most of these pieces are the equivalent of ballads, with only *Apache*, possibly *Telstar*, and just possibly *Mouldy Old Dough* – which is really a novelty instrumental – qualifying as rock music. The Acker Bilk and Simon Park entries were both UK million-sellers.

The Bellamy Brothers single's 50-letter title makes it only the second longest to achieve a chart place in the UK.

MUSIC

THE TOP 10 ALBUMS OF ALL TIME WORLDWIDE

	Title	Artist
1	Thriller	Michael Jackson
2	Saturday Night Fever	Soundtrack
3	Sgt Pepper's Lonely Hearts Club Band	Beatles
4	Grease	Soundtrack
5	Bridge Over Troubled Water	Simon and Garfunkel
6	Born In The USA	Bruce Springsteen
7	The Sound Of Music	Soundtrack
8	Rumours	Fleetwood Mac
9	Brothers In Arms	Dire Straits
10	Dark Side Of The Moon	Pink Floyd

Total worldwide sales of albums have traditionally been notoriously hard to gauge, but even with the huge expansion of the album market during the 1980s, and multiple million sales of many major releases, it is not thought that anything has overtaken any of this Top 10 in recent times, the sales of most of them being between 15,000,000 and 20,000,000 globally, with *Saturday Night Fever* near 25,000,000, and the apparently uncatchable *Thriller* on 40,000,000.

THE TOP 10 ALBUMS OF ALL TIME IN THE UK

	Title	Artist
1	Sgt Pepper's Lonely Hearts Club Band	Beatles
2	Bad	Michael Jackson
3	Brothers In Arms	Dire Straits
4	Greatest Hits	Queen
5	Stars	Simply Red
6	Thriller	Michael Jackson
7	. . . But Seriously	Phil Collins
8	Bridge Over Troubled Water	Simon and Garfunkel
9	Greatest Hits	Simon and Garfunkel
10	Rumours	Fleetwood Mac

On the occasion of the album's 25th anniversary in 1992, EMI Records conducted new research into the sales of *Sgt Pepper* and concluded that it had sold over 4,250,000 copies in the UK, substantially more than *Brothers In Arms*, which was previously thought to have bettered it. Michael Jackson's *Bad* has now also overtaken *Brothers*, with UK sales of a fraction over 4,000,000 to Dire Straits' 3,600,000. The Queen (sales boosted hugely by Freddie Mercury's death), Simply Red and Michael Jackson *Thriller* albums have each sold over 3,000,000 copies, while all the others in this list have achieved UK sales in excess of 2,500,000.

THE TOP 10 WOMEN IN THE UK ALBUM CHARTS*

1	Madonna		6	Shirley Bassey
2	Barbra Streisand		7	Whitney Houston
3	Diana Ross		8 =	Elkie Brooks
4	Tina Turner		8 =	Nana Mouskouri
5	Kate Bush		10	Donna Summer

Based on total number of weeks their albums have stayed in the UK album charts; up to 31 March 1993.

Madonna leads the field by a long margin, her seven albums having spent a total of more than 520 weeks in the UK charts.

Michael Jackson's *Thriller* album is the bestselling of all time.

THE 10 ALBUMS THAT STAYED LONGEST IN THE UK CHARTS

	Album	Artist	First year in chart
1	Rumours	Fleetwood Mac	1977
2	Bat Out Of Hell	Meat Loaf	1978
3	The Sound Of Music	Original cast	1965
4	Greatest Hits	Queen	1981
5	Bridge Over Troubled Water	Simon and Garfunkel	1970
6	Dark Side Of The Moon	Pink Floyd	1973
7	South Pacific	Original cast	1958
8	Greatest Hits	Simon and Garfunkel	1972
9	Face Value	Phil Collins	1981
10	Tubular Bells	Mike Oldfield	1973

The 10 longest-staying records virtually took up residence in the album charts (the Top 50, 75 or 100, depending on the years during which the charts were compiled), remaining there for periods ranging from over five years for *Tubular Bells* to the astonishing eight-and-a-half-year occupation of Fleetwood Mac's *Rumours*.

Simply Red's *Stars* is the UK's bestselling CD of all time.

UNLIKELY BIRTHPLACES QUIZ

Link these music artists with their places of birth:

1	Holly Johnson (of Frankie Goes To Hollywood)	A	Lucknow, India
2	Glenn Medeiros	B	Dumbarton, Scotland
3	Stewart Copeland (of Police)	C	Kauai, Hawaii
4	Freddie Mercury	D	Khartoum, The Sudan
5	Denny Laine (of Moody Blues and Wings)	E	Zanzibar, Africa
6	Jackson Browne	F	Stockholm, Sweden
7	David Byrne (of Talking Heads)	G	McLeod, Canada
8	Neneh Cherry	H	Alexandria, Egypt
9	Cliff Richard	I	On a boat off the Jersey coast
10	Joni Mitchell	J	Heidelberg, Germany

10 UNLIKELY RECORDING ARTISTS

	Artist	Title	Year
1	Eamonn Andrews (TV presenter)	*Shifting Whispering Sands*	1956
2	Duchess of Bedford	*Luck's In Love With You*	1957
3	Joe Brady (of *Z Cars*)	*The Great Train Robbery*	1963
4	Senator Everett Dirksen	*Gallant Men*	1966
5	John F. Kennedy	*Sing Along With JFK*	1962
6	Freddie Lennon (John's dad)	*That's My Home*	1964
7	Marina (marionette in *Stingray*)	*Marina Speaks*	1965
8	Leonard Nimoy (of *Star Trek*)	*A Visit To A Sad Planet*	1967
9	Harvey Smith (equestrian)	*True Love*	1975
10	Godfrey Winn (journalist)	*I Pass*	1967

Through the years, various figures from public life, including actors, sportsmen, TV personalities and politicians have been persuaded to make pop singles, of which this list is a random selection; one of them, *Gallant Men* (a spoken piece by a serving US Senate member), actually made the US charts at the end of 1966. The only involuntary effort was by JFK: an enterprising arranger named Hank Levine heard some tapes of Kennedy quoting some song lyrics during a speech, and dubbed a rock backing track on to these. The resulting tongue-in-cheek *Sing Along* EP was withdrawn immediately after the President's assassination, and is now exceedingly rare.

THE TOP 10 CDs OF ALL TIME IN THE UK

	Title	Artist
1	*Stars*	Simply Red
2	*Bad*	Michael Jackson
3	*Brothers In Arms*	Dire Straits
4	*Greatest Hits*	Queen
5	*Thriller*	Michael Jackson
6	*. . . But Seriously*	Phil Collins
7	*The Immaculate Collection*	Madonna
8	*Whitney*	Whitney Houston
9	*Tango In The Night*	Fleetwood Mac
10	*'The Bodyguard'* Original Soundtrack	Whitney Houston

After two years as the UK bestselling album, most of those sales being on the CD format, Simply Red's *Stars* became, by the end of 1992, the top UK CD seller to date. Meanwhile, new to the Top 10 is a second Whitney Houston entry, in the shape of the soundtrack to her film with Kevin Costner, *The Bodyguard*.

THE FIRST 10 TRACKS BROADCAST ON VIRGIN 1215

	Track	Artist
1	Born To Be Wild	INXS
2	Purple Haze	Cure
3	A Day In The Life	Beatles
4	A Hard Rain's Gonna Fall	Bob Dylan
5	A Kind Of Magic	Queen
6	A New Flame	Simply Red
7	A Sort Of Homecoming	U2
8	Abacab	Genesis
9	Abracadabra	Steve Miller
10	Accidents Will Happen	Elvis Costello

Virgin 1215, Britain's first national commercial pop station, broadcasting on the 1215 AM waveband, went on air on Friday 30 April 1993 – appropriately at 12.15 pm. Introduced by Richard Skinner, the first few minutes of the station's life were marked by its first gaffe when Cure's version of the Jimi Hendrix track *Purple Haze* was announced as *Hey Joe*.

THE TOP 10 CLASSICAL COMPOSERS IN PERFORMANCE, 1992

	Composer	Performances
1	Ludwig van Beethoven	50
2	Wolfgang Amadeus Mozart	33
3	Joseph Haydn	29
4	Gustav Mahler	$25^1/_5$
5 =	Antonin Dvorák	$20^1/_4$
5 =	Peter Tchaikovsky	$20^1/_4$
7	Johannes Brahms	20
8	Dmitri Shostakovich	16
9	Jean Sibelius	15
10	Franz Schubert	12

David Chesterman has been writing to *The Times* every year since 1952, reporting on the 10 composers whose symphonies have been most performed at the Royal Albert, Royal Festival, Barbican and Queen Elizabeth Halls and at St John's, Smith Square, London. His analysis is based on the number of times each composer's work is played, with individual movements counted as fractions of the whole symphony. In 1990 Beethoven took a temporary back seat when Mozart outperformed him – for only the third time in 40 years, the 1991 celebration of the bicentenary of his death resulting in even more concerts featuring his work. Beethoven regained his pre-eminence in 1992, with his 7th Symphony alone performed nine times. In 1991 Dvorák, who had ranked 5th in 1989 but was not even in the Top 10 in 1990, regained his position, maintaining it in 1992, while Sergei Prokofiev and Anton Bruckner, both in the 1991 list, dropped out in 1992. No English composer has ever made the Top 10 but, to apply the jargon of pop music, Ralph Vaughan Williams (11th in 1992) is 'bubbling under'.

THE TOP 10 CLASSICAL ALBUMS OF 1992 IN THE UK

	Title	Artist
1	Essential Opera	Various
2	The Essential Mozart	Various
3	Essential Ballet	Various
4	Beethoven Violin Concerto	Nigel Kennedy/Klaus Tennstedt
5	Vivaldi: The Four Seasons	Nigel Kennedy/ECO
6	Pavarotti In The Park	Luciano Pavarotti
7	The Essential Kiri	Kiri Te Kanawa
8	Brahms Violin Concerto	Nigel Kennedy/LPO/Klaus Tennstedt
9	Three Tenors In Concert	Carreras, Domingo, Pavarotti
10	Tavener: The Protecting Veil	Isserlis/Rozhdestvensky/LSO

Inevitably, the biggest classical music sellers represent the extreme populist end of the market – specifically, in 1992, several 'Essential' samplers of classic repertoire, Nigel Kennedy and the *Three Tenors*. The John Tavener work at number 10 was given a high profile when nominated alongside several rock and jazz albums in the prestigious Mercury Awards for outstanding contemporary music.

The magnificent three: the celebrated 'Three Tenors', Domingo, Carreras and Pavarotti, have maintained a place in the classical albums Top 10 since 1990.

THE 10 MOST PROLIFIC CLASSICAL COMPOSERS

	Composer	Dates	Nationality	Hrs
1	Joseph Haydn	1732–1809	Austrian	340
2	George Handel	1685–1759	German-English	303
3	Wolfgang Amadeus Mozart	1656–91	Austrian	202
4	Johann Sebastian Bach	1685–1750	German	175
5	Franz Schubert	1797–1828	German	134
6	Ludwig van Beethoven	1770–1827	German	120
7	Henry Purcell	1659–95	English	116
8	Giuseppe Verdi	1813–1901	Italian	87
9	Anton Dvorák	1841–1904	Czechoslovakian	79
10 =	Franz Liszt	1811–86	Hungarian	76
10 =	Peter Tchaikovsky	1840–93	Russian	76

The Top 10 ranks classical composers by the total number of hours of music each composed. If the length of the composer's working life is brought into the calculation, Schubert wins: his 134 hours were composed in a career of 18 years, giving an average of 7 hours 27 minutes per annum. The same method would place Tchaikovsky ahead of Liszt: although both composed 76 hours of music, Tchaikovsky worked for 30 years and Liszt for 51, giving them respective annual averages of 2 hours 32 minutes and 1 hour 29 minutes.

THE TOP 10 COMPOSERS ON CLASSIC FM

	Composer	Works played	Total plays*
1	Wolfgang Amadeus Mozart	306	681
2	Johann Sebastian Bach	190	500
3	Ludwig van Beethoven	186	476
4	Georg Friedrich Handel	121	400
5	Frederic Chopin	213	380
6	Peter Tchaikovsky	132	373
7	Franz Schubert	126	339
8	Antonio Vivaldi	174	335
9	Franz Liszt	96	293
10	Antonin Dvorák	93	287

*7 September to 31 December 1992.

The 'Mendelssohn' Stradivarius violin realized £902,000 at auction.

THE 10 MOST EXPENSIVE MUSICAL INSTRUMENTS EVER SOLD AT AUCTION

	Instrument/sale	Price (£)*
1	'Mendelssohn' Stradivarius violin Christie's, London, 21 November 1990	902,000
2	'Cholmondley' Stradivarius violoncello Sotheby's, London, 22 June 1988	682,000
3	Jimi Hendrix's Fender *Stratocaster* guitar Sotheby's, London, 25 April 1990	198,000
4	Steinway grand piano, designed by Lawrence Alma-Tadema and Edward Poynter for Henry Marquand, 1884–87 Sotheby Parke Bernet, New York, 26 March 1980 ($390,000)	163,500
5	Verne Powell platinum flute Christie's, New York, 18 October 1986 ($187,000)	126,200
6	Flemish single-manual harpsichord made by Johan Daniel Dulken of Antwerp, 1755 Sotheby's, London, 27 March 1990	82,280
7	Kirkman double-manual harpsichord Christie's, London, 26 June 1987	77,000
8	Columnar alto recorder made by Hans van Schratt, mid-16th century Christie's, London, 16 March 1988	44,000
9	'Portable Grand Piano' made by John Isaac Hawkins, c1805 (a very early example of an upright piano, considerably pre-dating the modern type, and one of only three examples known) Sotheby's, London, 4 July 1985	14,300
10	Miniature silver horn made by Johann Wilhelm Haas of Nuremberg, 1681 Sotheby's, Geneva, 5 May 1981 (SF46,200)	11,800

*Including 10 per cent buyer's premium, where appropriate.

This list represents the most expensive example of each type of musical instrument only. The two harpsichords and the two pianos are actually of different types, but as each belongs to the same family, it may be argued that numbers 7 and 9 should be disqualified from the ranking – in which case, the contenders for the new numbers 9 and 10 would be a pair of German kettle drums, c1700, formerly the property of the Counts von Geich, sold at Sotheby's, London, on 21 November 1974 for £3,900 – the record price for a percussion instrument – and a Swiss sachbut made by J. Steimer of Zofinger in the early eighteenth century (Sotheby's, London, 6 May 1976, £3,080), which holds the record for a brass instrument (other than the current number 10, which is an unusual miniature model).

MUSIC

THE 10 MOST EXPENSIVE MUSIC MANUSCRIPTS EVER SOLD AT AUCTION

	Manuscript/sale	Price (£)*
1	Nine symphonies by Wolfgang Amadeus Mozart	
	Sotheby's, London, 22 May 1987	2,350,000
2	Ludwig van Beethoven's *Piano Sonata in E Minor*, Opus 90	
	Sotheby's, London, 6 December 1991	1,000,000
3 =	Robert Schumann's *Piano Concerto in A Minor*, Opus 54	
	Sotheby's, London, 22 November 1989	800,000
3 =	Wolfgang Amadeus Mozart's *Fantasia in C Minor* and *Sonata in C Minor*	
	Sotheby's, London, 21 November 1990	800,000
5	Ludwig van Beethoven's first movement of the *Sonata for Violoncello and Piano in A Major*, Opus 69	
	Sotheby's, London, 17 May 1990	480,000
6	Johann Sebastian Bach's cantata *Auf Christi Himmelfahrt allein*	
	Sotheby's, London, 22 November 1989	390,000
7	Igor Stravinsky's *Rite of Spring*	
	Sotheby's, London, 11 November 1982	300,000
8	Franz Schubert's Quartet in B flat Major (No. 8) D.112, Opus 168	
	Christie's, London, 24 June 1992	270,000
9	Johann Sebastian Bach's cantata *O Ewigkeit, Du Donnerwort*	
	Sotheby's, London, 11 November 1982	190,000
10	Franz Schubert's overture to the opera *Fierabras*	
	Sotheby's, London, 28 May 1986	150,000

*'Hammer prices', excluding premiums.

The collection of nine symphonies by Mozart not only holds the record for the highest price ever paid for a music manuscript, but also for any post-medieval manuscript.

THE 10 MOST REQUESTED RECORDS ON *DESERT ISLAND DISCS*

	Composer	Work
1	Ludwig van Beethoven	'O Freunds, nicht diese Tone' (choral) from *Symphony* No. 9
2	Claude Debussy	*Claire de Lune*
3	Edward Elgar	*Pomp and Circumstance*, March No. 1
4	Richard Wagner	'Liebestod' from *Tristan Und Isolde*
5	George Gershwin	*Rhapsody in Blue*
6	Johann Christian Bach/Charles François Goundod	*Ave Maria*
7	Felix Mendelssohn	'Nocturne' from *A Midsummer Night's Dream*
8	Ludwig van Beethoven	*Symphony* No. 5
9	Georg Friedrich Handel	'Hallelujah Chorus' from *Messiah*
10	Giuseppi Verdi	'Dies Irae' from *Requiem*

The Beethoven at number one has been requested by more than 60 'castaways' in the programme's 50-year history.

'Alas! poor Yorrick. I knew him, Horatio' is just one of the 1,422 lines an actor playing Hamlet must remember.

SHAKESPEARE'S 10 MOST DEMANDING ROLES

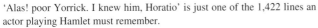

	Role	Play	Lines
1	Hamlet	*Hamlet*	1,422
2	Falstaff	*Henry IV*, Parts I and II	1,178
3	Richard III	*Richard III*	1,124
4	Iago	*Othello*	1,097
5	Henry V	*Henry V*	1,025
6	Othello	*Othello*	860
7	Vincentio	*Measure for Measure*	820
8	Coriolanus	*Coriolanus*	809
9	Timon	*Timon of Athens*	795
10	Antony	*Antony and Cleopatra*	766

Hamlet's role comprises 11,610 words – over 36 per cent of the total number of lines spoken in the play, but if multiple plays are considered, he is beaten by Falstaff who, as well as appearing in *Henry IV*, Parts I and II, also appears in *The Merry Wives of Windsor* where he has 436 lines. His total of 1,614 lines thus makes him the most talkative of all Shakespeare's characters. By the same criterion, Henry V appears (as Prince Hal) in *Henry IV*, where he speaks 117 lines – hence making his total 1,142.

SHAKESPEARE'S FIRST 10 PLAYS

	Play	Approximate year written
1	Titus Andronicus	1588–90
2	Love's Labour's Lost	1590
3	Henry VI, Parts I–III	1590–91
4 =	The Comedy of Errors	1591
4 =	Richard III	1591
4 =	Romeo and Juliet	1591
7	The Two Gentlemen of Verona	1592–93
8	A Midsummer Night's Dream	1593–94
9	Richard II	1594
10	King John	1595

Few authorities agree on the precise dating of Shakespeare's plays. There are only scanty contemporary records of their early performances, and only half of them appeared in print in his lifetime – and even those that were published before his death in 1616 were generally much altered from his originals. It was not until after 1623, with the publication of the so-called 'Folios', that Shakespeare's complete works were progressively published. There is much argument over the dating of Romeo and Juliet, in particular, which may have been written as early as 1591 or as late as 1596–97; if the latter, it would be pre-dated by numbers 7–10 on the list and by The Merchant of Venice (c1596).

THE 10 WORDS MOST USED BY SHAKESPEARE

	Word	Frequency
1	The	27,457
2	And	26,285
3	I	21,206
4	To	19,938
5	Of	17,079
6	A	14,675
7	You	14,326
8	My	13,075
9	That	11,725
10	In	11,511

In his complete works, William Shakespeare wrote a total of 884,647 words – 118,406 lines comprising 31,959 separate speeches. He used a total vocabulary of 29,066 different words, some – such as 'America' – appearing only once (The Comedy of Errors, III.ii), while at the other end of the scale the Top 10 accounts for all those words that he used on more than 10,000 occasions. Perhaps surprisingly, their relative frequency is not dissimilar to what we might encounter in modern usage: supposedly 'Shakespearean' words such as 'prithee' and 'zounds!' actually make a poor showing in the frequency table. A further 18 words appear more than 5,000 times, in descending order: is, not, me, for, it, with, be, his, this, your, he, but, have, as, thou, so, him and will. It should be noted that these statistics are derived from a computer analysis of Shakespeare's works conducted in the late 1960s – which, although comprehensive, was rather ahead of its time, since the software for such a monumental task was much less sophisticated than it would be today – and it is possible that the odd instance of a word's use may have slipped through the net. Reports of missing examples will be gratefully received . . .

SHAKESPEARE'S 10 MOST PRODUCED PLAYS

	Play	Productions
1	As You Like It	62
2	Twelfth Night	58
3	The Merchant of Venice	57
4	Hamlet	56
5	Much Ado About Nothing	55
6	The Taming of the Shrew	54
7	A Midsummer Night's Dream	49
8 =	The Merry Wives of Windsor	46
8 =	Macbeth	46
10	Romeo and Juliet	45

This list, which is based on an analysis of Shakespearean productions at Straford-upon-Avon from 31 December 1878 to 1 January 1991, provides a reasonable picture of his most popular plays. Records do not, however, indicate the total number of individual performances during each production.

SHAKESPEARE'S 10 LONGEST PLAYS

	Play	Lines
1	Hamlet	3,901
2	Richard III	3,886
3	Coriolanus	3,820
4	Cymbeline	3,813
5	Othello	3,672
6	Antony and Cleopatra	3,630
7	Troilus and Cressida	3,576
8	Henry VIII	3,450
9	Henry V	3,368
10	The Winter's Tale	3,354

10 ACTORS WHO HAVE PLAYED HAMLET

1 Sarah Bernhardt

French actress, appeared as Hamlet at the Adelphi Theatre, London, in 1899, and in a French silent film version in 1900.

2 Edwin Booth

American actor, opened as Hamlet in the USA in 1864 for a record run.

3 Richard Burton

British actor, appeared in the role at the Old Vic in 1953 and on film in 1964.

4 Richard Chamberlain

American actor, previously best known for his TV role as Dr Kildare, appeared in a television version of *Hamlet* in 1970. Ian McKellen (1972) and Derek Jacobi (1980) have also played TV Hamlets.

5 Mel Gibson

American film actor, appeared in the 1991 film directed by Franco Zeffirelli, with Glenn Close as Ophelia.

6 Paul Jones

British singer-turned-actor (formerly of rock group Manfred Mann), took the role on stage.

7 Stacy Keach

American film actor, made his stage debut in 1964 in a New York production of *Hamlet*.

8 Laurence Olivier

British actor, appeared in both the title role and directed the 1948 film, the first British production to win a 'Best Picture' Oscar.

9 Innokenti Smoktunovski

Russian actor, starred in a 1964 Soviet film of *Hamlet*, translated by *Doctor Zhivago* author Boris Pasternak.

10 Nicol Williamson

British actor, starred in the 1969 film, with pop singer Marianne Faithfull as Ophelia.

Les Misérables is one of five Andrew Lloyd Webber musicals in the all-time UK Top 10.

THE 10 LONGEST-RUNNING MUSICALS OF ALL TIME IN THE UK

	Show	Performances
1	The Black and White Minstrel Show	6,464
2	Me and My Girl	5,524
3	Cats	4,974 *
4	Oliver!	4,125
5	Starlight Express	3,734 *
6	Jesus Christ, Superstar	3,357
7	Les Misérables	3,034 *
8	Evita	2,900
9	Phantom of the Opera	2,774 *
10	The Sound of Music	2,386

*Still running; total at 31 March 1993.

The Black and White Minstrel Show total includes both the original 10-year run (1962–72) and the 1973 revival. *Me and My Girl* opened at the Victoria Palace on 16 December 1937 and, apart from a brief closure when war was declared in 1939, ran until 29 June 1940, by which time it had achieved 1,646 performances. Revivals in 1941, 1945–46, 1949–50 and 1985–16 January 1993 boosted the total to the present figure, making it the UK's longest-running musical comedy of all time. Total performances of *Oliver!* include runs at different theatres from 1960–66, 1967–68, 1977–80 and 1983–84. On 12 May 1989 *Cats*, which opened in 1981, became the longest continuously running musical in British theatre history. In 1991 *My Fair Lady*, formerly at number 10 with 2,281 performances, was relegated from the list when the continuing run of *Les Misérables* overtook it, and the subsequent entry of *Phantom of the Opera* displaced *Salad Days* (2,283 performances).

THE 10 LONGEST-RUNNING NON-MUSICALS OF ALL TIME IN THE UK

	Show	Performances
1	The Mousetrap	16,796 *
2	No Sex, Please – We're British	6,761
3	Oh! Calcutta!	3,918
4	Run for Your Wife	2,638
5	There's a Girl in My Soup	2,547
6	Pyjama Tops	2,498
7	Sleuth	2,359
8	Boeing Boeing	2,035
9	Blithe Spirit	1,997
10	Worm's Eye View	1,745

*Still running; total at 31 March 1993.

Oh! Calcutta! is included here as it is regarded as a revue with music, rather than a musical.

THE 10 LONGEST-RUNNING COMEDIES OF ALL TIME IN THE UK

	Show	Performances
1	No Sex, Please – We're British	6,761
2	Run for Your Wife	2,638
3	There's a Girl in My Soup	2,547
4	Pyjama Tops	2,498
5	Boeing Boeing	2,035
6	Blithe Spirit	1,997
7	Worm's Eye View	1,745
8	Dirty Linen	1,667
9	Reluctant Heroes	1,610
10	Seagulls Over Sorrento	1,551

THE 10 LONGEST-RUNNING SHOWS OF ALL TIME IN THE UK

	Show	Performances
1	The Mousetrap	16,796 *
2	No Sex, Please – We're British	6,761
3	The Black and White Minstrel Show	6,464
4	Me and My Girl	5,524
5	Cats	4,974 *
6	Oliver!	4,125
7	Oh! Calcutta!	3,918
8	Starlight Express	3,734 *
9	Jesus Christ, Superstar	3,357
10	Les Misérables	3,034 *

Still running; total at 31 March 1993.

All the longest-running shows in the UK have been London productions. *The Mousetrap* opened on 25 November 1952 at the Ambassadors Theatre. After 8,862 performances it transferred to St Martin's Theatre where it re-opened on 25 March 1974. It is not the only play in the world to have run continuously since the 1950s – Eugène Ionesco's *La Cantatrice Chauve et la Leçon* was first performed in Paris on 11 May 1950 and has run continuously since 16 February 1957, clocking up 11,130 performances (to 1 July 1991). It was seen by over 800,000 people – despite being staged in a theatre with just 90 seats.

THE 10 LONGEST-RUNNING MUSICALS OF ALL TIME ON BROADWAY

	Show	Performances
1	A Chorus Line (1979–90)	6,137
2	Cats (1982–)	4,378 *
3	42nd Street (1980–89)	3,486
4	Grease (1972–80)	3,388
5	Fiddler on the Roof (1964–72)	3,242
6	Hello Dolly! (1964–71)	2,844
7	My Fair Lady (1956–62)	2,717
8	Annie (1977–83)	2,377
9	Les Misérables (1987–)	2,463 *
10	Man of La Mancha (1965–71)	2,328

Still running; total at 31 March 1993.

Off Broadway, the musical show *The Fantasticks* by Tom Jones and Harvey Schmidt has been performed continuously at the Sullivan Street Playhouse, New York, since 3 May 1960 – a total of more than 13,500 performances.

THE 10 LONGEST-RUNNING NON-MUSICALS OF ALL TIME ON BROADWAY

	Show	Performances
1	Oh! Calcutta! (1976–89)	5,959
2	Life with Father (1939–47)	3,224
3	Tobacco Road (1933–41)	3,182
4	Abie's Irish Rose (1922–27)	2,327
5	Deathtrap (1978–82)	1,792
6	Gemini (1977–81)	1,788
7	Harvey (1944–49)	1,775
8	Born Yesterday (1946–49)	1,642
9	Mary, Mary (1961–65)	1,572
10	Voice of the Turtle (1943–47)	1,557

More than half the longest-running non-musical shows on Broadway began their runs before the Second World War; the others all date from the period up to the 1970s, before the long-running musical completely dominated the Broadway stage. Off Broadway, these records have all been broken by *The Drunkard*, which was performed at the Mart Theatre, Los Angeles, from 6 July 1933 to 6 September 1953, and then re-opened with a musical adaptation and continued its run from 7 September 1953 until 17 October 1959 – a grand total of 9,477 performances seen by some 3,000,000 people.

THE 10 LONGEST-RUNNING SHOWS OF ALL TIME ON BROADWAY

	Show	Performances
1	A Chorus Line (1975–90)	6,137
2	Oh! Calcutta! (1976–89)	5,959
3	Cats (1982–)	4,974 *
4	42nd Street (1980–89)	3,486
5	Grease (1972–80)	3,388
6	Fiddler on the Roof (1964–72)	3,242
7	Life with Father (1939–47)	3,224
8	Tobacco Road (1933–41)	3,182
9	Hello Dolly! (1964–71)	2,844
10	My Fair Lady (1956–72)	2,717

Still running; total at 31 March 1993.

A Chorus Line is unbeaten as Broadway's longest-running musical.

THE FIRST 10 PLAYS STAGED AT THE NATIONAL THEATRE*

	Play	Author	Director	Opening date
1	*Hamlet*	William Shakespeare	Peter Hall	16 Mar 1976
2	*John Gabriel Borkman*	Henrik Ibsen	Peter Hall	17 Mar 1976
3	*Plunder*	Ben Travers	Michael Blakemore	19 Mar 1976
4	*Watch It Come Down*	John Osborne	Bill Bryden	20 Mar 1976 †
5	*Happy Days*	Samuel Beckett	Peter Hall	20 Mar 1976 #
6	*No Man's Land*	Harold Pinter	Peter Hall	12 Apr 1976
7	*The Playboy of the Western World*	John Millington Synge	Bill Bryden	3 Jun 1976
8	*Blithe Spirit*	Noël Coward	Harold Pinter	24 Jun 1976
9	*Weapons of Happiness*	Howard Brenton	David Hare	14 Jul 1976
10	*Jumpers*	Tom Stoppard	Peter Wood	21 Sep 1976

At the South Bank.   †Matinée performance.   #Evening performance.

A British National Theatre was first proposed in 1848, but it was not until the National Theatre Bill was passed more than 100 years later that the project received serious attention. Under this act of 1949, a grant of £1,000,000 was made available and a committee set up under Sir Laurence Olivier and Norman Marshall. The National Theatre thus came into existence, but had no permanent home. Denys Lasdun was appointed to design a building, but although the Queen Mother (then Queen Elizabeth) laid a foundation stone on the South Bank in 1951, subsequent development proceeded very slowly. The Old Vic was used as temporary home from 1963 onwards, and building started in earnest in 1969. It was plagued by a series of industrial disputes and construction costs rose finally to exceed £16,000,000. The Lyttelton Theatre (named after Oliver Lyttelton, Lord Chandos, chairman of the National Theatre Board from 1963–71), the first of the three stages in the building to be completed, was inaugurated on 15 March 1976 with a special charity production of the Ben Travers farce *Plunder* – which began its 'official' run four days later. *Hamlet*, starring Albert Finney, transferred to the National from its run at the Old Vic (as did the next six productions: *Jumpers* was the first production to commence its run at the new site). All the first 10 National Theatre productions took place at the Lyttelton and the theatre was formally opened by The Queen on 25 October 1976. The first production at the Olivier was Christopher Marlowe's *Tamburlaine the Great*, directed by Peter Hall, which opened on 4 October 1976, and the first at the Cottesloe (named after Lord Cottesloe, the then chairman of the South Bank Theatre Board) was Ken Campbell and Christopher Langham's *Illuminatus!*, directed by Ken Campbell, which opened on 4 March 1977. The National Theatre was awarded the prefix 'Royal' in 1988.

FILM

	Actor/actress/nomination years	Nominations
1	**Katharine Hepburn**	
	1932–33*; 1935; 1940; 1942; 1951; 1955; 1956; 1959; 1962; 1967*; 1968*(shared); 1981*	12
2 =	**Bette Davis**	
	1935*; 1938*; 1939; 1940; 1941; 1942; 1944; 1950; 1952; 1962	10
2 =	**Jack Nicholson**	
	1969†; 1970; 1973; 1974; 1975*; 1981†; 1983†; 1985; 1987; 1992†	10
2 =	**Laurence Olivier**	
	1939; 1940; 1946; 1948*; 1956; 1960; 1965; 1972; 1976†; 1978	10
5	**Spencer Tracy**	
	1936; 1937*; 1938*; 1950; 1955; 1958; 1960; 1961; 1967	9
6 =	**Jack Lemmon**	
	1955†; 1959; 1960; 1962; 1973*; 1979; 1980; 1982	8
6 =	**Al Pacino**	
	1972†; 1973; 1974; 1975; 1979; 1990†; 1992*; 1992†	8
6 =	**Geraldine Page**	
	1953†; 1961; 1962; 1966; 1972; 1978; 1984; 1985*	8
9 =	**Ingrid Bergman**	
	1943; 1944*; 1945; 1948; 1956*; 1974†*; 1978	7
9 =	**Marlon Brando**	
	1951; 1952; 1953; 1954*; 1957; 1972*; 1973	7
9 =	**Richard Burton**	
	1952†; 1953; 1964; 1965; 1966; 1969; 1977	7
9 =	**Jane Fonda**	
	1969; 1971*; 1977; 1978; 1979; 1986; 1981†	7
9 =	**Greer Garson**	
	1939; 1941; 1942*; 1943; 1944; 1945; 1960	7
9 =	**Paul Newman#**	
	1958; 1961; 1963; 1967; 1981; 1982; 1986*	7
9 =	**Peter O'Toole**	
	1962; 1964; 1968; 1969; 1972; 1980; 1982	7

*Won Academy Award.   Oscar® is a Registered Trade Mark.

†Nomination for Best Supporting Actor or Actress.

#Also won an honorary Oscar in 1985.

As the Top 10 shows, a number of actors and actresses have received numerous nominations without actually winning many (or, in Richard Burton's and Peter O'Toole's cases, any) Oscars. Two actresses and two actors tie in first place with totals of eight *unsuccessful* nominations for Best Actor/Actress or Best Supporting Actor/Actress: Bette Davis, Katharine Hepburn, Jack Nicholson and Laurence Olivier. Deborah Kerr was nominated as Best Actress and Thelma Ritter six times as Best Supporting Actress, but neither ever won. It is clearly worth persevering, however: up to 1992, Al Pacino had been nominated four times as Best Actor and twice as Best Supporting Actor without winning, but in that year he found himself nominated in both categories and broke his losing streak by winning Best Actor Oscar for *Scent of a Woman*.

Apart from the awards to actors and actresses, certain individuals in other areas of film-making have been nominated and won on numerous occasions. Outstanding among them are the 32 secured by Walt Disney in a wide variety of categories, with five other individuals heading their respective fields by achieving notable tallies of both nominations and awards:

Name	Award	Nominations (wins)
Alfred Newman	Best Score	41 (9)
Edith Head	Costume Design	35 (8)
Sammy Cahn	Best Song	26 (4)
Billy Wilder	Best Screenplay	12 (3)
William Wyler	Best Director	12 (3)

Bette Davis is presented with her Oscar for *Jezebel* in 1938, her last win despite receiving a further eight nominations.

TOP 10 FILM LISTS

Films that appear in the various lists of '10 Most Successful' and Top 10s of films in which various stars have appeared are ranked according to the total rental fees paid to distributors by cinemas in North America (USA and Canada). This is regarded by the film industry as a reliable guide to what a film has earned in those markets, while as a rough rule of thumb – also used by the industry itself – doubling the North American rental receipts gives a very approximate world total.

It should be noted that rental income is not the same as 'box office gross', which is another commonly used way of comparing the success of films. While the latter method is certainly valid over a short period – for example, to compare films released in the same year – it indicates what the cinemas rather than the films themselves earned and, of course, varies according to ticket price.

Inflation is a key factor in calculating 'success', whichever method of assessment is used: as cinema ticket prices go up, so do box office income and the rental fees charged by distributors. This means that the biggest earners tend to be among the most recent releases. If inflation were taken into account, the most successful film ever would be *Gone With the Wind*; while it has earned actual rental fees of almost $80,000,000 (ranking it in only 37th place in the all-time list), inflation since the film's release in 1939 makes this worth over $500,000,000 in today's money.

Attempts have been made elsewhere to compile precise comparative lists by building in factors for increases in ticket prices and inflation, but with such changes taking place so frequently in recent years, and with a total lack of uniformity in box office prices even in one country, it is virtually impossible to achieve consistent or meaningful results, and rental fees remain the most satisfactory index for comparing the success of one film against another. However, even the dollar rental amounts are extremely volatile, with new information constantly emerging about not only newly released films but also many older ones. The order of those in the various Top 10 lists should therefore be taken only as a guide based on the best evidence currently available. Actual amounts are given only for the 'All-Time Film Rental Blockbusters' category, as an indication of the exceptional earning power of this elite group of films. To put this into perspective, only 16 films have made more than $100,000,000 (the total earned by these is more than $2,000,000,000), while of *all* the films ever made, fewer than 100 have earned total rental fees of more than $50,000,000.

It must not be forgotten that over recent years additional income has been derived by distributors from sales of video recordings and TV broadcasting rights. As this is not generally included in rental fees, it may alter the overall earnings of certain films, and hence their order in the Top 10 lists.

Especially in recent years, some films that were enormously expensive to make have also been among the highest earners, while others have failed disastrously at the box office; conversely, certain films that were produced with relatively low budgets have gone on to earn huge sums. It is ultimately the differential between the cost of making a film and its income – which is notoriously difficult to estimate – that determines whether it has been a success or a 'flop'.

THE 10 YOUNGEST OSCAR WINNERS

	Actor/actress	Award/film (where specified)	Award year	Age
1	Shirley Temple	Special Award – outstanding contribution during 1934	1934	6
2	Margaret O'Brien	Special Award (*Meet Me in St Louis*, etc)	1944	8
3	Vincent Winter	Special Award (*The Little Kidnappers*)	1954	8
4	Jon Whitely	Special Award (*The Little Kidnappers*)	1954	9
5	Ivan Jandl	Special Award (*The Search*)	1948	9
6	Tatum O'Neal	Best Supporting Actress (*Paper Moon*)	1973	10
7	Claude Jarman Jr	Special Award (*The Yearling*)	1946	12
8	Bobby Driscoll	Special Award (*The Window*)	1949	13
9	Hayley Mills	Special Award (*Pollyanna*)	1960	13
10	Peggy Ann Garner	Special Award (*A Tree Grows in Brooklyn*)	1945	14

The Academy Awards ceremony usually takes place at the end of March in the year following that in which the film was released, so the winners are generally at least a year older when they receive their Oscars than when they acted in their award-winning films. Hayley Mills, the 12th and last winner of the 'Special Award' miniature Oscar (presented to her by its first winner, Shirley Temple), won her award precisely one day before her 14th birthday. Subsequent winners have had to compete on the same basis as adult actors and actresses for the major awards of Best Actor/Actress and Best Supporting Actor/Actress. Tatum O'Neal is thus the youngest winner of – as well as the youngest ever nominee for – an 'adult' Oscar. Jackie Cooper was nine at the time of his nomination as Best Actor for his part in *Skippy* (1930–31 Academy Awards), but the youngest winner was, surprisingly, more than 20 years older, Richard Dreyfuss (for *The Goodbye Girl* in the 1977 Awards). Eight-year-old Justin Henry is the youngest ever Oscar nominee for Best Supporting Actor, for his role in *Kramer* vs *Kramer* (1979), but the youngest winner in this category is Timothy Hutton, who was aged 20 when he won in the 1980 Awards for his role in *Ordinary People*. The youngest Best Actress Award winner is Marlee Matlin, aged 21, for *Children of a Lesser God* (1986), and the youngest nominee Isabelle Adjani, 20, for *The Story of Adèle H* (1975).

The oldest Best Actress Oscar-winner (and also oldest nominee) is Jessica Tandy (for *Driving Miss Daisy*, 1989 Awards), who was in her 80th year at the time of the ceremony. The oldest Best Actor Oscar-winner (and nominee) is Henry Fonda, who was 76 at the time of his 1981 win for *On Golden Pond*. The oldest Best Supporting Actor is George Burns, aged 80 (*The Sunshine Boys*, 1975). Ralph Richardson was 82 when he was nominated as Best Supporting Actor for his role in *Greystoke: The Legend of Tarzan* (1984), as was Eva Le Gallienne, nominated as Best Supporting Actress for her part in *Resurrection* (1980), but the oldest winner in the latter category is Peggy Ashcroft, aged 77, for *A Passage to India* (1984).

Shirley Temple was the youngest-ever Oscar winner.

COLOUR FILM QUIZ

Fill in the missing colours:

1 *The Creature from the _____ Lagoon*

2 *Electra Glide in _____*

3 *How _____ Was My Valley*

4 *The Color _____*

5 *Heller in _____ Tights*

6 *The Man in the _____ Flannel Suit*

7 *_____ Fang*

8 *The _____ Badge of Courage*

9 *The _____ Rolls-Royce*

10 *The _____ Pimpernel*

THE 10 FILMS TO WIN THE MOST OSCARS

	Film	Year	Awards
1	Ben Hur	1959	11
2	West Side Story	1961	10
3 =	Gigi	1958	9
3 =	The Last Emperor	1987	9
5 =	Gone With the Wind	1939	8 *
5 =	From Here to Eternity	1953	8
5 =	On the Waterfront	1954	8
5 =	My Fair Lady	1964	8
5 =	Cabaret	1972	8
5 =	Gandhi	1982	8
5 =	Amadeus	1984	8

Plus two special awards.

Eight other films have won seven Oscars each: *Going My Way* (1944), *The Best Years of Our Lives* (1946), *The Bridge on the River Kwai* (1957), *Lawrence of Arabia* (1962), *Patton* (1970), *The Sting* (1973), *Out of Africa* (1985) and *Dances With Wolves* (1991). *All About Eve* (1950) was nominated for 14 awards and won six while *The Turning Point* (1977) and *The Color Purple* (1985) each had 11 nominations and did not win any.

THE TOP 10 WOODY ALLEN FILMS

Woody Allen (born Allen Stewart Konigsberg, 1 December 1935, Brooklyn, New York) began his professional career as a gag-writer for other performers. He moved to scriptwriting and acting, the 1965 film *What's New, Pussycat?* providing him with the first opportunity to do both. He has also been directing films since 1969.

	Film	Year
1	Annie Hall	1977
2	Hannah and Her Sisters	1986
3	Manhattan	1979
4	Casino Royale	1967
5	Everything You Always Wanted to Know About Sex	1972
6	What's New, Pussycat?	1965
7	Sleeper	1973
8	Crimes and Misdemeanors	1989
9	Love and Death	1975
10	Zelig	1983

This list includes films which Woody Allen has either written, starred in or directed. *Annie Hall* was the first occasion since 1941 that one individual has been nominated for Best Film, Best Actor, Best Director and Best Screenplay (the previous nominee was Orson Welles for *Citizen Kane*). The film won him Best Picture Oscar – which, characteristically, he did not bother to collect.

THE TOP 10 'BEST PICTURE' OSCAR WINNERS

	Film	Year
1	Rain Man	1988
2	The Godfather	1972
3	Dances With Wolves	1990
4	The Sound of Music	1965
5	Gone With the Wind	1939
6	The Sting	1973
7	Platoon	1986
8	Kramer vs Kramer	1979
9	One Flew Over the Cuckoo's Nest	1975
10	The Silence of the Lambs	1991

Winning the Academy Award for 'Best Picture' is no guarantee of box-office success: the award is given for a picture released the previous year, and by the time the Oscar ceremony takes place, the filmgoing public has already effectively decided on the winning picture's fate. Receiving the Oscar may enhance a successful picture's continuing earnings, but it is generally too late to revive a film that may already have been judged mediocre. In recent years, *The Last Emperor*, winner of the 1987 Oscar for Best Picture, actually earned less than several winners from the 1950s and 1960s. The presence in this list of such films as *Gone With the Wind*, made over half a century ago, and *The Sound of Music* alongside such recent blockbusters as *Dances With Wolves* eloquently testifies to the box-office staying power of certain 'classic' movies, whereas other 'Best Pictures' have faded into cinematic history.

THE TOP 10 WARREN BEATTY FILMS

Warren Beatty (born Warren Beaty (with one 't'), 30 March 1937, Richmond, Virginia), had his first film role in *Splendor in the Grass* (1961), since when his output has been fewer than 20 films. As well as his acting, he has been successful as a producer, most recently for *Bugsy* (1991), which was nominated for 10 Oscars, winning two.

	Film	Year
1	Dick Tracy*†	1990
2	Heaven Can Wait*	1978
3	Bugsy	1991
4	Shampoo†	1975
5	Bonnie and Clyde	1967
6	Reds*†	1981
7	Ishtar	1987
8	Splendor in the Grass	1961
9	McCabe and Mrs Miller	1971
10	The Fortune	1975

Also director or co-director.

†Also co-writer.

Warren Beatty also made an appearance in Madonna's 1991 'documentary' *Truth Or Dare* (retitled *In Bed With Madonna* in the UK), which, if included, would be placed 8th in this list.

THE TOP 10 CHEVY CHASE FILMS

Chevy (real name Cornelius Crane) Chase (born 8 October 1943, New York) made his name as a comedian on the anarchic US TV show *Saturday Night Live* before starring in comedy films including the hugely successful *National Lampoon* series.

	Film	Year
1	National Lampoon's Christmas	1989
2	Spies Like Us	1985
3	National Lampoon's Vacation	1983
4	Foul Play	1978
5	National Lampoon's European Vacation	1985
6	Fletch	1985
7	Seems Like Old Times	1980
8	Caddyshack	1980
9	Three Amigos!	1986
10	Fletch Lives	1989

THE TOP 10 KEVIN COSTNER FILMS

Ten years after his first film, Costner (born 18 January 1955, Lynwood, California) received huge acclaim (and seven Oscars) for *Dances With Wolves*, which was the first film he also directed. He followed it with the smash commercial success *Robin Hood: Prince of Thieves,* and is now ranked by *Premiere* magazine as the most powerful actor in Hollywood.

	Film	Year
1	Robin Hood: Prince of Thieves	1991
2	Dances With Wolves	1990
3	The Bodyguard	1992
4	The Untouchables	1987
5	JFK	1991
6	Field of Dreams	1989
7	Bull Durham	1988
8	Silverado	1985
9	No Way Out	1987
10	Night Shift	1982

THE TOP 10 TOM CRUISE FILMS

Tom Cruise (real name Thomas Cruise Mapother IV; born 3 July 1962, Syracuse, New York), while often playing handsome all-American heroes and military roles (*Taps, Top Gun, Born on the Fourth of July, A Few Good Men*) and light comedy (*Risky Business*) has shown himself equally at home with dramatic parts, such as in *Rain Man*.

	Film	Year
1	Rain Man	1988
2	Top Gun	1986
3	A Few Good Men	1992
4	Days of Thunder	1990
5	Born on the Fourth of July	1989
6	Cocktail	1988
7	Risky Business	1983
8	Far and Away	1992
9	The Color of Money	1986
10	Taps	1981

THE TOP 10 MICHAEL DOUGLAS FILMS

Michael Douglas (born 25 September 1944, New Brunswick, New Jersey) is the son of actor Kirk Douglas. Winner of Best Actor Oscar for *Wall Street* and star of blockbusters *Fatal Attraction* and *Basic Instinct*, Douglas is one of the most 'bankable' of all Hollywood stars, although it is often forgotten that his first major success was not as an actor but as multi-Oscar-winning director of *One Flew Over the Cuckoo's Nest*.

	Film	Year
1	Fatal Attraction	1987
2	Basic Instinct	1992
3	The War of the Roses	1989
4	The Jewel of the Nile	1985
5	Romancing the Stone	1984
6	The China Syndrome	1979
7	Black Rain	1989
8	Wall Street	1987
9	Coma	1978
10	Shining Through	1992

Rain Man is Tom Cruise's No. 1 film.

Kevin Costner's *Robin Hood: Prince of Thieves* has earned even more than his Oscar-winning *Dances With Wolves*.

THE TOP 10 CLINT EASTWOOD FILMS

After his early bit parts Clint Eastwood (born 31 May 1930, San Francisco, California) spent several years as Rowdy Yates in the popular TV series *Rawhide*, thereby establishing the image that was employed to great effect in Sergio Leone's 'spaghetti Westerns' (*A Fistful of Dollars* and its sequels). The 'Dirty Harry' films followed, but he has also ventured into comedy and the occasional successful return to his roots in the Westerns that remain his forte.

	Film	Year
1	Every Which Way But Loose	1978
2	Any Which Way You Can	1980
3	Unforgiven	1992
4	Sudden Impact	1983
5	Firefox	1982
6	The Enforcer	1976
7	Tightrope	1984
8	Heartbreak Ridge	1986
9	Escape from Alcatraz	1979
10	City Heat	1984

Unforgiven, Eastwood's 1992 multi-Oscar-winning film (Best Picture, Director, Editing, Supporting Actor), rapidly cut a swathe through his now considerable oeuvre and by the end of the year was well on its way to becoming his highest-earning film ever. Eastwood would probably prefer to forget some of his early films (which almost everyone else has), such as his first role in *Revenge of the Creature* (1955), *Lady Godiva* (1955), in which he is credited as 'First Saxon', *The First Traveling Saleslady* (1956), a film about two female barbed-wire saleswomen, and *Tarantula* (1957), a film about giant spiders.

The Top 10 films directed by Eastwood presents a somewhat different picture:

	Film	Year
1	Unforgiven	1992
2	Sudden Impact	1983
3	Firefox	1982
4	Heartbreak Ridge	1986
5	Pale Rider	1985
6	The Gauntlet	1977
7	Bronco Billy	1980
8	The Outlaw Josey Wales	1976
9	The Rookie	1990
10	High Plains Drifter	1973

His directorial debut was of a single scene in *Dirty Harry* (1971). If this were included, it would appear in 6th place.

THE TOP 10 DANNY DEVITO FILMS

Danny DeVito (born 17 November 1944, Asbury Park, New Jersey) has taken advantage of his lack of stature and physical appeal and has built his screen career playing irascible and often villainous characters, culminating in his memorable performance as The Penguin in *Batman Returns*. He appeared alongside Jack Nicholson (who, coincidentally, played the villain in the original *Batman*) in *One Flew Over the Cuckoo's Nest* and has since been in three more films with Nicholson: *Goin' South*, *Terms of Endearment* and *Hoffa*.

	Film	Year
1	Batman Returns	1992
2	One Flew Over the Cuckoo's Nest	1975
3	Twins	1988
4	Terms of Endearment	1983
5	The War of the Roses*	1989
6	The Jewel of the Nile	1985
7	Romancing the Stone	1984
8	Ruthless People	1986
9	Throw Momma from the Train*	1987
10	Other People's Money	1991

*Also director.

Danny DeVito had a relatively minor role in *One Flew Over the Cuckoo's Nest*. If this is discounted from the reckoning, his 10th most successful film becomes *Hoffa* (1992).

THE TOP 10
MIA FARROW FILMS

Mia Farrow (born 9 February 1945, Los Angeles, California) is the daughter of Australian film director John Farrow and actress Maureen O'Sullivan and was previously married to Frank Sinatra and to conductor André Previn. Her cinema career spans almost 30 years, 10 of them in on- and off-screen partnership with Woody Allen, a relationship which ended in a much publicized legal action in 1993.

	Film	Year
1	Hannah and Her Sisters	1986
2	Rosemary's Baby	1968
3	The Great Gatsby	1974
4	Death on the Nile	1978
5	Zelig	1983
6	Radio Days	1987
7	Supergirl	1984
8	Broadway Danny Rose	1984
9	The Purple Rose of Cairo	1984
10	New York Stories	1989

THE TOP 10
RICHARD GERE FILMS

Abandoning his ambition to be a musician, Richard Gere (born 31 August 1948, Syracuse, New York) began his acting career in London where he appeared in the stage version of Grease and in Shakespeare at the Young Vic. His film career has spanned almost 20 years and has ranged from drama to comedy – not to mention biblical (he was oddly cast in the title role of the unmemorable 1985 mini-epic King David).

	Film	Year
1	Pretty Woman	1990
2	An Officer and a Gentleman	1982
3	Sommersby	1993
4	Looking for Mr Goodbar	1977
5	Final Analysis	1992
6	The Cotton Club	1984
7	American Gigolo	1980
8	Internal Affairs	1990
9	Breathless	1983
10	No Mercy	1986

THE TOP 10
CARRIE FISHER FILMS

Carrie Frances Fisher (born 21 October 1956, Beverly Hills, California) is the daughter of actress Debbie Reynolds and actor Eddie Fisher. She is perhaps best known for her role as Princess Leia in the Star Wars trilogy, but is also a bestselling author whose book Postcards from the Edge was made into a film starring Meryl Streep.

	Film	Year
1	Star Wars	1977
2	Return of the Jedi	1983
3	The Empire Strikes Back	1980
4	When Harry Met Sally	1989
5	The Blues Brothers	1980
6	Shampoo	1975
7	Hannah and Her Sisters	1986
8	The 'Burbs	1989
9	Soapdish	1991
10	Sibling Rivalry	1990

Along with Mark Hamill and Harrison Ford, Carrie Fisher has had the remarkable good fortune to appear in three of the Top 5 highest-earning films of all time. If she had managed to negotiate a 10 per cent stake in just the North American rental income of these three, she would have received more than $50,000,000. Her part in Shampoo was very minor; if excluded, her 10th entry would be Under the Rainbow (1981).

THE TOP 10
JODIE FOSTER FILMS

After a career as a child TV star, Jodie Foster (born 19 November 1962, Los Angeles, California) moved into films at the age of 10, oscillating roles between childish innocence and street-wise 'bad girl'. She won a Best Actress Oscar for The Accused and for The Silence of the Lambs, since when she has launched into directing with Little Man Tate.

	Film	Year
1	The Silence of the Lambs	1990
2	Sommersby	1993
3	The Accused	1988
4	Taxi Driver	1976
5	Freaky Friday	1976
6	Little Man Tate*	1991
7	Alice Doesn't Live Here Any More	1975
8	Candleshoe	1977
9	Tom Sawyer	1973
10	The Hotel New Hampshire	1984

*Also directed.

The Silence of the Lambs is by far the most profitable of all the films in which Jodie Foster has appeared.

Mel Gibson and Goldie Hawn teamed in *Bird on a Wire*, his third and her most successful film.

THE TOP 10 MEL GIBSON FILMS

Mel Gibson was born in Peekskill, New York, on 3 January 1956, but grew up in Australia where he began his acting career. The two *Mad Max* sequels (the original film was not an international success) established his reputation and led to the blockbusting *Lethal Weapon* films (so successful that a 'homage', *National Lampoon's Loaded Weapon 1*, has been released) and, less predictably, his critically acclaimed *Hamlet*. Gibson is rated one of Hollywood's top stars, reputedly earning more than $50 million from *Forever Young*.

	Film	Year
1	Lethal Weapon 3	1992
2	Lethal Weapon 2	1989
3	Bird on a Wire	1990
4	Lethal Weapon	1987
5	Forever Young	1992
6	Tequila Sunrise	1988
7	Mad Max Beyond Thunderdome	1985
8	Air America	1990
9	Mad Max 2: The Road Warrior	1981
10	Hamlet	1990

THE TOP 10 TOM HANKS FILMS

During the 1980s, Tom Hanks (born 9 July 1956, Concord, California) attained star status through a succession of popular romantic comedies, with *Splash!* standing out as his breakthrough film, and *Big*, appropriately, one of the biggest smashes of 1988. His successful run was sadly later overshadowed by the much-criticized *Bonfire of the Vanities*.

	Film	Year
1	A League of Their Own	1992
2	Big	1988
3	Turner & Hooch	1989
4	Splash!	1984
5	Dragnet	1987
6	Bachelor Party	1984
7	Joe Versus the Volcano	1990
8	The 'Burbs	1989
9	The Money Pit	1986
10	Nothing in Common	1986

THE TOP 10 GOLDIE HAWN FILMS

Goldie Hawn (born Goldie Jean Studlendgehawn, 21 November 1945, Washington, DC) made her first appearance in 1968 in the long-running TV series *Rowan and Martin's Laugh-In*. She has effectively reprised her role as a zany, eternally youthful blonde in comedy films ever since, with *Private Benjamin* earning her a Best Actress Oscar nomination.

	Film	Year
1	Bird on a Wire	1990
2	Private Benjamin	1980
3	Death Becomes Her	1992
4	Housesitter	1992
5	Foul Play	1978
6	Shampoo	1975
7	Seems Like Old Times	1980
8	Best Friends	1982
9	Protocol	1984
10	Wildcats	1986

THE TOP 10 AUDREY HEPBURN FILMS

Audrey Hepburn (born Edda van Heemstra Hepburn-Ruston, 4 May 1929, Brussels, Belgium; died 20 January 1993) had a British father and a Dutch mother. She began as a dancer and stage actress and appeared in minor parts before achieving acclaim and a Best Actress Oscar for *Roman Holiday* (1954). After 1967 her roles were few and far between, and her last years were devoted to charity work with UNICEF.

	Film	Year
1	*My Fair Lady*	1964
2	*Always*	1989
3	*Wait until Dark*	1967
4	*Charade*	1963
5	*War and Peace*	1956
6	*The Nun's Story*	1959
7	*Bloodline*	1979
8	*How to Steal a Million*	1966
9	*Breakfast at Tiffany's*	1961
10 =	*Sabrina*	1954
10 =	*Robin and Marian*	1976

Audrey Hepburn in *My Fair Lady*, the most successful of all her films.

The part-animated *Who Framed Roger Rabbit?* is Bob Hoskins' top film.

THE TOP 10 BOB HOSKINS FILMS

Bob Hoskins was born (26 October 1942) in Bury St Edmunds, Suffolk – despite which he achieved fame fulfilling Hollywood's stereotypical image of a gruff cockney. He has often found himself cast as a gangster, but has also played roles as diverse as romance, comedy and (on stage) Shakespeare.

	Film	Year
1	*Who Framed Roger Rabbit?*	1988
2	*Hook*	1991
3	*Mermaids*	1990
4	*The Cotton Club*	1984
5	*Pink Floyd The Wall*	1982
6	*Lassiter*	1984
7	*Sweet Liberty*	1986
8	*Brazil*	1985
9	*The Honorary Consul*	1983
10	*Mona Lisa*	1986

THE TOP 10 STEVE MARTIN FILMS

Like Woody Allen, Steve Martin (born 18 August 1945, Waco, Texas) began his career writing comedy material for others before deciding to use it himself, first on stage, then in TV and finally films, with *The Jerk* marking his breakthrough and leading to a run of (mostly) successful comedy films.

	Film	Year
1	*Parenthood*	1989
2	*The Jerk**	1979
3	*Father of the Bride*	1991
4	*Housesitter*	1992
5	*Planes, Trains and Automobiles*	1987
6	*Three Amigos!**	1986
7	*Little Shop of Horrors*	1986
8	*Dirty Rotten Scoundrels*	1988
9	*Roxanne*	1987
10	*Grand Canyon*	1991

*Also co-writer.

Steve Martin was also one of the many 'guest stars' in *The Muppet Movie* (1979). If included, it would appear in 5th place.

THE TOP 10 PAUL NEWMAN FILMS

Paul Newman (born 26 January 1925, Cleveland, Ohio) has been making films for 40 years, but had to wait until 1985 before receiving the recognition of an honorary Oscar – followed by one for Best Actor the next year for his part in *The Color of Money* (repeating the role he had played 25 years earlier in *The Hustler*). Newman is a noted philanthropist, donating large sums of money to various causes – including the royalty income from a range of sauces and salad dressings that bear his name.

	Film	Year
1	*The Sting*	1973
2	*The Towering Inferno*	1974
3	*Butch Cassidy and the Sundance Kid*	1969
4	*The Verdict*	1982
5	*The Color of Money*	1986
6	*Absence of Malice*	1981
7	*Fort Apache, the Bronx*	1980
8	*Slap Shot*	1977
9	*Blaze*	1989
10	*Cat on a Hot Tin Roof*	1958

If Paul Newman's unbilled cameo appearance in *Silent Movie* (1976) were included, it would be in 6th place.

THE TOP 10 JACK NICHOLSON FILMS

Jack Nicholson (born 22 April 1937, Neptune, New Jersey) served a long apprenticeship in minor film parts for a decade before the hugely successful *Easy Rider*. He won an Oscar for *One Flew Over the Cuckoo's Nest* and is today one of Hollywood's biggest – and certainly biggest-earning – stars: he received a substantial share of the profits from *Batman*, the fourth highest-earning film ever.

	Film	Year
1	*Batman*	1989
2	*A Few Good Men*	1992
3	*One Flew Over the Cuckoo's Nest*	1975
4	*Terms of Endearment*	1983
5	*The Witches of Eastwick*	1987
6	*The Shining*	1980
7	*Broadcast News*	1987
8	*Reds*	1981
9	*Easy Rider*	1969
10	*Carnal Knowledge*	1971

THE TOP 10 RICHARD PRYOR FILMS

Richard Pryor (born 1 December 1940, Peoria, Illinois) has scored well in frenetic comedy romps and adventure films, as well as in his occasional sorties into more dramatic roles. Along with another perennially popular black actor, Eddie Murphy, the multi-talented Pryor is one of the few Hollywood stars who has also made hugely successful films of his stand-up comedy routines.

	Film	Year
1	*Stir Crazy**	1980
2	*Superman III*	1983
3	*The Muppet Movie*	1979
4	*Harlem Nights*	1989
5	*Silver Streak**	1976
6	*California Suite*	1978
7	*The Toy*†*	1983
8	*See No Evil, Hear No Evil*	1989
9	*Brewster's Millions*	1985
10	*Richard Pryor Live on the Sunset Strip**	1982

*Also writer or co-writer. †Also director.

Richard Pryor also co-wrote but did not appear in *Blazing Saddles* (1974). If included as part of his output, it would rank second in this list.

THE TOP 10 ARNOLD SCHWARZENEGGER FILMS

Arnold Schwarzenegger was born (30 July 1947) in Graz, Austria. He moved to the USA and won numerous body-building contests before entering films in 1969 (in the *Hercules in New York* title role). His subsequent films have been ever more successful, with *Terminator 2: Judgment Day* only just falling short of a place among the 10 highest-earning films of all time and contributing to *Premiere* magazine's ranking of him as the eighth most powerful man in Hollywood – and that's not just for his muscles . . .

	Film	Year
1	*Terminator 2: Judgment Day*	1991
2	*Total Recall*	1990
3	*Twins*	1988
4	*Kindergarten Cop*	1990
5	*Predator*	1987
6	*Conan the Barbarian*	1981
7	*Commando*	1985
8	*The Terminator*	1984
9	*The Running Man*	1987
10	*Red Heat*	1988

THE TOP 10 MERYL STREEP FILMS

Meryl Streep (born 22 June 1949, Summit, New Jersey) attained seemingly effortless stardom, receiving an Oscar nomination (one of a total of nine) for only her second film, *The Deer Hunter*, and winning 'Best Actress' Oscar for *Sophie's Choice*, a harrowing drama far removed from her comedy performance in the recent *Death Becomes Her*.

	Film	Year
1	*Kramer vs Kramer*	1979
2	*Out of Africa*	1985
3	*Death Becomes Her*	1992
4	*The Deer Hunter*	1978
5	*Silkwood*	1983
6	*Manhattan*	1979
7	*Postcards from the Edge*	1990
8	*Sophie's Choice*	1982
9	*Julia*	1982
10	*Heartburn*	1986

It is perhaps surprising that *Sophie's Choice*, the film for which Meryl Streep won an Oscar, scores so far down this list, while one of her most celebrated films, *The French Lieutenant's Woman* (1981), does not make her personal Top 10 at all.

Robin Williams (confronting Dustin Hoffman) in *Hook*, his most lucrative film to date.

THE TOP 10 SIGOURNEY WEAVER FILMS

Sigourney Weaver (born Susan Weaver, 8 October 1959, New York) has made something of a speciality of playing vulnerable-but-tough parts, her roles in the two *Ghostbusters* and three *Aliens* films bringing her greatest fame and fortune.

	Film	Year
1	*Ghostbusters*	1984
2	*Ghostbusters II*	1989
3	*Aliens*	1986
4	*Alien*	1979
5	*Aliens³*	1992
6	*Working Girl*	1988
7	*Gorillas in the Mist*	1988
8	*The Deal of the Century*	1983
9	*The Year of Living Dangerously*	1982
10	*Eyewitness/The Janitor*	1981

Sigourney Weaver also had a fleeting minor part in *Annie Hall* (1977). If included, this would appear in 7th position.

THE TOP 10 ROBIN WILLIAMS FILMS

Robin Williams (born 21 July 1952, Chicago, Illinois) first came to public attention on TV through his appearances in *Rowan and Martin's Laugh-In* and as the alien Mork in *Mork and Mindy*, since when he has made 15 films, typically playing crazed individuals – such as the DJ in *Good Morning, Vietnam*, and the certifiable down-and-out in *The Fisher King*. Williams has also played some impressive dramatic roles, as in *Dead Poets Society* and *Awakenings*.

	Film	Year
1	*Hook*	1991
2	*Good Morning, Vietnam*	1987
3	*Dead Poets Society*	1989
4	*Popeye*	1980
5	*Awakenings*	1990
6	*The Fisher King*	1991
7	*Dead Again*	1991
8	*The World According to Garp*	1982
9	*Cadillac Man*	1990
10	*Moscow on the Hudson*	1984

Robin Williams' voice appears in the 1992 animated blockbuster *Aladdin*. If this were included, its earnings would easily place it at the head of the list. If his minor cameo role in *Dead Again* is excluded, his 10th most successful film would be *Toys* – even though it has been both commercially and critically a resounding flop.

THE TOP 10 BRUCE WILLIS FILMS

Bruce Willis was born (19 March 1955) in West Germany, but grew up in New Jersey. He first appeared in minor film roles in the early 1980s, but did not become well known until *Die Hard*, one of a small group of movies (including the *Terminator* and *Mad Max* series) whose sequels have been even more successful than the original films that spawned them. He has made only a dozen films to date, their success running the complete spectrum from 'blockbuster' to 'flop'.

	Film	Year
1	Look Who's Talking*	1989
2	Die Hard 2	1990
3	Die Hard	1988
4	Death Becomes Her	1992
5	The Last Boy Scout	1991
6	Blind Date	1987
7	The Bonfire of the Vanities	1990
8	Hudson Hawk	1991
9	Mortal Thoughts	1991
10	Billy Bathgate	1991

*Voice only.

It is somewhat ironic to consider that the most successful film role of an actor whose screen persona is of a tough-guy should be that of a baby in *Look Who's Talking* – and that consisting only of Willis's dubbed voice. If discounted, either of two other films, *Sunset* (1988) and *In Country* (1989) could be considered as contenders for 10th place, although neither can be regarded as in any sense high-earning films.

THE 10 BIGGEST FILM FLOPS OF ALL TIME*

	Film	Year	Loss ($)
1	The Adventures of Baron Munchausen	1988	48,100,000
2	Ishtar	1987	47,300,000
3	Hudson Hawk	1991	47,000,000
4	Inchon	1981	44,100,000
5	The Cotton Club	1984	38,100,000
6	Santa Claus – The Movie	1985	37,000,000
7	Heaven's Gate	1980	34,200,000
8	Billy Bathgate	1991	33,000,000
9	Pirates	1986	30,300,000
10	Rambo III	1988	30,000,000

*To end of 1992.

Since the figures shown here are based upon North American rental earnings balanced against the films' original production cost, some in the list will eventually recoup a proportion of their losses via overseas earnings, video and TV revenue, while for others, such as *Inchon* and *Pirates*, time has run out. The recent entry of *Hudson Hawk* and *Billy Bathgate*, two newcomers to the 'flops' league table, means that the British-produced *Raise the Titanic* (1980), reputed to have lost $29,200,000, has finally sunk from the Top 10.

Home Alone is the highest-earning comedy film ever made and is also the most successful film of the 1990s to date.

THE TOP 10 FILMS OF THE 1990s

	Film	Released
1	Home Alone	1990
2	Terminator 2	1991
3	Home Alone 2: Lost in New York	1992
4	Batman Returns	1992
5	Ghost	1990
6	Robin Hood: Prince of Thieves	1991
7	Aladdin	1992
8	Pretty Woman	1990
9	Dances With Wolves	1990
10	Lethal Weapon 3	1992

Just two years into the decade, all 10 of these films have amassed rental income from the North American market alone in excess of $80,000,000, a feat achieved by only 15 films in the whole of the 1980s and just seven in the 1970s. *Home Alone* has been so successful that it now ranks as one of the Top 10 films of all time, with its 1992 sequel *Home Alone 2: Lost in New York* ranked 15th in the all-time list. A further 15 films released since 1990, including several released as recently as 1992 (*Sister Act, The Bodyguard, Wayne's World, A League of Their Own* and *Basic Instinct*) have each earned more than $50,000,000.

THE TOP 10 FILMS AT THE UK BOX OFFICE IN 1992

1   *Basic Instinct*
2   *Hook*
3   *Lethal Weapon 3*
4   *Batman Returns*
5   *Cape Fear*
6   *The Addams Family*
7   *Beauty and the Beast*
8   *Wayne's World*
9   *My Girl*
10 *The Hand that Rocks the Cradle*

Although three of the top five films here (*Basic Instinct*, *Lethal Weapon 3* and *Cape Fear*) carry 18 certificates, possibly the most significant aspect of this Top 10 is the amount of whole-family viewing it represents, featuring two 'U' certificates (Spielberg's *Hook* and Disney's animated *Beauty and the Beast*) and three PGs (*The Addams Family*, *Wayne's World* and *My Girl*). This ties in with the perceived growth in cinema audiences of all ages during the 1990s, thanks to multi-screen cinemas offering a wide choice of viewing.

THE TOP 10 FILM RENTAL BLOCKBUSTERS OF ALL TIME

	Film	Year	Total rental ($)
1	*E.T.: The Extra-Terrestrial*	1982	228,618,939
2	*Star Wars*	1977	193,777,000
3	*Return of the Jedi*	1983	169,193,000
4	*Batman*	1989	150,500,000
5	*The Empire Strikes Back*	1980	141,672,000
6	*Home Alone*	1990	140,099,000
7	*Ghostbusters*	1984	132,720,000
8	*Jaws*	1975	129,549,325
9	*Raiders of the Lost Ark*	1981	115,598,000
10	*Indiana Jones and the Last Crusade*	1989	115,500,000

The order of the all-time Top 10 is unchanged since the previous year, when *Home Alone* made its first appearance, with only the dollar totals increased. Only six other films have earned more than $100,000,000 in North American rentals: *Terminator 2* (1991; $112,500,000), *Indiana Jones and the Temple of Doom* (1984; $109,000,000), *Beverly Hills Cop* (1984; $108,000,000), *Back to the Future* (1985; $105,496,267), *Home Alone 2: Lost in New York* (1992; $102,000,000) and *Batman Returns* (1992; $100,100,000). *Gone With the Wind* (1939), once regarded as the highest-earning film of all time (which it would still be if its income were index-linked), has been overtaken by so many films from the more recent period that it now occupies a lowly 37th place in the all-time list.

Carrie Fisher and friends in the blockbuster *Return of the Jedi*.

THE TOP 10 FILMS AT THE US BOX OFFICE IN 1992

	Film	Gross ($)
1	*Batman Returns*	162,831,698
2	*Beauty and the Beast*	145,863,363
3	*Lethal Weapon 3*	144,731,527
4	*Sister Act*	139,538,294
5	*Home Alone 2: Lost in New York*	124,942,522
6	*Wayne's World*	121,436,898
7	*Hook*	118,965,084
8	*Basic Instinct*	117,208,217
9	*The Addams Family*	113,379,166
10	*A League of Their Own*	107,277,391

A reminder that 'box office gross' and rental income are not the same, and lists based on the two statistics cannot be compared.

THE 10 MOST SUCCESSFUL ANIMATED FILMS OF ALL TIME

	Film	Year
1	*Aladdin*	1992
2	*Who Framed Roger Rabbit?**	1988
3	*Beauty and the Beast*	1991
4	*One Hundred and One Dalmatians*	1961
5	*Snow White and the Seven Dwarfs*	1937
6	*Jungle Book*	1967
7	*Bambi*	1942
8	*Fantasia*	1940
9	*Cinderella*	1949
10	*Pinocchio*	1940

*Part-animated, part live action.

For more than 50 years the popularity of animated films has been so great that they stand out among the most successful films of each decade: *Snow White* was the second highest-earning film of the 1930s (after *Gone With the Wind*); *Bambi*, *Fantasia* and *Cinderella* – and through the success of its recent re-release joined by *Pinocchio* – were the four most successful films of the 1940s; *Lady and the Tramp*, though just outside the Top 10, was the second most successful of the 1950s (after *The Ten Commandments*); and *One Hundred and One Dalmatians* second and *Jungle Book* third most successful films of the 1960s (after *The Sound of Music*). Among runners-up are, in descending order: *Lady and the Tramp* (1955); *The Little Mermaid* (1989); *Peter Pan* (1953); *The Rescuers* (1977); the part-animated *Song of the South* (1946); *The Aristocats* (1970); *Oliver and Company* (1988); *The Land Before Time* (1988), *An American Tail* (1986) and *Sleeping Beauty* (1989).

One Hundred and One Dalmatians remains one of the top animated films of all time.

THE TOP 10 JAMES BOND FILMS

	Film	Year
1	Octopussy	1983
2	Moonraker	1979
3	Thunderball	1965
4	Never Say Never Again	1983
5	The Living Daylights	1987
6	For Your Eyes Only	1981
7	A View to a Kill	1985
8	The Spy Who Loved Me	1977
9	Goldfinger	1964
10	Diamonds Are Forever	1967

Ian Fleming wrote 12 James Bond novels that have miraculously become the basis of 18 films. After his death in 1964, *Octopussy*, *The Living Daylights* and *For Your Eyes Only* were developed by other writers from his short stories; *Never Say Never Again* was effectively a remake of *Thunderball*, while *A View to a Kill* and *Licence to Kill* (1989, in 11th place) were written by others without reference to Fleming's writings. Of the 10 most successful James Bond films, Roger Moore starred as Bond in five (Nos. 1, 2, 6, 7 and 8), Sean Connery in four (3, 4, 9, 10) and Timothy Dalton in one (5) (he was also in *Licence to Kill*). *Casino Royale*, the 13th highest-earning Bond film, with David Niven as Bond, is an oddity in that it was presented as an avowed comedy, rather than an adventure with comic elements. Outside the Top 10, George Lazenby played Bond in a single film, *On Her Majesty's Secret Service*, which ranks next to bottom in the earnings league; the very first Bond film, *Dr No* (1963), has earned the least – less, in fact, than *Chitty Chitty Bang Bang*, the film based on Ian Fleming's children's book of this title.

The ranking order for the 10 most successful Bond films that were based on Ian Fleming's novels is:

	Novel	Book	Film
1	Moonraker	1955	1979
2	Thunderball	1961	1965
3	The Spy Who Loved Me	1962	1977
4	Goldfinger	1959	1964
5	Diamonds Are Forever	1956	1971
6	Live and Let Die	1954	1973
7	Casino Royale	1953	1967
8	From Russia with Love	1957	1963
9	You Only Live Twice	1964	1967
10	The Man with the Golden Gun	1965	1974

The other two novels, *On Her Majesty's Secret Service* (book published 1963/film 1969) and *Dr No* (1958/1962), earned the least.

Sean Connery appeared as James Bond seven (or 007) times.

THE TOP 10 FILMS DIRECTED BY STEVEN SPIELBERG

	Film	Year
1	E.T.: The Extra-Terrestrial	1982
2	Jaws	1975
3	Raiders of the Lost Ark	1981
4	Indiana Jones and the Last Crusade	1989
5	Indiana Jones and the Temple of Doom	1984
6	Close Encounters of the Third Kind	1977/80 *
7	Hook	1991
8	The Color Purple	1985
9	Always	1989
10	1941	1979

*Re-edited and re-released as 'Special Edition'.

Steven Spielberg has directed some of the most successful films of all time (the top five in this list appear among the top dozen films of all time). If his credits as producer are included, further blockbusters, such as the *Back to the Future* trilogy, *Gremlins*, the animated film *An American Tail* and part-animated *Who Framed Roger Rabbit?*, would also score highly. *Jurassic Park* will without doubt rank prominently next time this list is updated. Almost inevitably, considering his prolific output, he has also directed a few that have been less successful, including *Twilight Zone – The Movie* (1983) and *Empire of the Sun* (1987), while *The Sugarland Express* (1974) has probably earned the least of all the films Spielberg has directed.

THE 10 MOST SUCCESSFUL CHILDREN'S FILMS* OF ALL TIME

	Film	Year
1	*Honey, I Shrunk the Kids*	1989
2	*Hook*	1991
3	*Teenage Mutant Ninja Turtles*	1990
4	*The Karate Kid Part II*	1986
5	*Mary Poppins*	1964
6	*The Karate Kid*	1984
7	*Teenage Mutant Ninja Turtles II*	1991
8	*WarGames*	1983
9	*The Muppet Movie*	1979
10	*The Goonies*	1985

*Excluding animated films.

Some of the most successful films of all time, such as *E.T.*, *Star Wars* and its two sequels, the two *Ghostbusters* films, *Home Alone* and *Home Alone 2: Lost in New York* have been those that are unrestricted by classification, appeal to the broadest possible base of the 'family audience', and consequently thus attract the greatest revenue. This list is of films that are aimed primarily at a young audience – though some are no doubt also appreciated by accompanying adults.

THE 10 MOST SUCCESSFUL COMEDY FILMS OF ALL TIME

	Film	Year
1	*Home Alone*	1990
2	*Beverly Hills Cop*	1984
3	*Ghost*	1990
4	*Home Alone 2: Lost in New York*	1992
5	*Tootsie*	1982
6	*Pretty Woman*	1990
7	*Three Men and a Baby*	1987
8	*Beverly Hills Cop II*	1987
9	*The Sting*	1973
10	*National Lampoon's Animal House*	1978

The two *Beverly Hills Cop* films are regarded by certain purists as 'action thrillers' rather than comedies. If they are excluded, Nos. 9 and 10 become *Crocodile Dundee* (1986), recently ousted from the list by the phenomenal success of *Home Alone 2: Lost in New York*, and *Look Who's Talking* (1989). If *Ghost* and *Pretty Woman*, which are arguably either comedies or romances with comedy elements, are also excluded, the next two on this list are *Coming to America* (1988) and the recent smash *Sister Act* (1992). Other high-earning comedy films include *City Slickers* (1991), *Nine to Five* (1980), *Smokey and the Bandit* (1977), *Stir Crazy* (1980), *Crocodile Dundee II* (1988) and *The Addams Family* (1991).

THE TOP 10 FILM SEQUELS OF ALL TIME

1	*Star Wars/The Empire Strikes Back/Return of the Jedi*
2	*Raiders of the Lost Ark/Indiana Jones and the Temple of Doom/Indiana Jones and the Last Crusade*
3	*Rocky I–VI*
4	*Star Trek I–VI*
5	*Batman/Batman Returns*
6	*Home Alone 1–2*
7	*Back to the Future I–III*
8	*Jaws I–IV*
9	*Ghostbusters I–II*
10	*Superman I–IV*

Based on total earnings of the original film and all its sequels up to the end of 1992, the *Star Wars* trilogy stands head and shoulders above the rest, having made more than $500,000,000 in the North American market alone. All the other films in the Top 10 have achieved total earnings of around $200,000,000 or more, with *Lethal Weapon 1–3* and *Beverly Hills Cop I–II* lagging just outside the Top 10. A successful film does not guarantee a successful sequel, however: although their total earns them a place in the Top 10, each of the four *Superman* films actually earned less than the previous one, with *Superman IV* earning just one-tenth of the original. *Smokey and the Bandit Part III* earned just one-seventeenth of the original, and although the 1973 film *The Sting* was a box-office blockbuster, its 1983 sequel earned less than one-fifteenth as much, while *Grease 2* earned less than one-tenth of the original *Grease*. Sometimes the situation is reversed, however:

Terminator 2 has already earned six times as much as its 'prequel'. The James Bond films are not presented as sequels, but if they were taken into account, their total earnings would place them in 2nd position in this list.

The cumulative income of *Batman* and *Batman Returns* makes them the highest-earning two-film series of all time.

THE 10 MOST SUCCESSFUL WAR FILMS OF ALL TIME

	Film	Year
1	Platoon	1986
2	Good Morning, Vietnam	1987
3	Apocalypse Now	1979
4	M*A*S*H	1970
5	Patton	1970
6	The Deer Hunter	1978
7	Full Metal Jacket	1987
8	Midway	1976
9	The Dirty Dozen	1967
10	A Bridge Too Far	1977

Surprisingly few war films have appeared in the high-earning bracket for more than five years, suggesting that the days of big-budget epics in this genre may be over. This list, however, excludes successful films that are not technically 'war' films but which have military themes, such as A Few Good Men (1992), The Hunt for Red October (1990) and An Officer and a Gentleman (1982), which would otherwise be placed in the top five, or Top Gun (1986) which would actually head the list.

THE 10 LONGEST FILMS EVER SCREENED

	Title	Country/year	Duration hr	min
1	The Longest and Most Meaningless Movie in the World	UK, 1970	48	0
2	The Burning of the Red Lotus Temple	China, 1928–31	27	0
3	****	USA, 1967	25	0
4	Heimat	West Germany, 1984	15	40
5	Berlin Alexanderplatz	West Germany/Italy, 1980	15	21
6	The Old Testament	Italy, 1922	13	0
7	Comment Yukong déplace les montagnes	France, 1976	12	43
8	Out 1: Noli me Tangere	France, 1971	12	40
9	Ningen No Joken (The Human Condition)	Japan, 1958–60	9	29
10	Shoah	France, 1985	9	26

The list includes commercially screened films, but not 'stunt' films created solely to break endurance records (particularly those of their audiences), among which are the 85-hour The Cure for Insomnia and the 50-hour Mondo Teeth. Those in the list are no more watchable: The Longest and Most Meaningless Movie in the World was later cut to a more manageable 1 hr 30 min, but remained just as meaningless. Outside the Top 10, Abel Gance's Napoleon has not been shown at its full length of nine hours since it was first released, but as new segments of it have been discovered, it has been meticulously reassembled to a length approaching that of the original version. Among more conventional yet extremely long films of recent times are Wagner (GB/Hungary/Austria, 1983; 9 hr 0 min), Little Dorrit (UK, 1987; 5 hr 57 min), the colossally expensive and commercially disastrous Cleopatra (USA, 1963; 4 hr 3 min) and the Greatest Story Ever Told (USA, 1965), which was progressively cut from 4 hr 20 min to 2 hr 7 min, but was no less tedious as a result.

THE 10 HIGHEST GROSSING FILMS OF ALL TIME IN THE UK

	Film	Approx. gross (£)
1	Ghost	23,300,000
2	Crocodile Dundee	21,300,000
3	Robin Hood: Prince of Thieves	19,900,000
4	Terminator 2: Judgment Day	18,100,000
5	E.T.: The Extra-Terrestrial	17,800,000
6	The Silence of the Lambs	17,200,000
7	Who Framed Roger Rabbit?	15,600,000
8	Indiana Jones and the Last Crusade	15,000,000
9	Fatal Attraction	14,400,000
10	Return of the Jedi	14,100,000

Inevitably, bearing inflation in mind, the top-grossing films of all time are releases from the 1980s and 1990s, though it is also true that UK cinema admissions have risen sharply through these decades too. From the nadir of the late 1960s and 1970s, today's films are both more widely viewed (even excluding video) than those of 15 to 25 years ago, as well as grossing considerably more at the box office.

THE 10 MOST SUCCESSFUL WESTERNS OF ALL TIME

	Film	Year
1	Butch Cassidy and the Sundance Kid	1969
2	Unforgiven	1992
3	Jeremiah Johnson	1972
4	How the West Was Won	1962
5	Pale Rider	1985
6	Young Guns	1988
7	Young Guns II	1990
8 =	Little Big Man	1970
8 =	Bronco Billy	1980
10	True Grit	1969

Clint Eastwood is in the unusual position of directing and starring in a film that has forced another of his films out of the Top 10, since the success of Unforgiven has ejected The Outlaw Josey Wales (1976). Although it has a Western setting, Back to the Future, Part III (1990) is essentially a science-fiction film (if it were a true Western, it would rate in 2nd place). If Dances With Wolves were regarded as a Western, it would head the Top 10 by a considerable margin, and if the same classification were applied to The Last of the Mohicans (1992), it would be in 3rd position.

THE 10 MOST EXPENSIVE ITEMS OF FILM MEMORABILIA SOLD AT AUCTION

	Item/sale	Price (£)*
1	James Bond's Aston Martin from *Goldfinger* Sotheby's, New York, 28 June 1986 ($275,000)	179,793
2	Herman J. Mankiewicz's scripts for *Citizen Kane* and *The American* Christie's, New York, 21 June 1989 ($231,000)	139,157
3	Judy Garland's ruby slippers from *The Wizard of Oz* Christie's, New York, 21 June 1988 ($165,000)	104,430
4	Piano from the Paris scene in *Casablanca* Sotheby's, New York, 16 December 1988 ($154,000)	97,469
5	Charlie Chaplin's hat and cane Christie's, London, 11 December 1987	82,500
6	Clark Gable's script from *Gone With the Wind* Sotheby's, New York, 16 December 1988 ($77,000)	48,734
7	Charlie Chaplin's boots Christie's, London, 11 December 1987	38,500
8	A special effects painting of the Emerald City from *The Wizard of Oz* Camden House, Los Angeles, 1 April 1991 ($44,000)	29,944
9	A 1932 Universal poster for *The Old Dark House*, starring Boris Karloff Christie's, New York, 9 December 1991 ($48,400)	26,600
10	16mm film of the only meeting between Danny Kaye and George Bernard Shaw Christie's, London, 27 April 1989	20,900

*$/£ conversion at rate then prevailing.

This list excludes animated film celluloids or 'cels' – the individually painted scenes that are shot in sequence to make up cartoon films – which are now attaining colossal prices: just one of the 150,000 colour cels from *Snow White* (1937) was sold in 1991 for $209,000/£115,000, and in 1989 $286,000/£171,250 was reached for a black and white cel depicting Donald Duck in *Orphan's Benefit* (1934). If memorabilia relating to film stars rather than films is included, Orson Welles' annotated script from the radio production of *The War of the Worlds* ($143,000/£90,500 in 1988) would qualify for the Top 10, while among near-misses are the witch's hat from *The Wizard of Oz* ($33,000/£20,886 in 1988), Marilyn Monroe's 'shimmy' dress from *Some Like It Hot* (£19,800 in 1988) and the stand-in model of Boris Karloff as Frankenstein's monster from the 1935 film *The Bride of Frankenstein* (£16,500 in 1988).

THE 10 MOST EXPENSIVE FILMS EVER MADE*

	Film	Year	Cost ($)
1	*Terminator 2: Judgment Day*	1991	95,000,000
2	*Total Recall*	1990	85,000,000
3 =	*Die Hard 2*	1990	70,000,000
3 =	*Who Framed Roger Rabbit?*	1988	70,000,000
3 =	*Hook*	1991	70,000,000
6	*The Godfather, Part 3*	1990	65,000,000
7	*Rambo III*	1988	58,000,000
8 =	*Superman*	1979	55,000,000
8 =	*Ishtar*	1987	55,000,000
8 =	*Tango and Cash*	1989	55,000,000
8 =	*Days of Thunder*	1990	55,000,000

*To 31 December 1992.

One Arnold Schwarzenegger sci-fi film replaces another as the most expensive movie ever made. However, by 1993, *Terminator 2* had earned $112,500,000 in North American rental income alone, making it the 11th highest earner of all time, so its makers Tristar are unlikely to be concerned by its enormous costs. *Hook*, another costly 1991 release, has proved less commercially successful, but by 1993 had earned $65,000,000 in rental income and is thus not liable for entry into the 'flops' table.

Guess whose? Charlie Chaplin's boots, hat and cane are among the Top 10 items of film memorabilia sold at auction.

THE TOP 10 ELECTRICITY SURGES OF ALL TIME IN THE UK

	TV programme	Channel	Date	Time	Pick-up (MW)
1	World Cup Semi-final:	BBC1	4 Jul 90	21.38	
	West Germany *v* England	ITV		21.48	2,800
2	*The Thornbirds*	BBC1	22 Jan 84	21.07	2,600
3 =	*The Thornbirds*	BBC1	16 Jan 84	21.30	2,200
3 =	*Dallas*	BBC1	8 May 85	20.56	
	This is Your Life	ITV		21.00	2,200
3 =	*The Darling Buds of May*	ITV	28 Apr 91	20.40	2,200
6 =	*Dallas*	BBC1	1 May 85	20.56	
	This is Your Life	ITV		21.00	2,100
6 =	*The Colbys*	BBC1	19 Feb 86	21.00	2,100
8 =	*Coronation Street*	ITV	2 Apr 84	19.57	
	Blue Thunder	BBC1		20.00	2,000
8 =	*Dallas*	BBC1	15 May 84	20.50	2,000
8 =	*EastEnders*	BBC1	1 Apr 86	20.00	2,000
8 =	*Coronation Street*	ITV	2 Apr 86	19.57	
	A Song for Europe	BBC1		20.00	2,000
8 =	*Dallas*	BBC1	30 Apr 86	20.57	
	Minder	ITV		21.00	2,000
8 =	*EastEnders*	BBC1	4 Sep 86	20.00	2,000
8 =	World Cup Semi-final:	BBC1	3 Jul 90	21.51	
	Italy *v* Argentina	ITV		21.57	2,000
8 =	*The Darling Buds of May*	ITV	12 May 91	20.44–50	2,000

Demand for electricity in the UK varies gradually during the day: as it gets dark, progressively more lights are switched on, or, during the winter, heating comes on at varying times during the morning, and the National Grid responds to such increases by steadily increasing the supply. The effect of television programmes is far more dramatic, however. It is not the programmes themselves but when they end that causes surges in demand (known as 'TV pick-ups'), as millions of viewers get up and switch on electric kettles and other appliances (even the action of flushing lavatories has an effect, as demand for electricity from water pumping stations increases). Because barely a few minutes separates the ends of certain programmes on BBC1 and ITV, it is not possible to differentiate between them, but all those listed contributed to national TV pick-ups of 2,000 megawatts or more. The end of *Elizabeth R* (at 21.50 on BBC1 on 6 February 1992) resulted in a 1,200-megawatt surge that was widely reported in the Press the following day, but was in fact unremarkable when compared with those in the Top 10. With the increasing spread of viewing across BBC, ITV, satellite and cable channels and the use of video recorders, however, such notable TV pick-ups will probably be less evident in the future.

THE 10 LONGEST-RUNNING PROGRAMMES ON BBC RADIO

	Programme	First broadcast
1	The Week's Good Cause	24 January 1926
2	Choral Evensong	7 October 1926
3	Daily Service	2 January 1928*
4	The Week in Westminster	6 November 1929
5	Sunday Half Hour	14 July 1940
6	Desert Island Discs	29 January 1942
7	Saturday Night Theatre	3 April 1943
8	This Week's Composer	2 August 1943
9	Letter From America (originally American Letter)	24 March 1946
10	From Our Own Correspondent	4 October 1946

*Experimental broadcast; national transmission began December 1929.

In addition to these 10 long-running programmes, a further six that started in the 1940s are still on the air: *Woman's Hour* (first broadcast 7 October 1946 – although the BBC's London station 2LO had previously first broadcast a programme with this name on 2 May 1923), *Down Your Way* (29 December 1946), *Round Britain Quiz* (2 November 1947), *Any Questions?* (12 October 1948), *Book at Bedtime* (6 August 1949) and *Morning Story* (17 October 1949). *Gardeners' Question Time* was first broadcast on 9 April 1947 as *How Does Your Garden Grow?* Its name was changed in 1950. A pilot for *The Archers* was broadcast in the Midland region for a one-week trial beginning on 29 May 1950, but the serial began its national run on 1 January 1951.

THE TOP 10 BBC 1 AUDIENCES, 1992

	Programme	Day	Date	Audience
1	EastEnders	Thu/Sun	2/5 Jan	24,320,000 *
2	Only Fools and Horses	Fri	25 Dec	20,130,000
3	Neighbours	Mon	17 Feb	19,410,000 *
4	More of Auntie's Bloomers	Sun	27 Dec	18,450,000
5	Elizabeth R	Thu	6 Feb	17,860,000
6	Birds of a Feather	Fri	25 Dec	16,880,000
7	Casualty	Sun	6 Dec	16,640,000
8	One Foot in the Grave	Sun	8 Mar	16,200,000
9	Grand National	Sat	4 Apr	16,000,000
10	Noel's Xmas House Party	Sat	26 Dec	15,930,000

*Aggregates two screenings of the same programme.

Only the highest audience figures are given for programmes in series.

THE TOP 10 RADIO STATIONS IN THE UK IN 1992

	Station	Listener hours*
1	BBC Radio 1	196,041,000
2	BBC Radio 2	114,231,000
3	BBC Radio 4	94,349,000
4	Capital Radio†	51,583,000
5	Atlantic 252	32,553,000
6	Metro Tyne Tees†	27,506,000
7	Classic FM	24,881,000
8	Metro Yorkshire†	21,100,000
9	LBC†	17,955,000
10	Radio Clyde†	14,816,000

*Total number of hours spent by all adults (over 15) listening to the station in an average week.

†Split frequency stations; listener hours are totals for all frequencies.

Source: RAJAR/RSL.

Cause for celebration: *Birds of a Feather* was one of BBC 1's top programmes in 1992.

THE TOP 10 BBC 2 AUDIENCES, 1992

	Programme	Day	Date	Audience
1	Wimbledon Men's Final	Sun	5 Jul	10,890,000
2	World Snooker Final	Mon	4 May	8,890,000
3	British Grand Prix	Sun	12 Jul	8,140,000
4	Olympic Grandstand	Wed	5 Aug	8,110,000
5	Absolutely Fabulous	Thu	17 Dec	8,010,000
6	Top Gear	Wed/Thu	26/27 Aug	7,930,000 *
7	Neighbours	Sat	1 Aug	7,870,000
8	Harry Enfield	Thu	30 Apr	7,550,000
9	Film: Mad Max 2	Sun	24 May	7,460,000
10	Benny Hill – Clown Imperial	Tue	26 May	7,240,000

THE TOP 10 ITV AUDIENCES, 1992

	Programme	Day	Date	Audience
1	Coronation Street	Wed/Sun	8/12 Jan	21,350,000 *
2	The Worst of It'll Be Alright on the Night	Sat	1 Feb	19,920,000
3	You've Been Framed	Sun	19 Jan	19,330,000
4	The Trouble with Mr Bean	Wed	1 Jan	18,740,000
5	The Darling Buds of May	Sun	26 Jan	18,730,000
6	Merry Christmas, Mr Bean	Tue	29 Dec	18,480,000
7	Film: Taggart: The Movie	Wed	1 Jan	18,330,000
8	Film: Three Men and a Baby	Sat	15 Feb	18,270,000
9	Mr Bean Rides Again	Mon	17 Feb	17,110,000
10	The Bill	Tue	28 Jan	16,940,000

THE TOP 10 CHANNEL 4 AUDIENCES, 1992

	Programme	Day	Date	Audience
1	Cutting Edge	Mon/Fri	23/27 Mar	8,690,000 *
2	The Camomile Lawn	Thu	5 Mar	7,590,000
3	Inspector Morse	Wed	16 Sep	7,090,000
4	Female Parts	Mon	11 May	7,060,000
5	Film: A Nightmare on Elm Street	Sun	31 Mar	6,800,000
6	Brookside	Wed/Sat	16/19 Sep	6,730,000 *
7	Film: Stand By Me	Sun	5 Jan	6,360,000
8	Coast of Dreams	Mon/Fri	24/28 Feb	6,190,000 *
9	Crystal Maze	Sun	27 Dec	5,950,000
10	Film: Rita, Sue and Bob Too	Sun	19 Apr	5,710,000

*Aggregates two screenings of the same programme.

Only the highest audience figures are given for programmes in series.

THE FIRST 10 PROGRAMMES ON BBC TELEVISION

	Time	Programme
		Monday 2 November 1936
1	15.02	Opening ceremony by Postmaster General G.C. Tryon
2	15.15	*British Movietone News* No. 387 (repeated several times during the next few days)
3	15.23	*Variety* – Adele Dixon (singer), Buck and Bubbles (comic dancers) and the Television Orchestra (15.31 close; 15.32 Television Orchestra continues in sound only with music by Arthur Bliss from the film, *Things To Come*, *Folk Song Suite* by Vaughan Williams and extracts from *The Beggar's Opera* by Frederick Austin)
4	21.05	Film: *Television Comes to London*
5	21.23	*Picture Page* (magazine programme featuring interviews with transatlantic flyer Jim Mollison, tennis champion Kay Stammers, King's Bargemaster Bossy Phelps and others, ghost stories from Algernon Blackwood and various musical interludes)
6	22.11	Speech by Lord Selsdon, followed by close
		Tuesday 3 November 1936
7	15.04	Exhibits from the Metropolitan and Essex Canine Society's Show – 'Animals described by A. Croxton Smith, OBE'
8	15.28	*The Golden Hind* – 'a model of Drake's famous ship, made by L. A. Stock, a bus driver'
9	15.46	*Starlight* with comedians Bebe Daniels and Ben Lyon (followed by repeat of items 7 and 8)
10	21.48	*Starlight* with Manuela Del Rio

Although there were earlier low-definition experimental broadcasts, BBC television's high-definition public broadcasting service – the first in the world – was inaugurated on a daily basis on 2 November 1936. During the first three months, two parallel operating systems were in use: the opening programmes were thus broadcast twice, first on the Baird system, and repeated slightly later on the Marconi-EMI system. After 5 February 1937, only the Marconi-EMI system was used.

THE FIRST 10 PROGRAMMES BROADCAST ON BBC 2

	Time	Programme
		Tuesday 21 April 1964
1	11.00	*Play School*
2	19.15	*Zero Minus Five* (introductory programme)
3	19.20	*Line-Up* (arts programme)
4	19.30	*The Alberts' Channel Too* (variety show)
5	20.00	*Kiss Me Kate* (musical starring Howard Keel and Millicent Martin)
6	21.35	Arkady Raikin (Soviet comedian)
7	22.20	*Off With a Bang* (fireworks from Southend pier)
8	22.35	*Newsroom*
9	23.02	*Jazz 625* (Duke Ellington in Concert)
		Wednesday 22 April 1964
10	11.00	*Play School*

The programmes for the official opening night on Monday 20 April 1964 were postponed after much of central London was blacked out by a powercut, and only a handful of announcements and news items were actually transmitted. Originally broadcast only in the London area, BBC 2 was the first British station to broadcast exclusively on the 625-line system for sharper definition, but a survey published on 9 June 1964 indicated that only 7.6 per cent of homes in the area had a television set capable of receiving such transmissions. By 6 December 1964 viewers in the Birmingham area were able to tune in to BBC 2, and the service was steadily extended to the rest of the country.

Play School was the first programme broadcast on BBC 2.

THE FIRST 10 PROGRAMMES ON ITV

	Time	Programme
		Thursday 22 September 1955
1	19.15	*The Ceremony at the Guildhall* (The Hallé Orchestra conducted by Sir John Barbirolli playing *Cockaigne* by Sir Edward Elgar and inaugural speeches by the Lord Mayor of London, Sir Seymour Howard, the Postmaster General, Dr Charles Hill and Chairman of the Independent Television Authority, Sir Kenneth Clark)
2	20.00	*Channel Nine* variety show from ABC's television theatre, featuring Shirley Abicair (Australian zither-player), Reg Dixon (organist), Hughie Green, Harry Secombe and other stars
3	20.40	Drama: Robert Morley introduces extracts from Oscar Wilde's *The Importance of Being Earnest* (starring Dame Edith Evans and Sir John Gielgud), Saki's *Baker's Dozen* and Noël Coward's *Private Lives*
4	21.10	Professional boxing from Shoreditch, Terence Murphy *v* Lew Lazar
5	22.00	*News and Newsreel*
6	22.15	*Gala Night at the Mayfair* (fashion show from the Mayfair Hotel, London)
7	22.30	*Star Cabaret* with Billy Ternant and his Orchestra
8	22.50	Preview of future Independent Television programmes
9	23.00	*Epilogue* (followed by National Anthem and close)
		Friday 23 September 1955
10	10.45	*Sixpenny Corner* (the first episode of a daily 'soap' set in a rural garage)

The first-ever TV commercial broadcast in the UK was an advertisement for Gibbs SR Toothpaste shown in the first break in the *Channel Nine* programme, at 20.12.

THE FIRST 10 PROGRAMMES BROADCAST ON CHANNEL 4

	Time	Programme	Audience
1	16.45	*Countdown* (quiz game introduced by Richard Whiteley)	3,681,000
2	17.15	*Preview* (review of forthcoming programmes)	2,724,000
3	17.30	*The Body Show* (keep-fit programme)	2,124,000
4	18.00	*People's Court* (Californian court cases re-enacted)	1,508,000
5	18.30	*Book Four* (book review programme featuring Len Deighton, William Boyd and Fay Weldon)	984,000
6	19.00	*Channel 4 News* (presented by Trevor McDonald, Peter Sissons, etc)	1,239,000
7	20.00	*Brookside* (first episode of the long-running soap)	2,779,000
8	20.30	*The Paul Hogan Show* (Australian comedy series)	3,598,000
9	21.00	*Walter* (feature film commissioned by Channel 4, starring Ian McKellen)	3,737,000
10	22.15	*The Comic Strip Presents: Five Go Mad in Dorset*	3,360,000

Channel 4 first went on the air on Tuesday 2 November 1982. Of the four terrestrial British TV stations, it is unique in having detailed audience figures for its first programmes. The final programme broadcast on the first night was The Raving Beauties' In the Pink (an all-female cabaret), from 22.45 to 23.45, which attracted an audience of 1,031,000.

THE FIRST 10 SUBJECTS FEATURED ON *THIS IS YOUR LIFE*

	Name	Profession	Programme
1	Eamonn Andrews	TV presenter	20 Jul 1955
2	Yvonne Bailey	French Resistance heroine	25 Sep 1955
3	Ted Ray	Entertainer	23 Oct 1955
4	Rev James Butterworth	Children's social worker	20 Nov 1955
5	C.B. Fry	Cricketer and writer	18 Dec 1955
6	Johanna Harris	British Red Cross worker	1 Jan 1956
7	Donald Campbell	Speed record-breaker	15 Jan 1956
8	Joe Brannelly	Music publisher	29 Jan 1956
9	Stanley Matthews	Footballer	12 Feb 1956
10	Henry Starling	Billingsgate Market porter	26 Feb 1956

Eamonn Andrews, himself the subject of the pilot *This Is Your Life* programme, went on to present it, first on BBC and, after 1969, on ITV, until his death in 1987, when it was taken over by Michael Aspel.

THE 10 LONGEST-RUNNING PROGRAMMES ON BRITISH TELEVISION

	Programme	Channel	First shown
1	Come Dancing	BBC	29 September 1950
2	Panorama	BBC	11 November 1953
3	This Week	ITV	6 January 1956
4	What the Papers Say	BBC	5 November 1956
5	The Sky at Night	BBC	24 April 1957
6	Grandstand	BBC	11 October 1958
7	Blue Peter	BBC	16 October 1958
8	Coronation Street	ITV	9 December 1960
9	Songs of Praise	BBC	1 October 1961
10	Dr Who	BBC	23 November 1963

Only programmes appearing every year since their first screenings are listed. Several other BBC programmes, such as *The Good Old Days* (1953–83), ran for many years but are now defunct. *The Sky at Night* has the additional distinction of having had the same presenter, Patrick Moore, since its first programme. Although *The Sooty Show* has been screened intermittently, Sooty is the longest-serving TV personality. The puppet's show, started by Harry Corbett in 1952, was transferred to Thames in 1968 where it has been presented since 1975 by its creator's son, Matthew Corbett. *This Is Your Life* was started by the BBC in 1953 and, after a break, was taken over by Thames in 1973. ITV has also presented a number of long-running programmes that are no longer with us, among them *Opportunity Knocks* (1956–77), *University Challenge* (1962–87) and *Crossroads* (1964–88). Among other programmes that have been running since the 1960s are *Top of the Pops* (BBC; first screened 1 January 1964), *Horizon* (BBC; 2 May 1964) and *Match of the Day* (BBC; 22 August 1964).

THE TOP 10 VIDEO RENTALS OF 1992 IN THE UK

1	Terminator 2: Judgment Day
2	Basic Instinct
3	Robin Hood, Prince of Thieves
4	Point Break
5	Backdraft
6	The Silence of the Lambs
7	City Slickers
8	Naked Gun 2¹/₂ – The Smell of Fear
9	Hot Shots!
10	The Commitments

Basic Instinct was actually the biggest-renting video title released during 1992, but, released fairly late in the year, it did not overtake *Terminator 2* until the early weeks of 1993. The title with the greatest longevity was *The Silence of the Lambs*, which had also emerged as the eighth-biggest renter of 1991. Unusually for the top annual renters, all these titles carried 18 certificates, theoretically giving them the most restricted viewing audience available.

A scene from *Point Break*, one of the most rented videos of 1992.

THE 10 BESTSELLING VIDEOS OF ALL TIME IN THE UK*

1 Fantasia
2 Cinderella
3 The Little Mermaid
4 Lady and the Tramp
5 Dirty Dancing
6 The Three Tenors Concert
7 Pretty Woman
8 Callanetics
9 Watch with Mother
10 Sleeping Beauty

*To February 1993.

Twelve months after an enormously successful marketing exercise which brought it the UK's biggest-selling video in *Fantasia* (3,200,000 copies sold), Walt Disney gave similar limited-availability treatment, including a Christmas season, to the classic 1950s animation *Cinderella*. While its sales were not in the *Fantasia* class, they topped 1,750,000, and have seen the newcomer safely into this Top 10 at number two, easing Disney stablemate *Pinocchio* from the bottom of the chart.

THE 10 MOST-RENTED VIDEOS OF ALL TIME IN THE UK*

1 Crocodile Dundee
2 Dirty Dancing
3 Ghost
4 Pretty Woman
5 A Fish Called Wanda
6 Robocop
7 Back to the Future
8 Police Academy
9 Home Alone
10 Beverly Hills Cop

*To February 1993.

Although this list is unchanged from 12 months ago, and video rentals generally are declining from the peaks they achieved during the 1980s, three titles – *Basic Instinct*, *Terminator 2: Judgment Day* and *The Silence of the Lambs* – are all knocking on the door of the Top 10, and were still renting healthily at the end of February 1993, indicating a possible entry for any or all of them at the time of the next update.

THE 10 BESTSELLING CHILDREN'S VIDEOS OF ALL TIME IN THE UK

1 Cinderella
2 The Little Mermaid
3 Lady and the Tramp
4 Watch with Mother
5 Sleeping Beauty
6 Pinocchio
7 The Rescuers
8 Hook
9 The Rescuers Down Under
10 Teenage Mutant Hero Turtles: How It All Began

With huge UK sales in excess of 1,750,000, Walt Disney's *Cinderella* bounds to the top of this chart just as *The Little Mermaid* did the previous year, with Steven Spielberg's *Hook* and Disney's *The Rescuers Down Under* as the list's other new entries.

THE FIRST 10 FILMS TO TOP THE UK VIDEO RENTAL CHART

1 Jaws
2 Star Trek: The Motion Picture
3 Scanners
4 The Exterminator
5 Superman: The Movie
6 The Jazz Singer
7 Monty Python's Life of Brian
8 Watership Down
9 Chariots of Fire
10 Star Wars

The UK Video Rental Chart was inaugurated in March 1981, when the industry itself was still in its infancy, and the regular release of recent major cinema films for rental was not yet established practice. Several of the 10 earliest chart-toppers (which cover the period until September 1982) did not come to video until some years after their big-screen success: six in the case of *Jaws*, and five for *Star Wars*.

THE 10 LARGEST MARKS & SPENCER STORES IN THE UK

	Location	Area sq m	Area sq ft
1	Marble Arch, London	11,947	128,600
2	Pantheon, Oxford Street, London	8,965	96,500
3	MetroCentre*, Gateshead, Tyne & Wear	8,872	95,500
4	Manchester	8,463	91,100
5	Kingston-upon-Thames, London	8,166	87,900
6	Thurrock, Essex	7,878	84,800
7	Bromley, Kent	7,757	83,500
8	Argyle Street, Glasgow	7,692	82,800
9	Croydon, London	7,664	82,500
10	Leeds, West Yorkshire	7,646	82,300

*The largest single-level store.

THE 10 OLDEST-ESTABLISHED MARKS & SPENCER STORES IN THE UK

	Location	Year opened
1	Leeds	1884
2 =	Wakefield	1890
2 =	Birkenhead	1890
2 =	Castleford	1890
5	Wigan	1891
6	Bolton	1892
7 =	Ashton-under-Lyne	1894
7 =	Manchester	1894
7 =	Scarborough	1894
10	Newcastle	1895

Polish refugee Michael Marks set up his first stall, 'Marks' Penny Bazaar', in Leeds market in 1884. Its success meant that it was followed by a succession of shops, initially in the north of England, but gradually spreading southwards. The company name Marks & Spencer was first adopted in 1926 and in 1928 the brand name St Michael came into use: various saints' names were considered before the chairman of the company, Simon Marks, decided upon St Michael, in honour of his father. Today the company is one of the UK's top three retailers and occupies a unique place in both its clothing and food.

Above The Marble Arch branch of M&S, the largest in the UK.

THE TOP 10 GROCERY BRANDS IN THE UK

Brand (product)/ Manufacturer	Annual sales (£)*

1 Persil (washing powder)
Lever Brothers — 237,200,000

Persil, the first-ever household detergent, originally went on the market in Germany on 6 June 1907. Its name may derive either from the parsley trademark of a French inventor ('persil' is French for parsley), or from two ingredients, *per*borate and *sil*icate, used by Professor Hermann Geissler and Dr Hermann Bauer, the German inventors of dry soap powder. The product has been made in Great Britain since 1909.

2 Coca-Cola (soft drink)
Coca-Cola — 237,000,000

Coca-Cola, invented by Dr John S. Pemberton of Atlanta, Georgia, first went on sale there on 8 May 1886. The name was registered in the USA in 1893 and the drink was first sold in London in 1900. Pemberton, who died in 1888, and his son sold all their rights to what is today regarded as the most widely known and powerful brand name in the world.

3 Ariel (washing powder)
Procter & Gamble — 224,400,000

Ariel, a revolutionary new product combining soap, synthetic detergents and enzymes, was introduced nationally in January 1969 followed by Ariel Automatic in October 1981, Ariel Ultra in October 1989, and various other Ariel products. Ariel is the name of various mythological characters, the best known being the 'airy spirit' in Shakespeare's *Tempest*.

4 Andrex (toilet paper)
Scott — 193,000,000

The name Andrex comes from the location of the factory where it was first made in 1945 (or relaunched – its 1942 launch was thwarted by wartime rationing): St Andrews Road, Walthamstow, London. It was originally called 'Androll' and changed to Andrex in 1954. By 1962 it had become the bestselling toilet tissue in the UK – a market that is today worth some £600,000,000 per annum – and has steadily moved up this Top 10 list, in 1992 gaining one place. The popular TV advertisements featuring the Andrex puppy started in 1972, and more than 70 have been made to date. About 16,898,112 km/10,500,000 miles of Andrex are produced every year – equivalent to more than 40 times the distance from the Earth to the Moon.

5 Nescafé (instant coffee)
Nestlé — 177,800,000

Nescafé was the original instant coffee, first sold in 1938 by the Swiss firm, Nestlé.

6 Whiskas (catfood)
Pedigree Petfoods — 150,300,000

Whiskas is now the bestselling petfood brand in the world.

7 Silver Spoon (sugar)
British Sugar — 140,200,000

Silver Spoon claims 55 per cent of the white granulated sugar market – a total of 300,000 tonnes a year.

8 PG Tips (tea)
Brooke Bond Foods (Unilever) — 135,600,000

'PG Tips' comes from the abbreviation of its earlier name, *Pre-gestee*, referring to its supposed 'before digestion' medicinal properties: the tips are the best parts of tea leaves. The company calculates that 35,000,000 cups of PG Tips tea are drunk every day – six Olympic-sized swimming pools of liquid or the equivalent of more than two cups a year for every person in the world. PG Tips' TV advertising featuring chimpanzees has been seen on British television for 36 years – the longest-running campaign in television history.

9 Flora (margarine)
Van den Berghs & Jurgens (Unilever) — 131,400,000

More than 60,000 tonnes of Flora, which was launched in 1964, are sold every year – equivalent to the weight of almost 160 jumbo jets or 4,800 double-decker buses.

10 Walkers Crisps
PepsiCo — 125,000,000

Walkers Crisps, a newcomer to this Top 10, is the bestselling brand of a product that has been around for 140 years: there is much dispute about how potato crisps began, but it is probable that they were adapted from a French recipe for what in Britain were once known as 'game chips' (because they were eaten with pheasant and other game fowl). In the USA, it is claimed that 'potato chips' were devised by George Crum, an American Indian working as a chef at Moon Lake Lodge at the New York spa resort of Saratoga Springs. Although popular, they remained a specialized dish on both sides of the Atlantic and did not take off as a commercially available snack until the invention of the mechanical potato-peeler in the 1920s. Walkers Crisps were first made in 1949 by Walkers Pork Butchery of Leicester, in order to diversify as a response to post-war meat shortages. Today the product has a dominant 37.8 per cent of the UK crisp market, which has total sales of 30,000,000 bags of crisps a day (equivalent to 347 bags per second of every day) weighing 900 tonnes, or more than twice the weight of a Jumbo jet.

*Through grocery outlets only; total brand sales may be higher.

Coca-Cola is the bestselling food grocery brand in the UK.

THE TOP 10 RETAILERS IN THE UK

	Retailer	Sales (£)* 1990–91	1991–92
1	J. Sainsbury	6,849,383,000	7,665,500,000
2	Tesco	6,346,300,000	7,097,400,000
3	Marks & Spencer	4,897,400,000	4,863,000,000
4	Argyll Group	4,496,100,000	4,729,200,000
5	Asda Group	4,348,500,000	4,526,300,000
6	Kingfisher	3,111,599,000	3,301,600,000
7	The Boots Company	2,982,000,000	3,037,400,000
8	Isosceles	3,118,700,000	2,788,000,000
9	Kwik Save Group	1,784,534,000	2,319,000,000
10	John Lewis Partnership	1,978,100,000	2,066,700,000

Excluding VAT.

Based on The Retail Rankings (1993) published by The Corporate Intelligence Group Ltd.

The increased sales of the UK's Top 10 retailers – up by more than six per cent in a year – would appear to contradict the cuts that have been widespread during the recession. In fact, the principal retailers are supermarkets with most sales in the food sector, which has been little affected by cutbacks in other areas. By contrast, stores that rely on sales of consumer goods such as home furnishings and do-it-yourself products have clearly been feeling the pinch.

THE TOP 10 DUTY-FREE SHOPS IN THE WORLD

	Shop location	Annual sales (US$)
1	Honolulu Airport	320,000,000
2	London Heathrow Airport	278,000,000
3	Tokyo Narita Airport	275,000,000
4	Amsterdam Schiphol Airport	221,000,000
5	Paris Charles de Gaulle Airport	211,000,000
6	Singapore Changi Airport	200,000,000
7	Frankfurt Airport	194,000,000
8	Viking Line Ferries (Finland)	190,000,000
9	Hong Kong Airport	160,000,000
10	DSB Ferries (Denmark)	137,000,000

Total sales in the Top 500 duty-free shops in the world in 1991 were $8,410,707,120, of which the Top 10 accounted for about 26 per cent. Honolulu is not only the world's top duty-free shop in terms of total annual sales, but also one of the highest per passenger ($125.49 – only Guam Airport is higher at $161.75), compared with Heathrow's average of $16.58. However, in line with the recessionary experience throughout the world, even Honolulu's figures are down from its 1990 total of $400,000,000 and per passenger sales of $160.90.

THE TOP 10 SUPERMARKET GROUPS* IN THE UK

	Retailer	Sales (£)** 1990–91	1991–92
1	Tesco	6,346,300,000	7,097,000,000
2	J. Sainsbury	6,208,400,000 †	6,944,000,000 †
3	Argyll Group (Safeway, etc)	4,325,700,000	4,729,000,000
4	Asda Group	4,142,600,000	4,308,000,000
5	Isosceles (Gateway, etc)	3,118,700,000	3,024,000,000
6	Kwik Save	1,784,500,000	2,273,000,000
7	William Morrison	909,600,000	1,118,000,000
8	Waitrose	995,700,000	1,067,000,000
9	Iceland (including Bejam)	724,600,000	889,000,000
10	William Low	384,000,000	420,000,000

*Excluding Co-ops.   **Excluding VAT.   †Excluding Savacentre.*

Based on The Retail Rankings (1993) published by The Corporate Intelligence Group Ltd.

THE TOP 10 DUTY-FREE PRODUCTS

	Product	Sales (US$)
1	Cigarettes	1,750,000,000
2	Women's fragrances	1,660,000,000
3	Scotch whisky	1,240,000,000
4	Women's cosmetics and toiletries	1,190,000,000
5	Cognac	1,170,000,000
6	Men's fragrances and toiletries	780,000,000
7	Leather goods (handbags, belts, etc)	700,000,000
8	Accessories	670,000,000
9	Confectionery	650,000,000
10	Jewellery and pearls	500,000,000

In 1991 total world duty-free sales were estimated to have reached $15,000,000,000, of which the Top 10 comprise $10,310,000,000 – a marginal reduction on the previous year and a reflection of the global recession and decline in international air traffic.

THE TOP 10 DUTY-FREE SHOPS IN THE UK

	Shop location	Annual sales (US$)
1	London Heathrow Airport	278,000,000
2	London Gatwick Airport	131,000,000
3	Sealink Ferries	125,000,000 *
4	P & O European Ferries	100,000,000
5	British Airways	64,700,000
6	Manchester Ringway Airport	52,800,000
7	Britannia Airways (charter airline)	42,700,000
8	Sally Line (ferry operator)	30,000,000 *
9	Monarch Airlines (charter airline)	23,000,000
10	Dan-Air (charter airline)	22,600,000

Estimated.

THE TOP 10 DUTY-FREE AIRLINES IN THE WORLD

	Airline/country	Annual sales (US$)
1	British Airways (UK)	64,700,000
2	Japan Air Lines (Japan)	57,000,000
3	Sterling Airways (Denmark)	51,500,000
4	Scanair (Scandinavia)	50,000,000 *
5	Korean Air (Korea)	45,000,000
6	Britannia Airways (UK)	42,700,000
7	Alitalia (Italy)	38,600,000
8	Lufthansa (Germany)	35,950,000
9	China Airlines (Taiwan)	34,000,000
10	Conair (Denmark)	30,000,000 *

Estimated.

THE TOP 10 DUTY-FREE FERRY OPERATORS IN THE WORLD

	Ferry operator/country	Annual sales (US$)
1	Viking Line Ferries (Finland)	190,000,000
2	DSB Ferries (Denmark)	137,000,000
3	Stena Line (Sweden)	135,000,000 *
4	Sealink Ferries (UK)	125,000,000 *
5	Silja Line (Finland)	106,000,000
6	P & O European Ferries (UK)	100,000,000
7	Sweferry/Scandlines (Sweden/Denmark)	88,600,000
8	DB/Puttgarden-Rödby (Germany)	78,200,000
9	Scandinavian Seaways (Denmark)	76,800,000
10	Color Line (Norway)	59,300,000

Estimated.

Sealink is the UK's top duty-free ferry operator.

THE TOP 10 DUTY-FREE AIRPORTS IN THE WORLD

	Shop location	Annual sales (US$)
1	Honolulu Airport	320,000,000
2	London Heathrow Airport	278,000,000
3	Tokyo Narita Airport	275,000,000
4	Amsterdam Schiphol Airport	221,000,000
5	Paris Charles de Gaulle Airport	211,000,000
6	Singapore Changi Airport	200,000,000
7	Frankfurt Airport	194,000,000
8	Hong Kong Airport	160,000,000
9	Osaka Airport	134,000,000
10	Copenhagen Airport	132,000,000

THE TOP 10 DUTY-FREE COUNTRIES IN THE WORLD

	Country	Total annual duty- and tax-free sales
1	USA	1,900,000,000
2	UK	1,250,000,000
3	Germany	820,000,000
4	Singapore	610,000,000
5	Hong Kong	600,000,000
6 =	Denmark	570,000,000
6 =	Japan	570,000,000
8	France	550,000,000
9	Spain	530,000,000
10	Sweden	510,000,000

THE TOP 10 FUND-RAISING CHARITIES IN THE UK

	Charity	Voluntary income (£)
1	National Trust	63,042,000
2	Oxfam	51,494,000
3	Royal National Lifeboat Institution	46,953,000
4	Imperial Cancer Research Fund	44,118,000
5	Cancer Research Campaign	40,207,000
6	Save the Children Fund	38,719,000
7	Salvation Army	35,188,000
8	British Red Cross Society	32,636,000
9	Help the Aged	31,625,000
10	Barnardos	31,513,000

There are over 167,000 registered charities in England and Wales alone, but the Top 10 remains similar from year to year. The order of the Top 10 is for voluntary income only. Most charities also receive income from other sources, such as rents and interest on investments – the National Trust leading the field with income from all sources totalling £116,621,000 in 1991, while both the Salvation Army and Barnardos received totals of more than £70,000,000.

THE TOP 10 ANIMAL CHARITIES IN THE UK

	Charity	Voluntary income (£)
1	Royal Society for the Prevention of Cruelty to Animals	27,298,000
2	World Wide Fund for Nature	17,343,000
3	Royal Society for the Protection of Birds	15,951,000
4	People's Dispensary for Sick Animals	13,920,000
5	Donkey Sanctuary	4,558,000
6	Blue Cross Animals' Hospital	4,150,000
7	National Canine Defence League	3,896,000
8	Dogs' Home Battersea	2,767,000
9	Cats Protection League	2,579,000
10	Wildfowl and Wetlands Trust	2,238,000

THE TOP 10 CHILDREN'S CHARITIES* IN THE UK

	Charity	Voluntary income (£)
1	Save the Children Fund	38,719,000
2	Barnardos	31,513,000
3	National Society for the Prevention of Cruelty to Children	26,580,000
4	Church of England Children's Society	13,051,000
5	National Children's Home	10,674,000
6	Romanian Orphanage Trust	7,738,000
7	Variety Club Children's Charity	4,072,000
8	Plan International (UK)	3,050,000
9	Christian Children's Fund of Great Britain	2,624,000
10	Malcolm Sargent Cancer Fund for Children	2,361,000

*Excluding charities that aid both children and adults.

The Save the Children Fund, here at work in war-torn Mozambique, is the UK's top children's charity.

THE TOP 10 GRANT-MAKING TRUSTS IN THE UK IN 1991

	Trust	Grants (£)
1	Wellcome Trust	71,700,000
2	Tudor Trust	19,836,000
3	Gatsby Charitable Foundation	19,249,000
4	Royal Society	14,223,000
5	Henry Smith (Estates Charities)	11,687,000
6	Leverhulme Trust	10,990,000
7	Garfield Weston Foundation	9,944,000
8	Wolfson Foundation	8,636,000
9	Baring Foundation	7,666,000
10	Monument Trust	6,571,000

THE TOP 10 BRITISH COMPANIES DONATING TO CHARITY IN 1991–92

	Company	Donations
1	British Telecom	14,498,000
2	British Petroleum	14,100,000
3	National Westminster Bank	11,700,000
4	British Gas	10,000,000
5	Barclays Bank	8,594,000
6	Shell UK	6,352,000
7	Grand Metropolitan	6,041,000
8	Glaxo Holdings	6,000,000
9	TSB Group	5,519,000
10	Marks & Spencer	5,485,000

THE TOP 10 BROADCAST APPEALS IN THE UK IN 1991–92

	Appeal	Station	Year	Amount raised (£)
1	Children in Need Appeal	BBC TV	1991	26,779,000
2	Telethon '92	ITV	1992	15,000,000 *
3	Help a London Child Appeal	Capital Radio	1992	514,000
4	Blue Peter Appeal	BBC TV	1991	200,000
5	Victoria House Appeal	BBC GMR	1992	190,000
6	Snowball Trust	Mercia Sound Radio	1992	131,000
7	Walkathon Appeal	BRMB	1991	121,000
8	Christmas Appeal	GWR FM	1991	116,000
9	Go for Gold Appeal	BBC Radio Lincolnshire	1991	86,000
10	Money Mountain Appeal	BBC Radio Derby	1991	52,000

*To August 1992, but income continuing.

THE 10 COUNTRIES THAT REGISTER THE MOST PATENTS

	Country	Patents
1	USA	96,514
2	Germany	43,190
3	Japan	36,100
4	France	35,581
5	UK	34,074
6	Italy	19,503
7	Netherlands	17,610
8	Switzerland	16,808
9	Sweden	16,767
10	Canada	14,473

A patent is an exclusive licence to manufacture and exploit a unique product or process for a fixed period. The figures refer to the number of patents actually *granted* during 1991 – which in most instances represents only a fraction of the patents applied for: a total of 380,453 applications were registered in Japan, for example, but the process of obtaining a patent can be tortuous, and many are refused after investigations show that the product is too similar to one that has already been patented. This international list, based on data from the World Intellectual Property Organization, provides a yardstick of the state of each nation's technological development. A further 26,643 patents were granted by the European Patent Office, which has no national affiliation.

PATENTS QUIZ
Who patented what and when?

	Inventor		Invention		Year*
1	Paul Von Korosy	A	Road 'cat's-eyes'	i	1960
2	Thomas Loud	B	Phonograph	ii	1874
3	Hubert Booth	C	Teabags	iii	1902
4	Walter Wingfield	D	Hovercraft	iv	1951
5	Edwin Land	E	Vacuum cleaner	v	1877
6	Gideon Sundback	F	Upright piano	vi	1930
7	Hippolyte Magee	G	Zip fastener	vii	1936
8	Thomas Alva Edison	H	Lawn tennis	viii	1802
9	Peter Shaw	I	Polaroid camera	ix	1869
10	Christopher Cockerell	J	Margarine	x	1915

*Issue of UK patent.

10 TRADE NAMES THAT HAVE ENTERED THE LANGUAGE

Many words that are in common use were – or still are – registered trademarks, and it may be surprising to discover that using them to apply to other manufacturers' products can technically render the user liable to legal action for trademark infringement. Companies often fight legal battles to ensure that their products do not become used generically – in its early years as the pioneer of popular photography Kodak, for example, went to a great deal of trouble to prevent its memorable name becoming synonymous with 'camera'. Such names as Fibreglass, Nylon, Perspex, Portakabin, Tannoy, Tarmac and Yo-Yo are all jealously protected by owners, but for some, such as aspirin, cellophane, gramophone and launderette, all originally trade names, it is too late. A classic case is that of 'tabloid', which the British drug company Burroughs, Wellcome & Co registered as a trade name on 14 March 1884. It was derived from the word 'tablet' and applied originally to various concentrated types of drugs marketed by the firm. By the end of the nineteenth century, it had acquired a secondary meaning, as almost anything small and compressed came to be called 'tabloid' (just as 'mini' came into widespread use in the 1960s for everything from small cars to short skirts). The phrase 'tabloid journalism', which described the content of small-format newspapers (in contrast to large 'broadsheet' papers), soon became so established that by 1903 Burroughs, Wellcome & Co felt obliged to instigate legal proceedings in an attempt to protect their trademark. It was, however, concluded that the independent use of the word had become so much a part of the language that no damaging infringement could be claimed. Since then, it is the Press usage that has superseded the first meaning of 'tabloid'. The following list is of 10 products whose names have become part of the English language – even though some continue to be registered trademarks:

1 Biro

Hungarian sculptor, painter, hypnotist and journalist, László J. and his brother Georg Biró, a chemist, developed the idea of the ballpoint pen in the 1930s and 1940s from their base in Argentina. The French BiC company (itself derived from its founder, Marcel Bich) today owns the rights to the trade name 'Biro'.

2 Escalator

The moving staircases developed in the 1890s and patented in 1900 were made in the USA for the Manhattan Elevated Railway by the Otis Elevator Company and originally bore the name 'Escalator' (from 'escalading elevator'), a word that rapidly entered everyday usage.

3 Hoover

In 1908 American leather goods and harness manufacturers William Henry 'Boss' Hoover (1849–1932) and his son set up the Hoover Suction Co to sell a vacuum cleaner that had been invented by J. Murray Spangler, first exporting them from their Canadian factory to the UK after the First World War. The British company was established in the 1930s and expanded into making other domestic appliances after the Second World War. Although the name Hoover is a trademark of the company, the word has come into use as both noun and verb equivalent to 'vacuum cleaner' and 'vacuum cleaning' – undoubtedly enhancing the public's awareness of the product.

4 Jacuzzi

The 'whirlpool bath' is named after Candido Jacuzzi (1903–86), an Italian immigrant to the USA and manufacturer of hydraulic pumps. His son was crippled with rheumatoid arthritis, so he hit on the idea of using one of the firm's jet pumps for hydromassage. Developed in the 1950s, the revolutionary bath which became known as the 'Jacuzzi' began the cult of the hot tub, particularly in California, and was the basis of a multi-million dollar manufacturing empire.

5 Linoleum

Linoleum was patented in the UK in 1863 by Frederick Walton and the Linoleum Manufacturing Company was formed the following year. The word, and its abbreviation 'lino', soon became so widely used that in 1878 it was removed from the Trade Marks Register.

6 Plasticine

The modelling clay invented by William Harbutt (1844–1922) was originally manufactured on a small scale for art students, then for children, with commercial manufacturing beginning in 1900 in a converted flour mill in Bathampton near Bath.

7 Pullman carriages

In 1864, after several years of experimentation with converted railway carriages, American inventor George Mortimer Pullman (1831–97) built the first railway sleeping car which bears his name. They first came into use in the UK in 1874 and continued to be manufactured by Pullman's British company, but the name became applied to any train with sleeping accommodation.

8 Thermos flask

'Thermos' is a trademark registered after a competition held in Germany by the firm that produced vacuum flasks for their British inventor, Sir James Dewar (1843–1923). Thermos Ltd was set up in the UK in 1907, when the brand name was registered internationally.

9 Vaseline

'Petroleum jelly' was developed and patented in 1870 by US chemist Robert Augustus Chesebrough (1837–1933) as a bi-product of the oil industry; it was patented in the UK in 1874. Chesebrough reputedly ate a spoonful of Vaseline every day – and lived to the age of 96.

10 Xerox

The name comes from the Greek *xeros*, dry, as the Xerox copying process patented by American inventor Chester Carlson (1906–68) does not involve liquid developer. In 1952 it was registered as a trademark by the Rochester, New York, Haloid Company, which later became the Xerox Corporation.

THE FIRST 10 PATENTS IN THE UK

Pat. no.	Patentee	Patent	Date*
1	Aaron Rathburne and Roger Burges	Making maps of English cities	11 Mar 1618
2	Nicholas Hillyard	Engraving and printing the king's head on documents	5 May 1617
3	John Gason	Locks, mills and other river and canal improvements	1 Jul 1617
4	John Miller and John Jasper Wolfen	Oil for suits of armour	3 Nov 1617
5	Thomas Murray	Sword blades	11 Jan 1618
6	Thomas Wildgoose and David Ramsey	Ploughs, pumps and ship engines	17 Jan 1619
7	Abram Baker	Smalt (glass) manufacture	16 Feb 1619
8	Robert Crumpe	Tunnels and pumps	9 Jan 1618
9	John Gilbert	River dredger	16 Jul 1618
10	Clement Dawbeney	Water-powered engine for making nails	11 Dec 1618

*Of patent being granted; these do not correspond precisely with the order of registration and issue of patent number.

The world's first patent, by which the architect Filippo Brunelleschi was granted the exclusive licence to make a barge crane to transport marble, was issued in Florence in 1421. The first granted in England dates from 1449, when John of Utynam received a patent by Henry VI for making glass for the windows of Eton College. Patents were occasionally granted during the sixteenth century, such as that issued in 1596 by Queen Elizabeth I to Sir John Harington for a water closet, but the system was not codified until 1617. From then on, each new patent that was granted was given a number, and this list of the first 10 issued under this system gives some indication of the diverse range of inventions being developed even at this early date.

THE 10 COUNTRIES THAT REGISTER THE MOST TRADEMARKS

	Country	Trademarks
1	Japan	95,329
2	France	90,549
3	USA	46,647
4	China	40,330
5	UK	30,421
6	Germany	26,471
7	Portugal	25,505
8	Republic of Korea	23,876
9	Brazil	22,333
10	Switzerland	15,975

This list includes all trademarks (product names that are thereby legally protected) and service marks (which apply to company and other names applied to services rather than products) that were actually registered in 1991. As with patents, more applications are filed than are granted, since many are rejected, for example through being too similar to an existing trademark or service mark, and the business of creating unique names for new goods and services has become a major international industry.

The Frankfurt headquarters of Deutsche Bank, one of Europe's foremost banks.

THE TOP 10 BANKS IN EUROPE

	Bank	Country	Capital ($)
1	Crédit Agricole	France	14,663,000,000
2	Union Bank of Switzerland	Switzerland	13,131,000,000
3	Barclays Bank	UK	11,637,000,000
4	Deutsche Bank	Germany	11,258,000,000
5	Compagnie Financière de Paribas	France	10,463,000,000
6	Crédit Lyonnais	France	10,459,000,000
7	National Westminster Bank	UK	10,453,000,000
8	Banque Nationale de Paris	France	10,231,000,000
9	ABN Amro Bank	Netherlands	9,344,000,000
10	Swiss Bank Corporation	Switzerland	9,262,000,000

THE 10 COUNTRIES PRODUCING THE MOST ELECTRICITY FROM NUCLEAR SOURCES

	Country	Nuclear power stations in operation	Nuclear % of total	Output (megawatt-hours)
1	USA	111	21.7	99,757
2	France	56	72.7	56,873
3	Former USSR	45	12.6	34,673
4	Japan	42	23.8	32,044
5	Germany	21	27.6	22,390
6	Canada	20	16.4	13,993
7	UK	37	20.6	11,710
8	Sweden	12	51.6	9,817
9	South Korea	9	47.5	7,220
10	Spain	9	35.9	7,067

THE 10 LARGEST NUCLEAR POWER STATIONS IN THE WORLD

	Station	Country	Reactors in use	Output (megawatts)
1	Bruce	Canada	1–8	6,910
2	Gravelines	France	1–6	5,706
3	Paluel	France	1–4	5,528
4	Washington	USA	1–5	5,326
5	Fukushima Daichi	Japan	1–6	4,696
6	Fukushima Daini	Japan	1–4	4,400
7	Pickering	Canada	1–8	4,328
8	Chinon	France	A3; B1–B4	4,051
9 =	Kursk	Russia	1–4	4,000
9 =	St Petersburg	Russia	1–4	4,000

THE 10 OLDEST NUCLEAR PLANTS IN THE WORLD

	Plant/country	Commissioned
1	Obninsk, Russia	Dec 1954
2	Calder Hall, UK	Oct 1956
3	Troitsk, Russia	Sep 1958
4	Chapel Cross, UK	Mar 1959
5	Yankee Rowe, USA	Jul 1961
6	Bradwell, UK	Jul 1962
7	Hunterskin, UK	Feb 1964
8	EBR2, USA	Aug 1964
9	Dungeness, UK	Oct 1965
10	Big Rock Point, USA	Nov 1965

THE TOP 10 URANIUM PRODUCERS IN THE WORLD

	Country	Annual production (tonnes)
1	Canada	11,700
2	South Africa	4,500
3	USA	4,200
4	Australia	4,000
5	France	3,225
6	Namibia	3,200
7	Niger	2,960
8	Gabon	900
9	Brazil	782
10	Spain	200

The amount of uranium produced in the former Soviet Union has always been a closely guarded secret, but as the country's nuclear power production is ranked third in the world, it is assumed to be several thousand tonnes per annum. It is estimated that Australia has the greatest reserves of uranium – some 463,000 tonnes.

THE 10 COUNTRIES WITH MOST NUCLEAR REACTORS*

	Country	Reactors
1	USA	114
2	Former USSR	57
3	France	55
4	UK	40
5	Japan	38
6	Germany	24
7	Canada	18
8	Sweden	12
9	Spain	10
10	South Korea	9

*Civilian nuclear power reactors only, excluding those devoted to military purposes.

THE 10 OLDEST NUCLEAR PLANTS IN THE UK

	Plant	Commissioned
1	Calder Hall	Oct 1956
2	Chapel Cross	Mar 1959
3	Bradwell	Jul 1962
4	Hunterskin	Feb 1964
5	Transfynydd	Feb 1965
6	Hinkley Point	May 1965
7	Dungeness	Oct 1965
8	Sizewell	Mar 1966
9 =	Oldbury	Jan 1968
9 =	Winfrith	Jan 1968

THE 10 OLDEST NUCLEAR PLANTS IN THE USA

	Plant	Commissioned*
1	Yankee Rowe, Massachusetts	Jul 1961
2	EBR2, Idaho	Aug 1964
3	Big Rock Point, Michigan	Nov 1965
4	San Onofre Island, California	Jan 1968
5	Haddam Neck, Connecticut	Jan 1968
6	Oyster Creek Island, New Jersey	Dec 1969
7	Nine Mile Point Island, New York	Dec 1969
8	Dresden 2, Illinois	Jun 1970
9	Ginna, New York	Mar 1970
10	Millstone Island	Dec 1970

Where identical months are given, the plant that was powered up first takes precedence.

Commissioned in 1959, Chapel Cross, Dumfriesshire, is the UK's second oldest nuclear power station.

THE TOP 10 CATEGORIES OF CONSUMER SPENDING IN THE UK

	Category	Total expenditure (£)
1	Transport and communications	62,579,000,000
2	Housing	51,614,000,000
3	Food	44,053,000,000
4	Recreation, entertainment and education	34,915,000,000
5	Hotels and catering	31,049,000,000
6	Alcoholic drinks	23,555,000,000
7	Household goods and services	22,796,000,000
8	Clothing and footwear	21,034,000,000
9	Fuel and power	14,272,000,000
10	Life assurance and pension scheme administration costs	11,803,000,000

Some of these categories, as computed by the Central Statistical Office in 1991, are fairly broad, 'transport and communications', for example, encompassing such items as bus travel, post and telephone charges, with the purchase of cars, motorcycles and other vehicles the largest single item at £16,426,000,000. Within the food category, the biggest single item is meat and bacon (£9,941,000,000) and among alcoholic drinks more than half (£12,775,000,000) is devoted to beer. Tobacco, at £9,746,000,000, does not quite make the Top 10.

THE TOP 10 COSTS OF CHILDREN IN THE UK

	Item	Cost %
1	Food	23
2	Housing and fuel	16
3	Clothing	13
4	Childcare	12
5	Household effects	10
6	Transport	8
7 =	Leisure activities	6
7 =	Leisure goods	6
9 =	Personal care	3
9 =	Pocket money	3

The Family Budget Unit has calculated that to achieve a modest-but-adequate living standard, the cost of a child under 11 in a two-child family is £59.90 a week and that for children between 10 and 16 the cost rises to £61.55. These costs increase with age, and boys are significantly more expensive than girls: a family with two boys aged 10 and 16 needs to spend £5.50 a week more than one with girls of the same ages.

THE 10 COUNTRIES THAT MAKE THE MOST INTERNATIONAL PHONE CALLS

	Country	Calls per head	Total calls
1	USA	5.2	1,281,103,000
2	Germany	12.8	1,018,200,000
3	UK	7.8	435,600,000 *
4	Italy	5.7	331,000,000
5	Netherlands	19.6	294,000,000
6	Switzerland	42.6	285,880,000
7	Canada	10.1	275,000,000 *
8	Belgium	21.9	217,166,000
9	Japan	1.6	200,640,000
10	Denmark	35.2	180,600,000

Estimated.

THE 10 MOST EXPENSIVE TELEPHONE CALL CHARGES IN THE EC

	Country	Cost of 5-minute local call (£)
1	UK	0.25
2	Austria	0.16
3	Switzerland	0.14
4	Denmark	0.13
5	Ireland	0.11
6	Belgium	0.10
7	Germany	0.08
8	France	0.07
9	Spain	0.06
10	Italy	0.05

	Country	Cost of 5-minute long-distance call (£)
1	Austria	1.61
2	Italy	1.58
3	Ireland	1.55
4	France	1.32
5	Spain	1.26
6	Germany	1.17
7	UK	0.79
8	Belgium	0.78
9	Switzerland	0.67
10	Denmark	0.33

In 1992 the Brussels-based European Consumers' Union compared call charges throughout the EC and showed that the UK was by far the most expensive, while the Netherlands was cheapest at 4p for a five-minute local call and 31p for a long-distance call. The UK fared better in charges for long-distance calls – and better still via Mercury, rather than BT, at 66p.

THE 10 COUNTRIES WITH THE MOST TELEPHONES

	Country	Telephones
1	USA	139,658,302
2	Japan	57,060,000
3	Germany	33,559,719
4	France	28,609,173
5	UK	26,240,000
6	Italy	23,070,821
7	Russia	20,468,000
8	Canada	15,814,928
9	Republic of Korea	14,831,659
10	Spain	13,264,360

	Country	Telephones per 100 inhabitants
1	Sweden	69.00
2	Switzerland	59.48
3	Canada	58.52
4	Denmark	57.71
5	USA	55.27
6	Finland	54.24
7	Iceland	52.14
8	Norway	51.60
9	Luxembourg	51.14
10	France	50.15
	UK	45.74

It is estimated that there are some 545,984,000 telephone lines in use in the world, of which 222,896,000 are in Europe, 185,925,000 in North and South America, 117,515,000 in Asia, 10,032,000 in Oceania and 9,616,000 in Africa. It is remarkable that, given its population, the whole of China has only 8,450,000 telephones – not many more than the Netherlands. For comparison, the population of China (1,143,330,000) is 76 times that of the Netherlands (15,009,000).

Ranking countries according to number of telephones per 100 inhabitants produces the following list:

Contrasting with the Top 10 countries, where the ratio is around two people per telephone or better, there are many countries in the world with fewer than one telephone per 100 inhabitants, among them Pakistan (0.83 phones per 100), China (0.72), India (0.65) and Indonesia (0.58), while most of Central and West Africa possesses fewer than 0.50, or one telephone for every 200 people.

THE 10 HIGHEST-EARNING ACTORS IN THE WORLD

	Actor	1991–92 income ($)
1	William H. Cosby Jr	98,000,000
2	Kevin Costner	71,000,000
3	Arnold Schwarzenegger	43,000,000
4	Eddie Murphy	40,000,000
5	Tom Cruise	33,000,000
6	Mel Gibson	32,000,000
7 =	Michael Douglas	30,000,000
7 =	Dustin Hoffman	30,000,000
9	Robin Williams	27,000,000
10	Sylvester Stallone	26,000,000

Used by permission of Forbes Magazine.

In the 1991–92 period William H. Cosby Jr maintained his longstanding place at the head of the highest-earning actors league, while Kevin Costner held on to 2nd place. Temporary emigres from the list Mel Gibson and Sylvester Stallone made a triumphant return, but four actors failed to make the grade: Bruce Willis and Robert De Niro (each of whom earned $25,000,000), Jack Nicholson ($24,000,000) and Sean Connery ($22,000,000). Former 10th place holder Michael J. Fox, whose principal source of income had been his earnings from the *Back to the Future* trilogy, not only dropped out of the Top 10 but slipped altogether from *Forbes Magazine*'s annual list of the Top 40 highest-paid entertainers.

With a two-year income approaching $100 million, Bill Cosby maintained his pre-eminent position among the world's highest-earning actors.

WEALTH

THE 10 HIGHEST-EARNING POP STARS IN THE WORLD

	Artist(s)	Income ($) 1991	1992	Total
1	New Kids on the Block	54,000,000	8,000,000	62,000,000
2	Michael Jackson	25,000,000	26,000,000	51,000,000
3 =	Madonna	24,000,000	24,000,000	48,000,000
3 =	Julio Iglesias	23,000,000	25,000,000	48,000,000
5	Guns N' Roses	21,000,000	26,000,000	47,000,000
6	Prince	10,000,000	35,000,000	45,000,000
7	Garth Brooks	20,000,000	24,000,000	44,000,000
8	U2	9,000,000	27,000,000	36,000,000
9	Grateful Dead	16,000,000	15,000,000	31,000,000
10	ZZ Top	11,000,000	18,000,000	29,000,000

Used by permission of Forbes Magazine.

Forbes Magazine's survey of top entertainers' income covers a two-year period in order to iron out fluctuations, especially those caused by successful tours. In 1991 both Aerosmith and Grateful Dead entered the Top 10 as a result of sell-out tours, but only the latter maintained their income over the subsequent year, while the Rolling Stones, having earned $44,000,000 in 1990 when they were touring, saw this fall to $11,000,000 in 1991 and $14,000,000 in 1992, thus evicting them from the Top 10. Conversely, after a relatively quiet 1991, the income from U2's massive global tour during 1992 reinstated them in the Top 10. In 1990 New Kids on the Block (previously at number three) sold almost $75,000,000 worth of concert tickets and over $1,000,000,000 worth of merchandise – hence their elevation in that year to number one, which they sustained in 1991, although they will clearly never be seen again in this list. In the 1990–91 period, Michael Jackson's income actually halved, but it remains so huge that he nevertheless remains a prominent member of this elite (his sister Janet lies just outside the Top 10 with a 1991–92 income of $22,000,000). Other runners-up are Hammer ($28,000,000) and Frank Sinatra ($23,000,000), while recent refugees from *Forbes'* Top 40 list (which encompasses entertainers in other fields) include Bon Jovi and Pink Floyd and, perhaps most surprisingly of all, Paul McCartney.

THE 10 HIGHEST-EARNING ENTERTAINERS IN THE WORLD*

	Entertainer	Profession	1991–92 income ($)
1	Oprah Winfrey	TV host/producer	88,000,000
2	Steven Spielberg	Film producer/director	57,000,000
3	Charles M. Schulz	'Peanuts' cartoonist	49,000,000
4	Johnny Carson	TV host/producer	45,000,000
5	David Copperfield	Illusionist	35,000,000
6	Siegfried & Roy	Illusionists	30,000,000
7	Tom Clancy	Novelist	29,000,000
8	Stephen King	Novelist/screenwriter	28,000,000
9	Cameron Mackintosh	Theatrical producer	27,000,000
10	Andrew Lloyd Webber	Composer	26,000,000

Oprah Winfrey increased her two-year earnings to keep her safely at the top of the pile. Newcomers to the list include illusionist David Copperfield – notable for performances that include levitating trains and escaping from exploding buildings – who joins regular Top 10 entrants Siegfried & Roy (the illusionist as megastar seems a uniquely North American phenomenon that has yet to find a British counterpart). British producer Cameron Mackintosh gains a toehold in the Top 10, but John Hughes (author of *The Breakfast Club* and writer/producer of the blockbuster *Home Alone* films) just slips from the list, not because he has earned less (he actually increased his earnings to $24,000,000), but simply because other members of this elite group have done even better.

*Other than actors and pop stars.

Used by permission of Forbes Magazine.

THE 10 HIGHEST-EARNING SPORTSMEN IN THE WORLD

	Name	Sport	Salary/ winnings	Income Other*	Total 1992 ($)
1	Michael Jordan	Basketball	3,900,000	32,000,000	35,900,000
2	Evander Holyfield	Boxing	27,000,000	1,000,000	28,000,000
3	Ayrton Senna	Motor racing	17,500,000	5,000,000	22,500,000
4	Nigel Mansell	Motor racing	12,500,000	2,000,000	14,500,000
5	Arnold Palmer	Golf	100,000	11,000,000	11,100,000
6	Andre Agassi	Tennis	2,000,000	9,000,000	11,000,000
7	Joe Montana	American football	3,500,000	6,000,000	9,500,000
8	Jack Nicklaus	Golf	200,000	9,000,000	9,200,000
9	Jim Courier	Tennis	3,000,000	6,000,000	9,000,000
10	Monica Seles	Tennis	2,500,000	6,000,000	8,500,000

*From sponsorship and royalty income from endorsed sporting products.

Used by permission of Forbes Magazine.

Some $20,000,000 of list-leader Michael Jordan's income is reckoned to come from his sponsorship deal with sports footwear manufacturer Nike, which is the most valuable in sporting history. Boxing is the sport perhaps most affected by the peaks and troughs of success and failure, exemplified by three boxers who ranked in the Top 10 in 1991 but were absent in 1992: Mike Tyson (whose income has declined from $31,500,000 in 1991 to the standard prison pocket money rate), George Foreman (formerly number four, but who is now rated 19th with total income of $7,000,000) and Razor Ruddock (7th in 1991, now unplaced in the Top 40). Two other boxers, Larry Holmes and Julio Cesar Chavez, earned $8,200,000 and $7,000,000 respectively. Also in 1992, several other sports stars found themselves outside the Top 10 but nevertheless earned total incomes in excess of $5,000,000, among them basketball players David Robinson, Magic Johnson and Patrick Ewing; motor racing drivers Gerhard Berger and Riccardo Patresi; golfers Greg Norman, Fred Couples, Nick Faldo and Lee Trevino; tennis players Michael Chang, Steffi Graf, Stefan Edberg, Gabriela Sabatini, Pete Sampras and Ivan Lendl, ice hockey player Wayne Gretzky and six baseball players led by Bobby Bonilla of the New York Mets with total income of $6,300,000 – most of it from his substantial salary.

Richard Branson (born 1951) is the youngest entrant in the list of the UK's 10 richest men.

THE 10 RICHEST MEN IN THE UK

	Name	Principal sources	Assets (£)
1	George Soros	Finance	2,000,000,000
2 =	Paul Raymond	Property and publishing	1,500,000,000
2 =	Gad Rausing	Packaging	1,500,000,000
2 =	Hans Rausing	Packaging	1,500,000,000
5	David Sainsbury	Retail trade	1,300,000,000
6	Galen Weston	Food production	1,000,000,000
7	Richard Branson	Airlines, etc	880,000,000
8	Charles Feeney	Duty-free shops	750,000,000
9 =	Simon Keswick	Finance and Far East trade	700,000,000
9 =	Sir John Swire	Finance and Far East trade	700,000,000

THE 10 RICHEST PEOPLE IN THE USA

In 1992 *Forbes Magazine*, which annually surveys the 400 wealthiest people in the USA, ranked some 73 Americans as dollar billionaires – that is, with assets in excess of $1,000,000,000. The *Forbes 400* includes both the inheritors of great family fortunes and self-made individuals. A placing in the list is extremely volatile, however, particularly during recent times, when many who made vast fortunes in a short period lost them with even greater rapidity, while stock market falls have led to a decline in the assets of many members of this elite club. Even the Top 10 undergoes changes from year to year, and now stands as:

Name(s)	Assets ($)
1 William Henry Gates III	**6,300,000,000**

In 1975, at the age of 19, Gates left law college to co-found (with Paul G. Allen, who rates 9th place in this list) the Microsoft Corporation of Seattle, now one of the world's leading computer software companies. Gates, a self-described 'hard-core technoid' was elevated to number one position in 1992. Formerly a bachelor devoted only to his business and fast cars, in 1993 he announced his engagement to Melinda French, one of his employees.

2 John Werner Kluge	**5,500,000,000**

Founder of the Metromedia Company of Charlottesville, Virginia. The family of German-born Kluge settled in Detroit in 1922, where he worked on the Ford assembly line. He won a scholarship to Columbia University and gained a degree in economics. He started a radio station and in 1959, with partners, acquired the Metropolitan Broadcasting Company, developing it into Metromedia, a corporation that owns TV and radio stations and cellular telephone franchises but with other properties as varied as the Chock Full O'Nuts Corporation and, formerly, the Harlem Globetrotters basketball team. Kluge has diversified his interests into such areas as films, printing and a chain of steak houses. He also owns an 80,000-acre estate and castle in Scotland.

3 Helen Walton, S. Robson Walton, John T. Walton, Jim C. Walton and Alice L. Walton	
(shared) **25,300,000,000**	

Samuel Moore Walton, the founder of Wal-Mart Stores, headed the list of America's richest people for several years. One of the largest retail chains in the USA, his 1,700 stores achieved sales of $43,900,000,000 in 1991. Sam Walton died on 5 April 1992 and his widow Helen and four children share his fortune.

4 Warren Edward Buffett	**4,400,000,000**

Buffet was born and still lives in Omaha, Nebraska. His professional career started as a pinball service engineer, after which he published a horse race tip sheet. His diverse business interests include the New England textile company, Berkshire Hathaway which has in turn acquired major stakes in the *Washington Post*, Coca-Cola and other companies.

5 Samuel Irving Newhouse Jr and brother Donald Edward Newhouse	
(shared) **7,000,000,000**	

The New York City-based Newhouse brothers are owners of America's largest privately owned chain of 29 newspapers with a total circulation of 3,000,000, with interests that include cable television and book publishing. Samuel ('Si') Newhouse runs book publishers Random House and magazine publishers Condé Nast, the publishers of *Vogue*, bought by their father in 1959 as an anniversary gift for his wife ('She asked for a fashion magazine and I went out and got her *Vogue*'). Donald controls their newspaper group.

6 Sumner Murray Redstone	**3,250,000,000**

Redstone, who comes from a theatre-owning family, built up his own cinema company, National Amusements, Inc, which now has more than 750 screens across the USA, coining the word 'multiplex' for his multi-screen cinema complexes, and acquired the cinema company Viacom.

7 Ronald Owen Perelman	**2,900,000,000**

Perelman is a wide-ranging entrepreneur who acquired Revlon, Max Factor and other cosmetics businesses, was the former owner of Technicolor and has professional interests that encompass firms from Marvel Comics to a camping goods company.

8 Ted Arison	**2,850,000,000**

Born to a shipowning family in Tel Aviv (where he now lives in retirement, while retaining various US business interests), Arison derives his wealth from his Carnival Cruise Lines fleet of cruise ships.

9 Paul Gardner Allen	**2,800,000,000**

Former partner of the richest American Bill Gates, Allen developed computer operating system MS-DOS and Basic programme and today retains shares in Microsoft that are the basis of his wealth.

10 (Keith) Rupert Murdoch	**2,600,000,000**

Son of *Melbourne Herald* owner Sir Keith Murdoch, Australian-born newspaper tycoon Rupert Murdoch, now a US citizen, has expanded his News Corporation empire to encompass magazines, book publishing, cinema and broadcasting interests, including Sky satellite TV.

Close runners-up in the billionaire league include recent presidential candidate Henry Ross Perot ($2,400,000,000), the Mars (of Mars bar fame) family (four members sharing $9,000,000,000), broadcasting magnate and husband of Jane Fonda Ted Turner ($1,900,000,000) and the former Ambassador to Great Britain Walter Annenberg ($1,600,000,000).

Microsoft chairman William Gates is the richest man in the USA.

THE 10 RICHEST FAMILIES IN THE UK

Family	Principal sources	Assets (£)
1 = David Sainsbury and family	Retail trade	3,000,000,000
1 = The Rausing family	Packaging	3,000,000,000
3 = George Soros and family	Finance	2,000,000,000
3 = The Weston family	Food production	2,000,000,000
3 = The Guinness family	Investment	2,000,000,000
3 = The Moores family	Mail order and football pools	2,000,000,000
7 The Hinduja family	Commodity trading	1,500,000,000
8 The Grosvenor family	Property	1,200,000,000
9 The Keswick family	Finance and Far East trade	900,000,000
10 The Royal Family	Investment	850,000,000

THE 10 RICHEST WOMEN IN THE UK

Name	Assets (£)
1 Donatella Moores Littlewoods heiress	234,500,000
2 Viscountess Boyd Guinness family heiress	210,000,000
3 Lady Brigid Ness Guinness family heiress	205,000,000
4 Patricia Martin Littlewoods heiress	195,000,000
5 Lady Grantchester Littlewoods heiress	170,000,000
6 Lady Elisabeth Nugent Guinness family heiress	128,000,000
7 Princess Victoria von Preussen Guinness family heiress (daughter of 3)	125,000,000
8 HM The Queen Heiress and landowner	100,000,000
9 Duchess of Roxburgh Heiress (daughter of Duke of Westminster)	98,000,000
10 Lady Jane Willoughby D'Eresby Heiress	97,000,000

THE 10 RICHEST INDIVIDUALS ON THE LONDON STOCK EXCHANGE

Name	Shareholding (£)
1 David Sainsbury	1,800,000,000
2 Conrad Black	385,000,000
3 Lord Sainsbury	262,000,000
4 Viscount Rothermere	249,000,000
5 Stephen Rubin	243,000,000
6 Kevin Leach	179,000,000
7 Paul Hamlyn	155,000,000
8 David Wilson	154,000,000
9 Kenneth Morrison	151,000,000
10 A.A. Luksic	106,000,000

THE 10 LARGEST LANDOWNERS IN THE UK

Name	Acres
1 Duke of Buccleuch	277,000
2 Wills family	268,000
3 HM The Queen	267,000
4 Earl of Seafield	185,000
5 Duke of Westminster	150,000
6 Prince of Wales	143,000
7 Duke of Atholl	130,000
8 Countess of Sutherland	126,000
9 A.A. Farquerson	119,000
10 Earl of Stair	110,000

THE TOP 10 GOLD PRODUCERS IN THE WORLD

	Country	Annual production (tonnes)
1	South Africa	614.1
2	USA	322.2
3	Australia	240.0
4	Former USSR	237.0
5	Canada	157.4
6	China	118.0
7	Brazil	76.5
8	Papua New Guinea	71.2
9	Indonesia	40.4
10	Chile	39.5
	World total	*2,216.5*

After experiencing a recent decline, world-dominating gold producer South Africa saw its output marginally up again in 1992. Australia's output has increased dramatically over recent years: the country's record annual production had stood at 119 tonnes since 1903, but in 1988 it rocketed to 152 tonnes, and in 1992 for the first time overtook that of the former Soviet Union.

GOLD QUIZ

1 To the nearest kilogram/two pounds, what is the weight of a standard gold bar?

2 In the James Bond novel and film, is 'The Man With the Golden Gun' called Scaramouche, Scaramanga or Scarabaeus?

3 In what Swiss town is a 'Golden Rose' awarded to television programmes?

4 Between which cities did the *Golden Arrow* train run?

5 When was San Francisco's Golden Gate Bridge opened – 1897, 1917 or 1937?

6 What is the Goldfish Club?

7 What is the name often given to iron pyrites?

8 Who, in legend, turned everything he touched to gold?

9 Who was knighted in 1581 aboard his ship the *Golden Hind*?

10 Which group had a 1983 hit single with *Gold*?

Gold reserves, mostly in the form of ingots, remain a significant measure of national economies.

THE TOP 10 GOLD RESERVES IN THE WORLD

	Country	Reserves (Troy ounces)
1	USA	262,010,000
2	Germany	95,180,000
3	Switzerland	83,280,000
4	France	81,850,000
5	Italy	66,670,000
6	Netherlands	43,940,000
7	Belgium	30,230,000
8	Japan	24,230,000
9	Austria	20,390,000
10	UK	18,970,000

Gold reserves are the government holdings of gold in each country – which are often far greater than the gold owned by private individuals. In the days of the 'Gold Standard', this provided a tangible measure of a country's wealth, guaranteeing the convertibility of its currency, and determined such factors as exchange rates. Though less significant today, gold reserves remain a component in calculating a country's international reserves, alongside its holdings of foreign exchange and SDRs (Special Drawing Rights).

THE 10 MOST EXPENSIVE COINS EVER SOLD BY SPINK COIN AUCTIONS, LONDON

	Coin/sale	Price (£)
1	George V 1920 Sydney Mint sovereign 1 March 1992	104,000
2	Henry III gold penny 13 June 1985	65,000
3	Brazilian Coronation peca, 1822 18 June 1986	58,000
4	George III pattern five guineas, 1773 9 November 1989	57,000
5	George III pattern five pounds, 1820 9 November 1989	47,500
6	Charles I triple unite, Oxford Mint, 1643 31 May 1989	44,000
7	Charles II gold pattern crown, 1662 19 November 1990	41,000
8	Edward VIII proof sovereign, 1937 7 December 1984	40,000
9	Anne Vigo five guineas, 1703 9 November 1989	39,000
10	Henry VIII sovereign 2 June 1983	36,000

Founded in 1666, the year of the Great Fire of London, Spink & Son Ltd is the world's oldest-established firm of antique dealers and numismatists. In addition to the coins appearing in the list, on 3 July 1988 in Tokyo Spink & Son, in association with the Taisei Stamp and Coin Co, achieved the world record price for a British coin when they sold a Victoria proof gothic crown, dating from 1847 and one of only two known, for the equivalent of £126,000.

THE 10 MOST EXPENSIVE WATCHES AVAILABLE FROM WATCHES OF SWITZERLAND

	Watch	Price (£)
1	Patek Philippe gents' 18ct yellow gold chronograph strap watch	112,675
2	Piaget ladies' 18ct yellow gold quartz bracelet watch with sapphire- and diamond-set dial	95,000
3	Patek Philippe gents' 18ct yellow gold manual chronograph moonphase strap watch	64,000
4	Patek Philippe gents' 18ct yellow gold manual chronograph	61,000
5	Chopard ladies' 18ct yellow gold quartz bracelet watch with diamond-set dial, bezel and bracelet	59,500
6	Patek Philippe gents' 18ct rose gold manual chronograph strap watch	55,000
7	Patek Philippe platinum moonphase manual pocket watch with diamond-set dial	54,500
8	Piaget ladies' 18ct yellow gold quartz bracelet watch with diamond-set dial	51,000
9	Chopard ladies' 18ct gold quartz 'Happy Diamond' bracelet watch with mother-of-pearl dial and diamond bezel	49,500
10	Breguet gents' 18ct yellow gold moonphase automatic power reserve strap watch	47,100

THE TOP 10 COINS AND NOTES IN CIRCULATION IN THE UK

	Unit	Units in circulation	Value in circulation (£)
1	£10	574,300,000	5,743,000,000
2	£20	264,400,000	5,288,000,000
3	£50	50,300,000	2,515,000,000
4	£5	323,200,000	1,616,000,000
5	£1 coins	1,007,000,000	1,007,000,000
6	50p	604,000,000	302,000,000
7	20p	1,370,000,000	274,000,000
8	10p (old)*	1,470,000,000	147,000,000
9	5p (new)	2,440,000,000	122,000,000
10	2p	3,600,000,000	72,000,000

*No longer legal tender.

Together, £20 notes and £1 coins account for more than £6 billion worth of the currency in circulation in the UK.

Notes in circulation on 23 December 1992 (which included a total of £1,350,000,000 'other notes', such as the high value notes used internally by the Bank of England) totalled £18,558,402,353 – the equivalent of a pile of £5 notes 294 km/183 miles high. Surprising though it may seem, although they were last issued on 31 December 1984 and ceased to be legal tender on 11 March 1988, the value of £1 notes still in circulation (£59,000,000) is greater than that of 1p coins (5,800,000,000 units worth £58,000,000), which are hence not in the Top 10. There is thus more than one unspendable £1 note for every person in the UK.

THE 10 BESTSELLING NON-CHOCOLATE SWEETS IN THE UK

	Product	Manufacturer	Sales per annum (£)
1	Fruit Pastilles	Rowntree	40,000,000
2	Extra Strong Mints	Trebor	35,000,000
3	Polo	Rowntree	30,000,000
4	Opal Fruits	Mars	26,000,000
5	Softmints	Trebor	25,000,000
6	Tunes	Mars	24,000,000
7	Gum/Orbit	Wrigley	22,000,000
8	Liquorice Allsorts	Bassett	20,000,000
9 =	Chocolate Eclairs	Cadbury	18,000,000
9 =	Lockets	Mars	18,000,000

The Top 10 brands had a market value of £258,000,000 in 1991, with the rest of the non-chocolate based market worth a total of £912,000,000. Outside the Top 10, the leading boiled sugar product is Fox's Glacier Mints, manufactured by Rowntree's and with sales of about £10,000,000 a year.

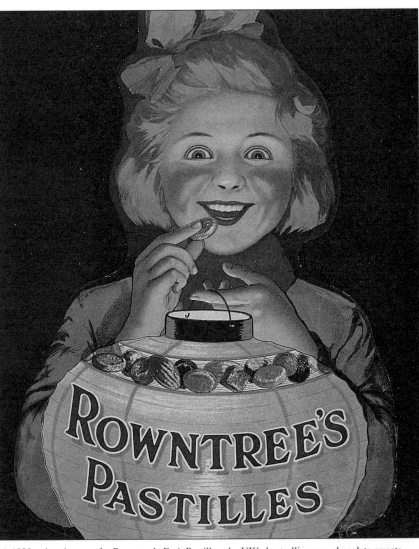

A 1920s advertisement for Rowntree's Fruit Pastilles, the UK's bestselling non-chocolate sweets.

THE TOP 10 CHOCOLATE-CONSUMING NATIONS IN THE WORLD

	Country	Total cocoa consumption (tonnes)
1	USA	566,200
2	Germany	277,600
3	UK	182,500
4	France	156,400
5	Japan	109,300
6	Former USSR	93,200
7	Brazil	81,200
8	Italy	68,300
9	Spain	56,800
10	Canada	46,900

Cocoa is the principal ingredient of chocolate, and its consumption is therefore closely linked to the production of chocolate in each consuming country. Like coffee, the consumption of chocolate tends to occur mainly in the Western world and in more affluent countries. Since some of the Top 10 consuming nations also have large populations, the figures for cocoa consumption *per head* present a somewhat different picture, led by those countries with a long-established tradition of manufacturing high-quality chocolate products:

	Country	Consumption per head kg	lb	oz
1	Switzerland	5.096	11	4
2	Belgium/Luxembourg	4.515	9	15
3	Iceland	3.687	8	2
4	Austria	3.591	7	15
5	Germany	3.444	7	9
6	UK	3.169	7	0
7	Norway	2.874	6	5
8	France	2.742	6	1
9	Netherlands	2.403	5	5
10	USA	2.241	4	15

THE TOP 10 ITEMS OF CONSUMER SPENDING ON FOOD IN THE UK

	Item	% of total food spending 1985	1991
1	Meat and bacon	25.8	22.7
2	Bread and cereals	13.6	14.3
3	Milk, cheese and eggs	14.3	13.1
4	Vegetables	7.6	9.2
5	Confectionery	8.8	8.6
6	Soft drinks	5.5	7.5
7	Fruit	5.4	6.6
8	Potatoes	3.9	4.6
9	Fish	3.5	3.8
10	Tea and coffee	3.8	3.0

In the past five years there has been a definite move toward foods regarded as 'healthy'. As a result, the proportion of grocery bills spent on bread, cereals, fish, fruit and vegetables has increased while spending on meat, dairy products, sugar and fats has declined. Although the soft drink market has grown, it should be noted that this category of spending also includes mineral water and other health-related drinks.

THE TOP 10 FOOD AND DRINK ITEMS CONSUMED IN THE UK

	Product	Average consumption per head per week g	oz
1	Milk and cream	2,121	74.80
2	Beer	1,356	47.82
3	Vegetables	1,169	41.23
4	Meat	962	33.93
5	Potatoes	958	33.81
6	Bread	752	26.53
7	Fruit	702	24.75
8	Biscuits, cakes, cereals, etc	418	14.74
9	Fruit juices	249	8.80
10	Butter, oils and fats	248	8.75

The 1991 National Food Survey, on which this list is partly based, revealed that a number of changes in British eating habits had taken place during the 1980s, in line with increasing awareness of 'healthy diets'. Most notable was a move from whole milk to other types, such as semi-skimmed, and a more than 50 per cent reduction in the amount of butter and sugar consumed (sugar, honey and glucose together account for 217 g/7.67 oz per week). Among other categories not represented in the Top 10 are eggs (an average of 2.25 per week), fish (138 g/4.88 oz) and cheese (117 g/4.11 oz). Apples are the most-eaten fruit (190 g/6.7 oz) and poultry the most consumed meat (216 g/7.63 oz).

THE TOP 10 FOOD AND DRINK ITEMS CONSUMED IN THE USA

	Product	Average consumption per head per annum		
		kg	lb	oz
1	Meat	115.2	254	0
2	Milk and cream	104.6	230	8
3	Vegetables	91.6	201	14
4	Beer	89.3	196	14
5	Grain products (bread, breakfast cereals, etc)	68.6	151	3
6	Sugar, honey and glucose	60.5	133	5
7	Potatoes	55.9	123	5
8	Fruit	49.9	109	14
9	Oils and fats	27.5	60	11
10	Eggs	13.5	29	11

Cheese comes next on the list (10.8 kg/23 lb 11 oz), followed by low-calorie sweeteners, the US consumption per head of which (9.1 kg/20 lb) is greater than that of fish (7.1 kg/15 lb 11 oz). Also high on the list come the great American staple foodstuffs, ice cream (7.3 kg/16 lb) and coffee (4.6 kg/10 lb 3 oz).

THE 10 MOST-ADVERTISED FOOD PRODUCTS IN THE UK*

	Product	Annual advertising expenditure (£)
1	Chocolate confectionery	83,327,000
2	Ready-to-eat cereals	71,728,000
3	Coffee and coffee extracts	37,415,000
4	Frozen ready-to-eat meals	33,358,000
5	Sauces, pickles and salad cream	29,110,000
6	Potato crisps and snacks	27,932,000
7	Tea	27,657,000
8	Margarine and low-fat spreads	23,210,000
9	Cheese	17,114,000
10	Milk and milk products	15,935,000

*Excluding soft drinks and alcohol.

In addition to those items in the Top 10, sums in excess of £10,000,000 were spent on advertising five further food categories: biscuits, fresh and frozen meat and poultry, ice cream and lollies, yoghurt, and sugar confectionery. In 1991 total expenditure on all products, ranging from the £83,227,000 on chocolate (equivalent to £1.45 for every inhabitant of the UK) down to those where spending is measured in thousands rather than millions, such as cake mixes and jellies, was £558,600,000, or £9.70 per head of the population.

MARKS & SPENCER'S 10 BESTSELLING FOOD LINES

	Food type	Bestselling items
1	Fresh chicken	Whole and portions
2	Delicatessen	Roast chicken and ham
3	Sandwiches	Prawn mayonnaise, ham, cheese and pickle
4	Fruit	Bananas, strawberries, peaches
5	Ready-prepared recipe dishes	Lasagne, chicken Kiev, chicken tikka masala
6	Pies	Cottage pies, pork pies
7	Quiches	Quiche Lorraine
8	Salads	Tomato, crispheart lettuce
9	Fish	Prawns, smoked salmon
10	Orange juice	Freshly squeezed, Jaffa orange

Though Britain's best-known retailers of clothing, Marks & Spencer is, perhaps surprisingly, also the country's largest fishmonger, while their overall bestselling line for many years has not been knickers, but chickens! The firm pioneered a number of food developments: iceberg lettuces, for example, were previously grown in California until Marks & Spencer encouraged British growers to produce them, and cherry tomatoes were strictly a garden variety until the company arranged for them to be grown commercially.

Cereals are second only to chocolate among the UK's most advertised food products.

THE TOP 10 FOOD COMPANIES IN THE UK

	Company	Best-known products	Annual sales (£)
1	Hillsdown Holdings	Buxted chickens, Blue Bird and Needlers confectionery	3,039,000,000
2	Associated British Foods	Sunblest bread, Ryvita	2,272,000,000
3	Unigate	St Ivel dairy products	2,165,000,000
4	Cadbury Schweppes	Cadbury's and Fry's chocolate, Coca-Cola, Schweppes soft drinks	2,031,000,000
5	United Biscuits	McVitie's and Crawfords biscuits, KP snacks, Wimpy and Pizzaland restaurants	1,955,000,000
6	Tate & Lyle	Sugar	1,819,000,000
7	Rank Hovis McDougall	Mother's Pride and Hovis bread, Mr Kipling cakes, McDougall's flour, Bisto	1,544,000,000
8	Rowntree	Kit Kat, Polo Mints and other confectionery	1,428,000,000
9	The Union International	Dewhurst butchers	1,213,000,000
10	Northern Foods	'Own-brand' foods for supermarkets, Bowyers meat products	1,009,000,000

THE 10 BESTSELLING BIRDS EYE FROZEN FOODS

1	Garden peas
2	MenuMaster prepared meals
3	Fish fingers
4	Original Beefburgers
5	Potato Waffles
6	Fish in sauce
7	Country Club Cuisine
8	MenuMaster platters
9	Sliced green beans
10	MenuMaster roast meats

Current sales figures are confidential, but when this list was previously compiled in 1989 it was revealed that our annual consumption of Birds Eye garden peas was 27,519 tonnes (equivalent to the weight of over 72 fully laden jumbo jets or 2,200 London buses) and that of fish fingers 13,000 tonnes (1,040 buses).

British housewives begin to discover the advantages of frozen food.

FROZEN FOOD

Francis Bacon, Viscount St Albans, had an eventful life which had included service as Attorney-General and imprisonment in the Tower of London. He was also a noted scientist, and during a spell of unseasonally late winter weather in March 1626, he was travelling to Highgate, London, when he got into a discussion over the possibility of preserving food by keeping it cold. He immediately bought a chicken and stuffed it with snow. Unfortunately, as a result Bacon caught a severe chill and died – in the arms of a relative, a judge with the remarkable name of Sir Julius Caesar.

After this pioneering experiment, the notion of frozen food was largely forgotten until the nineteenth century when an Australian newspaperman called James Harrison hit on the idea of freezing beef in order to ship it to London. Unfortunately, the refrigeration plant failed and a consignment of rotten meat arrived. No one else had dared risk freezing food on a large scale after this debacle, though some small-scale freezing of food had been attempted earlier in this century. In most cases, though, the slowness of the process created large ice crystals that broke up the texture of the food, making the thawed product soggy and robbing it of its flavour. It was Birdseye who first realized that quick freezing – which produces small ice crystals – was the key to the success of the process.

Clarence 'Bob' Birdseye, born in Brooklyn in 1886, always credited Eskimos with the invention of frozen food. In 1912, working as a fur-trader in Labrador, he had spotted them keeping fish and caribou meat for months in sub-zero conditions. After his marriage in 1915, he returned to Labrador with his wife and baby, conducted a fish and wildlife survey for the US Government and became a professional fisherman. While living in the Arctic, he copied the Eskimo method of preserving his family's precious food supply in the winter by freezing it in barrels, and after returning to the USA in 1917 became interested in the possibility of preserving food commercially by the same method.

In 1924 in Gloucester, Massachusetts, he opened a company, General Seafoods, and began preserving fish by rapid freezing. In the course of his experiments, he tried freezing anything he could get his hands on – including a whale and an alligator! Soon his company was also freezing bulk quantities of more conventional foods, including 500 tons of fruit and vegetables every year. It prospered and in 1929 was sold for $22,000,000 to the firm that became the giant General Foods Corporation (Birdseye himself became a millionaire and devoted the rest of his life to inventing, dying in New York in 1956). Individual packs of frozen food were first marketed in the USA by Birdseye in 1930, and in Britain by Smedley of Wisbech, who launched frozen asparagus in 1937. Birds Eye sold its first individual frozen meals – chicken fricassée and steak – in 1939, and the whole concept of frozen food quickly gained popularity in the USA in the 1940s, as other companies followed in Birdseye's footsteps. Fish fingers have a longer pedigree than most people realize: back in 1927 UK Patent No: 257,222 was granted to Birdseye for 'Improvements in Methods of Preserving Fish Foods' – which were fish fingers in all but name (although they were not in fact called that until they were launched in Britain in 1955).

THE 10 DEGREES OF HOTNESS OF CHILLIES

1	Delicate		6	Hot
2	Mild		7	Burning
3	Medium		8	Fiery
4	Warm		9	Incendiary
5	Piquant		10	Volcanic

It is said that Christopher Columbus 'discovered' chilli peppers on the island of Hispaniola in 1492, from where they spread to the rest of the world. Various scales have been devised for measuring the 'hotness' of chillies, of which this is one.

THE 10 BESTSELLING HARTLEY PURE FRUIT JAMS

1	Strawberry		6	Black cherry
2	Raspberry		7	Damson
3	Raspberry seedless		8	Blackberry
4	Blackcurrant		9	Pineapple
5	Apricot		10	Redcurrant jelly

An early advertisement for raspberry jam which (nowadays in somewhat less than scout troop-sized jars) remains one of Hartley's most popular flavours.

THE TOP 10 SUGAR-CONSUMING NATIONS IN THE WORLD

	Country	Consumption per head per annum kg	lb
1	Cuba	89.2	196.7
2	Swaziland	67.1	147.9
3	Singapore	65.3	144.0
4	Israel	59.9	132.1
5	Costa Rica	59.2	130.5
6	Iceland	58.6	129.2
7	Netherlands	57.9	127.7
8	Fiji	56.2	123.9
9	Austria	55.1	121.5
10	Hungary	54.1	119.3
	UK	43.4	95.7

Each citizen of Cuba, the world's leaders in the sweet-tooth stakes, would appear to consume a quantity equal to the familiar 1 kg/2.2 lb bag of sugar every four days. The commonly used method of comparing food consumption with the equivalent weight of an average person is perhaps misleading in this instance, since large proportions of the countries in the Top 10 are presumably so overweight as a result of their massive intake of sugar that it is impossible to state what an 'average' person weighs!

THE TOP 10 PROTEIN-CONSUMING NATIONS IN THE WORLD

	Country	Protein consumption (grams per head per day)
1	Iceland	127.6
2	Ireland	117.1
3	France	112.9
4	Greece	112.2
5	Bulgaria	110.2
6	USA	109.9
7	Italy	107.4
8	Former USSR	107.3
9 =	Belgium/Luxembourg	106.4
9 =	Former Czechoslovakia	106.4
	UK	93.6
	World average	70.9

THE 10 BESTSELLING TYPES OF CHEESE IN THE UK

	Type	Annual sales (tonnes)
1	English Cheddar	89,484,000
2	Processed cheese	26,069,000
3	Cottage cheese	17,874,000
4	Irish Cheddar	14,845,000
5	Scottish Cheddar	12,247,000
6	Red Leicester	10,889,000
7	Edam	9,225,000
8	Cheshire	8,576,000
9	New Zealand Cheddar	5,741,000
10	Double Gloucester	5,009,000

A profusion of cheeses in alluring packaging – yet British consumers remain faithful to a small range of well-known varieties.

THE TOP 10 CHEESE-PRODUCING NATIONS

	Country	Annual production (tonnes)
1	USA	3,090,100
2	Former USSR	1,845,000
3	France	1,425,400
4	Germany	1,193,357
5	Italy	692,486
6	Netherlands	614,275
7	Egypt	318,750
8	UK	310,000
9	Poland	292,780
10	Canada	290,721
	World total	*14,163,370*

CHEESE QUIZ

From which countries do these cheeses come?

1 Gruyère
2 Ricotta
3 Edam
4 Serra
5 Jarlsberg
6 Munster
7 Quark
8 Caboc
9 Liederkrantz
10 Manchego

THE 10 LARGEST CHEESES EVER MADE

1 18,171 kg/40,060 lb

Making gigantic cheeses is not a modern eccentricity: in his *Natural History*, the Roman historian Pliny describes a 454-kg/1,000-lb cheese that was made in the Tuscan town of Luni. The current world record holder is this monster Cheddar manufactured on 13–14 March 1988 by Simon's Specialty Cheese of Little Chute, Wisconsin, USA. It was then taken on tour in a refrigerated 'cheesemobile'.

2 15,690 kg/34,591 lb

Made on 20–22 January 1964 for the World's Fair, New York, by the Wisconsin Cheese Foundation, it was 4.35 m/14½ ft long, 1.95 m/6½ ft wide and 1.8 m/6 ft high and took 183 tons of milk – equivalent to a day's output by a herd of 16,000 cows. It was toured and displayed until 1968 when it was cut up and sold. As late as 1978, the last two chunks were sold at a charity auction for $200 each.

3 6,096 kg/13,440 lb

Using the milk from 6,000 cows, production was started on 12 July 1937 and the cheese was exhibited at the New York State Fair in Syracuse.

4 5,359 kg/11,815 lb

This Cheddar was made in January 1957 in Flint, Michigan, from the milk pooled by a group of 367 farmers from their 6,600 cows.

5 3,629 kg/8,000 lb

This large Canadian Cheddar was made for the 1883 Toronto Fair.

6 669 kg/1,474 lb

A cheese 3.90 m/13 ft in circumference made by James Elgar of Peterborough, Northamptonshire, in 1849.

7 653 kg/1,400 lb

A Cheddar given to President Andrew Jackson. After maturing for two years in the White House, it was given to the people of Washington, DC, on Washington's birthday.

8 = 544 kg/1,200 lb

A huge Cheshire given in 1801 to President Thomas Jefferson by a preacher, John Leland, it was appropriately made by the town of Cheshire, Massachusetts.

8 = 544 kg/1,200 lb

Made on 3 March 1989 in the village of West Pennard, Somerset, by John Green, to recreate the 'Great Pennard Cheese' (see number 10) and as an exhibit at the May 1989 Festival of British Food and Farming. It took 5,455 litres/1,200 gallons of milk and measured 75 cm/3 ft in diameter and 2.7 m/9 ft in circumference.

10 499 kg/1,100 lb

This 2.7-m/9-ft circumference Cheddar, named the 'Great Pennard Cheese' after the Somerset village in which it was made, was presented to Queen Victoria as a wedding gift in 1840. It was taken to London and exhibited at the Egyptian Hall in Piccadilly, but on its return was found to have suffered so much in the heat of the exhibition that she refused to accept it.

THE TOP 10 ALCOHOL-CONSUMING NATIONS IN THE WORLD

	Country	Annual consumption per head (100% alcohol) litres	pints
1	France	12.7	22.4
2	Luxembourg	12.2	21.5
3	East Germany*	11.8	20.8
4 =	Hungary	10.8	19.0
4 =	Spain	10.8	19.0
4 =	Switzerland	10.8	19.0
7	West Germany*	10.6	18.7
8	Austria	10.4	18.3
9 =	Belgium	9.9	17.4
9 =	Denmark	9.9	17.4
21	UK	7.6	13.4
24	USA	7.5	13.2

*Figures for united country not yet available.

Even though its total consumption has declined from its peak of 17.4 litres/30.6 pints per head, France has held its lead in this list for many years.

THE TOP 10 BEER-DRINKING NATIONS IN THE WORLD

	Country	Annual consumption per head litres	pints
1	Germany	143.1	251.8
2	Czechoslovakia	135.0	237.6
3	Denmark	126.2	222.0
4	Luxembourg	121.4	213.6
5	Austria	121.3	213.5
6	Belgium	120.7	212.4
7	Ireland	117.0	205.9
8	New Zealand	110.8	195.0
9	UK	110.2	193.9
10	Australia	108.2	190.4

Perhaps surprisingly, despite its position as the world's leading producer of beer, the USA is ranked 12th in terms of consumption (90.8 litres/159.8 pints per head).

THE 10 MOST ADVERTISED BEER BRANDS IN THE UK

	Beer	Advertising expenditure (£)
1	Tennents	8,845,000
2	Guinness	8,535,000
3	Carling	8,072,000
4	Carlsberg	7,381,000
5	Heineken	5,312,000
6	Holsten	5,163,000
7	Fosters	4,719,000
8	Castlemaine	4,458,000
9	McEwan	4,171,000
10	John Smith	3,495,000

In 1991, total expenditure on beer advertising in the UK was estimated to be £93,359,000, of which the Top 10 accounted for £60,151,000, or 64 per cent.

An English-style pub in Denmark: the country finds a place among the world's leading consumers of alcohol, with beer high on the list of national preferences.

FOOD & DRINK

THE TOP 10 BEER-PRODUCING COUNTRIES IN THE WORLD

	Country	Annual production litres	pints
1	USA	23,226,500,000	40,872,900,000
2	Germany	11,704,300,000	20,596,700,000
3	UK	6,016,500,000	10,587,500,000
4	Japan	5,789,400,000	10,187,900,000
5	Former USSR	5,580,000,000	9,819,400,000
6	China	5,500,000,000	9,678,600,000
7	Brazil	4,780,000,000	8,411,600,000
8	Mexico	3,453,400,000	6,077,100,000
9	Spain	2,657,900,000	4,677,200,000
10	Canada	2,314,900,000	4,073,600,000
	World total	*107,700,000,000*	*189,525,400,000*

World beer production is almost sufficient to allow every person on the planet to drink 0.57 litres/1 pint every 10 days of the year. That of the UK is adequate to provide every UK inhabitant with the same quantity every two days.

THE TOP 10 IMPORTED BEER BRANDS IN THE UK

1	Holsten Diat Pils
2	Becks
3	Grolsch
4	Sol
5	San Miguel
6	Budweiser Budvar
7	Peroni
8	Michelob
9	Rolling Rock
10	Miller Genuine Draft

THE TOP 10 WINE-PRODUCING COUNTRIES IN THE WORLD

	Country	Annual production (tonnes)
1	France	6,200,000
2	Italy	5,915,000
3	Spain	3,107,000
4	Former USSR	1,800,000
5	USA	1,490,000
6	Argentina	1,465,000
7	Germany	1,015,000
8	Portugal	991,000
9	South Africa	963,000
10	Bulgaria	600,000
	World total	*27,767,000*

As predicted in the last edition of *The Top 10 of Everything*, Yugoslavia's internal problems have so severely damaged its important wine industry that it has now lost its longstanding position among the world's foremost producers, its place having been taken by Bulgaria, with Hungary a close runner-up.

THE TOP 10 WINE-DRINKING NATIONS IN THE WORLD

	Country	Litres per head per annum	Equiv. 75 cl bottles
1	France	73.1	97.5
2	Italy	61.4	81.9
3	Luxembourg	58.2	77.6
4	Argentina	54.2	72.3
5	Switzerland	49.4	65.9
6	Portugal	47.5	63.3
7	Spain	37.4	49.9
8	Austria	35.0	46.7
9	Greece	32.6	43.5
10	Uruguay	30.4	40.5
26	*UK*	*11.6*	*15.5*
29	*USA*	*7.7*	*10.3*

THE TOP 10 TEA-DRINKING NATIONS

	Country	Annual consumption per head			
		kg	lb	oz	cups*
1	Irish Republic	3.09	6	13	1,360
2	UK	2.74	6	1	1,206
3	Turkey	2.24	4	15	986
4	Qatar	2.17	4	13	955
5	Iraq	2.14	4	11	942
6	Hong Kong	1.82	4	0	801
7	Kuwait	1.62	3	9	713
8	New Zealand	1.58	3	8	695
9	Tunisia	1.47	3	4	647
10	Egypt	1.38	3	1	607
	USA	*0.34*	*0*	*12*	*150*

*Based on 440 cups per kg/2 lb 3 oz.

Notwithstanding the UK's traditional passion for tea, during the past decade its consumption has consistently lagged behind that of Ireland. In the same period, Qatar's tea consumption has dropped from its record 3.97 kg/8 lb 12 oz (1,747 cups) per head. Within Europe, consumption varies enormously from the current world-leading Irish figure down to just 0.07 kg/2.5 oz (31 cups) in Italy, while in the rest of the world, Thailand's 0.01 kg/0.4 oz (4 cups) is one of the lowest.

Ready for the grape harvest in Bordeaux: France is the world's leading wine producer.

THE TOP 10 COFFEE-DRINKING NATIONS

	Country	Annual consumption per head			
		kg	lb	oz	cups*
1	Finland	11.51	25	6	1,727
2	Sweden	11.13	24	9	1,670
3	Norway	10.66	23	8	1,599
4	Denmark	10.59	23	6	1,589
5	Austria	9.99	22	0	1,499
6	Netherlands	9.90	21	13	1,485
7	Switzerland	8.39	18	8	1,259
8	Germany	7.92	17	7	1,188
9	France	5.84	12	14	876
10	USA	4.52	9	15	660
	UK	*2.45*	*5*	*6*	*368*

*Based on 150 cups per kg/2 lb 3 oz.

The total coffee consumption of many countries declined during the 1980s – that of Belgium and Luxembourg for example more than halved from 7.17 kg/15 lb 13 oz (1,076 cups) in 1986 to 3.53 kg/7 lb 12 oz (530 cups) in 1991. That of both Finland and Sweden has remained high, however – the average Finn drinks almost five cups of coffee a day compared with just one for the UK. Ireland's consumption is the EC's lowest at 1.93 kg/4 lb 4 oz (293 cups).

THE TOP 10 BRANDS OF BOTTLED MINERAL WATER IN THE UK

	Brand	Type	% of market
1	Evian	Still	11
2	Buxton Spring	Still/sparkling	7
3 =	Highland Spring	Still/sparkling	6
3 =	Volvic	Still	6
5 =	Perrier	Sparkling	5
5 =	Strathmore	Still/sparkling	5
5 =	Sainsbury's Caledonian Spring	Still/sparkling	5
8	Chiltern Hills	Still/sparkling	4
9 =	Ballygowan	Still/sparkling	3
9 =	Tesco's Mountain Spring	Still/sparkling	3

It is estimated that the total value of the market for bottled mineral water in the UK rose from £130,000,000 in 1988 to £345,000,000 in 1992, and it is predicted to double by 1997. The UK currently drinks 435,000,000 litres/765,492,555 pints a year, or 7.56 litres/13.30 pints per head of the population. Consumption has a long way to go to rival that of Italy, however, which drinks the most per head of any country – 101.50 litres/178.61 pints per annum.

THE TOP 10 CONSUMERS OF COCA-COLA

1	Iceland
2	USA
3	Mexico
4	Australia
5	Norway
6	Germany
7	Canada
8	Spain
9	Argentina
10	Japan
59	*UK*

This ranking is based on consumption per capita in these countries – although the actual volumes are a closely guarded secret. The figures for many small countries are distorted by the influx of large numbers of tourists, but as Iceland is not noted for its tourist industry, the surprising conclusion must be that Icelanders drink huge quantities of Coke!

THE TOP 10 MILK-DRINKING NATIONS

	Country	Annual consumption per head	
		litres	pints
1	Former USSR	302.3	532
2	Iceland	299.6	527
3	Uruguay	294.3	518
4	Ireland	248.1	437
5	Norway	214.0	377
6	Finland	194.4	342
7	Israel	190.7	336
8	Bulgaria	190.0	334
9	Romania	180.0	317
10	Hungary	179.9	317

10 DISHES NAMED AFTER PEOPLE

1 Apple Charlotte

Known as 'the king of cooks and the cook of kings', the French master chef Marie Antonin was employed by the Prince Regent (later King George IV) at Brighton Pavilion (1816–19) when he created a new dessert, naming it Apple Charlotte after the Prince's daughter.

2 Châteaubriand

The Châteaubriand steak was named after François René, Vicomte de Châteaubriand (1768–1848), a Napoleonic statesman who fled France soon after the French Revolution. In 1822 he was appointed Ambassador to Britain. It was while he was living in London that his chef, Montmireil, perfected the method of cooking a piece of tender steak between two inferior pieces of meat, the juices of which it absorbed. He duly named it after his master.

3 Coquilles St Jacques

According to legend, a village in Portugal was converted to Christianity when one of its inhabitants was saved from drowning by those accompanying the body of St James (French *Jacques*) by sea to Galicia. The saved man emerged from the water covered with scallop shells (French *coquilles*) and the village adopted this as the symbol of St Jacques. Centuries later, the Coquilles St Jacques were embellished with mornay sauce to create the dish known today.

4 Eggs Benedict

One morning in 1894, suffering from a hangover, Samuel Benedict, a New York man-about-town, entered the Waldorf-Astoria hotel. He ordered the breakfast he habitually consumed as a cure-all – bacon, buttered toast, poached eggs and hollandaise sauce. On this occasion, however, Oscar, the maître d'hotel, modified the dish, substituting ham and a muffin for the bacon and toast, christening the concoction Eggs Benedict in Samuel's honour.

5 Eggs Arnold Bennett

Like the Pêche Melba, this omelette filled with haddock and cream originated at the Savoy Hotel in London. The writer and drama critic, Arnold Bennett, often took dinner there after visiting the theatre. Too hungry to wait for a more elaborate meal, Eggs Arnold Bennett was created for him as an 'instant' dish.

6 Melba Toast

Toast Melba or Melba Toast was named after the great Australian opera singer Dame Nellie Melba (1861–1931) but was actually suggested by Marie Louise Ritz, wife of César Ritz, manager of the Savoy Hotel in London. She suggested that head chef Auguste Escoffier should try toasting thin bread, then slicing it again and re-toasting it. Dame Nellie was staying in the Savoy and had been recommended to eat a light diet while she recuperated from a strenuous tour. Escoffier duly served her his newly created toast, which she adored. 'Call it "Toast Melba",' said the modest Marie Ritz.

7 Oysters Rockefeller

In 1899, Jules Alciatore of Antoine's Restaurant in New Orleans devised this oyster dish; a customer declared it tasted 'as rich as Rockefeller' and so it acquired its opulent name.

8 Pavlova

The Pavlova, a meringue made with various fruits topped with cream, was named in honour of the great Russian ballerina, Anna Pavlova (1885–1931), during a tour of Australia and New Zealand.

9 Praline

César de Choiseul, Comte du Plessis-Praslin (1598–1675), led the French army against Spain in 1650, and devoted his life to royal service – yet he is remembered less for his military achievements than for the fact that his chef prepared a dish composed of sugar and almonds which became known as *praslins* – and ultimately as praline.

10 Sandwich

John Montagu, 4th Earl of Sandwich (1718–92), is alleged to have had his servant put roast beef between slices of bread so that he could continue a marathon card game uninterrupted. Similar methods of eating were known at least as early as Roman times, but his name became irrevocably linked with this most familiar of foods.

THE 10 LARGEST PRISONS IN ENGLAND AND WALES

	Prison	Inmates
1	Wandsworth, London	1,274
2	Walton, Liverpool	1,239
3	Winson Green, Birmingham	977
4	Brixton, London	941
5	Wormwood Scrubs, London	924
6	Armley, Leeds	922
7	Durham	902
8	Pentonville, London	773
9	Wymott, Lancashire	733
10	Stafford	730

Figures are for average prison populations in 1991–92. Strangeways, Manchester, formerly England's largest prison, was wrecked during a prisoners' riot in April 1990 and has not been fully re-opened.

THE 10 LARGEST PRISONS IN SCOTLAND

	Prison	Inmates
1	Barlinnie, Glasgow	955
2	Edinburgh	570
3	Shotts, Lanarkshire	460
4	Glenochil, near Alloa	458
5	Polmont, near Falkirk*	415
6	Perth	374
7	Low Moss, near Glasgow	337
8	Greenock	237
9	Peterhead, near Aberdeen	192
10	Glenochil, near Alloa*	160

*Young Offenders' Institution.

The figures are as at 31 December 1992, when a number of prisoners would have been released on parole for Christmas, and are hence not representative of peak populations.

CRIMINALS IN FICTION QUIZ

1 Who is Sherlock Holmes's opponent, known as the 'Napoleon of Crime'?

2 Who is the feline master criminal who is also called the 'Napoleon of Crime'?

3 Who is the 'Amateur Cracksman'?

4 Which of James Bond's opponents has the first name 'Auric'?

5 Which criminal literary creation of Sax Rohmer was played on film by Peter Sellers?

6 What is the identity of the murderer in Edgar Allan Poe's *The Murders in the Rue Morgue*?

7 Which detective's opponents include Flattop, Pruneface and The Brow?

8 In G.K. Chesterton's *Father Brown* stories, is the giant French criminal turned detective known as (a) Flambeau, (b) Soufflé or (c) Brullée?

9 Who played the part of the villain Caspar Gutman in the 1941 film of Dashiell Hammett's *The Maltese Falcon*?

10 In Robert Louis Stevenson's novel, what are the first names of Dr Jekyll and Mr Hyde?

THE 10 MOST PROLIFIC MURDERERS IN THE UK

1 Mary Ann Cotton

Cotton (b.1832), a former nurse, is generally held to be Britain's worst mass murderer. Over a 20-year period, it seems probable that she disposed of 14–20 victims, including her husband, children and stepchildren by arsenic poisoning. She was hanged at Durham on 24 March 1873.

2 Michael Ryan

On 19 August 1987 in Hungerford, Berkshire, Ryan (b.1960), who had no previous convictions, armed himself with an AK47 Kalashnikov assault rifle, an M1 carbine and a 9mm Beretta pistol and went on a rampage, shooting 14 dead – including his mother – and wounding 16 others (two of whom died later) before shooting himself.

3 = William Burke and William Hare

Two Irishmen living in Edinburgh, Burke and Hare murdered at least 15 people in order to sell their bodies (for £8 to £14 each) to anatomists in the period before human dissection was legal. Burke was hanged on 28 January 1829 while Hare, having turned king's evidence against him, was released a week later and allegedly died a blind beggar in London in the 1860s.

3 = Bruce Lee

In 1981 Lee was convicted of arson that resulted in the deaths of 26 residents of an old people's home. He was later cleared by the Court of Appeal of 11 of the deaths. He is currently in a mental hospital.

3 = Dennis Andrew Nilsen

Nilsen (b.1948) admitted to murdering 15 men between 1978 and 1983. On 4 November 1983 he was sentenced to life imprisonment on six charges of murder and two attempted murders.

6 Dr William Palmer

Known as the 'Rugeley Poisoner', Palmer (b.1824) may have killed at least 13, probably 14 and perhaps as many as 16, including his wife, brother and children in order to claim insurance, and various men whom he robbed to pay off his gambling debts. He was hanged at Stafford on 14 June 1856. The true number of his victims remains uncertain.

7 Peter Sutcliffe

Known as the 'Yorkshire Ripper', Sutcliffe (b.1946) was caught on 2 January 1981 and on 22 May 1981 found guilty of murdering 13 women and seven attempted murders between 1975 and 1980. He was sentenced to life imprisonment on each charge and is currently in Parkhurst Prison.

8 Peter Thomas Anthony Manuel

Found guilty of murdering seven people, it is likely that Manuel killed as many as 12. He was hanged at Barlinnie Prison on 11 July 1958.

9 John George Haigh

The so-called 'Acid Bath Murderer' certainly killed six and may have disposed of up to nine victims. He was hanged at Wandsworth Prison on 10 August 1949.

10 'Jack the Ripper'

In 1888 in Whitechapel, London, 'Jack the Ripper' killed and mutilated five or six women. Despite more than a century of speculation and a list of possible candidates now running into dozens, his true identity and dates remain unknown.

Other multiple murderers in British history include John Reginald Halliday Christie who may have killed as many as six women at 10 Rillington Place, London, and was hanged at Pentonville Prison on 15 July 1953. On 7 May 1981 John Thompson was found guilty on one specimen charge of murder by arson during an incident in which a total of 37 died at the Spanish Club, Denmark Street, London.

Peter Manuel earned an unenviable place as one of the UK's most prolific murderers.

THE 10 MOST PROLIFIC MURDERERS IN THE WORLD*

1   Behram

The leader of the Thug cult in India, in the period 1790–1840 he was reputed to have committed over 931 ritual strangulations.

2   Countess Erszébet Báthory

In the period up to 1610 in Hungary, Báthory (1560–1614), known as 'Countess Dracula' – the title of a 1970 Hammer horror film about her life and crimes – murdered between 300 and 650 girls (her personal list of 610 victims was·described at her trial) in the belief that drinking their blood would prevent her from ageing. She was eventually arrested in 1611; tried and found guilty, she died on 21 August 1614 walled up in her own castle at Csejthe.

3   William Estel Brown

On 17 July 1961 Brown admitted that on 18 March 1937 he had deliberately loosened the gas pipes in his school basement in New London, Texas, thereby causing an explosion that killed 282 children and 24 teachers.

4   Pedro Alonso López

Known as the 'Colombian Monster' and the 'Monster of the Andes', up to his 1980 capture he murdered at least 300 young girls in Colombia, Ecuador and Peru. He was caught by Ayacucho Indians in Peru, whose children he had been abducting, and escorted to Ecuador by a female missionary. He was arrested and led police to 53 graves; further bodies were revealed when a river flooded, but others were devoured by wild animals or buried under roads and on construction sites and were never discovered. López was convicted and sentenced to life imprisonment.

5   Gilles de Rais

A fabulously wealthy French aristocrat, de Rais (b.1404) was accused of having kidnapped and killed between 60 and 200 children. He was strangled and his body burnt at Nantes on 25 October 1440.

6   Herman Webster Mudgett

Also known as 'H.H. Holmes', Mudgett (b.1860) was believed to have lured over 150 women to his 63rd Street, Chicago, 'castle', which was fully equipped for torturing and murdering them and disposing of the bodies. Arrested in 1894 and found guilty of murder, he confessed to killing 27. Mudgett, regarded as America's first mass murderer, was hanged at Moyamensing Prison, Philadelphia, on 7 May 1896.

7   Julio Gonzalez

On the morning of Sunday 25 March 1990, Gonzalez, a Cuban refugee who had lived in the USA for 10 years, allegedly firebombed Happy Land, a discotheque in The Bronx, New York (ordered closed in 1988 because it lacked basic fire safety measures), killing 87.

8   Bruno Lüdke

Lüdke (b.1909) was a German who confessed to murdering 85 women between 1928 and 29 January 1943. Declared insane, he was incarcerated in a Vienna hospital where he was subjected to medical experiments, apparently dying on 8 April 1944 after a lethal injection.

9   Wou Bom-Kon

An off-duty policeman, on 26–27 April 1982 in South Korea he went on a drunken rampage with guns and grenades, killing 57 and injuring 35 before blowing himself up with a grenade.

10   Andrei Chikatilo

Russia's worst serial killer was convicted in Rostov-on-Don in 1992 of killing 52 women and children between 1978 and 1990 and was sentenced to death by firing squad.

*Includes only individual murderers; excludes murders by bandits, those carried out by groups, such as political and military atrocities, and gangland slayings.

Among possible contenders for this grisly catalogue are several serial killers whose full list of victims will probably never be known, among them Henry Lee Lucas – the subject of the film, Henry, Portrait of a Serial Killer – who may have committed up to 200 murders (he admitted in 1983 to 360 and was convicted of 11) and Ted Bundy who, after spending nine years on death row, was executed at Florida State Prison on 24 January 1989 for the murder of 12-year-old Kimberly Leach. During his last hours Bundy confessed to 23 murders. Police linked him conclusively to the murders of 36 girls and he once admitted that he might have killed as many as 100 times.

There are some murderers whose identity has never been established: in California in 1968–74 the 'Zodiac Killer', so called because he used zodiacal signs at the scenes of his crimes and to sign letters to the Press, claimed to have murdered 37 times, but was never identified or caught.

On 13 March 1980 John Wayne Gacy was sentenced to death by electrocution for the Chicago murders of 33 men. The sentence was never carried out and he is currently in prison (in the USA there are currently more than 2,000 convicted murderers on death row). Also in the USA Dean Corll, a Houston, Texas, electrician and his accomplice Elmer Henley, with the participation of David Brooks, murdered about 32 boys before Henley finally shot and killed Corll on 8 August 1973. Henley was sentenced to 594 years in jail and Brooks to life imprisonment. Patrick Kearney, yet another American serial killer, was probably responsible for 28 murders. Jeffrey Dahmer was convicted on 15 February 1992 of murdering and dismembering 17 victims, although the actual total could well have been higher. Such serial killings are not an exclusively modern phenomenon: Earle Wilson, for example, murdered at least 22 mostly elderly women in the USA and Canada in the 1920s, for which crimes he was hanged in Winnipeg, Canada, on 13 January 1928.

Just outside the Top 10 are such killers as John Gilbert Graham: in order to claim a total of £87,500 insurance, Graham placed a time bomb in the luggage of his mother, Daisy King, as she boarded an airliner in Denver, Colorado, on 1 November 1955. En route for San Francisco, it blew up killing all 44 on board. On 11 January 1957, Graham was found guilty – only on the charge of murdering his mother – and executed in the gas chamber of Colorado State Penitentiary.

In Germany, at the end of the First World War, Fritz Haarmann, known as 'The Butcher of Hanover', may have murdered as many as 50 refugees in order to steal their clothes and sell their bodies as meat. He was charged with 27 murders and executed in 1924.

Dr Marcel Petiot, once sufficiently respected to have been elected mayor of Villeneuve, is known to have killed at least 27 but admitted to 63 murders at his Paris house during the Second World War. He claimed that they were Nazi collaborators, but it is probable that they were wealthy Jews whom he robbed and killed after pretending to help them escape from occupied France. He was guillotined on 26 May 1946.

Belle Gunness (1859–1908?), a Norwegian-born immigrant to the USA, is believed to have murdered her husband Peter Gunness for his life insurance (she claimed that an axe had fallen from a shelf and onto his head). After this, she lured 16–28 suitors through 'Lonely Hearts' advertisements, as well as numerous others, to her Laporte, Indiana, farm, where she murdered them. On 28 April 1908 she burned the farm down and either committed suicide or, according to some reports, faked her own death and disappeared.

THE 10 WORST GUN MASSACRES OF ALL TIME

Perpetrator/location/ date/circumstances	Killed
1 **Wou Bom-Kon**	
Sang-Namdo, South Korea, 26–27 April 1982	**57**

Off-duty policeman Wou Bom-Kon went on a drunken rampage with rifles and hand grenades, killing 57 and injuring 35 before blowing himself up with a grenade (see The 10 Most Prolific Murderers in the World).

2 = James Huberty	
San Ysidro, California, USA, 19 July 1984	**22**

Huberty, aged 41, opened fire in a McDonald's restaurant, killing 21 before being shot dead by police. A further 19 were wounded, including a victim who died the following day.

2 = George Hennard	
Killeen, Texas, USA, 16 October 1991	**22**

Hennard drove his pick-up truck through the window of Luby's Cafeteria, killed 22 with semi-automatic pistols and then shot himself dead.

4 = Charles Whitman	
Austin, Texas, USA, 1 August 1966	**16**

Whitman killed his mother and wife before taking the lift to the 27th floor of the campus tower and ascending to the observation deck above at the University of Texas at Austin, from where he shot 14 and wounded 34 before being shot dead by police officer Ramiro Martinez.

4 = Michael Ryan	
Hungerford, Berkshire, UK, 19 August 1987	**16**

Ryan, 26, shot 14 dead and wounded 16 others (two of whom died later) before shooting himself (see The 10 Most Prolific Murderers in the UK).

4 = R. Gene Simmons	
Russellville, Arkansas, USA, 28 December 1987	**16**

47-year-old Simmons killed 16, including 14 members of his own family, by shooting or strangling. He was caught and in February 1989 sentenced to death.

7 = Wagner von Degerloch	
Muehlausen, Germany, 3–4 September 1913	**14**

Wagner von Degerloch, a schoolteacher, murdered his wife and four children before embarking on a random shooting spree as a result of which nine were killed and 12 injured. He was committed to a mental asylum, where he died.

7 = Sandy 'Pat' Sherrill	
Edmond, Oklahoma, 20 August 1986	**14**

Sherrill, aged 44, shot 14 dead and wounded seven others at the post office where he worked before killing himself.

7 = Christian Dornier	
Luxiol, Doubs, France, 12 July 1989	**14**

Dornier, a thirty-one-year-old farmer, went on a rampage leaving 14 dead and nine injured, including several children, before being wounded and caught by police.

7 = Marc Lépine	
Montreal University, Canada, 6 December 1989	**14**

In Canada's worst gun massacre Lépine, a 25-year-old student, went on an armed rampage, killing only women, then shot himself.

Police attend one of the 16 victims of Michael Ryan, the perpetrator of the UK's worst gun massacre.

THE 10 COMMONEST OFFENCES IN ENGLAND AND WALES IN 1991

	Offence	Offenders found guilty
1	Motoring offences	724,400
2	Theft and handling stolen goods	133,500
3	Violence against the person	47,200
4	Burglary	46,100
5	Other offences	34,400
6	Drug offences	23,500
7	Fraud and forgery	21,200
8	Criminal damage	10,200
9	Sexual offences	5,500
10	Robbery	4,800
	Total (indictable 337,600/summary 1,167,500)	*1,505,100*

This list includes both indictable offences (those normally calling for a trial before a jury) and summary offences (usually tried before a magistrates' court). In the latter category, motoring offences comprise the largest proportion, but other offences are less precisely itemized and hence appear in official statistics under a general heading. Under the Criminal Justice Act of 1988, a number of offences were reclassified, and some, such as certain criminal damage offences, may be either indictable or summary, depending on the value of the property that is damaged. 'Other offences' includes groups of less specific offences grouped as 'breach of local and other regulations' and 'other summary offences' which in total make up large numbers. It should be noted that direct comparisons cannot be made with offences under Scottish legal jurisdiction, which employs different categories of offence, some bearing a ring of the age in which they were established, including 'theft by opening lockfast places' and 'lewd and libidinous practices'.

THE 10 COMMONEST REPORTED CRIMINAL OFFENCES IN ENGLAND AND WALES

	Offence	Offences 1981	Increase 1991	%
1	Burglary	718,400	1,219,500	70
2	Theft from a motor vehicle	379,600	913,300	140
3	Criminal damage	386,700	821,100	112
4	Other theft*	485,300	685,600	41
5	Theft of a motor vehicle	332,600	581,900	75
6	Theft from a shop	225,300	281,300	25
7	Theft of a pedal cycle	109,800	212,200	93
8	Violence against the person	100,200	190,300	90
9	Fraud and forgery	106,700	174,700	64
10	Handling stolen goods	40,800	51,500	26
	Total (including those not in list)	2,963,800	5,276,200	78

*Category not specified elsewhere.

Thefts from cars increased by 140 per cent in the 1980s.

10 CAPITAL OFFENCES OF THE PAST

1. Carrying of horses or mares into Scotland
2. Conjuring, sorcery, witchcraft and digging up crosses
3. Counterfeiting or 'trimming' coins
4. Cutting down a tree
5. Escaping from prison
6. Hunting by night
7. Impersonating a Greenwich pensioner
8. Robbing a rabbit warren
9. Stealing hawks' eggs
10. Theft of goods above the value of 40 shillings from a house or five shillings from a shop

William Harrison, a clergyman writing in 1587, left a vivid record of daily life in Britain, including a long list of offences, in addition to those such as murder and treason, for which capital punishment was ordained. The normal method of execution was hanging, but under certain circumstances more horrible punishments were decreed: women who poisoned their husbands, for example, were burned to death, while a man who poisoned another man could be boiled to death in water or lead. Gradually, the number of capital offences increased – between 1714 and 1830 no fewer than 156 new offences were added, so that the total stood at 220. In practice there were probably fewer than 25 crimes for which anyone was ever executed, but the law was extremely severe with certain crimes: in 1820, for example, 46 people were hanged for forging banknotes. In 1837 the total of capital offences was reduced to 15 and in 1861 to four: murder, treason, piracy with violence and setting fire to Admiralty ships and dockyards. It was not until 1908 that capital punishment in the UK was abolished for criminals under the age of 16. After further modifications, it was abolished altogether in 1965.

THE FIRST 10 COUNTRIES TO ABOLISH CAPITAL PUNISHMENT

	Country	Abolished
1	Russia	1826
2	Venezuela	1863
3	Portugal	1867
4	Costa Rica	1882
5	Ecuador	1897
6	Panama	1903
7	Norway	1905
8	Uruguay	1907
9	Colombia	1910
10 =	Austria	1921
10 =	Sweden	1921
	UK	1965

Some countries abolished capital punishment in peacetime only, or for all crimes except treason, generally extending it totally at a more recent date. Some countries retained capital punishment on their statute books, but effectively abolished it: the last execution in Liechtenstein, for example, took place in 1795, in Mexico in 1946 and in Belgium in 1950. Finland abolished the death penalty at the same time as Russia (under whose rule it was at the time), but reintroduced it in 1882 – although no prisoner has been executed in that country since 1824. One US state, Michigan, abolished capital punishment for every offence except treason in 1846.

CRIME & PUNISHMENT

THE TOP 10 LIBEL AWARDS BY JURIES IN THE UK

	To	Against	Libel	Year	Amount (£)
1	Lord Aldington	Count Tolstoy	Repatriating Cossacks to certain death during the Second World War	1989	1,500,000
2	Sonia Sutcliffe	*Private Eye*	Making money out of being the wife of the 'Yorkshire Ripper'	1989	600,000 *
3	Jeffrey Archer	*Daily Star*	Paying for the services of a prostitute	1987	500,000
4 =	Barney Eastwood	Barry McGuigan	Boxing manager accused of forcing his boxer to fight, despite illness	1992	450,000
4 =	Martin Packard	*Eleftheroutypia* (Greek newspaper)	Drug smuggling and involvement with Greek Colonels	1987	450,000
6	Wafic Said	Misbah Baki	Callousness and breaking promises during the Gulf War	1992	400,000
7	Mr & Mrs Johnson	Radio City, Liverpool	Caravan holiday business described as 'a swindle'	1988	350,000
8	Fox & Gibbons	*Sourakia* (Arabic magazine)	Solicitor's firm's integrity questioned	1988	310,000 †
9 =	Charles Freeman Group	*Stationery Trade News*	Envelope distributor accused of dishonest methods	1988	300,000
9 =	Koo Stark	*The People*	Seeing Prince Andrew after her marriage	1988	300,000

*Reduced to £60,000 after negotiations.

†Reduced after negotiations (amount unknown).

The highest known libel settlements negotiated between parties before the cases reached trial are £1,000,000 paid on 12 December 1988 to Elton John by the *Sun* after allegations about his private life, and £610,000 paid to Richard Branson and Virgin Airways in 1993 by British Airways, following its alleged 'dirty tricks' campaign in appropriating Virgin passengers.

THE 10 LARGEST ARMED FORCES OF WORLD WAR I

	Country	Personnel*
1	Russia	12,000,000
2	Germany	11,000,000
3	British Empire	8,904,467
4	France	8,410,000
5	Austria–Hungary	7,800,000
6	Italy	5,615,000
7	USA	4,355,000
8	Turkey	2,850,000
9	Bulgaria	1,200,000
10	Japan	800,000

*Total at peak strength.

THE 10 LARGEST ARMED FORCES OF WORLD WAR II

	Country	Personnel*
1	USSR	12,500,000
2	USA	12,364,000
3	Germany	10,000,000
4	Japan	6,095,000
5	France	5,700,000
6	UK	4,683,000
7	Italy	4,500,000
8	China	3,800,000
9	India	2,150,000
10	Poland	1,000,000

*Total at peak strength.

Italian troops during World War I: the Top 10 countries alone mobilized a total of some 63 million men.

THE 10 SMALLEST ARMED FORCES OF WORLD WAR II

	Country	Personnel*
1	Costa Rica	400
2	Liberia	1,000
3 =	El Salvador	3,000
3 =	Honduras	3,000
3 =	Nicaragua	3,000
6	Haiti	3,500
7	Dominican Republic	4,000
8	Guatemala	5,000
9 =	Bolivia	8,000
9 =	Paraguay	8,000
9 =	Uruguay	8,000

*Total at peak strength.

As well as mobilizing very small armed forces, several South American countries entered the Second World War at a very late stage: Argentina, for example, the 53rd country to enter the war, did not actually declare war on Germany and Japan until 27 March 1945 – six weeks before Germany was defeated. The smallest European armed force was that of Denmark, with a maximum strength of 15,000, just 13 of whom were killed during the one-day German invasion of 9 April 1940, when Denmark became the second country after Poland to be occupied.

MILITARY

10 OF THE WORST BATTLES ON BRITISH SOIL

1 Location unknown
Britons *v* Romans (AD 61)

Some 80,000 Britons under Queen Boadicea of the Iceni were alleged to have been killed, with the loss of just 400 Romans.

2 Evesham
Crown *v* Barons (4 August 1265)

Simon de Montfort's baronial army of 5,350 was annihilated.

3 Dunbar
English *v* Scots (27 April 1296)

The Scottish army was defeated with a (probably exaggerated) loss of 10,000 troops.

4 Falkirk
English *v* Scots (22 July 1298)

About 5,000 Scots and 200 English were said to have been killed, the disparity resulting from the superiority of the English archers.

5 Bannockburn
Scots *v* English (24 June 1314)

English losses were put at some 15,000, Scots about 4,000.

6 Neville's Cross (Durham)
English *v* Scots (17 October 1346)

The Scots were defeated and about 9,000 killed.

7 Towton
Yorkists *v* Lancastrians (29 March 1461)

Approximately 28–38,000 were reckoned to have been killed in reputedly the bloodiest battle on English soil since Roman times.

8 Flodden
Scots *v* English (9 September 1513)

10,000 Scots were killed, with similarly heavy losses on the English side.

9 Edgehill
Royalists *v* Parliamentarians (23 October 1642)

A total of about 5,000 were killed.

10 Naseby
Royalists *v* Parliamentarians (14 June 1645)

Almost all of the Royalist army of 9,000 was wiped out.

Perhaps the most famous of all British battles, Hastings (Saxons *v* Normans; 14 October 1066), does not qualify for this list. Both sides had approximately 7,000 troops and losses were said to have been about one-quarter on each side, hence a total killed of around 3,500 has been suggested. It should be noted that this list is inevitably non-definitive, since no precise figures for losses are available, particularly for early battles, and exaggeration for political advantage is commonplace. Many further conflicts from the Wars of the Roses and Civil War could equally command a place in this catalogue of bloody battles.

THE 10 TWENTIETH CENTURY WARS WITH MOST MILITARY FATALITIES

	War	Years	Military fatalities
1	Second World War	1939–45	15,843,000
2	First World War	1914–18	8,545,800
3	Korean War	1950–53	1,893,100
4 =	Sino–Japanese War	1937–41	1,000,000
4 =	Biafra–Nigeria Civil War	1967–70	1,000,000
6	Spanish Civil War	1936–39	611,000
7	Vietnam War	1961–73	546,000
8 =	India–Pakistan War	1947	200,000
8 =	USSR invasion of Afghanistan	1979–89	200,000
8 =	Iran–Iraq War	1980–88	200,000

Twelve years of the Vietnam War resulted in more than 500,000 military and countless civilian deaths.

Berlin, seen here four years after the war, still showing the devastation caused by Allied bombing.

THE 10 MOST HEAVILY BLITZED CITIES IN THE UK

	City	Major raids	Tonnage of high explosive dropped
1	London	85	23,949
2	Liverpool/Birkenhead	8	1,957
3	Birmingham	8	1,852
4	Glasgow/Clydeside	5	1,329
5	Plymouth/Devonport	8	1,228
6	Bristol/Avonmouth	6	919
7	Coventry	2	818
8	Portsmouth	3	687
9	Southampton	4	647
10	Hull	3	593

The list, which is derived from official German sources, is based on total tonnage of high explosive dropped in major night attacks during the 'Blitz' period, from 7 September 1940 until 16 May 1941. Seven additional urban centres – Manchester, Belfast, Sheffield, Newcastle/Tyneside, Nottingham and Cardiff – were also victims of significant air raids in the same period.

During nine months of the Blitz, London suffered 85 major raids and was ravaged by almost 24,000 tons of bombs.

THE 10 AREAS OF EUROPE MOST BOMBED BY ALLIED AIRCRAFT*, 1939–45

	Area	Bombs dropped (tons)
1	Germany	1,350,321
2	France	583,318
3	Italy	366,524
4	Austria, Hungary and the Balkans	180,828
5	Belgium and Netherlands	88,739
6	Southern Europe and Mediterranean	76,505
7	Czechoslovakia and Poland	21,419
8	Norway and Denmark	5,297
9	Sea targets	564
10	British Channel Islands	93

*British and US.

THE 10 CITIES MOST BOMBED BY THE RAF AND USAF, 1939–45

	City	Estimated civilian fatalities
1	Dresden	100,000 +
2	Hamburg	55,000
3	Berlin	49,000
4	Cologne	20,000
5	Magdeburg	15,000
6	Kassel	13,000
7	Darmstadt	12,300
8 =	Heilbronn	7,500
8 =	Essen	7,500
10	Wuppertal	6,000

The high level of casualties in Dresden resulted principally from the saturation bombing and the firestorm that ensued after Allied raids on the lightly defended city. Although their main objective was to destroy the railway marshalling yards, the scale of the raids was massive: 775 British bombers took part in the first night's raid, on 13 February 1945, followed the next day by 450 US bombers, with a final attack by 200 US bombers on 15 February, while the city was still blazing, with 28.5 sq km/11 sq miles already devastated by the firestorm. A total of 39,773 were 'officially identified dead' but many thousands more were incinerated in buildings and never identified.

THE 10 MOST HEAVILY BOMBED LONDON BOROUGHS

	Borough	High-explosive bombs per 100 acres
1	Holborn	39.75
2	City	29.53
3	Westminster	28.85
4	Shoreditch	23.56
5	Southwark	23.35
6	Stepney	20.02
7	Finsbury	19.11
8	Chelsea	18.51
9	Bethnal Green	17.26
10	Bermondsey	17.16

During the 'Blitz', German bombing was concentrated on the centre of London and the Docks, but also caused enormous damage in adjacent boroughs, including the densely populated East End, and to a lesser extent, in the outer suburbs. About 15,000 people were killed and some 3,500,000 houses in London were bombed during the Second World War. The worst period was between 7 September 1940 and 11 May 1941 when an estimated 18,800 tons of high explosive bombs were dropped. The last major raid, but one of the heaviest, occurred on Saturday 10 May 1941 when, in addition to 1,436 fatalities, many important buildings were gutted, including the churches of St Clement Danes, St Olave, Hart Street and All Hallows, Barking, the House of Commons, Lambeth Palace library, the Deanery of Westminster Abbey and the British Museum library, destroying 150,000 books.

THE 10 LONDON BOROUGHS RECEIVING THE MOST V1 HITS

	Borough	V1s
1	Croydon	141
2	Wandsworth	122
3	Lewisham	114
4	Camberwell	80
5	Woolwich	77
6	Lambeth	71
7	Beckenham	70
8	Orpington	63
9	West Ham	58
10	Coulsdon	54

During 1944, V1 flying bombs destroyed approximately 24,000 houses in London and damaged a further 800,000 – particularly in the southern suburbs, which were the nearest to the V1 launch sites on the Channel coast of France. Casualty figures were also very high: in one incident, on Sunday 18 June, 121 members of the congregation – 63 servicemen and 58 civilians – were killed when a V1 hit the Guards Chapel at the Wellington Barracks during a service, while on the same day V1s that fell in Putney and Battersea killed, respectively, 28 and 19 people.

THE 10 COUNTIES RECEIVING THE MOST V1 HITS*

	County	V1s
1	Kent	1,444
2	Sussex	880
3	Essex	412
4	Surrey	295
5	Suffolk	93
6	Hertfordshire	82
7	Hampshire	80
8	Buckinghamshire	27
9	Norfolk	13
10	Berkshire	12

*Excluding London.

The V1 was notoriously inaccurate: although most were targeted on London, one of them landed near Hitler's headquarters at Soissons, France, while others came down as far afield as Northampton.

THE TOP 10 V1 ACES

	Pilot	Nationality	V1s destroyed*
1	Sqdn Ldr J. Berry	British	61$\frac{1}{3}$
2	Sqdn Ldr R. van Lierde	Belgian	40
3	Wg Cdr R.P. Beaumont	British	32
4	Wg Cdr E.D. Crew	British	31$\frac{1}{2}$
5	Flt Lt F.R.L. Mellersh	British	30
6	Sqdn Ldr A.E. Umbers	New Zealander	28
7	FO R.W. Cole	British	21$\frac{2}{3}$
8	Flt Lt A.R. Moore	British	21$\frac{1}{2}$
9 =	Lt D. Burgwal	Dutch	21
9 =	FO R.H. Clapperton	British	21
9 =	Sqdn Ldr R. Dryland	British	21
9 =	Flt Lt O.D. Eagleson	New Zealander	21

*Fractions are credited where a 'kill' is shared between two or more pilots, or between a pilot and a ground battery.

THE V1

Seldom has a weapon had as many different names as the V1: originally called the Fi-103 (Fi from Fiesler, its main manufacturer) or *Flakzeitlgerät 76* (anti-aircraft aiming device 76) or FZG 76, it was developed under the code name *Kirschkern*, 'Cherry Stone', but became known to the Germans as the V1 (from *Vergeltungswaffe Eins* – vengeance weapon 1) and to its British victims as 'flying bombs', 'buzz bombs' or 'doodlebugs'. Pilotless jet-propelled aircraft measuring 7.7 m/25 ft 4½ in, they were made of sheet steel and plywood and carried 850 kg/1,874 lb of high explosive. Using 1,591 litres/150 gallons of petrol oxidized by compressed air, they achieved an average speed of 563 kph/350 mph and a range of about 209 km/130 miles, which they reached in 20 to 25 minutes. Their engines then cut out, and most eyewitness accounts tell of the 'ominous silence' between this and the explosion that followed some 12 seconds later.

The first 10 V1 rockets were launched against England on 13 June 1944. Of these, five crash-landed near their launch site in Watten, France, one vanished (probably falling into the Channel) and four reached England, landing at Swanscombe, Kent, Cuckfield, Sussex and Platt near Sevenoaks, Kent. Only one reached its London target and caused casualties – six killed in Grove Road, Bethnal Green. The second wave, on the night of 15/16 June, was more successful: 244 missiles were launched, of which 45 crashed immediately, killing 10 French civilians, a number disappeared, presumably crashing into the sea, one landed in Framlingham, Suffolk and one near Chichester in Sussex, but a further 73 reached their target of London, where 11 were shot down.

In subsequent months more than 8,000 were launched. Many were erratic and strayed off course or crashed, and of those that continued toward London, a large proportion were brought down by barrage balloons, anti-aircraft fire and particularly by fighter pilots either shooting them down or flying alongside and 'tipping their wings' to send them away from their targets. In the initial week of attack, some 33 per cent were destroyed, but within three months this figure had risen to 70 per cent, with only 9 per cent reaching London. On 28 August 1944, 97 of the 101 V1s that approached England were brought down. Of those that were ground-launched in June to September 1944 (others were later air-launched from Heinkel 111 aircraft), 3,765 were destroyed: 1,902½ brought down by Royal Air Force pilots, 1,564½ by anti-aircraft fire, 278 by balloons and 20 by Royal Navy artillery. Many V1s were destroyed on the ground, their concrete launching ramps being easily spotted from the air and hence vulnerable to bombing. The V1 was, however, the precursor of the far deadlier V2.

The last two V2 rockets were launched on 27 March 1945. One hit Amsterdam, killing 27 people, and the other exploded between Court Road and Kynaston Road, Orpington, Kent, at 4.54 p.m., causing much damage and injury, but killing just one person, 34-year-old Ivy Millichamp of 88 Kynaston Road, who thus became the last British civilian casualty of the Second World War. Mrs Millichamp was uncommemorated until 1989 when a memorial tombstone was erected at All Saints Churchyard, Orpington.

THE 10 LONDON BOROUGHS RECEIVING THE MOST V2 HITS

	Borough	V2s
1	Woolwich	33
2	West Ham	27
3	Greenwich	22
4	Barking	21
5	Dagenham	19
6 =	Erith	17
6 =	Chislehurst	17
8	Waltham	15
9 =	East Ham	14
9 =	Wanstead	14

Masterminded by Wernher von Braun (1912–77), later leader of the US space programme, the 14 m/46 ft long V2 rocket (known to its German developers as 'A4'), was more accurate and far more powerful than the V1, producing a thrust of 25,400 kg/56,000 lb capable of carrying 1,016 kg/1 ton of explosive a range of up to 362 km/225 miles, while its speed of 5,794 kph/3,600 mph made it virtually impossible to combat with anti-aircraft fire or to intercept with fighter aircraft. The first two were launched from Holland against Paris on 6 September 1944, and on 8 September two fell on London, followed by more than 1,000 over the next seven months, resulting in a total of 2,855 fatalities (an even larger number was directed at Belgium with 4,483 killed). On 25 November 1944 a V2 hit Woolworth's in Deptford, killing at least 160 shoppers, and on 8 March 1945 one hit Smithfield Market, killing 110. On the morning of 27 March one of the last V2s – and the last explosive of the war in London – hit a block of flats in Stepney, killing 131.

THE 10 COUNTIES RECEIVING THE MOST V2 HITS

	County	V2s
1	London	517
2	Essex	378
3	Kent	64
4	Hertfordshire	34
5	Norfolk	29
6	Suffolk	13
7	Surrey	8
8	Sussex	4
9	Bedfordshire	3
10	Buckinghamshire	2

10 WEAPONS NAMED AFTER PEOPLE

1 Big Bertha

The name given to the 142-ton cannon used by the German army to shell Paris from a distance of 76 miles during the First World War was derived from Bertha Krupp von Bohlen und Halbach (1886–1957), who inherited the German Krupp armaments business from her father Friedrich Alfred who had committed suicide in 1902. The name was originally applied to the army's much smaller howitzers – but this itself was a mistake, since they were made by another firm, Skoda.

2 Bowie Knife

The large hunting knife was supposedly invented by Col James Bowie (1799–1836), a Texan adventurer who died during the siege of the Alamo, but it has been claimed that it was actually invented by his older brother Rezin Pleasant Bowie (1793–1841).

3 Colt Revolver

Samuel Colt (1814–62), the revolver's American inventor, is said to have whittled the original design in wood. The 'six-shooter' made him rich and was significant in the conquest of the American West.

4 Derringer Pistol

The small pistol, as used by John Wilkes Booth to assassinate Abraham Lincoln, was designed by Henry Deringer (spelled with one 'r') (1786–1868), a Philadelphia gunsmith, in 1835. When pirated European copies became widely sold, they attempted to circumvent Deringer's name by using two 'r's – and it is ironically Derringer that has stuck.

5 Gatling Gun

Dr Richard Jordan Gatling (1818–1903) patented the hand-cranked machine gun with a fire rate of up to 350 rounds per minute in 1862 – somewhat too late to be widely used in the American Civil War, and it was soon superseded by more efficient weapons. The slang term 'gat' for any gun derives from the name.

6 Maxim Gun

Sir Hiram Stevens Maxim (1840–1916), US-born but a naturalized British citizen, invented the gun in 1883 – as well as a flying machine, a mousetrap and many other gadgets.

7 Molotov Cocktail

The crude but effective petrol-filled bottle and fuse was originally so called by Finns in about 1940 during the war against Russia, as a 'cocktail for Molotov'. Vyacheslav Mikhailovich Molotov (real name Skriabin) (1890–1986) was the Soviet prime minister at the time.

8 Shrapnel

The exploding shells were devised by British inventor Lt Gen Henry Shrapnel (1761–1842) and used to great effect in Wellington's defeat of Napoleon at Waterloo in 1815. The name was later applied to any exploding shell or bomb fragments.

9 Sten Gun

The name comes from the first letters of the names of the weapon's inventors, Major R.V. Sheppard and H.J. Turpin, combined with the first two letters of England (or, according to some authorities, Enfield), where it was first made.

10 Tommy Gun

Invented by American army general John Taliaferro Thompson (1860–1940) and US Navy commander John N. Blish, the Thompson sub-machine gun became well known as the 'Tommy gun' – particularly when it became used by gangsters during the 1920s.

WAR FILMS QUIZ
Who appeared in which war film?

1	John Wayne	A	Platoon
2	Alec Guinness	B	The Guns of Navarone
3	Martin Sheen	C	Hope and Glory
4	Sarah Miles	D	A Bridge Too Far
5	Sean Connery	E	The Dam Busters
6	George C. Scott	F	The Bridge on the River Kwai
7	Gregory Peck	G	The Dirty Dozen
8	Charlie Sheen	H	Patton
9	Lee Marvin	I	The Longest Day
10	Richard Todd	J	Apocalypse Now

THE TOP 10 BRITISH GALLANTRY AWARDS*

1	Victoria Cross (VC)
2	George Cross (GC)
3	Distinguished Service Order (DSO)
4	Distinguished Service Cross (DSC)
5	Military Cross (MC)
6	Distinguished Flying Cross (DFC)
7	Air Force Cross (AFC)
8	Distinguished Conduct Medal (DCM)
9	Conspicuous Gallantry Medal (CGM)
10	George Medal (GM)

*In order of precedence, excluding defunct awards.

Fifty years of Queen Victoria's reign represented in an array of campaign medals and gallantry awards, including the Conspicuous Gallantry Medal and the pre-eminent Victoria Cross.

THE VICTORIA CROSS

Charles Davis Lucas's action, for which he received the first-ever Victoria Cross, was to pick up a live Russian shell fired at his ship, HMS *Hecla*, and heave it overboard, whereupon it exploded. He was promoted to Lieutenant on the spot, and received his VC three years later. The Royal Warrant inaugurating the Victoria Cross, Britain's highest gallantry award, was signed on 29 January 1856, but actions dating back to 1854 were included, thus encompassing the Crimean campaign. The names of the first recipients were announced in the *London Gazette* on 24 February 1857 and the first investiture of 62 men held on 26 June 1857 in Hyde Park, London, with Queen Victoria herself presenting the medals. The occasion marked two further firsts: it was the first time that both officers and men had received the same award, and the first when both had been present at the same ceremony. The sole criterion for receiving a VC was described as 'the merit of conspicuous bravery'; this was later modified to 'most conspicuous bravery or some daring pre-eminent act of valour or self-sacrifice or extreme devotion to duty in the presence of the enemy'. Up to the present day, 1,350 VCs have been awarded. The Falklands War was the last conflict for which VCs were awarded; prior to that, the last had been received by Warrant Officer Keith Payne of Australia for an action in Vietnam on 24 May 1969. The total includes eight that were forfeited in the period 1856 to 1914 under various, but undocumented, 'discreditable circumstances'. Subsequently, King George V expressed the view that no VC should ever be forfeited, remarking, 'Even were a VC to be sentenced to be hanged for murder, he should be allowed to wear his VC on the scaffold.' Although there are no records of such an event, no subsequent VCs have been rescinded.

Queen Victoria chose the design of the decoration herself. It comprises a Maltese Cross with the royal crest and a scroll inscribed 'For Valour', with the recipient's name on the reverse. The bronze from which it is made comes from cannons captured at Sebastopol during the Crimean War. The ribbon from which it is suspended was originally red for the Army and blue for the Navy, but since 1920 has been red for all services.

Three VCs top the league table of the most expensive medals ever sold at auction in the UK. They are: the VC Group awarded to Lieutenant W.B. Rhodes Moorhouse of the Royal Flying Corps (the first VC ever awarded to an airman), sold at Sotheby's, London, in 1990 for a record £126,600, the VC (and DFC) Group awarded to Wing Commander E.J.B. Nicolson, Royal Air Force (the only VC awarded for service during the Battle of Britain or to a fighter pilot in the Second World War), sold by Glendinning's, London, in 1983 (£110,000), and the VC Group awarded to Captain W. Leefe-Robinson, Royal Flying Corps (the first airman to bring down a Zeppelin over England), sold at Christie's, London, in 1988 (£99,000).

THE FIRST 10 VCs TO BE AWARDED

	Name	Rank	Action	Date
1	Charles Davis Lucas	Mate (later Rear-Admiral)	HMS *Hecla*, the Baltic	21 Jun 1854
2	John Bythesea	Lt (later Rear-Admiral)	HMS *Arrogant*, the Baltic	9–12 Aug 1854
3	William Johnstone	Stoker	HMS *Arrogant*, the Baltic	9–12 Aug 1854
4	James McKechnie	Sgt, Scots Guards	Crimea	20 Sep 1854
5	John Grieve	Sgt-Maj (later Lt and Adjt)	Crimea*	25 Oct 1854
6	Samuel Parkes	Private, Light Dragoons	Crimea*	25 Oct 1854
7	Alexander Roberts Dunn	Lt (later Col), Scots Guards	Crimea*	25 Oct 1854
8	Gerald Littlehales Goodlake	Major (later Lt Gen), Coldstream Guards	Crimea	28 Oct 1854
9	James Owens	Cpl (later Sgt), 1st Battalion, 49th Regiment	Crimea	30 Oct 1854
10	William Hewett	Lt (later Vice-Admiral)	Crimea	26 Oct/5 Nov 1854

Charge of the Light Brigade.

THE 10 CAMPAIGNS IN WHICH THE MOST VICTORIA CROSSES HAVE BEEN WON

	Campaign	Year	VCs
1	First World War	1914–18	634
2 =	Indian Mutiny	1857–58	182
2 =	Second World War	1939–45	182
4	Crimean War	1854–56	111
5	Second Boer War	1899–1902	78
6	Zulu War	1879	23
7	Second Afghan War	1878–80	16
8	Waikato–Hauhau Maori War	1863–66	13
9	Third China War	1860	7
10 =	Basuto War	1879–82	6
10 =	First Boer War	1880–81	6

The Top 10 accounts for all but 92 of the 1,350 VCs ever awarded, up to the 1982 Falklands conflict in which two VCs were awarded, posthumously, to Lt-Col 'H' Jones and Sgt Ian McKay, both of the Parachute Regiment.

THE TOP 10 COMBAT AREAS FOR VC WINNERS DURING WORLD WAR II

	Combat area	VCs
1	Burma	31
2	North Africa	27
3	Air missions	26
4	Naval missions	24
5	Northwest Europe (1944–45)	22
6	Italy	20
7	Pacific	11
8	France and Belgium (1940)	6
9	St-Nazaire raid	5
10	East Africa	4

Of the total of 182 VCs awarded in the Second World War, 176 were received for gallantry in the Top 10 areas listed, with the remaining six for actions in the Dieppe raid (3), Syria (2) and Crete (1).

THE TOP 10 NATIONALITIES OF VC WINNERS DURING WORLD WAR II

	Nationality	VCs
1	British and Irish	109
2	Australian	19
3	Indian	17
4	Canadian	13
5	Nepalese (Gurkha)	10
6	New Zealander	8
7	South African	3
8 =	Danish	1
8 =	Fijian	1
8 =	Rhodesian	1

Of the total of 182 Victoria Crosses awarded during the Second World War, 88 were awarded posthumously.

THE 10 REGIMENTS OF THE BRITISH ARMY THAT HAVE WON THE MOST VCs

	Regiment	VCs
1	Royal Artillery	51
2	Royal Engineers	44
3	Royal Army Medical Corps	29 *
4	Rifle Brigade	27
5 =	South Wales Borderers	22
5 =	King's Royal Rifle Corps	22
7	Royal Fusiliers	19
8 =	Lancashire Fusiliers	18
8 =	Seaforth Highlanders	18
10	Gordon Highlanders	17

*Including two bars.

THE 10 YOUNGEST WINNERS OF THE VC

	Name	Campaign/action date	Age yrs	mths
1	Andrew Fitzgibbon	Taku Forts, China, 21 Aug 1860	15	3
2	Thomas Flinn	Indian Mutiny, 28 Nov 1857	15	3
3	John Travers Cornwall	Battle of Jutland, 31 May 1916	16	4
4	Arthur Mayo	Indian Mutiny, 22 Nov 1857	17	6
5	George Monger	Indian Mutiny, 18 Nov 1857	17	8
6	Thomas Ricketts	Belgium, 14 Oct 1918	17	9
7	Edward St John Daniel	Crimean War, 5 Nov 1854; 18 Jun 1855*	17	10
8	William McWheeny	Crimean War, 20 Oct 1854; 5 Dec 1854; 18 Jun 1855*	17	? †
9	Basil John Douglas Guy	Boxer Rebellion, 13 Jul 1900	18	2
10	Wilfred St Aubyn Malleson	Gallipoli, 25 Apr 1915	18	7

*VC awarded for actions on more than one date; age based on first date.

†Precise date of birth unknown; said to have been 'aged 17' at the time of his award.

Andrew Fitzgibbon beats Thomas Flinn into 2nd place by being just 10 days younger at the time of the action for which he received his VC.

THE 10 MOST AWARDED BRITISH MEDALS

	Medal	Total awarded*
1	Military Medal	132,045
2	Military Cross	48,459
3	Distinguished Conduct Medal	29,227
4	Distinguished Flying Cross	22,249
5	Distinguished Service Order	16,838
6	Distinguished Service Medal	11,249
7	Distinguished Flying Medal	6,959
8	Distinguished (formerly Conspicuous) Service Cross	6,617
9	Indian Meritorious Service Medal†	5,814
10	Indian Distinguished Service Medal	5,611

*To end of 1979, excluding bars and foreign awards.

†Awarded 1917–25 only.

The Military Medal which heads this list was instituted by a Royal Warrant dated 25 March 1916 issued by George V. The medal was originally awarded for acts of gallantry performed by 'non-commissioned officers and men of Our Army in the Field'. Three months later it was extended to women of any nationality – a wording that, perhaps inadvertently, meant that only British soldiers but women civilians of any country were eligible. It consists of a medal bearing a profile of the monarch's head on one side and the words 'For bravery in the Field' on the other. It is worn suspended from a dark blue ribbon with red and white stripes. The first awards were retrospective and referred to actions in 1914 and 1915. Of the total of 132,045 medals awarded up to 1979, 115,577 date from the First World War, 311 from actions during the period 1920–1939, 15,225 from the Second World War and 932 from the period 1947–79.

With the reduction of Iraq's military strength following the Gulf War, Iran joins the Top 10 as a world military power.

THE 10 LARGEST ARMED FORCES IN THE WORLD

	Country	Estimated active forces			
		Army	Navy	Air	Total
1	China	2,300,000	260,000	470,000	3,030,000
2	Russia	1,400,000	320,000	300,000	2,720,000 *
3	USA	674,800	739,650 †	499,300	1,913,750
4	India	1,100,000	55,000	110,000	1,265,000
5	North Korea	1,000,000	40,000	92,000	1,132,000
6	Vietnam	700,000	42,000	15,000	757,000
7	South Korea	520,000	60,000	53,000	633,000
8	Pakistan	515,000	20,000	45,000	580,000
9	Turkey	450,000	52,300	58,000	560,300
10	Iran	305,000	18,000	35,000	358,000
	UK	145,400	62,100	86,000	293,500

*Balance of total comprises Strategic Deterrent Forces, Paramilitary, National Guard, etc.

†Navy 546,650, Marines 193,000.

In addition to the active forces listed here, many of the world's foremost military powers have considerable reserves on standby, South Korea's estimated at some 4,500,000, Vietnam's 3–4,000,000, Russia's 3,000,000, the USA's 1,784,050, China's 1,200,000 and Turkey's 1,107,000.

THE TOP 10 CHRISTIAN DENOMINATIONS IN THE WORLD

	Denomination	Adherents
1	Roman Catholic	872,104,646
2	Slavonic Orthodox	92,523,987
3	United (including Lutheran/Reformed)	65,402,685
4	Pentecostal	58,999,862
5	Anglican	52,499,051
6	Baptist	50,321,923
7	Lutheran (excluding United)	44,899,837
8	Reformed (Presbyterian)	43,445,520
9	Methodist	31,718,508
10	Disciples (Restorationists)	8,783,192

The Top 10 is based on mid-1980s estimates supplied by MARC Europe, a Christian research and information organization. A subsequent estimate by the Vatican increased the figure for Roman Catholics to 911,000,000 while retaining the 52,000,000 figure for Anglicans – which indicates something of the problem of arriving even at 'guesstimates' when it comes to global memberships. More recent estimates are not yet available.

The Roman Catholic Church remains the largest denomination of the world's largest religion.

RELIGION

THE 10 LARGEST CHRISTIAN POPULATIONS IN THE WORLD

	Country	Total Christian population
1	USA	218,133,000
2	Brazil	143,969,000
3	Former USSR	105,469,000
4	Mexico	79,742,000
5	Germany	60,963,000
6	Nigeria	60,652,000
7	UK	49,996,000
8	Philippines	58,737,000
9	Italy	47,915,000
10	France	45,611,000

Although Christian communities are found in almost every country in the world, it is difficult to put a precise figure on nominal membership rather than active participation, and these figures therefore represent only approximations.

THE TOP 10 ORGANIZED RELIGIONS IN THE WORLD

	Religion	Followers
1	Christianity	1,833,022,000
2	Islam	971,328,700
3	Hinduism	732,812,000
4	Buddhism	314,939,000
5	Sikhism	18,800,000
6	Judaism	17,822,000
7	Confucianism	6,028,000
8	Baha'ism	5,517,000
9	Jainism	3,794,000
10	Shintoism	3,222,800

This list excludes the followers of various tribal and folk religions, new religions and shamanism, which together total more than 437,000,000. There are also perhaps more than 876,232,000 people who may be classified as 'non-religious' (having no interest in religion of any persuasion) and a further 240,310,000 atheists (opposed to religion of any kind, or followers of alternative, non-religious philosophies), including large proportions of the populations of China and the former USSR. However, since reforms in the former Soviet Union, many who practised Christianity in secret while following the Communist anti-religion line in public have now declared their faith openly. The list is based on the work of David B. Barrett, who has been monitoring world religions for many years.

THE 10 LARGEST JEWISH POPULATIONS IN THE WORLD

	Country	Total Jewish population
1	USA	5,700,000
2	Israel	3,659,000
3	Former USSR	2,236,000
4	France	530,000
5	UK	322,000
6	Canada	310,000
7	Argentina	220,000
8	South Africa	114,000
9	Brazil	100,000
10	Australia	85,000

The Diaspora or scattering of Jewish people has been in progress for nearly 2,000 years, and as a result Jewish communities are found in virtually every country in the world. In 1939 it was estimated that the total world Jewish population was 17,000,000. Some 6,000,000 fell victim to Nazi persecution, reducing the figure to about 11,000,000, but by 1992 it was estimated to have grown to exceed 17,000,000 again.

A traditional Jewish family meal in Israel: the country actually has a smaller Jewish population than the USA.

THE TOP 10 RELIGIOUS AFFILIATIONS IN THE USA

	Religion/organization	Membership
1	Roman Catholic Church	58,568,015
2	Southern Baptist Convention	15,038,409
3	United Methodist Church	8,904,824
4	Muslim	8,000,000 *
5	Jews	5,981,000 **
6	Evangelical Lutheran Church in America	5,800,000
7	National Baptist Convention, USA, Inc	5,500,000 *
8	Church of God in Christ	5,499,875
9	Church of Jesus Christ of Latter-day Saints (Mormons)	4,267,000
10	Presbyterian Church	3,788,009

*Estimated.

**Combined membership of several groups.

It is claimed that out of the total US population of 248,709,873 (1990 Census), 156,336,384, or 62.86 per cent, are members of a religious organization. Those represented in the Top 10 are the principal sects of often larger groups; if membership of all branches within the groups are combined (even though some do not actually recognize the others), the Top 10 would be:

	Religion/organization	Membership
1	Roman Catholic	58,568,015
2	Baptist	31,040,661
3	Methodist	12,418,110
4	Lutheran	8,347,519
5	Muslim	8,000,000 *
6	Jews	5,981,000 **
7	Churches of God	5,744,879
8	Eastern Orthodox	4,473,287
9	Latter-day Saints	4,459,231
10	Churches of Christ	4,362,395

THE 10 LARGEST MUSLIM POPULATIONS IN THE WORLD

	Country	Total Muslim population
1	Indonesia	157,681,000
2	Pakistan	122,235,000
3	India	98,876,000
4	Bangladesh	94,186,000
5	Turkey	57,909,000
6	Iran	56,765,000
7	Nigeria	55,700,000
8	Egypt	49,148,000
9	Former USSR	37,890,000
10	Algeria	25,655,000

THE TOP 10 RELIGIONS IN THE UK

	Religion	Membership
1	Roman Catholicism	1,946,000
2	Anglicanism	1,839,000
3	Presbyterianism	1,292,000
4	Islam	990,000
5	Methodism	483,000
6	Sikhism	390,000
7	Orthodox	265,000
8	Baptist	242,000
9	Mormonism	150,000
10	Hinduism	140,000

This list is based on figures for adult *membership*, as recorded in, for example, the electoral rolls of the Church of England. Adherents are thus held to be practising rather than nominal members of each religion – although they are not necessarily all regular attenders of their respective places of worship.

THE 10 WORDS MOST MENTIONED IN THE BIBLE

	Word	Frequency
1	The	24,123
2	And	23,872
3	Of	18,197
4	That	9,900
5	To	9,729
6	In	9,526
7	He	7,609
8	For	7,114
9	Lord	6,667
10	A	6,308

A computer search of the *King James Bible* (Old and New Testaments) indicates the number of *verses* in which a particular word occurs, but not the number of individual uses of the word. Thomas Hartwell Horne (1780–1862), a dogged biblical researcher a century before computers were invented, undertook a manual search of individual uses and concluded that 'and' appeared a total of 35,543 times in the Old Testament and 10,684 times in the New Testament.

BIBLICAL BLUNDERS

The 66 books of the Authorized Version of the Bible are divided into 1,189 chapters containing 31,173 verses with 774,746 words composed of 3,566,480 letters, making it about 10 times as long as an average novel. The task of typesetting, proof-reading and printing such a monumental work, especially in the days when it was undertaken entirely by hand, is an extremely daunting one, so it is scarcely surprising that a number of editions have contained glaring mistakes, some with disastrous consequences.

Some peculiarities resulted from mistranslations: Coverdale's Bible, the very first complete Bible in English, translated by Miles Coverdale and published in 1535, is also known as the 'Bug Bible' because one of the Psalms translates the word for terror as 'bugges', so we get the quaint 'Thou shalt not nede to be afrayd for eny bugges by night'. The 1560 'Breeches Bible' is so called because in it Adam and Eve 'sewed figge-tree leaves together and made themselves breeches', while the 1568 'Treacle Bible' derives its weird name from the mistranslation of the word 'balm' or ointment to produce the bizarre enquiry, 'Is there no treacle in Gilead?'

More serious have been some of the mistakes made by printers. The printers of the 1634 'Fool Bible', all copies of which were suppressed, were fined £3,000 after they made the error of omitting the word 'no' from before 'God' in one of the Psalms, making it read, 'The fool hath said in his heart, there is a God'. The so-called 'Wicked Bible' or 'Unrighteous Bible' of 1653 was said to contain 6,000 mistakes, among them the unfortunate omission of 'not' from the phrase, 'Know ye that the unrighteous shall inherit the kingdom of God?' Leaving out the same short word also produced perhaps the worst Bible misprint of all time, when a 1631 Bible converted the Seventh Commandment into 'Thou *shalt* commit adultery'. As a result, the king's printers, Barker and Lucas of Blackfriars, were heavily fined, which led to their bankruptcy.

Countless subsequent editions contain printers' errors like 'The Parable of the Vinegar' in place of 'Vineyard'; the one in a 1795 Bible which produced the alarming instruction, 'Let the children first be killed', rather than 'filled'; or the line in Luke announcing that 'Her sins, which are many, are forgotten', instead of 'forgiven'. Other Bibles have accidentally replaced Jesus with Judas, and in one 'Christ condemneth (instead of 'commendeth') the poore widdowe'. The 'Printers' Bible' of 1702 is so called because it contains the line 'Printers (rather than 'Princes') have persecuted me without a cause' – as well as the mistake 'For without are dogs, and scorers' (it should have been 'sorcerers'). Even more recent versions are not immune, the 'Affinity Bible' of 1923 warning us that 'A man may not marry his grandmother's wife.'

RELIGION QUIZ

Who founded which Christian denomination?

1	Society of Friends (Quakers)	A	John Wesley
2	Latter-Day Saints (Mormons)	B	Charles Taze Russell
3	Jehovah's Witnesses	C	Mary Baker Eddy
4	Shakers	D	John Thomas
5	Church of Christ (Scientist)	E	John Huss
6	Methodists	F	Menno Simons
7	Pentecostalists	G	George Fox
8	Christadelphians	H	Ann Lee
9	Mennonites	I	Joseph Smith
10	Moravians	J	C.F. Parham

THE 10 NUMBERS MOST MENTIONED IN THE BIBLE

	Number	Frequency*
1	One	1,695
2	Two	703
3	One hundred	517
4	Three	426
5	One thousand	395
6	Seven	391
7	Four	282
8	Five	270
9	Twenty	262
10	Ten	223

*Occurrences in verses in the King James Bible (Old and New Testaments).

THE 10 NAMES MOST MENTIONED IN THE BIBLE

	Name	Frequency*
1	Jesus (942) + Christ (536) – total:	1,478
2	David	983
3	Moses	784
4	Jacob	351
5	Aaron	334
6	Solomon	278
7	Joseph	236
8	Abraham	235
9	Ephraim	163
10	Benjamin	162

*Occurrences in verses in the King James Bible (Old and New Testaments), including possessive uses, such as 'John's'.

The name Judah also appears 776 times, but the total includes references to the territory as well as the individual with that name. At the other end of the scale, there are many names that, perhaps fortunately, appear only once or twice, among them Berodach-baladan and Tilgath-pilneser. The most mentioned place names produce few surprises, with Israel (2,305 references) heading the list, followed by Jerusalem (767), Egypt (559), Babylon (253) and Assyria (120).

THE TOP 10 GOALSCORERS IN THE FINAL STAGES OF THE WORLD CUP

	Player/country	Years	Goals
1	Gerd Müller (West Germany)	1970–74	14
2	Just Fontaine (France)	1958	13
3	Pelé (Brazil)	1958–70	12
4	Sandor Kocsis (Hungary)	1954	11
5 =	Helmut Rahn (West Germany)	1954–58	10
5 =	Teófilo Cubillas (Peru)	1970–78	10
5 =	Grzegorz Lato (Poland)	1974–82	10
5 =	Gary Lineker (England)	1986–90	10
9 =	Leónidas da Silva (Brazil)	1934–38	9
9 =	Ademir Marques de Menezes (Brazil)	1950	9
9 =	Vavà (Brazil)	1958–62	9
9 =	Uwe Seeler (West Germany)	1958–1970	9
9 =	Eusebio (Portugal)	1966	9
9 =	Jairzinho (Brazil)	1970–74	9
9 =	Paolo Rossi (Italy)	1978–82	9
9 =	Karl-Heinz Rummenigge (West Germany)	1978–86	9

Fontaine's 13 goals in the 1958 finals is a record for one tournament.

Gary Lineker's 10 World Cup goals make him England's top scorer.

THE TOP 10 INDIVIDUAL APPEARANCES IN THE FINAL STAGES OF THE WORLD CUP

Player/country	Years	Appearances
1 = Uwe Seeler (West Germany)	1958–70	21
1 = Wladislaw Zmuda (Poland)	1974–86	21
3 Grzegorz Lato (Poland)	1974–82	20
4 = Wolfgang Overath (West Germany)	1966–74	19
4 = Hans-Hubert Vogts (West Germany)	1970–78	19
4 = Karl-Heinz Rummenigge (West Germany)	1978–86	19
4 = Diego Maradona (Argentina)	1982–90	19
8 = Franz Beckenbauer (West Germany)	1966–74	18
8 = Sepp Maier (West Germany)	1970–78	18
8 = Mario Kempes (Argentina)	1974–82	18
8 = Antonio Cabrini (Italy)	1978–86	18
8 = Gaetano Scirea (Italy)	1978–86	18
8 = Pierre Littbarski (West Germany)	1982–90	18

While Seeler and Zmuda have both played in 21 matches, the West German's career is slightly longer at 1,980 minutes compared to the Pole's 1,807 minutes. The most appearances by a British player is 17 by Peter Shilton (England), 1982–90.

THE 10 MOST SUCCESSFUL COUNTRIES IN THE WORLD CUP

Country	Wins	Points
1 Germany/ West Germany	3	26
2 = Brazil	3	18
2 = Italy	3	18
4 Argentina	2	14
5 Uruguay	2	10
6 = Czechoslovakia	–	6
6 = Holland	–	6
8 = England	1	5
8 = France	–	5
8 = Sweden	–	5

This list is based on teams reaching the semi-finals and being awarded 4 points for winning the World Cup, 3 for runners-up, 2 for third place and 1 point for fourth place.

West Germany is the most successful World Cup country of all time.

THE 10 COUNTRIES THAT HAVE PLAYED THE MOST MATCHES IN THE FINAL STAGES OF THE WORLD CUP

	Country	Tournaments	Matches played
1	Germany/West Germany	12	68
2	Brazil	14	66
3	Italy	12	54
4	Argentina	10	48
5	England	9	41
6	Uruguay	9	37
7	France	9	34
8	Yugoslavia	8	33
9 =	Hungary	9	32
9 =	Spain	8	32

Mexico have also appeared in nine tournaments, while Belgium, the former Czechoslovakia and Sweden have all appeared in eight tournaments. Brazil is the only country to have appeared in the final stages of all 14 competitions.

THE 10 HIGHEST-SCORING WINS BY COUNTRIES ON THEIR DEBUT IN THE FINAL STAGES OF THE WORLD CUP

	Winners/losers	Year	Score
1	Italy v United States	1934	7–1
2	Germany v Belgium	1934	5–2
3	France v Mexico	1930	4–1
4	Hungary v Egypt	1934	4–2
5 =	Chile v Mexico	1930	3–0
5 =	USA v Belgium	1930	3–0
7 =	Romania v Peru	1930	3–1
7 =	Spain v Brazil	1934	3–1
7 =	Portugal v Hungary	1966	3–1
7 =	Tunisia v Mexico	1978	3–1

A total of 59 different countries have appeared in the final stages of the FIFA World Cup, with these achieving the most impressive starts to their World Cup careers.

THE 10 BIGGEST WORLD CUP ATTENDANCES

	Match	Venue	Year	Attendance
1	Brazil v Uruguay	Rio de Janeiro*	1950	199,854
2	Brazil v Spain	Rio de Janeiro	1950	152,772
3	Brazil v Yugoslavia	Rio de Janeiro	1950	142,409
4	Brazil v Sweden	Rio de Janeiro	1950	138,886
5	Mexico v Paraguay	Mexico City	1986	114,600
6	Argentina v West Germany	Mexico City*	1986	114,590
7 =	Argentina v England	Mexico City	1986	114,580
7 =	Mexico v Bulgaria	Mexico City	1986	114,580
9	Argentina v Belgium	Mexico City	1986	110,420
10	Mexico v Belgium	Mexico City	1986	110,000

*Final tie.

The biggest crowd outside Brazil or Mexico was that of 98,270 at Wembley in 1966 for England's game against France. The attendance for the final and deciding tie between Brazil and Uruguay in the 1950 World Cup finals is the world's highest for a soccer match.

THE 10 HIGHEST-SCORING MATCHES IN THE FINAL STAGES OF THE WORLD CUP

	Match	Year	Score
1	Austria v Switzerland	1954	7–5
2 =	Brazil v Poland	1938	6–5
2 =	Hungary v West Germany	1954	8–3
2 =	Hungary v El Salvador	1982	10–1
5	France v Paraguay	1958	7–3
6 =	Hungary v South Korea	1954	9–0
6 =	West Germany v Turkey	1954	7–2
6 =	France v West Germany	1958	6–3
6 =	Yugoslavia v Zaïre	1974	9–0
10 =	Italy v USA	1934	7–1
10 =	Sweden v Cuba	1938	8–0
10 =	Uruguay v Bolivia	1950	8–0
10 =	England v Belgium	1954	4–4
10 =	Portugal v North Korea	1966	5–3

Hungary's 8–3 victory over West Germany in 1954 was in the Group matches, where for tactical reasons West Germany fielded six reserves. When the two teams met again in the final, West Germany won 3–2. The highest-scoring World Cup final was in 1958 when Brazil beat Sweden 5–2.

THE 10 COUNTRIES WITH THE MOST PLAYERS SENT OFF IN THE FINAL STAGES OF THE WORLD CUP

	Country	Dismissals
1 =	Argentina	7
1 =	Brazil	7
3	Uruguay	6
4 =	Czechoslovakia	4
4 =	Germany/West Germany	4
4 =	Hungary	4
7	Yugoslavia	3
8 =	Cameroon	2
8 =	Chile	2
8 =	Holland	2
8 =	Italy	2
8 =	Soviet Union	2

A total of 60 players have received their marching orders in the final stages of the World Cup since 1930. The South American nations account for 23 of them.

THE 10 HIGHEST-SCORING DEFEATS BY COUNTRIES ON THEIR DEBUT IN THE FINAL STAGES OF THE WORLD CUP

	Losers/winners	Year	Score
1	South Korea v Hungary	1954	0–9
2	Dutch East Indies v Hungary	1938	0–6
3	Poland v Brazil	1938	5–6
4	New Zealand v Scotland	1982	2–5
5	Bolivia v Yugoslavia	1930	0–4
6 =	Mexico v France	1930	1–4
6 =	Turkey v West Germany	1954	1–4
8	Egypt v Hungary	1934	2–4
9 =	Belgium v USA	1930	0–3
9 =	El Salvador v Belgium	1930	0–3
9 =	Iran v Holland	1978	0–3
9 =	North Korea v Soviet Union	1966	0–3
9 =	Paraguay v United States	1950	0–3

THE 10 OLDEST MEMBERS OF THE 1966 ENGLAND WORLD CUP WINNING SQUAD

	Player	Club	Date of birth
1	Ron Flowers	Wolverhampton Wanderers	28 Jul 1934
2	Ray Wilson*	Everton	17 Dec 1934
3	Jack Charlton*	Leeds United	8 May 1935
4	Ron Springett	Sheffield Wednesday	22 Jul 1935
5	Jimmy Armfield	Blackpool	21 Sep 1935
6	George Eastham	Arsenal	23 Sep 1936
7	Bobby Charlton*	Manchester United	11 Oct 1937
8	Gordon Banks*	Leicester City	30 Dec 1937
9	John Connelly	Manchester United	18 Jul 1938
10	Roger Hunt*	Liverpool	20 Jul 1938

*Played in the final against West Germany.

The youngest member of the squad was Alan Ball (Blackpool), born 12 May 1945.

MANCHESTER UNITED'S 10 HIGHEST-SCORING WINS IN THE FA CUP

	Opponents	Home/away	Season	Round	Score
1	Yeovil Town	H	1948–49	5	8–0
2	Northampton Town	A	1969–70	5	8–2
3 =	West Manchester	H	1896–97	3Q	7–0
3 =	Accrington Stanley	H	1902–03	3Q	7–0
5	Brentford	H	1927–28	3	7–1
6	Staple Hill	H	1905–06	1	7–2
7	Bournemouth	H	1948–49	3	6–0
8	Blackburn Rovers	H	1908–09	3	6–1
9	Birmingham City	H	1968–69	5	6–2
10	Aston Villa	A	1947–48	3	6–4

3Q indicates 3rd Qualifying Round, a part of the competition in which United no longer have to take part. Prior to the 1925–26 season, the 1st Round was equivalent to the present day 3rd Round, the 2nd Round equivalent to the modern-day 4th Round and so on.

THE 10 CRICKETERS WITH MOST INNINGS OVER 50 IN A TEST CAREER*

	Player/country	Tests	50s
1	Allan Border (Australia)	141	85
2	Sunil Gavaskar (India)	125	79
3	Vivian Richards (West Indies)	121	69
4	Javed Miandad (Pakistan)	121	65
5	Geoffrey Boycott (England)	108	64
6	Colin Cowdrey (England)	114	60
7 =	Graham Gooch (England)	101	58
7 =	Clive Lloyd (West Indies)	110	58
9	David Gower (England)	117	57
10 =	Desmond Haynes (West Indies)	111	56
10 =	Gary Sobers (West Indies)	93	56

*To 1 June 1993.

Allan Border holds the triple record for the most runs in a Test career, most Test innings over 50 and most consecutive Test matches.

THE TOP 10 RUN-MAKERS IN A TEST CAREER*

	Player/country	Years	Runs
1	Allan Border (Australia)	1978–93	10,262
2	Sunil Gavaskar (India)	1971–87	10,122
3	Javed Miandad (Pakistan)	1976–93	8,689
4	Vivian Richards (West Indies)	1974–91	8,540
5	David Gower (England)	1978–92	8,231
6	Geoffrey Boycott (England)	1964–82	8,114
7	Gary Sobers (West Indies)	1954–74	8,032
8	Colin Cowdrey (England)	1954–75	7,624
9	Graham Gooch (England)	1975–93	7,620
10	Gordon Greenidge (West Indies)	1974–91	7,558

*To 1 June 1993.

THE 10 CRICKETERS TO HAVE PLAYED IN THE MOST CONSECUTIVE TEST MATCHES*

	Player/country	Years	Tests
1	Allan Border (Australia)	1979–93	138
2	Sunil Gavaskar (India)	1975–87	106
3	Gundappa Viswanath (India)	1971–83	87
4	Gary Sobers (West Indies)	1955–72	85
5	Desmond Haynes (West Indies)	1979–88	72
6	Ian Chappell (Australia)	1965–76	71
7	Kapil Dev (India)	1978–84	66
8 =	Alan Knott (England)	1971–77	65
8 =	Ian Botham (England)	1978–84	65
10 =	Rohan Kanhai (West Indies)	1957–69	61
10 =	Vivian Richards (West Indies)	1980–88	61

*To 1 June 1993.

THE 10 MOST RUNS CONCEDED BY A BOWLER IN A TEST INNINGS

	Player/country	Opponents	Year	Runs
1	Leslie Fleetwood-Smith (Australia)	England	1938	298
2	Oscar Scott (West Indies)	England	1930	266
3	Khan Mohammad (Pakistan)	West Indies	1958	259
4	Fazal Mahmood (Pakistan)	West Indies	1958	247
5	Stephen Boock (New Zealand)	Pakistan	1989	229
6	Vinoo Mankad (India)	West Indies	1953	228
7	Bishan Bedi (India)	England	1974	226
8	Kapil Dev (India)	Pakistan	1983	220
9	Ian Botham (England)	Pakistan	1987	217
10	Ian Peebles (England)	Australia	1930	204

The Test match innings in which Fleetwood-Smith conceded his runs was at The Oval when Len Hutton scored 364 and England scored 903 for 7 declared. Fleetwood-Smith's figures were 87–11–298–1. The Test match innings in which Khan Mohammad and Fazal Mahmood conceded their runs was in Jamaica when Gary Sobers made his record Test score of 365 not out and the West Indies scored 790 for 3 declared.

THE TOP 10 WICKET-TAKERS IN A TEST CAREER*

	Player/country	Years	Wickets
1	Richard Hadlee (New Zealand)	1973–90	431
2	Kapil Dev (India)	1978–93	420
3	Ian Botham (England)	1977–92	383
4	Malcolm Marshall (West Indies)	1978–91	376
5	Imran Khan (Pakistan)	1971–92	362
6	Dennis Lillee (Australia)	1971–84	355
7	Bob Willis (England)	1971–84	325
8	Lance Gibbs (West Indies)	1958–76	309
9	Fred Trueman (England)	1952–65	307
10	Derek Underwood (England)	1966–82	297

*To 1 June 1993.

THE FIRST 10 BOWLERS TO TAKE A WICKET WITH THEIR FIRST BALL IN TEST CRICKET

	Player/country	Opponents	Year
1	Arthur Coningham (Australia)	England	1894
2	Walter Bradley (England)	Australia	1899
3	Edward Arnold (England)	Australia	1903
4	George Macaulay (England)	South Africa	1923
5	Maurice Tate (England)	South Africa	1924
6	Matthew Henderson (New Zealand)	England	1930
7	Horace Smith (New Zealand)	England	1933
8	Tyrel Johnson (West Indies)	England	1939
9	Richard Howorth (England)	South Africa	1947
10	Intikhab Alam (Pakistan)	Australia	1959

Arthur Coningham took Archie MacLaren's wicket with his first ball in Test cricket, the first ball of the 2nd Test at Melbourne. Coningham never played another Test match. Only one other player has achieved the feat: Richard Illingworth (England) against the West Indies in 1991.

Andrew Sandham was the first cricketer to score a triple Test century.

THE FIRST 10 MEN TO SCORE TRIPLE CENTURIES IN TEST CRICKET

	Name/opponent	Score	Date
1	Andrew Sandham (Eng) v West Indies	325	4 Apr 1930
2	Don Bradman (Aus) v England	334	12 Jul 1930
3	Walter Hammond (Eng) v New Zealand	336 *	1 Apr 1933
4	Don Bradman (Aus) v England	304	23 Jul 1934
5	Len Hutton (Eng) v Australia	364	23 Aug 1938
6	Hanif Mohammad (Pak) v West Indies	337	23 Jan 1958
7	Gary Sobers (WI) v Pakistan	365 *	1 Mar 1958
8	Bobby Simpson (Aus) v England	311	25 Jul 1964
9	John Edrich (Eng) v New Zealand	310 *	9 Jul 1965
10	Bob Cowper (Aus) v England	307	16 Feb 1966

*Not out.

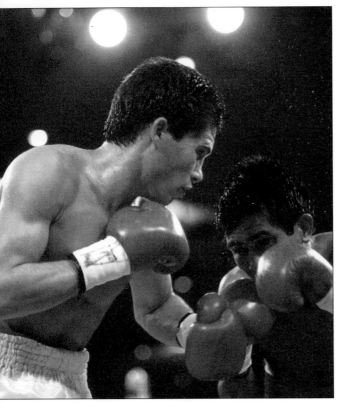

Julio César Chávez's 25 title fights put him in first place among non-American boxers with current careers.

THE 10 BOXERS WITH THE MOST WORLD TITLE FIGHTS

	Boxer/nationality	Years	Title fights
1	Joe Louis (USA)	1937–50	27
2	Henry Armstrong (USA)	1937–41	26
3 =	Muhammad Ali (USA)	1964–80	25
3 =	Julio César Chávez (Mexico)	1984–93	25
3 =	Larry Holmes (USA)	1978–92	25
6	Hilario Zapata (Panama)	1980–93	24
7 =	Wilfredo Gomez (Puerto Rico)	1977–86	23
7 =	Manuel Ortiz (USA)	1942–50	23
9 =	Alexis Arguello (Nicaragua)	1974–83	22
9 =	Tony Canzoneri (USA)	1927–37	22
9 =	George Dixon (Canada)	1890–1900	22
9 =	Emile Griffith (USA)	1961–76	22
9 =	Eusebio Pedroza (Pan)	1976–85	22
9 =	Sugar Ray Robinson (USA)	1946–61	22

Of those in the list Larry Holmes, Julio César Chávez and Hilario Zapata are still active. Julio César Chávez's overall record is 87 bouts and 87 wins, 74 of them inside the distance.

THE 10 SHORTEST WORLD TITLE FIGHTS OF MUHAMMAD ALI

	Opponent/nationality	Date	Result	Duration min	sec
1	Sonny Liston (USA)	25 May 1965	KO Rd.1	1	52
2	Cleveland Williams (USA)	14 Nov 1966	TKO Rd.3	7	08
3	Brian London (UK)	6 Aug 1966	KO Rd.3	7	40
4	Richard Dunn (UK)	24 May 1976	TKO Rd.5	14	05
5	Jean-Pierre Coopman (Bel)	20 Feb 1976	KO Rd.5	14	46
6	Henry Cooper (UK)	21 May 1966	TKO Rd.6	16	38
7	Sonny Liston (USA)	25 Feb 1964	TKO Rd.7	18	00
8	Zora Folley (USA)	22 Mar 1967	KO Rd.7	19	48
9	George Foreman (USA)	30 Nov 1974	KO Rd.8	23	58
10	Larry Holmes (USA)	2 Oct 1980	TKO Rd.11	30	00

KO – Knock-out.

TKO – Technical Knock-out.

Ali won all these fights except the one against Holmes. In all, Ali (formerly Cassius Clay) took part in 25 world heavyweight title fights between 1964 and 1980. He won 22 of them and was defeated only by Holmes, Leon Spinks (1978), and Joe Frazier (1971).

THE 10 MOST SUCCESSFUL RYDER CUP PLAYERS

	Player/country	Matches	Wins
1	Arnold Palmer (USA)	32	22
2	Billy Casper (USA)	37	20
3	Lanny Wadkins (USA)	30	18
4 =	Jack Nicklaus (USA)	28	17
4 =	Seve Ballesteros (Europe)	30	17
4 =	Lee Trevino (USA)	30	17
4 =	Nick Faldo (Europe)	31	17
8 =	Gene Littler (USA)	27	14
8 =	Peter Oosterhuis (Europe)	28	14
10 =	Hale Irwin (USA)	20	13
10 =	Tom Kite (USA)	24	13
10 =	Bernard Gallacher (Europe)	31	13
10 =	Tony Jacklin (Europe)	31	13

The Ryder Cup, first played in 1921, was between the USA and Great Britain until 1979 when European players were included.

Arnold Palmer is the most successful Ryder Cup player, with 22 wins out of 32 matches.

THE 10 BIGGEST WINNING MARGINS IN RYDER CUP MATCHES

	Winner(s)	Runner(s)-up	Year	Score
1 =	Walter Hagen/Denny Shute (US)	George Duncan/Arthur Havers	1931	10 & 9
1 =	Ed Oliver/Lew Worsham (US)	Henry Cotton/Arthur Lees	1947	10 & 9
3	George Duncan	Walter Hagen (US)	1929	10 & 8
4 =	Leo Diegel (US)	Abe Mitchell	1929	9 & 8
4 =	Abe Mitchell	Olin Dutra (US)	1933	9 & 8
4 =	Paul Runyan/Horton Smith (US)	Bill Cox/Ted Jarman	1935	9 & 8
7	Fred Daly	Ted Kroll (US)	1953	9 & 7
8 =	Johnny Golden (US)	Herbert Jolly	1927	8 & 7
8 =	Gene Sarazen/Johnny Farrell (US)	Archie Compston/Bill Davies	1931	8 & 7
8 =	Ralph Guldahl (US)	Alf Padgham	1937	8 & 7
8 =	Dutch Harrison (US)	Max Faulkner	1949	8 & 7
8 =	Skip Alexander (US)	John Panton	1951	8 & 7
8 =	Lloyd Mangrum/Sam Snead (US)	Eric Brown/John Panton	1953	8 & 7
8 =	Tom Kite (US)	Howard Clark	1989	8 & 7

American players are indicated. All other players either represented the Great Britain or European teams.

THE 10 LOWEST WINNING SCORES IN THE US MASTERS

	Player	Year	Score
1 =	Jack Nicklaus	1965	271
1 =	Raymond Floyd	1976	271
3	Ben Hogan	1953	274
4	Severiano Ballesteros (Spa)	1980	275
5 =	Arnold Palmer	1964	276
5 =	Jack Nicklaus	1975	276
5 =	Tom Watson	1977	276
8 =	Bob Goalby	1968	277
8 =	Gary Player (SAf)	1978	277
8 =	Ben Crenshaw	1984	277
8 =	Ian Woosnam (UK)	1991	277

All from USA unless otherwise stated.

As the Masters is the only Major played on the same course each year, it is uniquely possible to compare the winning scores.

THE 10 HEAVIEST WEIGHTS CARRIED BY WINNERS OF THE GRAND NATIONAL

	Horse	Year	Weight st	lb
1	Glenside	1911	13	3
2 =	Cloister	1893	12	7
2 =	Manifesto	1899	12	7
2 =	Jerry M	1912	12	7
2 =	Poethlyn	1919	12	7
6	Sprig	1927	12	4
7 =	Golden Miller	1934	12	2
7 =	Reynoldstown	1936	12	2
9 =	The Duke	1837	12	0
9 =	Sir William	1838	12	0
9 =	Lottery	1839	12	0
9 =	Jerry	1840	12	0
9 =	Charity	1841	12	0
9 =	Gay Lad	1842	12	0
9 =	Red Rum	1974	12	0

The Grand National was not run as a handicap until 1843.

THE 10 LIGHTEST WEIGHTS CARRIED BY WINNERS OF THE GRAND NATIONAL

	Horse	Year	Weight st	lb
1	Freetrader	1856	9	6
2 =	Half Caste	1859	9	7
2 =	Sunloch	1914	9	7
4	Wanderer	1855	9	8
5 =	Emigrant	1857	9	10
5 =	Anatis	1860	9	10
7 =	Abd-el-Kader	1850	9	12
7 =	Jealousy	1861	9	12
7 =	Ballymacad	1917	9	12
10	The Soarer	1896	9	13

Ballymacad won a wartime substitute race at Gatwick.

THE 10 LONGEST-PRICED WINNERS OF ENGLISH CLASSICS

	Horse	Race	Year	Odds
1 =	Otterington	St Leger	1812	100–1
1 =	Theodore	St Leger	1822	100–1
1 =	Jeddah	Derby	1898	100–1
1 =	Signorinetta	Derby	1908	100–1
1 =	Aboyeur	Derby	1913	100–1
6 =	Caller Ou	St Leger	1861	1,000–15
6 =	Hermit	Derby	1867	1,000–15
8 =	Psidium	Derby	1961	66–1
8 =	Rockavon	2,000 Guineas	1961	66–1
10 =	Azor	Derby	1817	50–1
10 =	Lap-Dog	Derby	1826	50–1
10 =	Spaniel	Derby	1831	50–1
10 =	Vespa	Oaks	1833	50–1
10 =	Little Wonder	Derby	1840	50–1
10 =	Throstle	St Leger	1894	50–1
10 =	Night Hawk	St Leger	1913	50–1
10 =	Ferry	1,000 Guineas	1918	50–1
10 =	Polemarch	St Leger	1921	50–1
10 =	Airborne	Derby	1946	50–1
10 =	Gilles de Retz	2,000 Guineas	1956	50–1
10 =	Mon Fils	2,000 Guineas	1973	50–1
10 =	Snow Knight	Derby	1974	50–1
10 =	Jet Ski Lady	Oaks	1991	50–1

THE 10 SHORTEST-PRICED WINNERS OF ENGLISH CLASSICS

	Horse	Race	Year	Odds
1	Pretty Polly	Oaks	1904	8–100
2 =	Crucifix	1,000 Guineas	1840	1–10
2 =	Galtee More	St Leger	1897	1–10
4	St Frusquin	2,000 Guineas	1896	12–100
5 =	Patron	2,000 Guineas	1829	1–8
5 =	Achievement	1,000 Guineas	1867	1–8
7 =	Ibrahim	2,000 Guineas	1835	1–7
7 =	Ormonde	St Leger	1886	1–7
9 =	Persimmon	St Leger	1896	2–11
9 =	Gay Crusader	St Leger	1917	2–11

THE 10 FASTEST WINNING TIMES OF THE EPSOM DERBY

	Horse	Year	Time min	sec
1	Mahmoud	1936	2	33.80
2	Kahyasi	1988	2	33.84
3	Reference Point	1987	2	33.90
4 =	Hyperion	1933	2	34.00
4 =	Windsor Lad	1934	2	34.00
4 =	Generous	1991	2	34.00
7	Golden Fleece	1982	2	34.27
8	Call Boy	1927	2	34.40
9	Captain Cuttle	1922	2	34.60
10	Nijinsky	1970	2	34.68

Electronic timing was first used in 1964.

Only races at Epsom are considered. Dante won the 1945 wartime substitute race at Newmarket in 2 minutes 26.6 seconds.

THE TOP 10 JOCKEYS IN THE BREEDERS' CUP

	Jockey*	Years	Wins
1 =	Pat Day	1984–91	6
1 =	Laffit Pincay Jr	1985–90	6
1 =	Pat Valenzuela	1986–92	6
4 =	Eddie Delahoussaye	1984–92	5
4 =	Chris McCarron	1985–92	5
4 =	José Santos	1987–90	5
7	Angel Cordero	1985–89	4
8 =	Craig Perrett	1984–90	3
8 =	Randy Romero	1987–89	3
10 =	Walter Guerra	1984–85	2
10 =	Yves St Martin (France)	1984–86	2
10 =	Jorge Velasquez	1985	2
10 =	Pat Eddery (GB)	1985–91	2
10 =	Freddy Head (France)	1987–88	2

American unless otherwise stated.

Reference Point leads the field in the third fastest Derby of all time.

THE 10 DRIVERS WITH THE MOST GRAND PRIX WINS IN A SEASON

	Driver/nationality	Year	Wins
1	Nigel Mansell (Great Britain)	1992	9
2	Ayrton Senna (Brazil)	1988	8
3 =	Jim Clark (Great Britain)	1963	7
3 =	Alain Prost (France)	1984	7 *
3 =	Alain Prost (France)	1988	7 *
3 =	Ayrton Senna (Brazil)	1991	7
7 =	Alberto Ascari (Italy)	1952	6
7 =	Juan Manuel Fangio (Argentina)	1954	6
7 =	Jim Clark (Great Britain)	1965	6
7 =	Jackie Stewart (Great Britain)	1969	6
7 =	Jackie Stewart (Great Britain)	1971	6
7 =	James Hunt (Great Britain)	1976	6
7 =	Mario Andretti (USA)	1978	6
7 =	Nigel Mansell (Great Britain)	1987	6 *
7 =	Ayrton Senna (Brazil)	1990	6

*Did not win world title that year.

Nigel Mansell's total of nine wins in the 1992 Grand Prix season stands as a world record.

THE 10 MANUFACTURERS WITH THE MOST GRAND PRIX WINS IN A SEASON

	Manufacturer	Year	Wins
1	McLaren–Honda	1988	15
2	McLaren–Porsche	1984	12
3 =	McLaren–Honda	1989	10
3 =	Williams–Renault	1992	10
5 =	Williams–Honda	1986	9
5 =	Williams–Honda	1987	9
7 =	Lotus–Ford	1978	8
7 =	McLaren–Honda	1991	8
9 =	Ferrari	1952	7
9 =	Ferrari	1953	7
9 =	Lotus–Climax	1963	7
9 =	Tyrell–Ford	1971	7
9 =	Lotus–Ford	1973	7
9 =	Williams–Renault	1991	7

THE 10 COUNTRIES PROVIDING THE MOST WORLD MOTOR RACING DRIVERS CHAMPIONS

	Country	Different champions*
1	Great Britain	7
2	Brazil	3
3 =	Australia	2
3 =	Austria	2
3 =	Italy	2
3 =	United States	2
7 =	Argentina	1
7 =	Finland	1
7 =	France	1
7 =	New Zealand	1
7 =	South Africa	1

*Multiple individual wins counted as one.

THE 10 MOST SUCCESSFUL TEAMS IN THE LE MANS 24-HOUR RACE

	Team	Years	Wins
1	Porsche	1970–87	12
2	Ferrari	1949–65	9
3	Jaguar	1951–90	7
4	Bentley	1924–30	5
5 =	Alfa-Romeo	1931–34	4
5 =	Ford	1966–69	4
7	Matra-Simca	1972–74	3
8 =	La Lorraine	1925–26	2
8 =	Bugatti	1937–39	2
8 =	Mercedes-Benz	1952–90	2

The first Le Mans 24-Hour Race was run in 1923.

THE 10 MOST SUCCESSFUL INDY CAR DRIVERS

	Driver	Years	Wins
1	A. J. Foyt	1960–81	67
2	Mario Andretti	1965–88	51
3	Al Unser	1965–87	39
4	Bobby Unser	1966–81	35
5	Rick Mears	1978–91	29
6 =	Johnny Rutherford	1965–86	27
6 =	Michael Andretti	1986–92	27
8	Rodger Ward	1953–66	26
9	Gordon Johncock	1965–83	25
10 =	Ralph DePalma	1909–21	24
10 =	Bobby Rahal	1982–92	24

THE TOP 10 POINTS-SCORERS IN A RUGBY LEAGUE MATCH

	Player	Match	Year	Points
1	George West	Hull Kingston Rovers v Brookland Rovers	1905	53
2	Jim Sullivan	Wigan v Flimby & Fothergill	1925	44
3	Sammy Lloyd	Castleford v Millom	1973	43
4	Dean Marwood	Workington Town v Highfield	1992	42
5 =	Paul Loughlin	St Helens v Carlisle	1986	40
5 =	Martin Offiah	Wigan v Leeds	1992	40
5 =	Shaun Edwards	Wigan v Swinton	1992	40
8 =	James Lomas	Salford v Liverpool City	1907	39
8 =	Major Holland	Huddersfield v Swinton Park Rangers	1914	39
10 =	John Woods	Leigh v Blackpool Borough	1977	38
10 =	Bob Beardmore	Castleford v Barrow	1987	38
10 =	John Woods	Leigh v Ryedale-York	1992	38

THE 10 BIGGEST RUGBY LEAGUE TEST MATCH WINS BY GREAT BRITAIN

	Opponents	Venue	Year	Score
1	France	Leeds	1993	72–6
2	France	Leeds	1991	60–4
3	Papua New Guinea	Wigan	1991	56–4
4	France	Leeds	1987	52–4
5	New Zealand	Auckland	1910	52–20
6	France	Leeds	1985	50–4
7	France	Leeds	1959	50–15
8	France	Carcassonne	1993	48–6
9 =	France	Bradford	1972	45–10
9 =	France	Perpignan	1991	45–10

THE TOP 10 TRY-SCORERS IN A RUGBY LEAGUE SEASON SINCE 1973–74*

	Player/club	Season	Tries
1	Ellery Hanley (Wigan)	1986–87	63
2	Martin Offiah (Widnes)	1988–89	60
3	Ellery Hanley (Bradford Northern)	1984–85	55
4	Paul Newlove (Featherstone Rovers)	1992–93	52
5 =	Keith Fielding (Salford)	1973–74	49
5 =	Steve Halliwell (Leigh)	1985–86	49
5 =	Martin Offiah (Widnes)	1990–91	49
8	Greg Austin (Halifax)	1990–91	47
9	Shaun Edwards (Wigan)	1992–93	46
10 =	Gary Prohm (Hull Kingston Rovers)	1984–85	45
10 =	Martin Offiah (Widnes)	1989–90	45

Two-division rugby reintroduced in this season.

Albert Rosenfeld (Huddersfield) holds the record for the most tries scored in a season with 80 in 1913–14.

Wigan's Ellery Hanley holds the record for most tries in a Rugby League season.

STEVE DAVIS'S FIRST 10 OPPONENTS IN THE WORLD PROFESSIONAL SNOOKER CHAMPIONSHIP

	Opponent	Year	Round	Result
1	Ian Anderson	1979	Qualifying Round 1	won 9–1
2	Patsy Fagan	1979	Qualifying Round 1	won 9–2
3	Dennis Taylor	1979	Round 1	lost 11–13
4	Chris Ross	1980	Qualifying Round 1	won 9–3
5	Paddy Morgan	1980	Qualifying Round 2	won 9–0
6	Patsy Fagan	1980	Round 1	won 10–6
7	Terry Griffiths	1980	Round 2	won 13–10
8	Alex Higgins	1980	Round 2	lost 9–13
9	Jimmy White	1981	Round 1	won 10–8
10	Alex Higgins	1981	Round 2	won 13–8

LILLYWHITES' 10 BESTSELLING ITEMS OF SPORTS CLOTHING

1	Polisox sports socks
2	Polisox ski socks
3	Sub 4 men's lycra shirts
4	Speedo latex hats
5	Jerzees jog pants
6	Russell Athletic T-shirts
7	Speedo anti-fog goggles
8	Reebok cotton dance socks
9	Cotton Traders England rugby shirts
10	Umbro rugby shorts

LILLYWHITES' 10 BESTSELLING TYPES OF SPORTS FOOTWEAR

1	Reebok Freestyle Hi Fitness shoes
2	Reebok Freestyle Lo Fitness shoes
3	Reebok Newport Classic tennis shoes
4	Reebok Transition tennis shoes
5	Nike Air Pegasus running shoes
6	Wilson Prostaff tennis shoes
7	HiTec Squash squash shoes
8	Converse All Stars basketball boots
9	Nike Air-Max running shoes
10	Reebok Ex-O-Fit fitness shoes

LILLYWHITES' 10 BESTSELLING ITEMS OF SPORTS EQUIPMENT*

1	Golf balls: Titleist 384 TT590
2	Tennis balls: Slazenger LTA
3	Squash balls: Dunlop XX Championship, yellow dot
4	Golf gloves: Mizuno Nick Faldo
5	Cricket balls: Reader League Special
6	Tennis rackets: Wilson Prostaff Classic
7	Squash rackets: Prince Extendel Lite 190
8	Footballs: Mitre Cosmic
9	Sportsbags and rucksacks: Head ATB backpack
10	Reebok Step

*Ranked in order of sales, with bestselling brand in each category.

James Lillywhite, a member of a notable cricketing family, opened the first-ever specialist sports shop in 1862 in London's Haymarket. As fashionable new sports such as croquet, lawn tennis, archery, cycling, skiing and even roller skating became popular in the late nineteenth century, so Lillywhites expanded its stock to provide the necessary equipment and clothing. The shop moved to the nearby Criterion Building in 1925, and in 1930 supplied Amy Johnson with the flying suit she wore on her epic solo flight to Australia.

Tennis balls and rackets feature among Lillywhites' Top 10 sporting equipment bestsellers.

THE TOP 10 PARTICIPATION SPORTS, GAMES AND PHYSICAL ACTIVITIES IN THE UK

	Activity	% participating
1	Walking	41
2	Snooker, pool and billiards	14
3 =	Keep-fit and yoga	12
3 =	Swimming	12
5	Cycling	9
6	Darts	7
7 =	Golf	5
7 =	Running, jogging, etc	5
7 =	Weight-lifting and training	5
10 =	Soccer	4
10 =	Tenpin bowling and skittles	4

Based on interviews with 17,574 people, the percentages represent those who had participated in the activity in question during the four weeks prior to the interview.

THE TOP 10 PARTICIPATION SPORTS, GAMES AND PHYSICAL ACTIVITIES IN THE USA

	Activity	No. participating
1	Walking*	71,431,000
2	Swimming*	67,469,000
3	Cycling*	55,245,000
4	Freshwater fishing	41,495,000
5	Bowling	40,117,000
6	Exercising with equipment*	35,329,000
7	Basketball	26,315,000
8	Running, jogging, etc*	23,817,000
9	Aerobic exercise*	23,252,000
10	Volleyball	23,195,000

*Engaged in more than six times during year.

Although using different statistical methods, the results of a National Sporting Goods Association survey in the USA produced results that are similar in some respects to those found in the UK, but with obvious national characteristics manifesting themselves (such as the British enthusiasm for snooker and darts and the American passion for basketball). Perhaps surprisingly, baseball as a participation (in contrast to spectator) sport scored relatively low in the USA (15,576,000), but soccer – perhaps in anticipation of the country's hosting of the 1994 World Cup – scored fairly high (10,920,000, compared with American football's 14,451,000). Perhaps more predictably, 'hunting with firearms' had 18,512,000 followers. In the same survey, camping, which most Britons would regard as a leisure activity rather than a form of exercise, attracted 46,177,000 American participants.

THE TOP 10 MEDAL-WINNING NATIONS IN THE COMMONWEALTH GAMES

	Nation	Gold	Medals Silver	Bronze	Total
1	England	420	368	368	1,156
2	Australia	397	374	322	1,093
3	Canada	287	301	299	887
4	New Zealand	94	121	161	376
5	Scotland	56	74	109	239
6	South Africa	60	44	47	151
7	Wales	32	39	60	131
8	India	37	36	31	104
9	Kenya	35	25	33	93
10	Nigeria	19	25	26	70

Other British Isles totals:

11	Northern Ireland	15	20	34	69
28 =	Isle of Man	2	0	3	5
28 =	Guernsey	1	3	1	5
31 =	Jersey	1	0	3	4

OLYMPIC GOLD MEDAL WINNERS QUIZ

1 Which athlete has won the most Olympic gold medals?

2 Which athlete has won the most track and field Olympic gold medals at one Games?

3 Which country has won the most gold medals at one summer Olympics?

4 Other than athletics, in which sport has Great Britain won most gold medals?

5 Which country has won the greatest number of golds in the modern pentathlon?

6 How many gold medals has Great Britain won for judo?

7 The swimmer Mark Spitz holds the record for the most gold medals at one Games. How many did he win in 1972 and how many of these were world records?

8 Which country is second only to the USSR/CIS for gymnastic golds?

9 Which country has won the most golds and most medals in total in the bobsleighing event?

10 How many gold medals has Great Britain won in total in the Summer and Winter Olympics: 185, 518 or 851?

England gained first, second and third place in the 1990 Commonwealth Games 200 metres, adding three medals to the country's supreme Games tally.

THE 10 BESTSELLING TOYS OF 1992

	Toy	Manufacturer
1	Sega TV-based video games	Sega
2	Nintendo TV-based video games	Bandai
3	Barbie	Mattel
4	Nintendo game boy	Bandai
5	Matchbox model wheeled vehicles	Matchbox
6	Tomy preschool toys	Tomy
7	Legoland Town	Lego
8	WWF range	Hasbro
9	Sega game gear	Sega
10	Sindy	Hasbro

W.H. SMITH'S TOP 10 GAMES IN 1992

1 Pictionary

2 Trivial Pursuit Genus III

3 Atmosfear

4 Scrabble

5 Taboo

6 Trivial Pursuit Television Edition

7 Monopoly

8 Balderdash

9 Trivial Pursuit Family Edition

10 Trivial Pursuit Genus II

HAMLEYS' 10 BESTSELLING TOYS AND GAMES IN 1992

1 Sega Video Games System

2 Nintendo Video Games System

3 Tomy Char-Gs (remote control car)

4 Trolls

5 Lego Pirate Island

6 Tobias (Hamley's limited edition Steiff teddy bear)

7 Atmosfear (board game)

8 Barbie's Magic House

9 Changeable Pens

10 Blitzer (airbrush and felt-tip pens)

THE 10 BESTSELLING COMPUTER GAMES IN THE UK

Console games

	Game	Manufacturer	Formats
1	*Sonic the Hedgehog 2*	Sega	MD/SG/GG
2	*Sonic the Hedgehog*	Sega	MD/SG/GG
3	*Super Mario Land 2*	Nintendo	GA
4	*Super Kick Off*	Various	SG/SN/NI/GA/GG
5	*Donald Duck*	Sega	MD/SG/GG
6	*Mickey Mouse*	Various	MD/SG/GA/GG
7	*Tazmania*	Sega	MD/SG/GG
8	*Desert Strike*	Electronic Arts	MD
9	*Super Mario Land*	Nintendo	GA
10	*European Club Soccer*	Virgin	MD

Formats: SN: Super Nintendo; NI: Nintendo Console; GA: Nintendo Gameboy; MD: Sega Megadrive; SG: Sega-8-Bit; GG: Sega Gamegear.

Home computer games

	Game	Manufacturer	Formats
1	*Formula 1 Grand Prix*	Microprose	ST/AG/PC
2	*Streetfighter 2*	US Gold	ST/AG
3	*Sensible Soccer*	Renegade/Mindscape	ST/AG
4	*Zool*	Gremlin Graphics	AG
5	*Jimmy White's Whirlwind Snooker*	Virgin	ST/AG/PC
6	*Monkey Island 2*	US Gold	AG/PC
7	*WWF Wrestlemania*	Ocean	ST/AG/PC
8	*Sensible Soccer 92/93*	Renegade/Mindscape	ST/AG
9	*Epic*	Ocean	ST/AG/PC
10	*Oh No More Lemmings*	Psygnosis	ST/AG/PC

Formats: ST: Atari ST; AG: Commodore Amiga; PC: PC compatible.

Trolls for Christmas: these seasonal creatures and their relatives were among Hamleys' bestsellers in 1992.

THE 10 MOST EXPENSIVE TOYS EVER SOLD AT AUCTION IN THE UK

	Toy/sale	Price (£)
1	*Titania's Palace*, a doll's house with 2,000 items of furniture (the record price for a doll's house) Christie's, London, 1978	135,000
2	Kämmer and Reinhardt bisque character doll, German, c1909 (the record price for a doll) Sotheby's, London, 1989	90,200
3	Hornby 00-gauge train set (the largest ever sold at auction) Christies, London, 1992	80,178
4	William and Mary wooden doll, English, c1690 Sotheby's, London, 1987	67,000
5	Russian carousel (tinplate ferris wheel), c1904 Sotheby's, London, 1993	62,500
6	Dual-plush Steiff teddy bear, c1920 (the record price for a teddy bear) Sotheby's, London, 1989	55,000
7 =	Tinplate carousel by Märklin, c1910 Sotheby's, London, 1992	47,300
7 =	Set of Märklin horse-drawn fire appliances, c1902 Sotheby's, London, 1992	47,300
9	Tinplate 4-volt electric ocean liner, *Augusta Victoria*, by Märklin Christie's, London, 1992	41,800
10	Tinplate clockwork battleship, *Maine*, by Märklin, c1904 Sotheby's, London, 1989	39,600

Models by the German tinplate maker Märklin, regarded by collectors as the Rolls-Royce of toys, similarly feature among the record prices of auction houses outside the UK, where high prices have also been attained. The most expensive tinplate toy ever sold, however, is a model of a fire hose-reel made by American manufacturer George Brown & Co, c1875, which was auctioned at Christie's, New York, in 1991 for $231,000/£128,330.

THE 10 MOST COLLECTED POSTAGE STAMP THEMES

1	Music	**6**	Boy Scouts
2	Flowers	**7**	Heraldry
3	Animals	**8**	Uniforms
4	Chess	**9**	Medicine
5	Art	**10**	Birds

THE 10 MOST LANDED-ON SQUARES IN MONOPOLY®

1	Trafalgar Square
2	Go
3	Fenchurch Street Station
4	Free Parking
5	Marlborough Street
6	Vine Street
7	King's Cross Station
8	Bow Street
9	Water Works
10	Marylebone Station

Monopoly® is a registered trade mark of Parker Brothers division of Tonka Corporation, USA, under licence to Waddington Games Ltd.

The *Augusta Victoria* by Märklin, which sold at auction for £41,800 in 1992.

THE 10 BEST POKER HANDS

	Hand	Specimen hand				
1	Royal flush	10D	JD	QD	KD	AD
2	Straight flush	4H	5H	6H	7H	8H
3	Four of a kind	9S	9H	9C	9D	2D
4	Full house	JC	JS	JD	6H	6C
5	Flush	2H	4H	5H	QH	KH
6	Straight	5C	6S	7D	8H	9C
7	Three of a kind	3D	3S	3C	5D	AS
8	Two pairs	2D	2C	QC	QS	JH
9	One pair	8D	8H	2C	3S	AD
10	Nothing	2S	6C	8D	10S	QC

H = Hearts; C = Clubs; D = Diamonds; S = Spades; A = Ace; J = Jack; Q = Queen; K = King.

THE 10 BIGGEST AIRSHIPS EVER BUILT

	Airship	Country	Volume (cu ft)	Length m	ft
1 =	*Hindenburg*	Germany	7,062,100	245	804
1 =	*Graf Zeppelin II*	Germany	7,062,100	245	804
3 =	*Akron*	USA	6,850,000	239	785
3 =	*Macon*	USA	6,850,000	239	785
5	*R101*	UK	5,508,800	237	777
6	*Graf Zeppelin*	Germany	3,995,000	236	775
7 =	*L70*	Germany	2,418,700	226	743
7 =	*L59*	Germany	2,418,700	226	743
9	*R100*	UK	5,156,000	216	709
10	*R38*	UK*	2,724,000	213	699

*UK-built, but sold to US Navy.

Although several of the giant airships in this list travelled long distances carrying thousands of passengers, they all ultimately suffered unfortunate fates: five (the *Hindenburg*, *Akron*, *Macon*, *R101* and *R38*) crashed with the loss of many lives, the *L70* was shot down and the *L59* exploded during bombing raids in 1918, and both *Graf Zeppelins* and the *R100* were broken up for scrap.

The *Hindenburg*, the world's largest airship, pictured over New York shortly before her fatal crash (*see* p.245).

AIR & SPACE

THE FIRST 10 FLIGHTS OF MORE THAN ONE HOUR

| | Pilot | Location | Duration | | | Date |
			hr	min	sec	
1	Orville Wright	Fort Meyer, USA	1	2	15.0	9 Sep 1908
2	Orville Wright	Fort Meyer, USA	1	5	52.0	10 Sep 1908
3	Orville Wright	Fort Meyer, USA	1	10	0.0	11 Sep 1908
4	Orville Wright	Fort Meyer, USA	1	15	20.0	12 Sep 1908
5	Wilbur Wright	Auvours, France	1	31	25.8	21 Sep 1908
6	Wilbur Wright	Auvours, France	1	7	24.8	28 Sep 1908
7	Wilbur Wright*	Auvours, France	1	4	26.0	6 Oct 1908
8	Wilbur Wright	Auvours, France	1	9	45.4	10 Oct 1908
9	Wilbur Wright	Auvours, France	1	54	53.4	18 Dec 1908
10	Wilbur Wright	Auvours, France	2	20	23.2	31 Dec 1908

*First-ever flight of more than one hour with a passenger (M.A. Fordyce).

Following Orville Wright's first-ever flight in a heavier-than-air aircraft (at Kitty Hawk, Carolina, on 17 December 1903), he and his brother Wilbur so mastered the art of flying that they totally dominated the air for the next few years. It was not until 1906 that anyone else could claim to have flown, and even then, while other novice pilots were making short hops of only a few minutes' duration, the Wrights were flying over long distances and for steadily increasing times. In 1908 Orville (at Fort Meyer, near Washington, DC) and Wilbur (at the Champ d'Auvours, a military base near Le Mans) made a total of 10 flights lasting more than an hour – the last of which, on the last day of the year, actually exceeded two hours and covered a distance of 77 miles. The first pilot other than one of the Wright Brothers to remain airborne for longer than an hour was Paul Tissandier who on 20 May 1909 flew for 1 hr 2 min 13 sec at Pont-Lond, near Pau, France – in an aircraft manufactured by the Wright Brothers. He was followed by Hubert Latham, an Anglo-French aviator, who on 5 June 1909, at Châlons, France, flew an *Antoinette IV* for 1 hr 7 min 37 sec – the first aeroplane other than a Wright Flyer and the first-ever monoplane flight of more than one hour – and by Henry Farman (20 July 1909, at Châlons), with a flight of 1 hr 23 min 3.2 sec duration, Roger Sommer (who broke Wilbur Wright's record on 7 August 1909 with a flight of 2 hr 27 min 15 sec) and Louis Paulhan. On 25 July 1909 Louis Blériot had made the first Channel crossing in a powered aircraft, but his epic flight lasted less than an hour. The first flight lasting over an hour in the UK was by Samuel Franklin Cody (an American, but later a naturalized British citizen, and the first person to fly in Britain), in London on 8 September 1909; the flight lasted 1 hr 3 min 0 sec.

10 CITIES IN WHICH BRITISH AIRWAYS CONCORDES HAVE LANDED

1	Bahrain
2	Bridgetown, Barbados
3	Christchurch, New Zealand
4	Kuwait*
5	London, UK
6	Miami, USA
7	New York, USA
8	Singapore
9	Sydney, Australia†
10	Toronto, Canada

*With The Queen on board, 12 Feb 1979.
†Landing perfectly, despite losing half its tail, 12 Apr 1989.

First flown in 1969, Concorde remains the only supersonic passenger aircraft in the world.

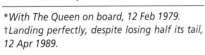

25 YEARS OF CONCORDE FLIGHTS

★ The 'droop-snoot' nose made familiar through Concorde was actually patented as early as 1955 by the Fairey Aviation Company (UK Patent No. 723,895).

★ *Concorde* was first named in a speech by General de Gaulle on 13 January 1963; the Anglo-French project was on the drawing board the following year.

★ The first prototype was shown at Toulouse on 11 December 1967.

★ The Soviet Tupolev Tu-144, nicknamed 'Concordski' for its similarity to Concorde, first flew on 31 December 1968, thus preceding Concorde into the air as the first supersonic airliner. However, while it was still undergoing tests, on 3 June 1973 a prototype appearing at the Paris Air Show fell apart and crashed in a Paris suburb, killing six on board and eight on the ground, further delaying its troubled development. Aeroflot's first Tu-144 flight – for freight and mail, but no passengers – took place on 1 November 1977, but the aircraft was withdrawn on 1 June 1978 and never flew again.

★ The first French flight took place on 2 March 1969.

★ The first British flight took place on 9 April 1969.

★ The first landing at Heathrow was on 13 September 1970.

★ The French Concorde carried out test flights to various South American destinations in September 1971.

★ The first Concorde landing in the USA was at Dallas-Fort Worth on 20 September 1973.

★ The first scheduled flight, inaugurating Concorde's commercial service, was from Paris to Rio on 21 January 1976.

★ The first scheduled flight to the USA (Washington, DC) involved the simultaneous landing of a British and French Concorde on 24 May 1976.

★ A number of scheduled routes have been suspended, but 25 years after its maiden flight both Air France and British Airways still each maintain seven Concordes in service.

10 CITIES IN WHICH AIR FRANCE CONCORDES HAVE LANDED

1	Acapulco, Mexico
2	Anchorage, USA
3	Bogota, Colombia
4	Caracas, Venezuela
5	Dakar, Senegal
6	Lima, Peru
7	Los Angeles, USA
8	Mexico City, Mexico
9	Paris, France
10	Rio de Janeiro, Brazil

THE 10 BUSIEST AIRPORTS IN THE WORLD

	Airport	City/country	Passengers per annum
1	Chicago O'Hare	Chicago, USA	59,900,000
2	DFW International	Dallas-Fort Worth, USA	48,200,000
3	LA International	Los Angeles, USA	45,700,000
4	Tokyo-Haneda International	Tokyo, Japan	42,000,000
5	London Heathrow	London, England	40,200,000
6	Hartsfield Atlanta International	Atlanta, USA	38,900,000
7	San Francisco International	San Francisco, USA	31,200,000
8	Stapleton International	Denver, USA	28,300,000
9	Frankfurt	Frankfurt, Germany	27,400,000
10	Miami International	Miami, USA	26,600,000

THE 10 BUSIEST AIRPORTS IN THE UK

	Airport	Passengers per annum
1	London Heathrow	40,248,000
2	London Gatwick	18,690,000
3	Manchester	10,150,000
4	Glasgow	4,154,000
5	Birmingham	3,251,000
6	Edinburgh	2,343,000
7	Belfast Aldergrove	2,169,000
8	Aberdeen	2,015,000
9	Luton	1,958,000
10	London Stansted	1,684,000

Only two other British airports handled more than 1,000,000 passengers in 1991: Jersey (1,638,000) and Newcastle-upon-Tyne (1,543,000).

THE 10 BUSIEST AIRPORTS IN EUROPE

	Airport	City/country	Passengers per annum
1	London Heathrow	London, England	40,248,000
2	Frankfurt	Frankfurt, Germany	27,369,000
3	Orly	Paris, France	23,195,000
4	Charles de Gaulle	Paris, France	21,612,000
5	London Gatwick	London, England	18,690,000
6	Fiumicino	Rome, Italy	16,727,000
7	Schiphol	Amsterdam, Netherlands	16,183,000
8	Madrid	Madrid, Spain	16,058,000
9	Arlanda	Stockholm, Sweden	12,793,000
10	Copenhagen	Copenhagen, Denmark	11,937,000

Seven further European airports – Dusseldorf, Milan, Palma, Stockholm, Munich, Manchester and Zurich – each handled over 10,000,000 passengers in 1991.

THE TOP 10 AIRLINE-USING COUNTRIES

	Country	Passenger-kms flown per annum*
1	USA	693,940,000,000
2	Former USSR	226,734,000,000
3	Japan	93,290,000,000
4	UK	92,283,000,000
5	France	51,471,000,000
6	Canada	50,372,000,000
7	Australia	37,028,000,000
8	Germany	36,316,000,000
9	Singapore	30,466,000,000
10	Brazil	27,854,000,000

*Total distance travelled by aircraft of national airlines multiplied by number of passengers carried.

THE FIRST 10 ANIMALS IN SPACE

	Animal/status	Country	Date
1	Laika (nickname of Kudrayavka, female Samoyed husky) Died in space	USSR	3 November 1957
2 3	Laska and Benjy (mice) Re-entered Earth's atmosphere, but not recovered	USA	13 December 1958
4 5	Able (female rhesus monkey) and Baker (female squirrel monkey) Successfully returned to Earth	USA	28 May 1959
6	Sam (male rhesus monkey) Recovered	USA	4 December 1959
7 8	Belka and Strelka (female Samoyed huskies) First to orbit and return safely	USSR	19 August 1960
9 10	Ptsyolka and Muskka (female Samoyed huskies) Capsule burned up on re-entry	USSR	1 December 1960

The first animal to be sent up in a rocket was Albert, a male rhesus monkey, in a US Air Force converted German V2 rocket in 1948. He died during the test, as did a monkey and 11 mice sent in a US Aerobee rocket in 1951. The earliest Soviet experiments with sending animals in rockets involved monkeys, dogs, rabbits, cats and mice, most of whom died as a result. Laika, the first dog in space, went up with no hope of coming down alive. Able and Baker were the first animals to be recovered (although Able died a few days later).

THE FIRST 10 US ASTRONAUTS TO WALK IN SPACE

	Astronaut	Spacecraft	EVA* hr:min	Launch date
1	Edward H. White	Gemini 4	0:23	3 Jun 1965
2	Eugene A. Cernan†	Gemini 9	2:08	3 Jun 1966
3	Michael Collins	Gemini 10	1:30	18 Jul 1966
4	Richard F. Gordon	Gemini 11	1:57	12 Sep 1966
5	Edwin E. ('Buzz') Aldrin**	Gemini 12	5:37	11 Nov 1966
6	David R. Scott§	Apollo 9	1:01	3 Mar 1969
7	Russell L. Schgweickart	Apollo 9	1:07	3 Mar 1969
8	Alfred M. Worden	Apollo 15	0:39	26 Jul 1971
9	Thomas K. Mattingly	Apollo 16	1:24	16 Apr 1972
10	Ronald E. Evans	Apollo 17	1:06	7 Dec 1972

*Extra Vehicular Activity.

†7 December 1972 – first to walk in space four times.

**16 July 1969 – first to walk in space twice.

§26 July 1971 – first to walk in space three times.

The first-ever space walk was that of Soviet cosmonaut Alexei Leonov, with an EVA of 12 minutes 9 seconds on 18 March 1965. Edward H. White, the first American to walk in space, was killed in the *Apollo* spacecraft fire of 27 January 1967, and the 10th man, Ronald E. Evans, died on 7 April 1990.

In 1960 Belka and her companion Strelka were the first living creatures to enter space and return safely to earth.

SPACE TRAVEL QUIZ

1 What record, released in 1969 but a No. 1 hit in 1975, concerned the space flight of Major Tom?

2 Place the US manned space programme in correct chronological order of first launch: *Discovery*; *Challenger*; *Mercury*; *Apollo*; *Gemini*; *Atlantis*; *Columbia*.

3 Who wrote the 1865 novel *From the Earth to the Moon*?

4 What space 'first' took place on 17 July 1975?

5 What, in space jargon, is an 'EMU'?

6 What was special about the April 1985 spaceflight of Jake Garn?

7 What was the name of the US communications satellite that, in 1962, inspired the Tornados' No. 1 hit record?

8 What was the appropriately named company for which Britain's first cosmonaut, Helen Sharman, previously worked?

9 What, approximately, is the furthest distance from the Earth that astronauts have yet travelled: 250,000, 500,000 or 1,000,000 miles?

10 In the film *2001 A Space Odyssey*, what is the name of the talking computer?

THE FIRST 10 MOONWALKERS

	Astronaut	Birthdate	Spacecraft	Total EVA* hr:min	Mission dates
1	Neil A. Armstrong	5 Aug 1930	*Apollo 11*	2:32	16–24 Jul 1969
2	Edwin E. ('Buzz') Aldrin	20 Jan 1930	*Apollo 11*	2:15	16–24 Jul 1969
3	Charles Conrad Jr	2 Jun 1930	*Apollo 12*	7:45	14–24 Nov 1969
4	Alan L. Bean	15 Mar 1932	*Apollo 12*	7:45	14–24 Nov 1969
5	Alan B. Shepard	18 Nov 1923	*Apollo 14*	9:23	31 Jan–9 Feb 1971
6	Edgar D. Mitchell	17 Sep 1930	*Apollo 14*	9:23	31 Jan–9 Feb 1971
7	David R. Scott	6 Jun 1932	*Apollo 15*	19:08	26 Jul–7 Aug 1971
8	James B. Irwin	17 Mar 1930	*Apollo 15*	18:35	26 Jul–7 Aug 1971
9	John W. Young	24 Sep 1930	*Apollo 16*	20:14	16–27 Apr 1972
10	Charles M. Duke	3 Oct 1935	*Apollo 16*	20:14	16–27 Apr 1972

*Extra Vehicular Activity (i.e. time spent out of the lunar module on the moon's surface).

Eugene A. Cernan (b.14 March 1934) and Harrison H. Schmitt (b.3 July 1935) in Apollo 17 (7–19 December 1972) were the last and only other astronauts to date who have walked on the surface of the moon; both spent a total of 22:04 in EVA. No further moon landings are planned by the USA. Although Russian scientists recently proposed sending a series of unmanned probes to land on Mars, which, if successful, would have led to a follow-up manned mission between 2005 and 2010, the entire Russian space programme is suffering from such severe financial problems that even its more routine current missions appear to be in jeopardy and such an ambitious project seems unlikely to be funded in the foreseeable future.

'One small step for man, but a giant leap for mankind': on 21 July 1969 (at 3.56 a.m. BST), Neil Armstrong became the first person to walk on the Moon.

THE 10 BESTSELLING CARS IN THE UK

	Make	Model	Total sales (1992)
1	Ford	Escort	121,140
2	Vauxhall	Cavalier	108,818
3	Ford	Fiesta	106,595
4	Vauxhall	Astra	86,858
5	Ford	Sierra	77,253
6	Rover	200 series	77,214
7	Rover	Metro	56,713
8	Peugeot	405	48,482
9	Vauxhall	Nova	42,779
10	Renault	Clio	34,701

Total sales of new cars in 1992 were 1,593,601 – just 0.08 per cent more than in the previous year (1,592,326), but far short of 1989's all-time record of 2,300,944.

The first seven cars in the Top 10 remained the same, but with adjustments in the order, the Ford Escort gaining the No. 1 position and the Fiesta falling to 3rd place. The Peugeot 205, formerly in 8th place, fell out of the Top 10 – perhaps losing out to the Renault Clio, a newcomer to the list, which clearly benefited from a massive and influential TV publicity campaign during the year (in which the only words spoken by the actors are 'Papa!' 'Nicole!').

Although Fords, Vauxhalls and Rovers (some of whose models are made overseas) dominate the Top 10, imported cars are hard on their heels in the rest of the Top 20. In 1992 the total sales of imported cars accounted for 54.93 per cent of the market.

The Vauxhall Astra is one of the UK's 10 bestselling cars.

ROAD, RAIL & SEA

THE 10 BESTSELLING CARS IN THE UK IN 1973

	Make	Model	Total sales
1	Ford	Cortina	181,607
2	Morris	Marina	115,041
3	Ford	Escort	114,296
4	British Leyland	Mini	96,383
5	Vauxhall	Viva	95,335
6	Hillman	Avenger	78,644
7	British Leyland	1100/1300	59,198
8	Hillman	Hunter	55,934
9	British Leyland	1600/Maxi	52,853
10	Ford	Granada/Consul	40,145

More than one-third of the world's motor vehicles run on the USA's roads.

THE TOP 10 MOTOR VEHICLE MANUFACTURERS IN THE WORLD

	Company	Country	Production Cars	Commercial vehicles	Total
1	General Motors	USA	5,208,221	1,936,335	7,144,556
2	Ford Motor Company	USA	3,703,646	1,831,639	5,535,285
3	Toyota	Japan	3,799,921	871,387	4,671,308
4	Nissan	Japan	2,349,165	716,124	3,065,289
5	Volkswagen	Germany	2,873,869	139,063	3,012,932
6	Peugeot-Citroën	France	2,459,139	241,916	2,701,055
7	Fiat	Italy	1,805,449	263,873	2,069,322
8	Renault	France	1,666,434	321,973	1,988,407
9	Honda	Japan	1,764,775	160,322	1,925,097
10	Chrysler	USA	859,245	954,048	1,813,293
	World total		35,773,462	12,501,708	48,275,170

Figures are for 1990 production, amalgamating worldwide production in all companies owned by the manufacturers. Two other Japanese companies, Mazda and Mitsubishi, actually produced more cars than Chrysler (1,302,464 and 870,112 respectively), but Chrysler's disproportionate commercial vehicle production provides the US company with a place in the Top 10. Nos. 1 to 9, plus Mazda, are the only manufacturers in the world to produce more than 1,000,000 cars a year. In this year, the output of the Rover Group, the only British-owned company in the world Top 40, a total of 527,807 vehicles, meant that it was placed 19th in the world league. The beginning of the global recession began to impact on the motor industry in this year, with total production down in all countries except Japan – although preliminary figures for 1991 indicate that Japan's seemingly inexorable annual rise in vehicle manufacture has at last been halted and is actually starting to decline.

THE TOP 10 CAR MANUFACTURERS IN THE UK

	Company	Total car production (1992)
1	Rover Group (Austin Rover and Land Rover)	378,797
2	General Motors (Vauxhall and IBC)	319,094
3	Ford	302,146
4	Nissan	179,009
5	Peugeot-Talbot	85,821
6	Jaguar Daimler	20,601
7	Carbodies (traditional 'black cab' taxis)	1,674
8	Rolls-Royce	1,258
9	Honda	1,001
10	Lotus	691

In 1992 General Motors' production of cars overtook that of Ford (although Ford's commercial vehicle production of 151,316 units led the field by a considerable margin). Honda arrived as a newcomer to the Top 10, but in response to the recession the output of sports car makers Lotus fell dramatically from 2,240 produced during the previous year, while TVR, the only other British manufacturer of consequence, failed to make the Top 10 at all. Specialist luxury sports car manufacturer Aston Martin produced just 60 cars in 1992.

THE TOP 10 VEHICLE-OWNING COUNTRIES IN THE WORLD

	Country	Total registered Cars	Commercial vehicles	Total
1	USA	143,549,627	45,105,835	188,655,462
2	Japan	34,924,172	22,773,497	57,697,669
3	Germany	35,512,083	2,764,191	38,276,274
4	Italy	27,300,000	2,427,000	29,727,000
5	France	23,550,000	4,910,000	28,460,000
6	UK	22,527,963	3,773,785	26,301,748
7	Former USSR	16,802,364	7,200,000	24,002,364
8	Canada	12,622,038	3,931,347	16,553,385
9	Spain	11,995,640	2,446,852	14,442,492
10	Brazil	12,127,562	935,783	13,063,345
	World	*444,899,624*	*138,082,153*	*582,981,777*

World motor vehicle ownership has increased more than fourfold from the 1960 total of 126,954,817. Of the world total, some 218,806,161 are in North America, 216,452,592 in Europe, 96,686,754 in Asia, 25,061,473 in South America, 11,926,997 in Oceania and 14,047,800 in Africa. As vehicles have proliferated, the ratio of people to vehicles has escalated from 23 in 1960 to close to nine people per vehicle today. In car-conscious and affluent countries the ratio is much higher: 1.3 per vehicle in the USA and 2.2 in the UK. San Marino, uniquely, claims the equivalent of one vehicle per person. The biggest disparities naturally occur in the least developed economies, with 922 people per vehicle in Bangladesh, for example, 803 in Ethiopia and an identical 194 in both India and China. In the car ownership stakes, Bangladesh also scores worst, with 1,788 people per car, contrasting with the UK's 2.6, with similar ratios prevailing in other Western European countries.

THE TOP 10 COUNTRIES DRIVING ON THE LEFT

	Country	Total vehicles registered
1	Japan	57,697,669
2	UK	26,301,748
3	Australia	9,776,600
4	South Africa	5,200,153
5	India	4,350,000
6	Thailand	2,813,865
7	Indonesia	2,591,087
8	Malaysia	2,426,799
9	New Zealand	1,867,745
10	Nigeria	1,410,000

While more countries drive on the right than on the left, there are 42 countries in the world that drive on the left, including the UK and most members of the British Commonwealth. The last country in Europe to change over from driving on the left to the right was Sweden, on 3 September 1967. At the time, it was estimated to have cost £41,000,000 to do so. There are innumerable explanations for keeping to the left, one being that it is common practice, especially among sword-wearing riders, to mount a horse from the left, and it is then simplest to remain on the left. Similarly, riding on the left facilitates right-handed sword defence against approaching riders. This does not explain, however, why other nations perversely drive on the right.

THE 10 COUNTRIES PRODUCING THE MOST MOTOR VEHICLES

	Country	Cars	Commercial vehicles	Total
1	Japan	9,753,069	3,492,363	13,245,432
2	USA	5,438,579	3,371,942	8,810,521
3	Germany	4,809,480	390,523	5,200,003
4	France	3,187,634	423,139	3,610,773
5	Spain	1,773,752	397,959	2,171,711
6	Former Soviet Union	1,170,000	759,000	1,929,000
7	Canada	1,072,352	833,103	1,905,455
8	Italy	1,631,941	245,385	1,877,326
9	South Korea	1,158,245	339,573	1,497,818
10	UK	1,236,900	217,141	1,454,041
	World total	*34,431,934*	*12,005,146*	*46,437,080*

In 1991 Spain's overall production overtook that of Italy for the first time ever, while South Korea, one of the few countries to increase its production in that year, moved ahead of the UK (other countries that went against the global trend and increased output marginally were Canada and a number of minor producers, such as Argentina, Brazil, Mexico, India and China). As a result, total world production dipped from 48,112,643 (35,675,329 cars and 12,437,314 commercial vehicles).

THE 10 BESTSELLING MAKES OF CAR IN THE UK

	Manufacturer/country	UK-built	Total sales
1	Ford (UK/Germany/Belgium/Spain/USA)	243,817	353,339
2	GM-Vauxhall (UK/Germany/Belgium/Spain/USA)	195,333	266,072
3	Rover (UK)	215,257	215,257
4	Peugeot-Talbot (UK/France/Spain)	33,526	124,019
5	Audi-Volkswagen (Germany/Belgium/Spain)	0	83,243
6	Nissan (UK/Japan/Spain)	18,381	74,188
7	Renault (France)	0	73,165
8	Citroën (France/Spain)	0	64,415
9	Volvo (Sweden/Netherlands/Belgium)	0	43,141
10	Toyota (Japan/USA)	0	42,213

Toyota entered the Top 10 for the first time in 1991. In the same year American-made Hondas were imported into the UK for the first time, and the company (UK/Japan/USA) was one of only four outside the Top 10 – all foreign-owned – achieving 1992 sales of more than 20,000 cars. The other three were: BMW (Germany), Fiat (Italy/Portugal), and Mercedes-Benz (Germany/Austria). 'Prestige' British-made cars such as Jaguar Daimler and Rolls-Royce/Bentley accounted for relatively small numbers of new registrations in 1992 (5,607 and 382 respectively).

THE TOP 10 EC COUNTRIES IMPORTING BRITISH-MADE CARS

	Country	Imports
1	France	145,864
2	Italy	145,512
3	Germany	92,135
4	Spain	45,473
5	Netherlands	32,599
6	Belgium/Luxembourg	30,631
7	Ireland	17,397
8	Portugal	16,031
9	Greece	6,677
10	Denmark	1,877

In 1991, while home sales slumped, British car manufacturers experienced an export sales boom, particularly in Europe, with every member country importing higher volumes: exports to France rose from 139,839 in 1990, those to Italy increased from 59,270 to a new record level and exports to Germany almost trebled. Total EC imports reached 532,196, compared with 321,025 the previous year.

THE TOP 10 MOTOR VEHICLE-OWNING COUNTRIES IN EUROPE

	Country	Cars	Total registered Commercial vehicles	Total
1	Germany	35,512,083	2,764,191	38,276,274
2	Italy	27,300,000	2,427,000	29,727,000
3	France	23,550,000	4,910,000	28,460,000
4	UK	22,527,963	3,773,785	26,301,748
5	Former USSR*	16,802,364	7,200,000	24,002,364
6	Spain	11,995,640	2,446,852	14,442,492
7	Poland	5,260,000	1,044,000	6,304,000
8	Netherlands	5,509,174	582,120	6,091,294
9	Former Yugoslavia	3,526,002	913,358	4,439,360
10	Belgium	3,833,294	443,443	4,276,737
	Europe total	184,324,277	32,128,315	216,452,592

*Includes non-European former USSR.

Up-to-date figures for the states that formerly constituted the USSR and Yugoslavia are not yet available. If these are discounted, Sweden (3,600,518 cars, 324,115 commercial vehicles, total: 3,924,633) and Austria (2,991,284 cars, 700,465 commercial vehicles, total: 3,691,749) occupy 9th and 10th positions.

THE TOP 10 NON-EC COUNTRIES IMPORTING BRITISH-MADE CARS

	Country	Imports*
1	Japan	14,757
2	USA	13,729
3	Austria	8,864
4	Switzerland	4,901
5	Finland	2,674
6	Sweden	2,498
7	Australia	1,845
8	Norway	1,735
9	Taiwan	1,513
10	Canada	860

*1991.

THE TOP 10 COUNTRIES OF ORIGIN OF CAR IMPORTS TO THE USA

	Country	Car imports (1991)
1	Japan	1,789,138
2	Canada	1,195,987
3	Mexico	249,499
4	South Korea	191,449
5	Germany	172,446
6	Sweden	62,905
7	Australia	21,649
8	Belgium	15,498
9	UK	14,874
10	Brazil	9,895
	Total imports	3,736,462

One curious anomaly in this list is that although the USA imported more cars from Australia than the UK, the total dollar value of the UK imports was more than double – $519,536,000 compared with Australia's $241,678,000. This is because a large proportion of purchases of UK-manufactured cars are in the luxury class (such as Rolls-Royce and Jaguar) which are significantly more expensive than the 'family' cars emanating from other territories. Another oddity is the number of countries whose exports to the United States for the year appear to have reached a grand total of one, among them India, Indonesia, Spain and Venezuela – and even the former USSR, from which we may conclude that somewhere in the USA there is a single eccentric collector driving a 1991-registered Russian Zil.

THE TOP 10 COMMERCIAL VEHICLE-OWNING COUNTRIES IN THE WORLD

	Country	Commercial vehicles
1	USA	45,105,835
2	Japan	22,773,497
3	Former USSR	7,200,000
4	France	4,910,000
5	China	4,171,855
6	Canada	3,931,347
7	UK	3,773,785
8	Mexico	3,063,185
9	Germany	2,764,191
10	Spain	2,446,852
	World	*138,082,153*

Four other countries have more than 2,000,000 commercial vehicles: Australia, India, Italy and Saudi Arabia, and four more have more than 1,000,0000: Argentina, Indonesia, South Africa and Thailand.

THE 10 LONGEST RAIL NETWORKS IN THE WORLD

	Country	Total rail length km	miles
1	USA	296,497	184,235
2	Former USSR	144,900	90,037
3	Canada	120,000	74,600
4	Germany	83,244	51,724
5	India	61,478	38,200
6	China	56,600	35,200
7	UK	39,448	24,512
8	Australia	39,251	24,349
9	France	34,676	21,557
10	Argentina	34,172	21,233

The extension of Washington, DC's metro now makes it the world's longest subway system.

THE 10 LONGEST RAIL TUNNELS IN THE WORLD

	Tunnel/country	Year completed	Length km	miles
1	Seikan, Japan	1988	53.9	33.5
2	Moscow Metro (Medved Kova/Belyaevo section), Russia	1979	30.7	19.1
3	London Underground (East Finchley/Morden Northern Line), UK	1939	27.8	17.3
4	Dai-Shimizu, Japan	1982	22.2	13.8
5 =	Simplon II, Italy/Switzerland	1922	19.8	12.3
5 =	Simplon I, Italy/Switzerland	1906	19.8	12.3
7	Shin-Kanmon, Japan	1975	18.7	11.6
8	Apennine, Italy	1934	18.2	11.5
9	Rokko, Japan	1972	16.3	10.1
10	Henderson, USA	1975	15.8	9.8

THE 10 LONGEST RAIL TUNNELS IN THE UK*

	Tunnel	County	km	Length m	miles	yd
1	Severn	Avon/Gwent	7	13	4	629
2	Totley	South Yorkshire	5	697	3	950
3	Standedge	Manchester/West Yorkshire	4	888	3	66
4	Sodbury	Avon	4	64	2	924
5	Disley	Cheshire	3	535	2	346
6	Ffestiniog	Gwynedd	3	528	2	338
7	Bramhope	West Yorkshire	3	429	2	241
8	Cowburn	Derbyshire	3	402	2	182
9	Sevenoaks	Kent	3	157	1	1,693
10	Morley	West Yorkshire	3	81	1	1,609

*Mainline, excluding London Underground system.

THE 10 LONGEST UNDERGROUND RAILWAY NETWORKS IN THE WORLD

	City	Built	Stations	Total track length km	miles
1	Washington, DC	1976–93	86	612	380
2	London	1863–1979	272	430	267
3	New York	1868–1968	461	370	230
4	Paris*	1900–85	430	301	187
5	Moscow	1935–79	115	225	140
6	Tokyo	1927–80	192	218	135
7	Berlin	1902–80	134	167	104
8	Chicago	1892–1953	142	156	97
9	Copenhagen	1934	61	134	83
10	Mexico City	1969–82	57	125	78

*Metro + RER.

The substantial extension of Washington DC's metro, completed in 1993, has lifted it from 10th to top position in this list. Other underground systems are also in the process of major development, among them Seoul, Korea, which currently comprises 116 km/72 miles and is expanding by 33 km/21 miles, which will put it into the Top 10.

100 YEARS OF LONDON'S ELECTRIC TUBE TRAINS

On 4 November 1890, Edward, the Prince of Wales, travelled from the City of London to the Oval. Short though it was, what was special about this particular royal journey was the Prince's mode of transport, for he went *under* the Thames seated inside the world's first-ever electric tube train. The line, which was opened to the public the following month, was called the South London and City Line, and ran between Stockwell and King William Street, stopping at just four stations. For a flat fare of twopence, passengers enjoyed the luxury of the world's first electrically illuminated underground trains, seated in heavily upholstered carriages nicknamed 'padded cells'.

King William Street station was closed 10 years later, when London Bridge station was added to the extended Northern Line, as it became known, running north to the Angel, Islington and south to Clapham Common. At the same time in 1900, the Central Line was opened – again by Prince Edward – with a ceremony at Bank Station (called 'City' until 1940). The fare on this line, which originally ran only as far as Shepherd's Bush, was also a bargain twopence, and it was once known as the 'Twopenny Tube'.

London's first 'tube train' under the river had been the cable car from the Tower of London to Bermondsey, inaugurated in 1870 and carrying 12 passengers who were winched across. It was said that if the car stopped in mid-journey, one could hear the sound of the paddleboats on the river above. It carried a million passengers a year until Tower Bridge was opened in 1894.

Prior to the first electric tube trains, those running on the Metropolitan Line, opened in 1863, and the Circle Line, completed in 1884, were steam trains fitted with a gadget to absorb smoke so that passengers were not suffocated in their gas-lit carriages. The 'cut-and-cover' method of digging trenches and arching them over was used on these first lines, but in built-up areas this was impossible and tunnelling was used instead. It was not until all the necessary inventions came together, making deep tunnelling, electric motors, electric lights and lifts or escalators possible, that the service could be electrified, which happened progressively during the 1890s. By the middle of the decade, about 90 million passengers were using the Tube every year.

After the South London and City Line, the next electric tube was 'The Drain' – officially the Waterloo and City Line – opened in 1898. Its trains were made in the USA and shipped over in parts, taken down to the tunnels by lift and assembled there.

By the end of the nineteenth century, the old steamy gaslit Metropolitan and District lines were looking distinctly old-fashioned, and by 1905 they were upgraded by electrification. The central London sections of the Bakerloo and Piccadilly lines were opened in 1906, and by the following year the deep tunnels of the Northern Line had reached Golders Green and Archway, with extensions to Morden by 1926 and High Barnet in 1940.

There is another little-known tube in London – the 6½-mile long Post Office Railway. Its tunnel was still being built during the First World War when it was used as a bomb shelter for national art treasures. Eventually opened in 1927, it runs between Paddington and Whitechapel, linking six sorting offices including Mount Pleasant. It is completely automated, with no driver – and, unlike the rest of London Underground, there is a train every four minutes.

THE 10 BUSIEST LONDON UNDERGROUND STATIONS

	Station	Annual passengers*
1	Victoria	56,990,000
2	Oxford Circus	48,490,000
3	King's Cross	37,800,000
4	Liverpool Street	34,920,000
5	Waterloo	30,650,000
6	Piccadilly Circus	29,330,000
7	Leicester Square	25,820,000
8	Tottenham Court Road	24,910,000
9	Charing Cross	24,340,000
10	Paddington	23,840,000

*Estimated total number of passengers using the station in both directions.

The total number of passengers using Victoria station is almost equivalent to the entire population of the UK. A 1991 survey calculated that a total of over 800,000,000 people a year travel on the London Underground (337,090,000 of them via the Top 10 stations), with an average (Monday–Friday) of 2,500,000 a day. The survey also revealed that the least-used station was North Weald (Central Line), with just 40 passengers per day.

THE 10 LONGEST PASSENGER LINERS IN THE WORLD

	Ship	Built year	Built country	Length m	Length ft	Length in
1	*France/Norway**	1961	France	315.53	1,035	2
2	*QEII*	1969	Scotland	293.53	963	0
3	*Sovereign of the Seas*	1987	France	268.33	880	4
4 =	*Monarch of the Seas*	1991	France	268.32	880	4
4 =	*Majesty of the Seas*	1992	France	268.32	880	4
6	*Ecstasy*	1991	Finland	262.00	859	7
7	*Fantasy*	1990	Finland	260.60	855	0
8	*Westerdam*	1986	Germany	243.20	797	11
9	*Crystal Harmony*	1990	Japan	240.90	790	4
10	*Starship Oceanic*	1965	Italy	238.44	782	3

*Renamed.

The *QEII* is the second longest but ninth heaviest liner in the world.

THE 10 LARGEST PASSENGER LINERS IN THE WORLD

	Ship	Built year	country	Passenger capacity	Gross tonnage
1	France/Norway*	1961	France	2,565	76,049
2 =	Majesty of the Seas	1992	France	2,766	73,937
2 =	Monarch of the Seas	1991	France	2,764	73,937
4	Sovereign of the Seas	1987	France	2,600	73,192
5 =	Ecstasy	1991	Finland	2,634	70,367
5 =	Fantasy	1990	Finland	2,634	70,367
7 =	Crown Princess	1990	Italy	1,590	69,845
7 =	Regal Princess	1991	Italy	1,900	69,845
9	QEII	1969	Scotland	1,877	69,053
10	Star Princess	1989	France	1,621	63,524

*Renamed.

THE PROGRESSION OF THE WORLD'S LARGEST LINERS

Ship	Gross tonnage	Years in service
Great Eastern	18,914	1858–88
Oceanic	17,274	1899–1914
Baltic	23,884	1904–33
Lusitania†	31,550	1907–15
Mauretania	31,938	1907–35
Olympic	45,300	1911–35
Titanic†	46,232	1912
Imperator/Berengaria*	52,022	1913–38
Vaterland/Leviathan*	54,282	1914–38
Bismarck/Majestic/ Caledonia*	56,621	1922–39
Normandie/Lafayette*†	79,301/83,102 **	1935–42
Queen Mary	80,774/81,237 **	1936–67
Queen Elizabeth	83,673/82,998 **	1938–72
France/Norway*	66,348/76,049 **	1961–
Sovereign of the Seas	73,192	1987–

*Renamed.

**Tonnage altered during refitting.

†Sunk.

After the fire and capsizing of the *Queen Elizabeth* in Hong Kong harbour (9 January 1972), and her eventual scrapping, the *France*, later renamed *Norway*, remained the largest passenger vessel in service until the *Sovereign of the Seas* was launched; she held the record only until 1990, however, when *Norway* was considerably enlarged during a refit, thus regaining her pre-eminence as the world's largest passenger liner afloat.

LINERS QUIZ

1 What famous liner did Edward J. Smith captain on its last voyage?

2 What was the nationality of steamship company founder Sir Samuel Cunard?

3 Where was the *Queen Mary* launched, by whom, and where is she now?

4 Who was the designer of the *Great Britain* and the *Great Eastern*?

5 What celebrated criminal attempted to flee Britain on the SS *Montrose*?

6 What 1972 film features an ocean liner that turns turtle?

7 What became of the *Queen Elizabeth*?

8 What was unique about the White Star Line's SS *Olympic*?

9 In the name of the shipping company, what do the letters 'P & O' stand for?

10 In what year did the *Great Western* begin its scheduled transatlantic service: 1837, 1853 or 1899?

THE 10 COMMONEST TYPES OF LOST PROPERTY ON LONDON TRANSPORT

	Type	1986–87	1987–88	Number 1988–89	1989–90	1990–91	1991–92
1	Books/cheque books/credit cards	19,013	19,329	19,148	20,006	20,270	20,436
2	'Value items' (handbags, purses, wallets, etc)	21,940	19,868	18,628	18,397	18,634	17,342
3	Clothing	16,497	15,211	14,954	15,088	14,624	13,704
4	Umbrellas	21,080	23,250	17,129	13,889	10,828	10,917
5	Cases and bags	9,222	9,317	9,155	9,272	9,034	8,513
6	Keys	9,923	9,265	8,793	8,595	8,348	7,559
7	Spectacles	5,975	5,754	5,756	5,985	5,944	5,362
8	Cameras, electronic articles and jewellery	5,550	5,304	5,493	5,352	5,732	5,298
9	Gloves (pairs)	5,625	4,402	3,770	3,428	3,446	3,268
10	Gloves (odd)	844	701	576	577	606	520
	Total items in Top 10:	115,669	112,401	103,402	100,589	97,466	92,919

As we have observed in every previous edition, there is an inexplicable consistency in the numbers of most categories of articles handed in to London Transport's Lost Property Office in Baker Street from year to year. Why, we may speculate, do an average of rather more than 100 individuals leave their spectacles on London's buses and tube trains every week? But also, why do only half as many people now lose their umbrellas? Alongside the mysterious pattern that emerges, a clear decline in the total can also be discerned, raising the question of whether the travelling public are becoming more careful with their property or less scrupulous about handing in finds. Books remain in the No. 1 position (oddly, cheque books and credit cards are now included with them) but changes in fashion have meant that hats, once one of the commonest lost items, no longer even warrant a separate category while electronic calculators, radios, tape recorders and cameras are now lost in large numbers. Among the stranger items that have been lost in recent years are a box of glass eyes, an artificial leg, a Yamaha outboard motor, part of a jump from the Horse of the Year Show, a complete double bed, a stuffed gorilla and an urn containing human ashes – the latter was never claimed and the ashes were eventually scattered in a Regent's Park flowerbed. This is chicken-feed, however, when compared with the plethora of bizarre items left on Japanese trains in a single year, among which were 500,000 umbrellas, £10,000,000 in cash, 29 small dogs, one live snake in a bag, 150 sets of false teeth and 15 urns containing ashes of the dead.

Along with books, cheque books and credit cards are the most frequently lost items on London Transport.

TOURISM

THE 10 MOST-VISITED NATIONAL TRUST PROPERTIES

	Property	Annual visitors
1	Fountains Abbey and Studley Royal, North Yorkshire	282,371
2	Stourhead Garden, Wiltshire	239,261
3	Polesden Lacey House and Garden, Surrey	222,931
4	Wakehurst Place, West Sussex	202,750
5	St Michael's Mount, Cornwall	197,894
6	Styal, Quarry Bank Mill, Cheshire	191,102
7	Chartwell, Kent	177,750
8	Bodnant Castle, Gwynedd	166,503
9	Bodiam Castle, East Sussex	165,500
10	Corfe Castle, Dorset	161,445

Over 10,000,000 people a year visit properties administered by the National Trust in England and Wales and Northern Ireland (the National Trust for Scotland is a separate organization). Of the more than 300 properties under the Trust's aegis, 77 are visited by 50,000 or more people a year.

Fountains Abbey is perennially the National Trust's most visited property.

THE TOP 10 TOURIST ATTRACTIONS IN SCOTLAND*

	Attraction	Annual visitors
1	Edinburgh Castle	973,620
2	Glasgow Museum and Art Gallery	892,865 F
3	Royal Botanic Gardens, Edinburgh	765,909 F
4	Museum of Transport, Glasgow	493,239 F
5	Edinburgh Zoo	486,324
6	Burrell Collection, Glasgow	486,085 F
7	Royal Museum of Scotland, Edinburgh	457,207 F
8 =	Old Blacksmith's Shop Visitor Centre, Gretna Green	400,000 †F
8 =	Royal Scots Regimental Museum, Edinburgh	400,000 †F
10	Rothiemurchus Estate, Aviemore	391,825 F

*Excluding country parks and leisure centres.

†Estimated.

F = free admission.

THE TOP 10 TOURIST ATTRACTIONS IN WALES*

	Attraction	Annual visitors
1	Ocean Beach Amusement Park, Rhyl	600,000 †
2	Erias Park, Colwyn Bay	500,000 †
3	Padarn Country Park, Llanberis	450,000 †
4	Barry Island Log Flume	430,185
5	Pembrey Country Park	386,000
6	James Pringle Weavers, Llanfair	385,854
7	Oakwood Leisure Park, Nr Narberth	370,000
8	Penscynor Wildlife Park, Neath	289,000
9	Welsh Folk Museum, St Fagans	287,826
10	Portmeirion, Penrhyndeudraeth	285,461

*Excluding leisure centres.

†Estimated.

THE TOP 10 HISTORIC PROPERTIES IN THE UK

	Property	1991 visits	1992 visits
1	Tower of London	1,923,520	2,235,199
2	St Paul's Cathedral	1,500,000 *	1,400,000 *
3	Edinburgh Castle	973,620	986,305
4	Roman Baths and Pump Room, Bath	827,214	895,948
5	Windsor Castle, State Apartments	627,213	769,298
6	Warwick Castle	682,621	690,000
7	Stonehenge, Wiltshire	615,377	649,442
8	Hampton Court Palace	502,377	580,440
9	Shakespeare's Birthplace, Stratford	516,623	577,704
10	Blenheim Palace, Oxfordshire	503,328	486,100

*Estimated.

The Tower of London is by far the most popular historic property in the UK.

THE TOP 10 TOURIST ATTRACTIONS CHARGING ADMISSION IN THE UK

	Attraction	1991 visits	1992 visits
1	Alton Towers, Staffordshire	1,968,000	2,501,379
2	Madame Tussaud's, London	2,248,956	2,263,994
3	Tower of London	1,923,520	2,235,199
4	Natural History Museum, London	1,571,681	1,700,000
5	St Paul's Cathedral, London	1,500,000 *	1,400,000 *
6	Tower World, Blackpool	1,300,000	1,300,000
7	Science Museum, London	1,327,503	1,212,504
8	Chessington World of Adventures	1,410,000	1,170,000
9	Thorpe Park, Surrey	921,014	1,026,000
10	Royal Academy, London	807,962	1,018,114

*Estimated.

THE TOP 10 MUSEUMS AND GALLERIES IN THE UK

	Museum/gallery	1991 visits	1992 visits
1	British Museum, London	5,061,287 F	6,309,349 F
2	National Gallery, London	4,280,139 F	4,313,988 F
3	Natural History Museum, London	1,571,682	1,700,000
4	Tate Gallery, London	1,816,421 F	1,575,637 F
5	Science Museum, London	1,327,503	1,212,504
6	Victoria and Albert Museum, London	1,066,428 F	1,182,402
7	Royal Academy, London	807,962	1,018,114
8	Glasgow Art Gallery and Museum	892,865 F	874,688 F
9	Jorvik Viking Centre, York	791,225	785,028
10	National Museum of Photography, Bradford	711,464 F	775,139 F

F = free admission.

Kew Gardens' 163-ft Pagoda dating from 1761–62, one of the attractions for almost one million visitors a year.

THE TOP 10 GARDENS IN THE UK

	Garden	1991 visits	1992 visits
1	Hampton Court Gardens	1,000,000 *	1,100,000 *F
2	Tropical World, Roundhay Park, Leeds	1,062,654 F	1,086,450 F
3	Kew Gardens	988,000	953,250
4	Royal Botanical Gardens, Edinburgh	765,909 F	662,459 F
5	Wisley Gardens, Surrey	630,000	616,970
6	Botanic Gardens, Belfast	350,000 *	400,000 *F
7	Sir Thomas and Lady Dixon Park, Belfast	320,000 *	400,000 *F
8	Botanic Gardens, Glasgow	350,000 *	350,000 *F
9	University of Oxford Botanic Gardens	324,800 *	282,000 *F
10	Stourhead Garden, Wiltshire	228,209	239,261

*Estimated.

F = free admission.

THE 10 MOST-VISITED CHURCHES AND CATHEDRALS IN THE UK

	Church	Estimated visitors (1992)
1	Westminster Abbey	2,750,000
2 =	Canterbury Cathedral	2,250,000
2 =	York Minster	2,250,000
4	St Paul's Cathedral	1,400,000 *
5	Chester Cathedral	1,000,000
6	King's College Chapel, Cambridge	550,000
7 =	Buckfast Abbey, Devon	500,000
7 =	Norwich Cathedral	500,000
7 =	Salisbury Cathedral	500,000
7 =	Winchester Cathedral	500,000

*Admission charged.

THE 10 COUNTRIES WITH MOST TOURIST ARRIVALS

	Country	Annual arrivals
1	France	51,462,000
2	USA	39,772,000
3	Spain	34,300,000
4	Italy	26,679,000
5	Hungary	20,510,000
6	Austria	19,011,000
7	UK	18,021,000
8	Germany	17,045,000
9	Canada	15,258,000
10	Switzerland	13,200,000

THE 10 ITEMS MOST COMMONLY BROKEN IN HOTELS

1	Glasses
2	Bathroom fittings
3	Crockery
4	Beds
5	Lights
6	Televisions
7	Basins
8	Mirrors
9	Telephones
10	Windows

THE 10 ITEMS MOST COMMONLY STOLEN FROM HOTELS

1	Towels
2	Teaspoons
3	Ashtrays
4	Pictures
5	Bathrobes
6	Hairdryers
7	Kettles
8	Televisions
9	Ornaments
10	Glasses

THE 10 ITEMS MOST COMMONLY LEFT BEHIND IN HOTELS

1	Nightdresses
2	Cosmetics
3	Jewellery
4	Shaving cream
5	Adult magazines
6	Clothes
7	Pens
8	Tights
9	Bags
10	Food

A survey of approximately 2,000 Automobile Association-appointed hotels in the UK and Ireland conducted in 1992 revealed evidence of visitors' clumsiness, (dis)honesty and forgetfulness, together with anecdotal reports of some of the commonest complaints and requests, some of them reminiscent of episodes of *Fawlty Towers*, the list headed by 'complaints about bad weather', followed by such incidents as 'bogus wives exposed', 'restaurant meals ordered for pets' and 'unreasonable requests about noise', among the latter such disturbances as birdsong, the sea, a hurricane (that actually ripped the hotel roof off) and a guest dying.

THE 10 WORST VOLCANIC ERUPTIONS IN THE WORLD

	Location	Year	Estimated no. killed
1	Tambora, Indonesia	1815	92,000
2	Mt Pelée, Martinique	1902	40,000
3	Krakatoa, Sumatra/Java	1883	36,380 *
4	Nevado del Ruiz, Colombia	1985	22,940 †
5	Mt Etna, Sicily	1669	20,000
6	Pompeii, Italy	79	16–20,000
7	Mt Etna, Sicily	1169	15,000
8	Mt Unzen-Dake, Japan	1792	10,400
9	Mt Laki, Iceland	1783	10,000
10	Kelut, Java	1919	5,110

Most killed by subsequent tidal wave.

†Most killed by resultant mud river that engulfed Armero.

The volcanic eruption that killed the greatest number of people was that of Tambora, Indonesia, in April 1815. The cataclysmic blast killed about 10,000 islanders immediately, with a further 82,000 dying subsequently from disease and famine resulting from crops being destroyed. An estimated 1,700,000 tons of ash was hurled into the atmosphere. This blocked out the sunlight and affected the weather over large areas of the globe during the following year. An interesting effect of this was to produce brilliantly coloured sunsets, depicted graphically in paintings from the period, especially in the works of J.M.W. Turner. It even had an influence on literary history: kept indoors by inclement weather at the Villa Diodati on Lake Geneva, Lord Byron and his companions amused themselves by writing horror stories, one of which was Mary Shelley's classic, *Frankenstein*.

The 1902 eruption of Martinique's Mt Pelée killed an estimated 40,000.

THE 10 WORST EARTHQUAKES IN THE WORLD

	Location	Date	Estimated no. killed
1	Near East/Mediterranean	20 May 1202	1,100,000
2	Shenshi, China	23 Jan 1556	830,000
3	Calcutta, India	11 Oct 1737	300,000
4	Antioch, Syria	20 May 526	250,000
5	Tang-shan, China	28 Jul 1976	242,419 *
6	Nan-Shan, China	22 May 1927	200,000
7	Yeddo, Japan	1703	190,000
8	Kansu, China	16 Dec 1920	180,000
9	Tokyo/Yokohama, Japan	1 Sep 1923	142,807
10	Hokkaido, Japan	30 Dec 1730	137,000

Official figure; the total could have been as high as 750,000.

Some authorities have suggested a death toll of up to 160,000 for the earthquake that devastated Messina, Italy, on 28 December 1908, but the true figure seems closer to 58,000. Several other earthquakes in China and Turkey resulted in deaths of 100,000 or more. In recent times, the Armenian earthquake of 7 December 1988 and that which struck northwest Iran on 21 June 1990 resulted in the deaths of more than 55,000 and 40,000 respectively. One of the most famous earthquakes, the one that destroyed San Francisco on 18 April 1906, killed between 500 and 1,000 – mostly in the fire that followed the shock.

THE 10 WORST TSUNAMIS ('TIDAL WAVES') IN THE WORLD

	Location	Year	Estimated no. killed
1	Atlantic coast (Morocco, west Europe, West Indies)	1775	60,000
2	Sumatra, Java	1883	36,000
3 =	Japan	1707	30,000
3 =	Italy	1783	30,000
5	Japan	1896	27,122
6	Chile, Hawaii	1868	25,000
7	Ryukyu Island	1771	11,941
8	Japan	1792	9,745
9 =	Japan	1498	5,000
9 =	Japan	1611	5,000
9 =	Peru	1756	5,000
9 =	Chile, Hawaii, Japan	1960	5,000
9 =	Philippines	1976	5,000

FIRES QUIZ

1 Which of these did not die as a result of fire: writer Hilaire Belloc, sculptor Barbara Hepworth, poet Percy Bysshe Shelley?

2 What London landmark was burned down on 16 October 1834?

3 Who, according to legend, 'fiddled while Rome burned'?

4 What is the USA's national fire prevention symbol?

5 Which British group had a No. 1 hit in 1968 with *Fire*?

6 The burning of which city was blamed on Mrs O'Leary's cow?

7 What 1991 film starring Kurt Russell features the work of firefighters?

8 What is the nickname of Paul Neal Adair, the oil well fire trouble-shooter?

9 What was a 'firemark'?

10 How many people were said to have been killed in the 1666 Great Fire of London – 9, 90, 900 or 9,000?

THE 10 WORST RAIL DISASTERS IN THE UK

Incident	No. killed

1 22 May 1915,
Quintinshill near Gretna Green **227**

A troop train carrying 500 members of the 7th Royal Scots Regiment from Larbert to Liverpool collided head-on with a local passenger train. The 15 coaches of the troop train, 195 m/213 yards long, were so crushed that they ended up just 61 m/67 yards long. Barely a minute later, the Scottish express, drawn by two engines and weighing a total of 600 tons, ploughed into the wreckage. The gas-lit troop train then caught fire. Since their records were destroyed in the blaze, the actual number of soldiers killed was never established, but was probably 215, as well as two members of the train's crew, eight in the express and two in the local train – a total of 227 killed and 246 injured, many very seriously. An enquiry established that the accident was caused by the negligence of the signalmen, George Meakin and James Tinsley, who were convicted of manslaughter and jailed.

2 8 October 1952,
Harrow and Wealdstone Station **122**

In patchy fog, Robert Jones, the relief driver of the Perth to Euston sleeping-car express, pulled by the *City of Glasgow*, failed to see a series of signal lights warning him of danger and at 8.19 a.m. collided with the waiting Watford to Euston train. Seconds later, the Euston to Liverpool and Manchester express (with two locomotives, *Windward Islands* and *Princess Anne*) hit the wreckage of the two trains. The casualties were 112 killed instantly, 10 who died later, and 349 injured.

3 4 December 1957,
Lewisham, South London **90**

A steam and an electric train were in collision in fog, the disaster made worse by the collapse of a bridge onto the wreckage, leaving 90 dead and 109 seriously injured.

4 28 December 1879, Tay Bridge, Scotland **80**

As the North British mail train passed over it during a storm, the bridge collapsed killing all 75 passengers and the crew of five. The bridge – the longest in the world at that time – had only been opened on 31 May the previous year, and Queen Victoria had crossed it in a train soon afterwards. The locomotive was salvaged from the bed of the Tay several months later. Surprisingly little-damaged, it was repaired and continued in service until 1919.

5 12 June 1889, Armagh, Northern Ireland **78**

A Sunday school excursion train with 940 passengers stalled on a hill. When 10 carriages were uncoupled, they ran backwards and collided with a passenger train, killing 78 and leaving 250 injured. Railway officials were charged with negligence.

6 5 November 1967,
Hither Green, South London **49**

The Hastings to Charing Cross train was derailed by a broken track. As well as those killed, 78 were injured, 27 of them very seriously.

7 28 February 1975,
Moorgate Station, London **43**

The Drayton Park to Moorgate tube ran into the wall at the end of the tunnel, killing 43 and injuring 74 in London Transport's worst rail disaster.

8 10 December 1937, Castlecary, Scotland **35**

In heavy snow the Edinburgh to Glasgow train ran into a stationary Dundee to Glasgow train and rode over the top of it, leaving 179 injured.

9 = 24 December 1874, Shipton near Oxford **34**

The Paddington to Birkenhead train plunged over the embankment after a carriage wheel broke, killing 34 and badly injuring 65.

9 = 12 December 1988,
Clapham Junction, London **34**

The 7.18 Basingstoke to Waterloo train, carrying 906 passengers, stopped at signals outside Clapham Junction; the 6.30 train from Bournemouth ran into its rear and an empty train from Waterloo hit the wreckage, leaving 33 dead (and one who died later) and 111 injured.

THE 10 WORST RAIL DISASTERS IN THE USA

Incident	No. killed

1 9 July 1918, Nashville, Tennessee **101**

On the Nashville, Chattanooga and St Louis Railway a head-on collision left 171 injured and a death-toll that remains the worst in US history.

2 1 November 1918, Brooklyn, New York **97**

A subway train was derailed in the Malbone Street tunnel.

3 = 7 August 1904, Eden, Colorado **96**

Train derailed on a bridge during a flood.

3 = 1 March 1910, Wellington, Washington **96**

An avalanche swept two trains into a canyon.

5 29 December 1876, Ashtabula, Ohio **92**

A bridge collapsed in a snow storm and the Lake Shore train fell into the Ashtabula river.

6 6 February 1951, Woodbridge, New Jersey **85**

A Pennsylvania Railroad commuter train crashed as a result of the collapse of a temporary bridge.

7 10 August 1887, Chatsworth, Illinois **81**

A trestle bridge caught fire and collapsed as the Toledo, Peoria & Western train was passing over. As many as 372 were injured.

8 = 6 September 1943,
Frankford Junction, Pennsylvania **79**

Pennsylvania's worst railway accident since that at Camp Hill on 17 July 1856 when two trains crashed head-on, resulting in the deaths of 66 school children on a church picnic outing.

8 = 22 November 1950, Richmond Hill, New York **79**

A Long Island Railroad commuter train rammed into the rear of another.

10 16 December 1943, Rennert, North Carolina **72**

Two Atlantic Coast Line trains collided.

The 1952 Harrow train crash left 122 dead in the UK's worst post-war rail accident.

THE 10 WORST RAIL DISASTERS IN THE WORLD

Incident	No. killed
1 6 June 1981, Bagmati River, India	**c800**

The carriages of a train travelling from Samastipur to Banmukhi in Bihar plunged off a bridge over the river Bagmati. Although the official death toll was said to have been 268, many authorities have claimed that the train was so massively overcrowded that the actual figure was in excess of 800, making it the worst rail disaster of all time.

2 3 June 1989, Chelyabinsk, Russia	**600+**

Two passenger trains travelling on the Trans-Siberian railway, laden with holidaymakers heading to and from Black Sea resorts, were destroyed by exploding liquid gas from a nearby pipeline.

3 12 December 1917, Modane, France	**573**

A troop-carrying train ran out of control and was derailed.

4 2 March 1944, Balvano, Italy	**521**

A train stalled in the Armi Tunnel, and many passengers were suffocated.

5 3 January 1944, Torre, Spain	**500–800**

A collision and fire in a tunnel resulted in many deaths.

6 3 April 1955, near Guadalajara, Mexico	**c300**

A train plunged into a ravine.

7 29 September 1957, Montgomery, Pakistan	**250–300**

A collision between an express and an oil train.

8 4 February 1970, near Buenos Aires, Argentina	**236**

A collision between an express and a standing commuter train.

9 23 December 1933, Lagny-Pomponne, France	**230**

France's second-worst rail disaster.

10 22 May 1915, Quintinshill, Scotland	**227**

Britain's worst rail disaster (*see* The 10 Worst Rail Disasters in the UK).

10 CELEBRITY AEROPLANE CRASH DEATHS

1   Amelia Earhart

An American flier, and the first woman to cross the Atlantic solo, is presumed to have been killed in 1937 when her plane disappeared in the South Seas during a round-the-world flight. Many theories have been proposed, one claiming that she was executed by Japanese soldiers as a spy.

2   Dag Hammarskjöld

The Secretary-General of United Nations died on 18 September 1961, the victim of an unexplained plane crash in the Congo.

3   Buddy Holly

This American rock singer, the Big Bopper (aka J.P. Richardson) and Richie Valens all died in the same accident aboard a Beechcraft Bonanza on 2 February 1959, on a flight from Clear Lake, Ohio to Moorhead, Minnesota.

4   Leslie Howard

The British actor was shot down by a German fighter that attacked the Douglas DC3 in which he was a passenger en route for Lisbon on 1 June 1943.

5   Amy Johnson

A record-breaking British aviator, she vanished during a flight over the Thames estuary on 5 January 1941.

6   Carole Lombard

The American actress was killed with her mother in a plane crash in Nevada on 16 January 1942.

7   Rocky Marciano

This world heavyweight boxing champion was killed in a plane crash at Newton, Iowa, on 31 August 1969.

8   Glenn Miller

The American big band leader was lost without trace on a wartime flight from England to France on 16 December 1944. Several fanciful explanations have since been suggested.

9   Kyu Sakamoto

This Japanese singer, who had a 1963 No. 6 UK hit with *Sukiyaki*, was killed in the crash in Japan of a Japan Air Lines Boeing 747 on 12 August 1985 (*see* The 10 Worst Air Disasters in the World).

10   Michael Todd

The American film producer and husband of Elizabeth Taylor was killed in a plane crash on 22 March 1958. His body was buried at Waldheim Cemetery, Forest Park, Illinois; in June 1977 his remains were stolen but later recovered and reburied.

THE 10 WORST AIR DISASTERS IN THE UK

	Incident	No. killed
1	21 December 1988, Lockerbie, Scotland	**270**

(see World List, No. 8)

2	18 June 1972, Staines, Middlesex	**118**

A BEA Trident crashed after take-off.

3	12 March 1950, Siginstone, Glamorgan	**81**

An Avro Tudor V crashed while attempting to land at Llandow; two were saved.

4	23 August 1944, Freckelton, Lancashire	**76**

A US Air Force B-24 crashed onto a school.

5	4 June 1967, Stockport, Cheshire	**72**

A British Midland Argonaut airliner carrying holidaymakers returning from Majorca crashed, en route to Manchester airport, killing all but 12 on board.

6	24 August 1921, off the coast near Hull	**62**

Airship *R38*, sold by the British Government to the USA, broke in two on a training and test flight.

7	22 August 1985, Manchester	**55**

A British Airtours Boeing 737 caught fire on the ground.

8	5 January 1969, near Gatwick Airport	**50**

An Ariana Afghan Airlines Boeing 727 crash-landed; the deaths include two on the ground.

9	8 January 1989, M1 Motorway	**47**

A British Midland Boeing 737-400 attempting to land without engine power crashed on the M1 Motorway embankment near East Midlands Airport.

10 =	15 November 1957, Isle of Wight	**45**

Following an engine fire, an Aquila Airlines Solent flying boat struck a cliff.

10 =	6 November 1986, off Sumburgh, Shetland Islands	**45**

A Boeing 234 Chinook helicopter ferrying oil rig workers ditched in the sea making it the worst-ever civilian helicopter accident.

In addition to disasters within the UK, a number of major air crashes involving British aircraft have occurred overseas. One of the earliest was that of British airship *R101* (see The 10 Worst Airship Disasters in the World). The Imperial Airways Argosy biplane *City of Liverpool* crashed near Dixmude in Belgium on 28 March 1933, killing all 12 passengers and three crew (one passenger fell out before the crash, and sabotage or attempted hijacking was suspected, as the aircraft was carrying silver bullion). On 4 March 1962 a chartered Caledonian DC-7C crashed near Douala, Cameroon, with the loss of 111 lives; at the time, this was the worst disaster involving a British airliner and the worst in Africa. A BOAC Boeing 707 crashed on Mount Fuji, Japan, on 5 March 1966, killing 124, and in the crash of a Dan-Air Boeing 727 at Santa Cruz de Tenerife, Canary Islands, on 25 April 1980 all 146 on board perished. The collison of a British Airways Trident heading from London to Istanbul and an Inex Adria DC-9 over Zagreb on 10 September 1976 left 176 dead, 54 passengers and nine crew in the British aircraft and 108 passengers and five crew in the Yugoslavian aircraft.

THE 10 WORST AIR DISASTERS IN THE USA

	Incident	No. killed
1	25 May 1979, Chicago	**275**

An American Airlines DC-10 crashed on take-off from Chicago O'Hare airport after an engine fell off, in the world's worst single aircraft disaster to date; as a result, all DC-10s were temporarily grounded.

2	16 August 1987, Romulus, Michigan	**156**

A Northwest Airlines McDonnell Douglas MD-80 crashed onto a road following an engine fire after take-off from Detroit. A girl aged four was the only survivor.

3	9 July 1982, Kenner, Louisiana	**154**

A Pan American Boeing 727 crashed after take-off from New Orleans for Las Vegas, killing all on board (138 passengers and the crew of eight) and eight on the ground.

4	25 September 1978, San Diego, California	**144**

A Pacific Southwest Boeing 727 collided in the air with a Cessna 172 light aircraft killing 135 in the airliner, two in the Cessna and seven on the ground.

5	16 December 1960, New York	**134**

A United Air Lines DC-8 with 77 passengers and a crew of seven and a TWA Super Constellation with 39 passengers and four crew collided in a snowstorm. The DC-8 crashed in Brooklyn killing eight on the ground, although one passenger, an 11-year-old boy survived; the Super Constellation crashed in Staten Island harbour, killing all on board.

6	2 August 1985, Dallas-Ft Worth Airport, Texas	**133**

A Delta Airlines TriStar crashed when a severe down-draught affected it during landing.

7	30 June 1956, Grand Canyon, Arizona	**128**

A United Air Lines DC-7 and a TWA Super Constellation collided in the air, resulting in the worst civil aviation disaster to that date.

8	24 June 1975, JFK Airport, New York	**113**

An Eastern Air Lines Boeing 727 on a flight from New Orleans crashed while attempting to land in a storm.

9	4 September 1971, Chilkoot Mountains, Alaska	**111**

An Alaska Airlines Boeing 727 crashed.

10	19 July 1989, Sioux City, Iowa	**107**

A United Air Lines DC-10 crashed en route from Denver to Chicago after an engine explosion.

The 1988 Lockerbie crash (see No. 8 The 10 Worst Air Disasters in the World) is the United States' worst air disaster not occurring within US territory. The previous worst was the 12 December 1985 crash of a chartered Arrow Air DC-8 during take-off from Gander, Newfoundland, killing all 256 on board, including 248 members of the 101st US Airborne Division. A domestic incident that could potentially have resulted in a huge number of casualties, but in fact killed only 14 with a further 25 injured, was the 28 July 1945 crash of a US Army B-25 bomber into the 78th and 79th floors of the Empire State Building, hurling blazing wreckage completely through the building and killing the crew of three and 11 office workers. The worst pre-war American air disaster was the 4 April 1933 crash into the sea off the New Jersey coast of the *Akron* dirigible airship, with the loss of 73 lives (see The 10 Worst Airship Disasters in the World).

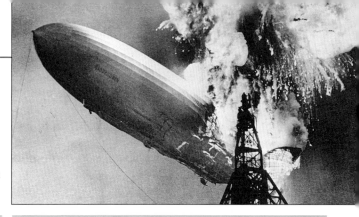

The last moments of the giant *Hindenburg*, the most vivid, though not the worst-ever airship disaster.

THE 10 WORST AIR DISASTERS IN THE WORLD

	Incident	No. killed
1	27 March 1977, Tenerife, Canary Islands	**583**

Two Boeing 747s (Pan Am and KLM, carrying 364 passengers and 16 crew and 230 passengers and 11 crew respectively) collided and caught fire on the runway of Los Rodeos airport after the pilots received incorrect control-tower instructions.

	Incident	No. killed
2	12 August 1985, Mt Ogura, Japan	**520**

A JAL Boeing 747 on an internal flight from Tokyo to Osaka crashed, killing all but four on board in the worst-ever disaster involving a single aircraft.

	Incident	No. killed
3	3 March 1974, Paris, France	**346**

A Turkish Airlines DC-10 crashed at Ermenonville, north of Paris, immediately after take-off for London, with many English rugby supporters among the dead.

	Incident	No. killed
4	23 June 1985, off the Irish coast	**329**

An Air India Boeing 747 on a flight from Vancouver to Delhi exploded in mid-air, perhaps as a result of a terrorist bomb.

	Incident	No. killed
5	19 August 1980, Riyadh, Saudi Arabia	**301**

A Saudia (Saudi Arabian) Airlines Lockheed Tristar caught fire during an emergency landing.

	Incident	No. killed
6	3 July 1988, off the Iranian coast	**290**

An Iran Air A300 airbus was shot down in error by a missile fired by the *USS Vincennes*.

	Incident	No. killed
7	25 May 1979, Chicago, USA	**275**

(*see* The 10 Worst Air Disasters in the USA)

	Incident	No. killed
8	21 December 1988, Lockerbie, Scotland	**270**

Pan Am Flight 103 from London Heathrow to New York exploded in mid-air as a result of a terrorist bomb, killing 243 passengers, 16 crew and 11 on the ground in the UK's worst-ever air disaster.

	Incident	No. killed
9	1 September 1983, Sakhalin Island, off the Siberian coast	**269**

A Korean Air Lines Boeing 747 that had strayed into Soviet airspace was shot down by a Soviet fighter.

	Incident	No. killed
10	11 July 1991, Jeddah, Saudi Arabia	**261**

A Canadian chartered DC-8 carrying Muslim pilgrims returning from Mecca to Nigeria crashed on take-off.

Two further air disasters have resulted in the deaths of more than 250 people: on 28 November 1979 an Air New Zealand DC-10 crashed near Mt Erebus, Antarctica, while on a sightseeing trip, killing 257 passengers and crew, and on 12 December 1985 an Arrow Air DC-8 crashed on take-off at Gander, Newfoundland, killing all 256 on board, including 248 members of the 101st US Airborne Division.

THE 10 WORST AIRSHIP DISASTERS IN THE WORLD

	Incident	No. killed
1	3 April 1933, off the Atlantic coast of USA	**73**

US Navy airship *Akron* crashed into the sea in a storm, leaving only three survivors in the world's worst airship tragedy.

	Incident	No. killed
2 =	21–26 December 1923, over the Mediterranean	**50**

French airship *Dixmude* was allegedly sighted over the Sahara five days after taking off from Toulon, out of control in a storm. It is assumed to have broken up and crashed into the sea; wreckage, believed to be from the airship, was found off Sicily 10 years later.

	Incident	No. killed
2 =	5 October 1930, near Beauvais, France	**50**

British airship *R101* crashed into a hillside leaving 48 dead, with two dying later, and six saved.

	Incident	No. killed
4	24 August 1921, off the coast near Hull	**44**

Airship *R38*, sold by the British Government to the USA and renamed *USN ZR-2*, broke in two on a training and test flight.

	Incident	No. killed
5	6 May 1937, Lakehurst, New Jersey, USA	**35**

German Zeppelin *Hindenburg* caught fire when mooring.

	Incident	No. killed
6	21 February 1922, Hampton Roads, Virginia, USA	**34**

Roma, an Italian airship bought by the US Army, crashed killing all but 11 men on board.

	Incident	No. killed
7	17 October 1913, Berlin, Germany	**28**

German airship *LZ18* crashed after engine failure during a test flight at Berlin-Johannisthal.

	Incident	No. killed
8	30 March 1917, Baltic Sea	**23**

German airship *SL9* was struck by lightning on a flight from Seerappen to Seddin, and crashed into the sea.

	Incident	No. killed
9	3 September 1915, mouth of the River Elbe, Germany	**19**

German airship *L10* was struck by lightning and plunged into the sea.

	Incident	No. killed
10 =	9 September 1913, off Heligoland	**14**

German Navy airship *L1* crashed into the sea, leaving six survivors out of the 20 on board.

	Incident	No. killed
10 =	3 September 1925, Caldwell, Ohio	**14**

US dirigible *Shenandoah*, the first airship built in the USA and the first to use safe helium instead of inflammable hydrogen, broke up in a storm, scattering sections over many miles of the Ohio countryside.

THE FIRST AIRSHIP TO BE
BROUGHT DOWN BY AN AIRCRAFT

On 7 June 1915 23-year-old Flight Sub-Lieutenant Reginald Warneford, serving in northern France, took off in his biplane in search of enemy Zeppelin airships. When he encountered one, designated *LZ37*, over Ostend, it promptly opened fire with its machine guns, but Warneford retaliated by flying over it and dropping his bombs. The resulting explosion turned his aircraft upside-down, but he managed to regain control and land. The Zeppelin was completely destroyed, the wreckage landing on the roof of a nearby convent and its unconscious helmsman conveniently falling through the roof onto a bed. Warneford was immediately awarded the Victoria Cross and the Legion of Honour, but survived for only 10 days before being killed in a plane crash. An overnight hero, Warneford's tomb in Brompton cemetery, London, depicting his exploit in a graphic stone carving, was paid for by readers of the *Daily Express*.

THE FIRST 10 AIRCRAFT FATALITIES

	Name	Nationality	Location	Date
1	Lt Thomas Etholen Selfridge	American	Fort Myer, USA	17 Sep 1908
2	Eugène Lefèbvre	French	Juvisy, France	7 Sep 1909
3	Captain Ferdinand Ferber	French	Boulogne, France	22 Sep 1909
4	Antonio Fernandez	Spanish	Nice, France	6 Dec 1909
5	Aindan de Zoseley	Hungarian	Budapest, Hungary	2 Jan 1910
6	Léon Delagrange	French	Croix d'Hins, France	4 Jan 1910
7	Hubert Leblon	French	San Sebastián, Spain	2 Apr 1910
8	Hauvette-Michelin	French	Lyons, France	13 May 1910
9	Thaddeus Robl	German	Stettin, Germany	18 Jun 1910
10	Charles Louis Wachter	French	Rheims, France	3 Jul 1910

Following the Wright Brothers' first flights in 1903, the first four years of powered flying remained surprisingly accident-free. Although there had been many fatalities in the early years of ballooning and among pioneer parachutists, it was not until 1908 that anyone was killed in an aeroplane. On 17 September at Fort Myer, Virginia, Orville Wright was demonstrating his Type A *Flyer* to the US Army. On board was a passenger, 26-year-old Lieutenant Thomas Etholen Selfridge of the Army Signal Corps. At a height of just 23 m/75 feet, one of the propellers struck a wire, sending the plane out of control. It crash-landed, injuring Wright and killing Lt Selfridge, who thus became powered flying's first victim. On 7 September 1909 Eugène Lefèbvre was the first pilot to be killed, also in a Type A Wright *Flyer*, when he crashed at Port Aviation, Juvisy, France, and on 22 September Captain Ferdinand Ferber was killed during an air show at Boulogne when his Voisin aeroplane hit a ditch during a manoeuvre on the ground. On 12 July 1910 the 11th fatal accident and the first involving a British citizen occurred when the Hon Charles Stewart Rolls (the 'Rolls' of Rolls-Royce) crashed a Type A Wright *Flyer* during an air show at Bournemouth. Later the same year, English pilot Cecil Grace was drowned when his Short biplane ditched in the English Channel during an attempted crossing. The first accident in which American pilots were killed were those involving Ralph Johnstone (Denver, Colorado, 19 November 1910) and Walter Archer (Salida, Colorado, 3 December 1910). Coincidentally, the next two accidents in which American pilots were killed both occurred on the same day, 31 December 1910; the victims were John Moisant in New Orleans and Arch Hoxsey in Los Angeles. The first woman killed was Denise Moore, piloting a Farman at Châlons, France, on 21 July 1911. The first qualified woman pilot and first American woman to be killed was Julie Clark on 17 June 1912 when her Curtiss biplane struck a tree at Illinois State Fair, Springfield.

THE FIRST 10 IN-FLIGHT SPACE FATALITIES

Name/date of birth

1   Vladimir M. Komarov (16 Mar 1927)

Launched on 24 April 1967, Soviet spaceship *Soyuz I* experienced various technical problems during its 18th orbit. After a successful re-entry, the capsule parachute was deployed at 7,010 m/23,000 ft, but its lines became tangled and it crash-landed near Orsk in the Urals, killing Komarov, who thus became the first-ever space fatality.

2 = Georgi T. Dobrovolsky (1 Jun 1928)

2 = Viktor I. Patsayev (19 Jun 1933)

2 = Vladislav N. Volkov (23 Nov 1933)

After a then record 23 days in space, including a link-up with the Salyut space station, the Soviet *Soyuz XI* mission ended in disaster on 29 June 1971 when the capsule depressurized during re-entry. Although it landed intact, all three cosmonauts – who were not wearing spacesuits – were found to be dead. The ashes of the three men were buried, along with those of Yuri Gagarin and Vladimir Komarov, at the Kremlin, Moscow. Spacesuits have been worn during re-entry on all subsequent missions.

5 = Gregory B. Jarvis (24 Aug 1944)

5 = Sharon C. McAuliffe (2 Sep 1948)

5 = Ronald E. McNair (21 Oct 1950)

5 = Ellison S. Onizuka (24 Jun 1946)

5 = Judith A. Resnik (5 Apr 1949)

5 = Francis R. Scobee (19 May 1939)

5 = Michael J. Smith (30 Apr 1945)

The *Challenger* STS 51-L, the 25th Space Shuttle mission, exploded on take-off from Cape Canaveral, Florida on 28 January 1986. The cause was determined to have been leakage of seals in the joint between rocket sections. The disaster, watched by thousands on the ground and millions on worldwide television, halted the US space programme until a comprehensive review of the engineering problems and revision of the safety methods had been undertaken, and it was not until 29 September 1988 that the next Space Shuttle, *Discovery* STS-26, was successfully launched.

The 11 cosmonauts and astronauts in this list are, to date, the only in-flight space fatalities. They are not, however, the only other victims of accidents during the space programmes of the former Soviet Union and the United States. On 24 October 1960, five months before the first manned flight, Field Marshal Mitrofan Nedelin, the commander of the Soviet Union's Strategic Rocket Forces, and an unknown number of other personnel (a total of 165 according to some authorities), were killed in the catastrophic launchpad explosion of an unmanned space rocket at the Baikanour cosmodrome, but the precise circumstances remain secret. Another explosion, during the refuelling of a Vostok rocket at the Plesetsk Space Centre on 18 March 1980, left some 50 dead. During a test countdown of *Apollo 1* on 27 January 1967, Roger B. Chaffee, Virgil I. 'Gus' Grissom and Edward H. White were killed in a fire, probably caused by an electrical fault. This tragedy led to greatly improved capsule design and safety procedures.

A number of former astronauts and cosmonauts have also been killed in accidents during other activities: Yuri Gagarin, the first man in space, was killed on 27 March 1968 in an aeroplane crash. The same fate befell a number of US astronauts who trained for but were killed before their space missions: Charles A. Bassett, Theodore C. Freeman, Elliot M. See and Clifton C. Williams all died during training in T-38 jet crashes in 1964–67, Stephen D. Thorne in a 1986 aeroplane accident and Edward G. Givens in a car crash. John L. Swigert, who had survived the ill-fated *Apollo 13* mission in 1970, died of cancer on 27 December 1982, thus becoming the first American space explorer to die of natural causes.

THE 10 WORST MOTOR VEHICLE AND ROAD DISASTERS IN THE WORLD

	Country/incident	No. killed
1	Afghanistan, 3 November 1982	**1,100+**
	A petrol tanker exploded in the Salang Tunnel.	
2	Colombia, 7 August 1956	**1,100**
	Seven army ammunition trucks exploded at Cali.	
3	Thailand, 15 February 1990	**150+**
	A dynamite truck exploded.	
4	Nepal, 23 November 1974	**148**
	Hindu pilgrims were killed when a suspension bridge over the River Mahahali collapsed.	
5	Egypt, 9 August 1973	**127**
	A bus drove into an irrigation canal.	
6	Togo, 6 December 1965	**125+**
	Two lorries collided with dancers during a festival at Sotouboua.	
7	Spain, 11 July 1978	**120+**
	A liquid gas tanker exploded in a camping site at San Carlos de la Rapita.	
8	Lesotho, 16 December 1976	**90**
	A bus fell into the Tsoaing River.	
9	India, 1 October 1978	**88**
	A bus skidded into floodwaters near Calcutta.	
10	Philippines, 6 January 1967	**84**
	Two ramshackle buses laden with Catholic pilgrims collided on a mountain pass at Terpate and fell over the edge.	

The worst-ever motor racing accident occurred on 13 June 1955, at Le Mans, France, when, in attempting to avoid other cars, French driver Pierre Levegh's Mercedes-Benz 300 SLR went out of control, hit a wall and exploded in mid-air, showering wreckage into the crowd and killing a total of 82 (*see also* The 10 Worst Disasters at Sports Venues). The worst British road accident occurred on 27 May 1975 when a coach crashed near Grassington, North Yorkshire, killing 33. The worst involving pedestrians was an incident when 24 Royal Marine Cadets were run down and killed by a double-decker bus in Gillingham, Kent, on 21 November 1971. It is believed that the worst-ever accident involving a single car occurred on 17 December 1956, when eight adults and four children were killed when the car in which they were travelling was hit by a train near Phoenix, Arizona. Although she was injured, 20-month-old Crucita Alires survived after being hurled into a tree by the impact.

10 CELEBRITY ROAD DEATHS

1 Duane Allman

This American guitarist (of Allman Brothers), who played with Eric Clapton on *Layla*, was killed in a motorcycle accident in Macon, Georgia, 29 October 1971. Berry Oakley from the same group was also killed in a motorcycle accident just three blocks away on 11 November 1972.

2 Marc Bolan

The British singer (T. Rex) died when a Mini driven by his American girlfriend, Gloria Jones, crashed into a tree on Barnes Common on 16 September 1977. The tree is now a shrine for T. Rex fans.

3 Pierre Curie

The co-discoverer (with his wife, Marie) of radium met his death in Paris on 19 April 1906 when he stepped out from behind a hansom cab and fell under the wheels of a wagon laden with military uniforms, the rear wheels of which crushed his skull.

4 James Dean

The American actor was killed at the age of 24, on 30 September 1955 at Paso Robles, California, when his Porsche Spyder collided with a car driven by Donald Gene Turnupseed (who was on the wrong side of the road). Recent evidence appears to refute the long-held belief that Dean was speeding at the time.

5 Isadora Duncan

The American dancer was strangled in Nice on 14 September 1927 when her scarf caught in the wheel of the Bugatti in which she was a passenger; her last words were, 'Goodbye, my friends, I am off to glory!'

6 T. E. Lawrence

'Lawrence of Arabia', British soldier and writer, was killed on 19 May 1935 in a mystery crash on a Brough motorcycle (given to him by George Bernard Shaw) near his home at Clouds Hill, Dorset.

7 Jayne Mansfield

The American actress was decapitated in a car crash near Biloxi, Mississippi, on 29 June 1967.

8 Margaret Mitchell

The American author of *Gone With the Wind* was knocked down and killed by a speeding car driven by Hugh D. Gravitt (who was convicted of manslaughter), on 16 August 1949, in Atlanta, Georgia.

9 George Patton

The American general known as 'Old Blood and Guts' survived the Second World War only to be killed in a car crash on 21 December 1945 in Heidelberg, Germany.

10 Jackson Pollock

The American action painter lost control and was hurled out of his convertible 1950 Oldsmobile and killed near East Hampton, New York, on 11 August 1956. His passenger Ruth Klingman, escaped with injuries, but Edith Metzger, a friend accompanying her, was also killed.

THE WORLD'S 10 WORST DISASTERS AT SPORTS VENUES*

	Location/disaster	Date	No. killed
1	Hong Kong Jockey Club (stand collapse and fire)	26 February 1918	604
2	Lenin Stadium, Moscow (crush in football stadium)	20 October 1982	340
3	Lima, Peru (football stadium riot)	24 May 1964	320
4	Hillsborough, Sheffield, UK (crush in football stadium)	15 April 1989	95
5	Le Mans, France (racing car crash)	11 June 1955	82
6	Katmandu, Nepal (stampede in football stadium)	12 March 1988	80
7	Buenos Aires, Argentina (riot in football stadium)	23 May 1968	73
8	Ibrox Park, Glasgow, Scotland (barrier collapse in football stadium)	2 January 1971	66
9	Bradford Stadium, UK (fire in football stadium)	11 May 1985	56
10	Heysel Stadium, Belgium (crush in football stadium)	29 May 1985	39

*Twentieth century only.

Such tragedies are not an exclusively modern phenomenon: during the reign of Roman Emperor Antoninus Pius (AD 138–161), a stand at the Circus Maximus collapsed during a gladiatorial spectacle and 1,162 spectators were killed.

THE 10 MOST ACCIDENT-PRONE CAR COLOURS

	Colour	Accidents per 10,000 cars of each colour
1	Black	179
2	White	160
3	Red	157
4	Blue	149
5	Grey	147
6	Gold	145
7	Silver	142
8	Beige	137
9	Green	134
10 =	Brown	133
10 =	Yellow	133

Figures released by the Department of Transport in 1992 appeared to refute the notion that white cars were safest because they were the easiest to see, especially at night. These statistics were immediately disputed by some car manufacturers, insurance companies and psychologists who pointed out that the type of vehicle and age and experience of drivers were equally salient factors, and until further surveys are conducted it would perhaps be misleading to consider any colour 'safer' than another.

THE WORLD'S 10 WORST DISASTERS AT THEATRE AND ENTERTAINMENT VENUES*

	Location/disaster	Date	No. killed
1	Canton, China (theatre fire)	25 May 1845	1,670
2	Lehmann Circus, St Petersburg, Russia (fire)	14 February 1836	800
3	Ring Theatre, Vienna (fire)	8 December 1881	620
4	Iroquois Theatre, Chicago (fire)	30 December 1903	602
5	Cocoanut Grove Night Club, Boston (fire)	28 November 1942	491
6	Abadan, Iran (arson in theatre)	20 August 1978	400
7	Niteroi, Brazil (circus fire)	17 December 1961	323
8	Brooklyn Theatre, New York (fire)	5 December 1876	295
9	Novedades Theatre, Madrid, Spain (fire)	23 September 1928	270
10	Sinceljo, Colombia (bullring collapse)	20 January 1980	222

*Nineteenth and twentieth centuries, excluding sports stadiums and race tracks.

The figure given for the first entry in this list is a conservative estimate, some sources putting the figure as high as 2,500; it is not the only major theatre fire in China: a June 1871 theatre fire in Shanghai is said to have left 900 dead and one on 13 February 1937 at Antoung is credited with causing 700 deaths. However, even in recent times, reports from China are generally scanty on detail and unreliable, so these reports are therefore excluded. The figure for the Ring Theatre fire also varies greatly according to source, some claiming it to be as high as 850. In addition to these disasters, a further 200 died in a fire at the Théâtre Royal, Quebec, Canada on 12 July 1846 and, coincidentally, 188 in a fire at the Theatre Royal, Exeter, on 5 September 1887. About 183 died during a panic caused by a fire at the Victoria Hall, Sunderland, on 16 June 1883, and a fire at a dance hall in Natchez, Mississippi, on 23 April 1940 killed 198; one at the Rhoads Opera House, Boyertown, Pennsylvania on 12 January 1903 left 170 dead, while the USA's worst circus fire (which precipitated a stampede) occurred at Ringling Brothers' Circus, Hartford, Connecticut, on 6 July 1944 when 168 lives were lost. More recently, a fire at the Beverly Hills Supper Club, Southgate, Kentucky on 28 May 1977 killed 165 and one in a dance hall at St-Laurent-du-Pont, France on 1 November 1970 resulted in 146 losing their lives.

INDEX

Quizzes appear in **BOLD CAPITALS**

ACKNOWLEDGEMENTS

I would like to thank the following organizations and individuals who kindly supplied me with information to enable me to compile many of the lists in **THE TOP 10 OF EVERYTHING**.

Academy of Motion Picture
    Arts and Sciences
AGB
Air France
Airport Operators Council
    International
Art Sales Index
Associated Examining Board
Audit Bureau of Circulations
    Ltd
Automobile Association
Backnumbers
Bank of England
BBC Publicity
BBC Radio 1
BBC Written Archives
Birds Eye
A. & C. Black
Bonhams
Bookwatch Ltd
Botanic Gardens Conservation
    International
The Brewers Society
British Airports Authority
British Bankers Association
British Broadcasting
    Corporation
British Cave Research
    Association
British Library
British Museum
British Rail
British Rate & Data
British Small Animal
    Veterinary Association
British Tourist Authority
Burke's Peerage
Business Age
Cadbury Schweppes Group
Canine Defence League
Capital Radio plc
The Governing Council of the
    Cat Fancy
Central Statistical Office
Channel Four Television
Charities Aid Foundation
Chivers/Hartley
Christie's East
Christie's London
Christie's South Kensington
Civil Aviation Authority

Classic FM
Classical Music
Coca-Cola Co
Cohn & Wolfe
Corporate Intelligence Group
    Ltd
Countryside Council for Wales
Daily Mail
Department of Transport
English Nature
Euromonitor Ltd
European Leisure Software
    Publishers Association
Family Budget Unit, Joseph
    Rowntree Foundation
Feste Catalogue Index
    Database
Food and Agriculture
    Organization of the
    United Nations
Forbes Magazine
The Forestry Commission
Gallup
Generation AB
Geological Museum
Gold Fields Mineral Services
Hamleys Ltd
Home Office
IMS
The Independent
Independent Broadcasting
    Authority
International Cocoa
    Organization
International Coffee
    Organization
International Hydrographic
    Organization
International Union of
    Geological Sciences
    Commission
Joint Council for the GCSE
The Kennel Club
Keynote Publications
Lillywhites
Lloyds Register of Shipping
London Regional Transport
London Theatre Record
London Underground
The Mail on Sunday
MARC Europe
Marks & Spencer plc
MEAL
Motor Vehicle Manufacturers
    Association of the United
    States, Inc
MRIB
NASA
National Alliance of Women's

Organizations
National Canine Defence
    League
National Dairy Council
The National Grid Company
    plc
National Theatre
National Trust
A.C. Nielsen Co Ltd
Nielsen Media Research
Nuclear Engineering
    International
Office of Population Censuses
    and Surveys
Organization for Economic
    Development and
    Cooperation
Oxford University Press
The Patent Office
Penguin Books Ltd
Phillips West Two
The Phobics Society
Produktschap voor
    Gedistilleerde Dranken
The Proprietary Association of
    Great Britain
The Public Lending Right
RAJAR/RSL
The Really Useful Group plc
The Red House
Release
The Royal Aeronautical
    Society
The Royal Astronomical
    Society
Royal Mint
The Royal Society for the
    Prevention of Cruelty to
    Animals
Scottish Home Office
Scottish National Heritage
Scottish Tourist Board
Screen Digest
Shakespeare Birthplace Trust
Siemens AG
W.H. Smith & Son Ltd
The Society of Authors
The Society of Motor Vehicle
    Manufacturers and
    Traders Ltd
Sotheby's London
Sotheby's New York City
Spink & Son Ltd
The Sugar Bureau
Swedish Embassy
Tea Council
Theatre Record
D.C. Thomson & Co Ltd
The Times

Trebor Bassett
UBS Phillips & Drew Global
    Pharmaceutical Review
United Nations
US Bureau of the Census
Variety
Virgin 1215
Watches of Switzerland
Water Services Association
Welsh Tourist Office
World Health Organization
World Intellectual Property
    Organization

Edward Abelson
Marcel Berlins
Alan Brett
Steve Butler
Kevin Cahill
Terry Charman
David Chesterman
Robert Clark
Ludo Craddock
Luke Crampton
Alexander Crum Ewing
Paul Dickson
Christopher Forbes
Monika Half
Max Hanna
Peter Harland
Robert Lamb
Barry Lazell
Dr Jacqueline Mitton
Giles Moon
Ian Morrison
Edward Nodder
Tim O'Donovan
Clive Perrott
Adrian Room
Alan Somerset
James Taylor
Carey Wallace
Tony Waltham

Extra special thanks to Caroline Ash, the book's picture researcher, Linda Silverman, and its editor, Lorraine Jerram.

PICTURE CREDITS

QUIZ ANSWERS

The Moon (p.9) **1** The Soviet probe *Lunik II*, on 13 September 1959. **2** Wilkie Collins. **3** 1959, by *Lunik III*. **4** Somerset Maugham. **5** Wiltshire. **6** The Marcels. **7** Cancer (21 June to 21 July). **8** Michael Jackson. **9** David Niven. **10** 2151 (14 June).

Caves (p.22) **1** Fingal's Cave. **2** A speleologist. **3** Altamira. **4** Jean Auel. **5** Former Beatle Ringo Starr. **6** Chislehurst Caves. **7** A troglodyte. **8** David. **9** Up. **10** The Mammoth cave system, Kentucky, USA.

Fruit (p.26) **1** It is not specified, but is traditionally said to have been an apple. **2** 1967. **3** The banana. **4** Oranges. **5** Pears. **6** Pineapples. **7** *Cherry Pink and Apple Blossom White*. **8** Apricots. **9** Avocado. **10** Varieties of plum.

Group Names (p.36) **1**–I. **2**–E. **3**–H. **4**–F. **5**–A. **6**–D. **7**–J. **8**–C. **9**–B. **10**–G.

Place Name Changes (p.74) **1**–F. **2**–G. **3**–E. **4**–J. **5**–I. **6**–H. **7**–C. **8**–A. **9**–B. **10**–D.

UK Cathedrals (p.78) **1** New Vaudeville Band. **2** Durham. **3** T.S. Eliot. **4** Lord Nelson. **5** Chichester. **6** Hereford. **7** Gloucester. **8** Lincoln. **9** Peterborough (Mary was moved to Westminster Abbey). **10** Southwark.

Photographers (p.88) **1** William Henry Fox Talbot. **2** Cecil Beaton. **3** Linda McCartney. **4** Denis Healey. **5** The Crimean War. **6** David Bailey. **7** Lord Snowdon. **8** David Hemmings. **9** Man Ray. **10** Ottawa.

Pen Names (p.103) **1**–C. **2**–H. **3**–I. **4**–G. **5**–B. **6**–A. **7**–D. **8**–E. **9**–J. **10**–F.

Unlikely Birthplaces (p.117) **1**–D. **2**–C. **3**–H. **4**–E. **5**–I. **6**–J. **7**–B. **8**–F. **9**–A. **10**–G.

Colour Film (p.128) **1** *Black*. **2** *Blue*. **3** *Green*. **4** *Purple*. **5** *Pink*. **6** *Grey*. **7** *White*. **8** *Red*. **9** *Yellow*. **10** *Scarlet*.

Patents (p.157) **1**–C–vi. **2**–F–viii. **3**–E–iii. **4**–H–ii. **5**–I–iv. **6**–G–x. **7**–J–ix. **8**–B–v. **9**–A–vii. **10**–D–i.

Gold (p.168) **1** 12.44 kg/27.43 lb. **2** Scaramanga. **3** Montreux. **4** London and Paris. **5** 1937. **6** A club for World War II RAF pilots who ditched in the sea. **7** Fool's gold. **8** King Midas. **9** Sir Francis Drake. **10** Spandau Ballet.

Cheese (p.176) **1** Switzerland. **2** Italy. **3** Netherlands. **4** Portugal. **5** Norway. **6** France (Münster is from Germany). **7** Germany. **8** Scotland. **9** USA. **10** Spain.

Criminals in Fiction (p.181) **1** Professor James Moriarty. **2** Macavity, the cat in T.S. Eliot's *Old Possum's Book of Practical Cats*. **3** A.J. Raffles, in the novels of E.W. Hornung. **4** Goldfinger. **5** Dr Fu Manchu. **6** An ape. **7** Dick Tracy. **8** (a). **9** Sydney Greenstreet. **10** Henry and Edward.

War Films (p.192) **1**–I. **2**–F. **3**–J. **4**–C. **5**–D. **6**–H. **7**–B. **8**–A. **9**–G. **10**–E.

Religion (p.200) **1**–G. **2**–I. **3**–B. **4**–H. **5**–C. **6**–A. **7**–J. **8**–D. **9**–F. **10**–E.

Olympic Gold Medal Winners (p.216) **1** Ray Ewry (USA), 10. **2** Paavo Nurmi (Finland), 5. **3** USA (83 in 1984). **4** Rowing (18). **5** Sweden (9). **6** None (although GB has won 6 silver and 10 bronze). **7** Seven; all of them. **8** Japan, with 27. **9** Switzerland (8 golds and 22 in all). **10** 185.

Space Travel (p.223) **1** David Bowie's *Space Oddity*. **2** *Mercury*; *Gemini*; *Apollo*; *Columbia*; *Challenger*; *Discovery*; *Atlantis*. **3** Jules Verne. **4** A US *Apollo* capsule docked with a Soviet *Soyuz* capsule. **5** An Extravehicular Mobility Unit, or spacesuit. **6** His trip was the first by a politician – Garn was a US Senator who travelled as an observer. **7** Telstar. **8** The confectionary company Mars. **9** 250,000 miles – by *Apollo* 13 on the aborted lunar mission, 15 April 1970. **10** HAL – which is one letter back in the alphabet from IBM.

Liners (p.234) **1** The *Titanic*. **2** Canadian. **3** Glasgow, Queen Mary, Los Angeles. **4** Isambard Kingdom Brunel. **5** Dr Crippen. **6** *The Poseidon Adventure*. **7** She was used as a floating university in Hong Kong, was burnt and finally scrapped. **8** In 1911, she was the first ocean liner with a swimming pool. **9** Peninsular & Oriental (Steam Navigation Company). **10** 1837.

Fires (p.241) **1** Shelley (he was drowned, although his body was later burned). **2** The Palace of Westminster (Houses of Parliament). **3** The Emperor Nero. **4** A bear called Smokey. **5** The Crazy World of Arthur Brown. **6** Chicago: the disastrous fire of 8 October 1871 was supposedly caused by the cow kicking over an oil lamp. **7** *Backdraft*. **8** 'Red'. **9** A metal plate attached to a building to indicate that it was insured against fire. **10** 9.